Sunflower Justice

Law in the American West

SERIES EDITOR

John R. Wunder, University of Nebraska–Lincoln

Sunflower Justice

A New History of the Kansas Supreme Court

R. ALTON LEE

University of Nebraska Press
Lincoln and London

Manufactured in the United States of America

Library of Congress Cataloging-in-Publication Data

Lee, R. Alton.
Sunflower justice: a new history of the
Kansas Supreme Court / R. Alton Lee.
pages cm. — (Law in the American West)
Includes bibliographical references and index.
ISBN 978-0-8032-4841-0 (cloth: alk. paper)—
ISBN 978-0-8032-5411-4 (epub)—
ISBN 978-0-8032-5412-1 (mobi)—
ISBN 978-0-8032-5410-7 (pdf)
1. Kansas. Supreme Court—History.
2. Courts of last resort—Kansas—History.
I. Title.
KFK512.L44 2014
347.781'035—dc23
2013036676

Set in Adobe Garamond Pro by Laura Wellington.

For Marilyn
Who made innumerable trips to the History Center in Topeka during the last decade. I cannot find the words to express my appreciation for her support of my research — but she knows.

Contents

Illustrations

Preface

Legal history has too often been left to lawyers to define, and one result is the paucity of works on local and state legal topics that appeared to many to be "unimportant." American legal historiography, until the recent development of "history from the bottom up," was devoted largely to the national government, where "the action took place." Political scientists, historians, economists, and sociologists studied the Constitution from their particular vantage points and produced studies with an appeal limited primarily to other members of their fields. "As a consequence," Francis Heller concluded, the US Supreme Court's work "was over-evaluated but seldom illuminated."[1]

State and local legal history in the nineteenth century was neglected in part because historians do not have the legal skills to read and to interpret technical documents and complicated legal jargon. One can study the relationship to economic forces or the concept of legal thought or an aspect of group activity, but the rigors of the historical process subject the aspects of these disciplines and others to its peculiar demands. As a result, only the histories of the high courts in Florida, Massachusetts, Missouri, Tennessee, Virginia, Nebraska, and Washington have been written, although other similar studies are now under way. This is unfortunate, because it is here that the "the meaningful, everyday judicial opinions" are dispensed.[2]

Michael H. Hoeflick asserts that "the work that has been produced [in Kansas] primarily has been written by lawyers writing for other lawyers," and he justly laments the fact that much of the sources for writing this study "have been destroyed or lost." His observations apply only tangentially to the Kansas Supreme Court, as he is referring to the disappearance of attorneys' papers and similar legal documents. Most of the vital evidence on the court is available, providing enough material for at least a sketchy history of the institution, and that is what I have attempted to do in this volume. It is not a legal history of Kansas, nor is it a definitive history of the court and its work. It is a brief overview, conveniently located in one volume, of the judges and the decisions they wrote that helped mold Kansas legal history within the context of Kansas constitutional, political, economic, legal, and social history. I hope the book will encourage future scholars to expand and build on this foundation. To try to be definitive would be foolhardy and would require the cooperation of many scholars and the writing of many volumes. Both of these options appear unfeasible at this time.[3]

The great twentieth-century legal scholar James Willard Hurst encouraged his students to understand "how the law has really worked in social experience." Yet another scholar has stressed the point that legal historians have insisted on "a radical separation between law and politics." I reject this latter distinction and support Hurst's injunction because this subject is a specialized form of political history. Politicians shape the law and use it for whatever type of social and economic policies their constituents want their government to pursue. Judges are citizens with their own political, social, and economic predilections, and these often, consciously or subconsciously, influence the writing of their decisions.[4]

From the territorial period to 1990, the supreme court produced 245 volumes of opinions. Each volume contains approximately 250 decisions. How does the historian master such productivity? How does one organize and illuminate this mass of legal thought and development? How can the major trends be condensed so that an author can write, and readers can absorb, with any confidence of comprehension? There are many approaches, of course, and everyone who researches state supreme court histories will follow a different scheme. I have elected to choose the cases that best demonstrate the historical, social, legal, political, and economic trends of the period covered in each chapter.

During the latter half of the twentieth century, for instance, a great change came about in our judicial system labeled "legal liberalism." This involved the concept that courts in general could, and should, be used to bring about social change, and it originated particularly in the "Brandeis Brief," developed in support of the Oregon law limiting working hours for women. Louis Brandeis, "the people's attorney," followed the unusual approach of writing a couple of pages of legal precedent for his brief and over one hundred pages of statistics demonstrating the impact of long hours on women's physical and mental well-being in order to have the law sustained. The concept of legal liberalism would be employed particularly in Kansas at midcentury, with the *Brown* public school case having a great impact on the justices in the course of desegregating American life because of the psychological influence racial segregation had on children.[5]

Alexis de Tocqueville paid scant attention to the role political parties played in selecting American judges, but from the beginnings political parties were crucial in the Kansas system of popular election. A half century after Tocqueville wrote, Lord Bryce believed this system of selection of justices, "nominally by popular election, practiced by the party of wirepullers," often kept "the most honorable men" from reaching the bench. This led, in the Kansas experience, to judges having to kiss babies and nail an inordinate number of posters to telephone poles during the campaign process and frequently continuing their political careers from the state's highest bench. This process finally culminated in a demand in the 1950s to change the system of selecting judges to follow the principles of the Missouri Plan, which established a nonpartisan commission of lawyers and laymen to propose names to the governor for appointment to the bench. They would subsequently stand for retention on a nonpartisan ballot.[6]

In studying the Kansas Supreme Court I decided first to consider the judges and the experiences that shaped their thinking. I then examined the decisions that molded Kansas law in the first century and a half of the court's existence. My examination focuses on both how the judges shaped legal history and how the cases they heard constituted a part of the political, economic, social, and legal story of the Sunflower State. Each chapter is introduced by a brief historical survey to set the scene for the era. Some biographical material on the judges follows, with a presentation of pertinent cases of the period. The historical background is vital not only because it was within this context that the judges shaped Kansas law but also because the political process involved them directly, as they were nominated by political parties, campaigned for elective office, and sometimes continued partisan activities while on the bench until the mid-twentieth century.

I am indebted to many people for their assistance in researching and writing this volume. Foremost are the staff of the History Center at the Kansas State Historical Society. Charles Warnica and Antoinette Satterfield of the Government Documents Division, Hale Library at Kansas State University, were of great assistance. The Manhattan Public Library was an important source for interlibrary loan. Ramon Powers has been highly supportive of my efforts in writing Kansas history. At his suggestion I contacted retired Justice Fred N. Six in the early stages of this study. He kindly gave me advice, based on his experience and interest in legal history, that greatly improved my approach. After the study was finished, he generously spent time reading the entire manuscript and offering many pertinent suggestions for improvement. I must also credit him with the title, although I acknowledge that the subtitle is mine. Professor Derek Hoff of Kansas State University took time from his busy schedule and read part of the manuscript, suggesting changes in format and organization for which I am grateful.

Of course, I cannot hold these scholars accountable for my decision to decline some of their suggestions, many of which might have made the study stronger.

Sunflower Justice

Introduction

Ad Astra per Aspera

To the stars through difficulties. Kansas was enduring Herculean challenges, even agony in some cases, in its first few years of existence as a territory. Although it suffered a shorter tenure as a territory than any of its surrounding neighbors, those seven years were tumultuous indeed. But the New England Emigrant Aid Company stocked the territory with sound settlers who knew how to endure adversity, and its citizens survived both the buffeting of Mother Nature and the battering of hostile neighbors.

"Bleeding Kansas," historian Nicole Etcheson calls it, was born out of the sectional conflict over slavery that was rending the nation in two during the 1850s. In 1820, with the admission of Missouri to the Union, politicians created an even balance in the Senate, and the issue of expansion of slavery was resolved by drawing a line at 36°30' through the Louisiana Purchase and prohibiting slavery above that line. From 1820 to 1850 the minority South managed to protect its "peculiar institution" by maintaining this balance of free and slave states in the Union, and thus equality in the Senate, to prevent passage of legislation inimical to its labor system. Then in 1854 Senator Stephen A. Douglas of Illinois introduced the Kansas-Nebraska Act to create those two territories north of the 36°30' line with popular sovereignty to determine their future status. Let the settlers decide whether they wanted slavery or free labor. This necessitated repealing the Missouri Compromise of 1820, and Douglas's act gave the South a chance to gain Kansas as a slave state after surrendering it three decades earlier. Migration normally moved directly westward, so, under Douglas's law, slave-holding Missourians slavery by force and considered their occupation of the White House as sufficient reason for secession from the Union. When Republican Abraham Lincoln narrowly won the Electoral College with a minority vote of 40 percent of the popular vote in November 1860, this severed the last great tie of the Deep South to the Union. Prior to this election several southern states adopted the Alabama Platform, which pledged their delegates to walk out of the Democratic national convention if the party did not approve a plank protecting slavery in the territories. The majority of the Democrats, wishing to win in 1860, compromised by promising a platform to abide by any "clear-cut decision" of the Supreme Court on the question. When "Black Republican" Lincoln won the election on a plank of no further extension of slavery in the territories, representatives of several southern states walked out of Congress, and the Republicans, now a majority there, admitted Kansas as a free state on 29 January 1861. As a contemporary politician expressed it, "the agony is now over" for Kansans.[5]

Meanwhile, Free Soilers were drafting the Wyandotte Constitution in anticipation of statehood. Section III of that document created a judicial branch and was influenced by the experience of Kansas during the territorial period. The Northwest Ordinance of 1787 created a governmental system for colonies, or "territories," as they were then called, that operated so efficiently that subsequent Congresses used it throughout the nineteenth and twentieth centuries. It created territorial governments consisting of a governor, a secretary, and three judges appointed by Congress to rule until statehood, when the area would be admitted to the Union on a basis of equality with the original states. Unfortunately, this excellent system had the built-in weakness of allowing the ruling party, by its appointments, to control the future politics of the territory. A Congress controlled by Democrats appointed Democrats for territorial government positions, and Republicans and Whigs appointed their supporters when they were in power. The territorial governor subsequently used his patronage to appoint fellow party members to assure supremacy of his party when statehood arrived. Of the six governors appointed for the territory, three fled the territory through fear of assassination, and two were removed or resigned under pressure. This system affected the thinking of Kansans with its plan of appointed judges.[6]

The territory of Kansas had three supreme court justices, who also served as judges of the three district courts. The courts experienced frequent changes in personnel. New judges, appointed by presidential commissions, claimed their positions sometimes over the vigorous protests of the current judges who had received no notice of their replacement. Sessions of the territorial supreme court usually lasted five to nine days annually, and often the judges failed to attend.

At one point Governor John Geary threatened the judges with "military law and he would supercede their courts unless they took measures to clear their dockets." Chief Justice Samuel E. Lecompte of Maryland "was a man of great force of character" who was "openly partisan in his support of slavery." Governor Geary charged "party bias" as an excuse for his attempt to remove Lecompte from office. Sometime later the chief justice responded to Geary's letter by admitting he was biased toward the Democratic Party, as he was a lifelong member. Yes, he agreed that he was proslavery, and he would continue to support that institution. He did deny Geary's charge of "criminal complicity with a state of affairs which terminated in a contempt of all authority," as the governor insisted. Lecompte became a leader of the proslavery forces, founded the town of Lecompton, and presided over the convention that wrote the Lecompton Constitution.[7]

President James Buchanan appointed John Pettit of Indiana to replace Lecompte. Pettit had served as a US senator and had a "quite high" reputation as a legal scholar. The free press, though, charged him "with being a hard drinker, time waster, and cigar smoker," with one journalist complaining with exaggeration that Pettit was "the staggering embodiment of all vices." Pettit rendered an interesting decision in the case of a slave who ran away from Kentucky to Kansas. Two infant children inherited Peter Fisher from their deceased father, and their guardian, Rain C. Hutchinson, pursued Fisher with an extradition order issued under the authority of the Fugitive Slave Act of 1850.

As Hutchinson was about to return to Kentucky with the runaway, Lewis Weld freed Fisher "with a club, knife, pistol, and other hurtful weapons" in violation of the federal law. Judge Pettit quashed Weld's indictment through a strict construction of the Fugitive Slave Act. The law must be enforced, Pettit averred, but it provided for recapture of the fugitive by the owner, his agent, or his attorney, and "all other persons are thereby excluded from doing the same thing as effectively as if they were positively forbidden." Hutchinson was neither the owner of the slave nor the "agent or attorney" of the owners, and thus the fugitive slave law was not violated, according to the judge. Pettit admitted that his opinion was "hastily written in the midst of turmoil, interruption, and confusion," and if he had been able to consult even an inadequate law library, he would have found that the guardian acted legally within the intent of the law. But Pettit was from Indiana, and his decision was popular with the Free Soilers. If former Chief Justice Samuel Lecompte of Maryland had heard the case, the decision would have been quite different. Another territorial judge, Sterling Cato, was strongly proslavery and "issued partisan decisions," being "completely destitute of a sense of justice."[8]

The president appointed these justices for four-year terms, yet they actually served at his pleasure. Appeals from their decisions went directly to the US Supreme Court, but only one such decision from the territory of Kansas ever arrived in Washington, and it involved a land-sale contract. Presidents Franklin Pierce and James Buchanan appointed "either nine or ten" of these judges. Eight served at least briefly, but only six served "more than a few days." None were from Kansas, all were Democrats, and at least one, Rush Elmore of Alabama, brought his nineteen slaves with him to the Sunflower Territory.[9]

The Kansas winters proved to be too severe for the slaves. Mrs. Elmore, who had never cooked before, spent the winter cooking for them, and the judge was kept busy cutting firewood to keep them warm. He later opened a legal practice in Topeka in partnership with Democrat John Martin, who would be elected to the US Senate in 1893 during the Populist era. Justices Sanders Johnston and Joseph A. Williams were proslavery Democrats, although President Abraham Lincoln later appointed Williams to a Memphis tribunal that tried civil cases.[10]

The territorial supreme court was early called upon to render an advisory opinion of the type that courts normally do not entertain. The first territorial governor, Andrew Reeder, exercised his power properly, although in his own pecuniary interest, in locating the first capital at Pawnee, where he and his associates were engaged in land speculation, and he called the legislature into session there. The legislators refused to meet in the unfinished building provided for them and petitioned President Franklin Pierce to remove Reeder from office. Both houses passed an act to gather in Shawnee. The governor vetoed it, the assembly passed it over his veto, and they adjourned to gather in Shawnee. This issue arrived at the supreme court in its first session. Justices Lecompte and Elmore sustained the legislature's actions but responded to the suit as judges, not as a sitting court. Johnston "declined to participate," as he thought the question was not a proper one to bring before the court. President Pierce soon replaced Reeder with Wilson Shannon as governor; Shannon also had a short tenure in office.[11]

John Geary, the competent third territorial governor, complained to President James Buchanan that peace in Kansas was impossible without "a complete administrative overhaul of territorial officials, including judges," and he "publicly quarreled" with Chief Judge Lecompte. The latter had thwarted the governor's attempts at making arrests of killers by deliberately moving the time and locations of his court. In addition, he had freed indicted Kickapoo ranger Charles Hays twice following his arrests by Geary. Democrat Geary had sought to be an even-handed administrator and help bring peace to Kansas by arresting the killer. Partisan southern Democrat Lecompte granted the accused Hays bail, and the sheriff supplied him with "bail-bond." Geary ordered Hays arrested again, but, in Geary's absence, Lecompte released him on a writ of habeas corpus. The governor concluded that neither Lecompte nor Judge Sterling Cato "made any pretense of impartiality." For Geary, the Hays episode proved "the last straw," and he decided that the people should elect territorial judges, a practice many of the states to the east followed.[12]

The experience of "Governor" Charles Robinson with Cato's court would substantiate Geary's conclusion that voters should elect judges. Under the Topeka "free state" Constitution, Dr. Robinson was elected governor, and Judge Cato issued a writ for his arrest on the grounds that he "had illegally attempted to assume state office." Robinson was acquitted on the basis that he could not "usurp" an office that Cato's court insisted did not exist. These unhappy experiences with an appointed judiciary were quite vivid in the minds of the delegates to the Wyandotte convention.[13]

Following the defeat of the Lecompton Constitution, the state Republican Party was organized at Osawatomie, with Horace Greeley addressing the delegates. When Greeley arrived in Kansas in late April the state was enduring copious rainfall. Travel was precarious and occasionally dangerous because of floodwaters. In typical Kansas weather fashion, a month later the state entered a period of extensive drought. The decision was made at Osawatomie to draw up a new state constitution. The territory had endured three constitutions — Topeka in 1855, Lecompton in 1857, and Leavenworth in 1858 — and this constitution smashing in three short years was not conducive to stable state building. Delegates, both Democratic and Republican, were chosen to attend the Wyandotte convention in July 1859. The convention took place during the severe drought, which lasted from June 1859 to November 1860. The temperature often rose to 105° in the shade in late July, and crops withered and died. Once again Kansas became an object of eastern charity. New York businessman Thaddeas Hyatt, who helped in the relief efforts of 1856, joined W. F. N. Arny and Samuel Pomeroy to organize a relief drive. Pomeroy and James H. Lane of Jayhawk fame were elected the first US senators. Pomeroy, one historian observed, was determined to ride to the Senate "on the famine horse."[14]

Democrats and Republicans faced each other directly for the first time in Kansas in electing delegates to attend the Wyandotte meeting. The Democrats won Doniphan, Jackson, Jefferson, and Leavenworth Counties for sixteen representatives, while Republicans carried the remaining counties with thirty-five delegates. Old free state men who wrote the three previous constitutions were "conspicuous for their absence." The delegates chose James Winchell, former *New York Times* newspaperman, as president and John A. Martin, current Atchison newspaperman, as secretary. The delegates were relatively young and neophytes at constitution writing but farsightedly determined to rely on proven experience. As with most constitutional conventions, they decided to follow tried and true examples from other states as a guide. Fourteen of the fifty-two delegates originally came from Ohio, and the convention decided to use that state's document as a frame of reference. The secretary later recalled that the combination of intense heat and the knowledge that territorial scrip, or paper money, "would be received by importunate landlords only at a usurious rate" led the delegates to conduct their business "in dispatch," if not in haste. They realized they needed to stabilize the territory's inflationary currency, heavy debts, and poor credit ratings in order to succeed.[15]

Only fifteen members were over forty years of age, and one-third were under thirty. John Martin, publisher of *Freedom's Champion* of Atchison, was a key player in this convention and also in the state's early political years. Born in 1839, Martin had to decline election to the territorial legislature because he was too young to qualify for the office. He was chosen secretary of the Republican Party at Osawatomie, and before he was eligible to vote he was elected secretary at the Wyandotte meeting. When he was twenty-two the governor appointed him a lieutenant colonel in the Eighth Kansas Volunteers. The Eighth joined the Army of the Cumberland during the Civil War and participated in the campaigns of Chickamauga, Chattanooga, and Sherman's March to the Sea. At age twenty-six Martin was brevetted brigadier general, and he returned to Atchison at war's end to resume publishing his newspaper, renamed the *Daily Champion*. His party would twice nominate him unanimously for governor.[16]

President Winchell appointed eleven members to the Judiciary Committee, whose report, when adopted by the convention, became Article III of the Kansas constitution. All but physician J. J. Blunt were lawyers. Two members were twenty-six years old, three were twenty-eight, one was twenty-nine, one was thirty, one was thirty-five, and two were thirty-eight. Four were Democrats from Leavenworth County, and one was from Doniphan. All of them refused to sign the final constitution. Agreeing with the decision of their caucus, none of the Democrats signed it, objecting that the convention curtailed the boundaries of Kansas too drastically; the legislative body was too large; Native Americans were denied the franchise; the requirement for registration of voters for approving the constitution was questionable; the refusal to exclude free Negroes from the state was immoral; and the apportionment of representatives was unfair. John Martin later expressed the view that both parties had committed a blunder they later regretted, the Republicans in refusing to include the South Platte country within the state's boundaries and the Democrats in refusing to sign the document "they had labored so diligently to perfect."[17]

Winchell named Samuel A. Kingman of Brown County as chairman of the Judiciary Committee. Kingman was a lawyer who later compiled a distinctive record in his fifteen years' service on the state supreme court. His committee report on Article III was mostly based on the Ohio Constitution of 1851. This determined the judicial branch to be composed of one chief justice and two associates elected by the voters for six-year terms with one specifically elected as chief justice. The provision for election, not appointment, came from the Ohio document, but the territorial experience lent emphasis to its importance, although, as will be seen, it did not eliminate politicking while on the bench. In addition, there would be five district courts with one judge, each elected by the people for four-year terms. The supreme court would appoint a secretary and a clerk, and each county would elect a clerk of the district court for two-year terms. (Much of this clause came from the Topeka Constitution.) Each county would elect a judge for its probate court, and that judge would also serve as its clerk. The supreme court was given original jurisdiction over "proceedings in quo warranto, mandamus, and habeas corpus; and such appellate jurisdiction as may be provided by law." The legislature would later establish the appellate jurisdiction of district courts. The state legislature also would set the salaries of all judges at a minimum of $2,000 annually, and this could not be reduced during their tenure. No judge could hold any other office "of profit or trust" nor practice law in any state court. State judges could be removed from office by resolutions approved by two-thirds of the members of both houses, but "the party charged shall have had notice and opportunity to be heard." The Judiciary Committee reported its work on the seventh day, and two days later its report was "perfected" and endorsed. The committee of the whole reduced the salaries of judges from the recommended $2,000 to $1,500 and approved Section III.[18]

On the seventeenth day the delegates approved Topeka as the capital city, and the document was signed by all the Republican delegates except one, who was ill. The convention directed that election returns on the document be made to J. M. Winchell, but Acting Governor Hugh Sleight Walsh issued a proclamation directing them to be made to him. The effect of this would be to divide the returns by sending them to both Winchell and Walsh for their interpretation and action. The Democratic Walsh would then proclaim the constitution rejected, and Republican Winchell would announce its adoption. This "doubt" would provide the Democrat-controlled US Senate "with a pretext" for postponing Kansas statehood. The Republican strategy, therefore, was to have each county send its election returns to both men. The Democrats in the Senate, however, needed no "pretext" to withhold statehood for a Republican Kansas that would upset the balance of power in the Senate.[19]

The constitution was submitted to the voters on 4 October 1859, and they approved it with a tally of 10,421 to 5,330 opposed. Every county except Johnson and Morris tendered a majority for the constitution. Kansans now had to await secession, and Congress admitted them to the Union on 29 January 1861, a cold day with temperatures below zero. These men wrought well, as their document lasted into the twenty-first century with only thirty-seven periodic amendments. This admission to the Union signified, optimistically, that the period of Kansas "bleeding" was over.[20]

1. The Kingman Court

The Union army placed Thomas Ewing, Jr., in command of the District of the Border to control and to pacify the "Bleeding Kansas" area. The Confederate guerrilla William Clarke Quantrill was ravaging eastern Kansas, and, following his infamous raid on Lawrence in 1863, Ewing issued his renowned Order no. 11, which evicted all southern sympathizers in three counties in western Missouri: Jackson, Cass, Bates, and part of Vernon. Union forces had already imposed loyalty oaths, instituted fines for disloyalty, required passports and trade permits, and suppressed newspapers in the vicinity. Order no. 11 truly brought the war home, as it made refugees of some twenty thousand people. Missouri artist George Caleb Bingham immortalized the order years later with his famous mural of the same name. The southern-sympathizing Truman family was directly affected by this border warfare. The order created so much havoc that it was soon suspended. Just two years earlier General Ewing had resigned as the first chief justice of Kansas to accept the post of commander of the District of the Border.[1]

The Judges

One authority concludes that the judges elected after statehood handed down decisions that "settled and determined" state law "in admirable fashion." The new court met in Topeka, designated as the state capital, and consisted of Chief Justice Thomas Ewing, Jr., with Samuel Kingman and Lawrence D. Bailey as the associates. They assembled in a little room in the basement of the capitol on 28 October 1861. Ewing was elected for a six-year term, Kingman for four years, and Bailey

Fig. 1. Samuel A. Kingman. Image from the Kansas State Historical Society.

for two. On 21 May 1861 the state legislature set the supreme court jurisdiction as being a court of record and added to the original jurisdiction by giving the court authority to issue writs of error and certiorari in criminal cases. Interestingly, no provision was made for the court to nullify acts of the state in conflict with the constitution. Indeed, the national Constitution is silent on this question, but the court soon assumed this power, as happened on the national level.[2]

The supreme court of the territory ceased to function after the admission of Kansas to the Union. The court's journal and dockets passed into the hands of the state court with the last journal entry of 11 January 1861. The state supreme court recorded its proceedings "in the unused pages" of the territorial court journal, published as volume 1 of the *Reports*.[3]

Thomas Ewing's overweening ambition was to serve in the US Senate. His first case involved Senator James Lane's attempt to remove Governor Charles Robinson to make way for Lane's candidate, George Crawford. When Lincoln issued his call for volunteers to fight the Civil War soon afterward, Ewing responded out of a belief that military service would assist his campaign later for the Senate. He was en route to Arkansas to fight the Confederates when he resigned his post as chief justice. In January 1865 he returned to Kansas to oppose Lane, unsuccessfully, for a Kansas seat in the Senate. Failing in this, he left the state, never to return. He later assisted President Andrew Johnson legally in his impeachment trial.[4]

Thus Ewing served only one year, writing nine opinions, and then resigned in October 1862 to accept command as a colonel in the Kansas Eleventh during the Civil War. He had a distinguished military career, advancing to brigadier general. Louis Carpenter, reporter for the supreme court, was killed during Quantrill's attack on Lawrence. He had begun preparation of the first volume of the *Reports* when this raid "swept away nearly all his labors." As a result, cases decided prior to August 1863 had to be constructed from materials supplied by justices and attorneys who had participated in them. After the war, Ewing practiced law in the New York City area.[5]

Samuel Austin Kingman emerged as a significant figure in this early chaotic period of Kansas law. Many labeled him the "John Marshall of Kansas" because he was to the state constitution what John Marshall had been to the national judiciary. He was born in Worthington, Massachusetts, in 1818 and educated in the common schools there before becoming a teacher. At age nineteen he migrated to Kentucky, where he taught school and studied law. He served in the state legislature for three years and had the good fortune (for Kansas) to help write a new state constitution. Because of poor health, he migrated to the territory of Kansas in 1857, first settling in Leavenworth, then staking a homestead claim in Brown County. The following summer he moved to Hiawatha and began practicing law. He had lived in the territory of Kansas scarcely eighteen months and was unknown outside of Brown County when his neighbors elected him as a delegate to the Wyandotte constitutional convention in July 1859.[6]

Not only was Kingman chosen to chair the judiciary committee that produced Article III of the new constitution, but he also perfected the significant homestead provision in that document. This concept was first introduced in Texas in 1839, and Robert C. Foster of Leavenworth included it in the Leavenworth Constitution. It ignited an "animated and earnest debate" among the delegates. It was discussed, referred, amended, voted down, revived, and ruled out of order. Finally, Kingman proposed an acceptable version with the phrase "all men are possessed of equal and inalienable rights, among which are those of life, liberty, and the pursuit of happiness." As finally adopted, the clause exempted a homestead of 160 acres of land or a house and lot of 1 acre in any town or city or a home "to every family that could not be alienated" without the joint consent of husband and wife. A man's home is his castle, and that home is exempt from forced sale "under process of law." Kingman fought against the original two-thousand-dollar limit on exemption for a city house, arguing that this mitigated against making improvements in homesteads or homes. He believed this told the owner that "his labor shall be in vain" and that he should waste no time or money in improvements. To Kingman "a home is a home—good or bad—the fireside around which a man may gather his family, with the certainty of assurance that neither the hand of the law nor any, nor all of the uncertainties of life can eject them from the possession of it." However this clause has been criticized, and it has been over the years, most Kansans consider it "the most beneficent provision of their organic law."[7]

"The homestead exemption," according to one authority, "is an American institution with no parallel in other lands." It has no roots in common law but is purely constitutional in origin. In effect it is an exemption law in terms of claims of creditors, but the home must be occupied as a residence by the family of the owner. It protects against the alienation of one spouse acting alone while the other is still living. Since the drafting of the Wyandotte Constitution, the supreme court has interpreted, applied, protected, and extended the doctrine so that it is "something toward which the eye of the creditor need never be turned." It was not until 1980 that the legislature made a change to remove the requirement that the homestead be occupied by a family.[8]

Kingman was nominated for reelection in 1864 on the Union Republican ticket but was defeated by Jacob Safford. He moved to Atchison, where he joined a law practice with future senator John J. Ingalls. The post–Civil War era in Kansas witnessed wild speculation and expansion in railroad construction, and even judges engaged in this gamble. Kingman joined another future chief justice, A. H. Horton, future Democratic governor George W. Glick, Peter T. Abels, and others in promoting the Atchison and Nebraska City Railroad in 1865. Two years later the same group organized the Atchison and Leavenworth Railroad, capitalized at $1 million.[9]

In 1866 Kingman was elected chief justice, receiving almost twenty thousand votes (Nelson Cobb, his opponent, received eight thousand), and he was reelected chief in 1872. During his thirteen and a half years on the high bench he wrote 226 opinions that were known for their "brevity and conciseness." He was so respected by his fellow jurists that they often conceded the difficult decisions for him to write. He endured a sickly physical condition all his life, and, as one colleague noted, he was "often wracked with pain." Perhaps it was this weakness that made him empathize with and be so considerate of others. A young lawyer, Leander Stillwell, described his encounter with the great judge in a homespun manner.[10]

In February 1870 Stillwell appeared before the high court, representing a town in Neosho County in one of the ubiquitous county seat fights of a newly developing state. He was a modest young attorney who had just moved to Kansas two years previously to practice his profession. He came before the supreme court to plead for a writ of mandamus to compel his county board of commissioners to remove the county records back to Erie, "the alleged county seat of said county." His first appearance was not auspicious, as he traveled by stagecoach day and night to the nearest railroad and thence to the capital, and he was "tired, sleepy, and, moreover, greatly awed by my surroundings." He briefly made his presentation, and Judge Kingman announced that the court would consider the matter. Stillwell discovered that the court would announce its decision that December, and because his "heart then was especially wrapped in the case," he returned to Topeka to hear the decision, which went against him.

> I was sitting in one corner of the court-room, reading and re-reading that fatal opinion, looking, I imagine, like the very incarnation of mental anguish and utter wretchedness, when Judge Kingman came in to get some papers from the clerk. He spied me sitting in my corner, in my loneliness and woe, and at once came and shook hands with me in the kindest and most fatherly manner. After a brief conversation he invited me to go with him to his room and visit a while. I tried to beg off, saying that his time was important, he was doubtless busy, etc., but the good old man silenced all my objections at once. He said the court had adjourned for that term and he had nothing to do; and taking me by the arm, he escorted me to his room; we went in and sat down. He lit his old corn-cob pipe, put his feet, encased in coarse white-yarn socks and old carpet slippers, on the seat of an adjacent chair, and then proceeded to chat with me and tell stories, some comical, some pathetic, and all interesting, of incidents of his early days

in Kansas territory and elsewhere. It soon cropped out in the conversation that the judge in his youthful days had practiced law for some years in the town of Hickman, Ky. It so happened that as a soldier boy in the Union army I had also been around and about Hickman to some extent; so a topic was struck where we both were in common ground, and the judge's anecdotes of his career there, and his reminiscences in general, touching the bench, bar and clientage of his time in that locality, were simply delicious.

> But all the time neither of us alluded to my ill-starred "lost cause." Of course, I wouldn't; and the old man on his part knew that some griefs are inconsolable, and, with consummate tact, he skillfully avoided the subject. But I have always been of the opinion that if I had gained the case, I should have lost this delightful interview.[11]

Justice David Brewer related an interesting story about his older colleague. An oil painting of Kingman was presented to the court and hung over the clerk's desk. James Legate remarked one day that it resembled John Brown, who also had a long, flowing white beard, and thus it acquired the name of the famous abolitionist. One day "Dr. Wyman" came into the courtroom, where Kingman was smoking his pipe. After a pause, the judge asked the doctor what he thought about the portrait of John Brown. The near-sighted doctor put on his spectacles and studied the picture a bit, recognized who it really was, then "very deliberately" said, "If John Brown looked like that I don't blame Governor Wise for hanging him." Kingman could only sputter that he wished he could think of something derogatory to say about the medical profession.[12]

In addition to his judicial career, Kingman was the first president of the Kansas State Historical Society and remained as a director, donating his personal tomes, which became the nucleus of the society's library. He served as president of the state Judges' Association and the state Bar Association, and he was president of the Ananais Club at the time of his death. He had to resign from the court in 1876 for health reasons. He was appointed state librarian for a time but again had to resign because of his health. He lived in Topeka until his death, and

Kingman County was named after him. David J. Brewer, later a justice of the US Supreme Court, declared that the early volumes of the *Reports* "will remain an enduring witness. They who were with him in conference know how wise were his counsels, how clear his views, and how discriminating and correct his analysis of difficult and confused cases." Kingman's interpretation of the state constitution is important in the cases of *Cobb* on Ewing's unexpired term; the *Judd* case on territorial taxes under state jurisdiction; the *Helm* case on his homestead provision; *Ephraim* on state/Indian jurisdiction; and the *Miller* and *Lang* cases on tax assessments. There were a number of justices serving with Kingman as he helped mold early Kansas law.[13]

Lawrence Bailey was born at Sutton, New Hampshire, in 1819 of Puritan stock. He was admitted to the bar in 1846, was a California forty-niner, and was active in the formation of that state government. He returned to New Hampshire to practice law and moved to Kansas in 1857, settling on a claim in Douglas County before migrating to Emporia. This occurred at the time Kansas was "bleeding" profusely. He was originally elected to a two-year term on the court and then to a six-year term in 1863. He wrote twelve opinions and was succeeded in that office in 1869 by Daniel M. Valentine, who observed that his predecessor "was an honest, honorable and conscientious man, and was also a man of strong convictions, of strong likes and dislikes."[14]

Nelson Cobb was appointed to serve out Ewing's term until a new election was held in 1863. Cobb was born in Greene County, New York, an isolated region that had no common schools. He was educated by his parents, who were former schoolteachers. He studied law and was admitted to that state's bar. He moved to Kansas in 1859 and, during his brief term of one year on the bench, wrote the opinions of fifteen cases that were noted for their "accurate analysis, clear and terse expression, exact and extensive knowledge of the law, and his high sense of justice."[15]

Nominated to the position of chief justice, Cobb lost his election race to Robert Crozier in 1863, then to Kingman in the following election. Crozier was born in Cadiz, Ohio, in 1828 and moved to Kansas in 1857. He published the first issue of the *Lawrence Times* on 5 October 1857 and served as US attorney for Kansas until his election to complete Ewing's six-year term. After later serving as district judge for four years, he died in 1895.[16]

Daniel Mulford Valentine was born in Shelby County, Iowa, in 1830. During his boyhood the family migrated to Indiana, where he taught school, studied law, and was admitted to the bar in 1859. He settled at Leavenworth and then moved to Peoria and then the county seat of Franklin. He served in both houses of the state legislature and as a district judge. As associate justice on the Kansas Supreme Court, he "did much to mold its present shape of the jurisprudence of the state." His opinions were "clear, explicit, matter of fact." He dissented in part from a Kingman opinion but never explained why, merely stating that he disagreed with the chief justice's "construction" of the plaintiff's responses. Dissents were rare in the early court, and only occasionally did judges file a concurring opinion.[17]

Jacob Safford was born in Royalton, Vermont, in 1827. He was educated at Oberlin and admitted to the bar in 1854. The next year he traveled west to Nebraska City to practice law and spent two winters in that state legislature. He moved to Lawrence in 1858, then to Tecumseh, and finally to Topeka when that town was named the county seat. Safford was elected district judge in the first election following admission to the Union. Elected to the supreme court in 1864, he fulfilled his six-year term before returning to his law practice. Lawyers, like doctors and other professionals, find it difficult to say anything negative about their colleagues. In Safford's memorial, Judge Kingman noted that "law is a jealous mistress." Safford, he thought, gave too much attention to his law practice and his financial interests in railroads to be a successful judge. In discussing Safford's career on the bench, Associate Justice Valentine observed that he was "probably better known, however, as an enterprising and public-spirited citizen of Topeka."[18]

David Brewer gained election to the supreme court in 1870. He was born in 1837 in Smyrna, Asia Minor, to Congregational missionaries. His mother, Emilia Field Brewer, was the sister of the famous David

Fig. 2. David J. Brewer. Image from the Kansas State Historical Society.

Field, who drafted the civil code of procedure for New York state, Cyrus Field, who laid the first transatlantic cable, Stephen Field, the respected Supreme Court justice of the late nineteenth century, and Henry Field, a noted clergyman. Brewer was educated at Wesleyan University and Yale, studied in his uncle's law office in Albany, and graduated from Albany Law School. Determined to go west, he reached Pike's Peak before returning to Kansas, where he settled down to practice law in Leavenworth in 1859. He served as district judge and county attorney and was elected to the supreme court in 1870, running against four other candidates. One biographer described him as "an intriguing combination of prairie progressive and laissez-faire dogmatist." His success on the Kansas bench led President Chester Arthur to appoint him to the Eighth Circuit Court, and in 1889 President Benjamin Harrison elevated him to the US Supreme Court.[19]

All these early jurists were Republicans, and most came from New England and New York. When Kingman returned as chief justice in 1867, his court began a period of significant transformation in Kansas law. During its first five formative years, the problem of making the new state government operational was a demanding task. Frequent changes in court personnel highlighted the difficulties of the judicial branch, and there were some obvious problems of inexperience while voters sorted out the election and performance process. Some judges during these formative years joined the court after cases were heard and thus could not participate in writing the decisions. Others served as counsel for the parties involved in the litigation. There was an obvious lack of teamwork that changed with the new court of Kingman, Valentine, and Brewer following Kingman's election as the chief justice in November 1866. By that time the nation was enjoying a peacetime prosperity; the state population was surging, growing tenfold from 1861 to 1882; and the court business increased correspondingly as a result. From 1867 onward an obvious esprit de corps developed on the high bench. Problems of county seat fights, the legal status of Indian tribes, and railroads occupied much of the attention of the early court.[20]

The Cases

The transition from territory to statehood created legal problems, and the first case in this category heard by Ewing's court concerned the first election held under the auspices of the state of Kansas. The territorial schedule called for a statewide election on Tuesday after the first Monday in November in 1861. George A. Crawford received some votes in that election, and he brought suit in *State of Kansas ex rel. George A. Crawford v. Charles Robinson et al.* for a writ of mandamus to require the state to canvass the returns again and count his votes. He had been elected governor by the voters of the territory, and Section I, Article I of the Wyandotte Constitution provided that the governor would be elected by state voters after admission to the Union in January 1861 to hold office for two years after taking the oath on the second Monday in January. Yet state officials had been elected on the first Tuesday in December 1859 before statehood and were to begin serving on 1 February 1861 immediately after admission to the Union.

The first state legislature provided for elections to be held in November 1862. The argument was presented that these first officers were chosen by the electors of the territory but not by state voters. In a "very carefully written opinion," the court rejected this argument and refused the writ, saying that this first government would complete terms in January 1863, when the next government would assume office. Charles Robinson then served as the state governor from 9 February 1861 to the second Monday in January 1863. He suffered a most unsuccessful term, enduring impeachment, but he was finally acquitted and left office under a cloud.[21]

The question of legislation enacted by the territorial solons between the admission to statehood on 29 January 1861 and 9 February 1861 also arose when the governor issued a proclamation to convene the state legislature. In *Kansas v. Meadows* the court affirmed the validity of the interim laws on the basis of the continuing schedule of the territory "until their successors are elected and qualified." The territorial legislature was legal until February 1861, when the new state government assumed power.[22]

When Ewing resigned, Governor Robinson appointed Nelson Cobb as his replacement. He held that office until 5 January 1864, when he yielded it to Robert Crozier, who was elected to complete Ewing's unexpired six-year term on 3 November 1863. The issue involved Ewing's resignation, dated 20 October 1861; Cobb's service, which began on 28 December; and the governor not receiving Ewing's resignation, which he sent from Pea Ridge, Arkansas, until 28 December. Meanwhile, though no specific election for chief justice was called, John Watson was elected to the office in the general election in November, and while the board of canvassers did not count the vote for chief justice, the state officers elected at that time made their canvass and declared Watson elected. In a quo warranto proceeding brought by the attorney general in *Kansas ex rel. Watson v. Cobb*, Justice Kingman held that Cobb's appointment legally entitled him to the office because Ewing's resignation came in less than thirty days prior to the 1862 election, and Robinson's selection of him was valid. The constitution, Kingman stated, clearly provides that temporary vacancies of judicial positions can be filled only by appointment of the governor and not by election.[23]

Legal issues of property taxes also carried over from territory to statehood. Tax laws of 1858 and 1860 provided for taxpayers to discharge their obligations in payment with warrants for the units to which payment was due. Sarah Driver owned real estate in Wyandotte township in fee simple and was assessed township and county taxes. Her property was forfeited for nonpayment of those taxes. In the absence of other bidders, the county treasurer bid in the land for the amount of the taxes in January 1860. On 1 January 1863 the treasurer sold the land for the taxes and interest and was paid in legal tender. The original owner, Driver, sought to redeem her land and paid in township scrip for the township taxes, county scrip for the county taxes, and legal tender for the interest and costs. The registrar refused to issue the redemption certificate and demanded legal tender for all the taxes due. Kingman sustained the district judge's writ of mandamus on the registrar ordering the issuance of the redemption certificate because he was "bound by law" to accept the various warrants, and the writ of mandamus was "a subject within the jurisdiction of the district court."[24]

The issue of legal tender created many legal issues at this time. In 1863, in an effort to raise revenue to fight the Civil War, Congress created $450 million by issuing that amount in legal tender, or paper money, and putting it into circulation. This was valid paper money, because Congress declared it to be "legal tender for all debts, public and private." Congress's next step was to tax out of existence all other currencies in the nation, leaving a sound national currency system that was of inestimable value to the emerging capitalist system. For a nation accustomed to only bullion as "money," these greenbacks (critics said they were backed only by the green paper they were printed on) were difficult to accept, and their value fluctuated with the fortunes of the Union army. Greenbacks also created legal problems, as they were circulating at about 68 cents per gold dollar at the time of Appomattox.[25]

In frontier country such as Kansas, paper money was important because of the scarcity of specie (gold or silver), and creditors were reluctant to accept it for debts or governmental units for taxes because of its depreciated value. Over a period of years, state courts sustained laws requiring greenbacks as legal tender for both debts and taxes by repudiating gold clause contracts. The national currency system in place during the Gilded Age was of great value in promoting the capitalist system.[26]

The various election laws also created confusion for county commissioners, who were charged with providing for elections and verifying their validity. The first state legislature decided elections should be held on 2 June 1861 to determine the permanent location of "the seat of justice" in Coffey County. At the first election no town received a majority, so the law provided for a second election on the first Monday in November between the two top vote-getters after the county commissioners announced the results of the first election. In 1858 the territorial legislature approved location of the seat at Burlington. The county clerk refused to accept this decision and moved his records to Leroy. After the first election resulted in neither town receiving a majority, the second election was held but without the necessary proclamation of the results of the first election, and Leroy won. Upon petition the district court issued a mandamus for the clerk to move the records to Burlington. Chief Justice Cobb, speaking for the court, held that, without the "important and necessary" proclamation, the county could not receive "a full and fair vote" without informing the electorate. The judgment of the district court was affirmed, and the seat of justice was returned to Burlington.[27]

Leander Stillwell's case for locating the Neosho County seat involved a good deal of fraud, as did many county seat wars, because location was a prize that meant growth and security for the winner. As Justice Brewer noted in a later case, roads and residences are built, lawyers become involved, and merchants and railroads make local decisions on the basis of the location of the county seat. "The public good," he observed, "requires a speedy transition [of the issue]." Kansas law provided that a county could be created by gubernatorial proclamation when its population reached six hundred. The governor could then name temporary officials and the county seat until elections were held for these as provided by the legislature. Even before this point in settlement the fight often began with some areas falsely certifying the number of required residents. In Comanche County a representative to the state legislature was elected, and several thousand dollars in bond issues were voted, but the county had "no inhabitants and never did." In the Stevens County conflict six men were killed before the governor could order the militia there to restore order.[28]

This issue in Stillwell's Neosho County produced the case of *Kansas ex rel. Wells v. Commissioners of Neosho County* in 1870. A June 1868 election produced 543 votes for Erie, 572 votes for Mission Town, and 2 for Osage Mission. The commissioners rejected the vote in Mission Town on the basis of fraud and kept the county seat in Erie. The district court approved a mandamus for a recanvass of the vote, but a new election was called instead. On 14 December 1869 no town received a majority, but a third election two weeks later produced 2,587 for Erie and 1,965 for Mission. The new county commissioners "caused the said county records to be removed and surreptitiously and clandestinely carried to

Erie." Justice Valentine, speaking for the court, observed that the case should be titled Joseph A. Wells without "Kansas ex rel." because the state cannot bring suit for such a writ. Valentine found that 4,552 votes were cast, yet there were only "about 1,700" legal voters in the county. While most of the fraud occurred at Erie, it was widespread, and the court had a duty "to go behind the canvass" and discover those 2,852 illegal votes. "Neither party [had] shown a clear right" to the county seat, so a new election was ordered to let the "people" decide the location. Erie eventually won the struggle.[29]

Kingman's homestead provision was also tested in the early courts. Mary Cusick owned three adjoining lots in Leavenworth with a large brick house that she lived in as her homestead. In August 1860 Sheriff John C. Douglas obtained a judgment against her for $100 and costs for tax delinquency and proceeded to advertise one of the lots for sale to satisfy that assessment. She argued that the homestead provision forbade this action. Chief Justice Crozier noted that the sheriff insisted that the clause was an impairment of contract because the state constitution provided for transition from territory to statehood, and "all suits, rights, actions, prosecutions, recognizances, contracts, judgments and claims . . . shall continue as if no change had taken place." The sheriff argued, therefore, that he could use the same means of enforcement that he had employed before adoption of the constitution. Crozier decided that this objection was "not well founded." The claim of protection against impairment of contract, Crozier stated, "was one of the most important questions ever addressed to this tribunal." Using the national precedent of *Bronson v. Kingle*, the chief justice noted that the homestead exemption and the common law extended from the protection of implements or tools to earn a livelihood to the concept of "a place of abode and shelter." The object was "reasonably necessary to protect the citizens in their pursuits necessary to their existence and well being."[30]

The title to John and Catherine Ward's homestead was in John's name. John mortgaged the homestead, and after the Wards sold it, the mortgagor foreclosed. Also, while they lived on their homestead another couple acquired title to the property through a sheriff's sale to satisfy the mortgage. Finally, the couple sold the homestead to Isaac Morris, claiming that the land was unencumbered. Catherine Ward was not a party to any of these proceedings except the sale to Morris. Valentine held that the homestead clause did not permit the husband alone to encumber the property, but as a couple they could sell, and the purchaser could take the title "free and clear from all encumbrances."[31]

When Samantha married James Helm on 15 April 1871 he owned eighty acres, and they lived on it as their homestead. In June 1871 William and his brother James plotted to defraud Samantha of the homestead by selling it to William for $900 when it was worth $1,500. She refused to agree to the sale until her husband purchased another homestead for a home. The brothers "menaced and threatened" her life and forced her to sign the deed. Two days later James abandoned Samantha, and she petitioned to have the deed set aside. Chief Justice Kingman and the court supported Samantha because the homestead clause requires the consent of both husband and wife to alienate it. She had that right of protection "with or without her husband." Because she was "compelled to sign away the interest by duress," her rights could not be lost "by the illegal conduct of those who attempt to profit by their violence."[32]

The plight of Native Americans also absorbed the early court's attention. These people on the Great Plains took advantage of white preoccupation with their civil war, and in the decades following hostilities, the Union army gained extensive experience in guerrilla warfare in subduing these tribes. During this process, federal and state officials attempted another "removal" of the tribes from lands white settlers wanted for farms to less desirable lands (until oil was discovered in Oklahoma). In 1867 a meeting of the various tribes in the area signed the Medicine Lodge Creek treaties, which required them to move to Oklahoma and other western areas. Following Indian raids and pitched battles, the Kansas frontier was largely pacified by 1869, and white migration into the area proceeded apace. The tribes received annuities for their lands, and the litigation of these treaties and land titles absorbed much of the time of the Kingman court.

A case involving these lands was first tried in a territorial district court under Judge Pettit and appealed to the Kansas Supreme Court, with Chief Justice Ewing writing the opinion before he went to war. The territories of Kansas and Nebraska were created by the act of 30 June 1854. Two weeks later the Delaware Tribe sold lands to the federal government for $10,000 and provided for the sheriff to sell its "surplus" lands and forward the proceeds to the tribe, which was then moving to Indian Territory. The territorial legislature created the county of Leavenworth and elected the sheriff, Green P. Todd, who failed to register his bond as a territorial official. His handling of the Delaware trust funds was challenged on this basis. Ewing, speaking for the court, ruled that Todd's proceedings were valid because the lands ceded came under the jurisdiction of the United States and thus also the state of Kansas. The writ of attachment of the sold property was invalid because Todd was sheriff from the time he accepted his commission, "and his neglect, or that of the court, to have the bond approved, did not vacate the office." His actions, therefore, "were binding and effectual."[33]

Louis Laurent sold a pint of whiskey, a pint of brandy, and a pint of wine to "one Check-wan," a Pottawatomie who was subject to tribal jurisdiction. A federal law of 1870 prohibited selling liquor to Native Americans who were tribal members, an attempt to protect them from the dangers of alcohol, to which they were particularly susceptible. Laurent sued to quash his grand jury indictment as there was not a "true bill": the jury foreman had presented it without the presence of the jury, and not all twelve members supported the indictment. The Kingman court rejected the plaintiff's plea, affirmed his conviction, and charged him with court costs. The indictment, the justice observed, met the intent of the rules prescribed by the legislature.[34]

A complex land title question regarding the Wyandotte treaty of 1855 soon arose. John Pipe, a Wyandotte, received title to land at the fork of the Kansas and Missouri Rivers allotted to him as head of the family, his wife, Mary, and his minor children, Maria and Winfield from a former marriage to Maria Pipe. His current wife, Mary, was the daughter of George Spybuck and the sister of James Spybuck, and she died childless in 1857. On 1 July 1859 John sold the land to Commodore P. Summers for $309.75. George and James Spybuck claimed to be heirs of Maria Pipe. The lower court determined that John Pipe held title to one-fourth of his land and the other three-fourths in trust for Mary, Maria, and Winfield. Was his sale of the land to Summers in conformity to the treaty of 1855? Chief Justice Cobb answered this in his opinion: when John Pipe patented his title it conveyed all 147 acres of land to him as head of family, and the lower court erred in excluding his lien.[35]

On 29 September 1869 the Osage Tribe signed a treaty to convey its land in Kansas to the national government. The lands were to be surveyed and sold by the secretary of the interior, and no homestead or preemption settlement on them would be recognized. In addition, the treaty provided that "not to exceed" twenty-five half-breeds who had made improvements on "the north half" of these lands should receive title in fee simple for eighty acres each. "The chiefs and the head men of the tribe" would designate the twenty-five men. William Tinker made his selection of land and received a title on 10 June 1870. On 30 September 1870 Tinker and his wife deeded the land to George Lounsberry, but in January 1866 J. W. Rakestraw had moved onto the land and built improvements. Rakestraw insisted that a mistake had been made and that Tinker's title was for a different eighty acres. Justice Brewer wrote that Rakestraw was "simply a naked trespasser" who had no claim to the land, and he remanded the case for a new trial. The error could have been corrected even after the title was issued, and when Tinker made no effort to correct it, "it was virtually a selection by him of the tract reported." The approval of the secretary of the interior "confirmed the title in him as of date prior to any rights Rakestraw would acquire by his occupancy."[36]

In 1865 Chief Justice Cobb answered a question that he termed "very important and delicate" involving the ascertainment of the boundary between the powers and functions of the national and state governments. In May 1854 the Shawnee, who had achieved a rather high level of "civilization" and whom the national government sought to domesticate further (a policy of "killing them with kindness"), signed a treaty selling their lands of 1.6 million acres to Washington for $829,000. In turn, the government ceded two hundred thousand acres back to them, and the tribe would then allocate two hundred acres for each tribal member. The individual could select his acreage under the traditional legal concept of "perpetual use and occupancy." Charles Blue-Jacket, a Shawnee living in Johnson County, selected his headrights, and a patent for 200 acres was assigned to him. All property within the state, except that exempted in the state constitution, the US Constitution, "and the laws and treaties made in pursuance thereof," was subject to taxation. What was the status of Blue-Jacket's land? He argued that the title in fee simple rested in the hands of the national government, and therefore it was exempt from taxation. The treaty contained the clause that the land "shall never be sold by the grantee or his heirs without the consent of the Secretary of Interior." Justice Cobb determined that under the terms of the treaty, Blue-Jacket held title to his lands, but the secretary of the interior had the power to exempt it from taxation. Yet the secretary of the interior deliberately did not insert the exemption in this instance. Blue-Jacket's property, therefore, was subject to state taxation. "The object of these patents," Cobb asserted, "was to convey to the individuals title to the land in fee simple" and thus gave Blue-Jacket the obligation to pay taxes.[37]

The state jurisdiction over Native Americans was clarified further the next year when George Hunt killed Mah-cah-tah-chin-quah. Both were members of the Wea Tribe, living in Miami County. The murder, however, took place outside the Wea Reservation. Hunt was convicted of fourth-degree manslaughter but appealed the decision on the grounds that both men came under tribal jurisdiction. Not so, responded Justice Bailey for the court, when the crime takes place outside the tribal jurisdiction. The state of Kansas had authority in this instance. He used the analogy that if a Frenchman kills another Frenchman "on the streets of Paola" in Miami County, the French government would not have jurisdiction. "Every civilized nation," he asserted, "claims and exercises the right to maintain order and punish crime within its territorial limits." This analogy was not far-fetched, as the national government still adhered to the strange policy of negotiating treaties with Indian tribes as though they were a foreign nation.[38]

Sac and Fox tribal member Keokuk received brutal treatment at the hands of a federal official in Lawrence. He was "willfully and with force, assaulted . . . beat, bruised, wounded, ill-treated, and kept in jail" with "thieves and other vile characters" for one night and two days. He asked for $10,000 in damages. Albert Wiley defended his actions on the grounds that he was the US agent for the Sac and Fox Tribe, and he had received orders from Acting Commissioner of Indian Affairs Charles Mix to prevent any Sac or Fox from traveling to the national capital. Keokuk, he said, "pretends to be a chief of said Indians," and Wiley acted with authority in detaining him by force. The jury awarded Keokuk $1,000, and Wiley appealed this decision. The Kingman court supported Keokuk's rights, saying that Mix's instructions did not justify illegal actions against him. Keokuk was a ward of the national government, and so agents could restrain him, but if he did not violate any laws, his rights must be respected.[39]

The Osage Tribe sold its Kansas lands to the US government and moved to Indian Territory on 28 September 1865. The treaty included the provision that preemption or homestead claims on tribal lands would not be recognized. James Wood preempted a quarter section of this land and made improvements, but the registrar of deeds refused to accept his application for title. The Katy Railroad acquired title to this land by a grant in assistance to construction. Justice Valentine declared that "all the departments of the federal government" have agreed on the concept that the national government retains all powers over the sale or conveyance of Indian lands under its treaty-making power. The lands were to be sold to raise a "civilization fund" for the members of the Osage Tribe for their "education and civilization." If their lands were open to preemption or homesteading, they would probably never raise "a dollar" for this purpose. The plaintiff could not legally preempt any of this land and therefore was "merely a trespasser upon government land." Valentine's decision affirmed the lower court's opinion.[40]

A suit was brought to determine the status of the Cherokee Strip.

When the Cherokee Nation was removed to Indian Territory, the treaty the tribe signed in 1835 ceded it an area containing some 7 million acres lying north of the 37th parallel. The Cherokees had abandoned this land following the treaty of 1866, and the state of Kansas exercised jurisdiction to the 37th parallel, or the northern boundary of Indian Territory. Henry Ephraim preempted 160 acres in this area in Labette County and built improvements, insisting that the land was "vacant and unoccupied" when he took possession. Theodore Garlick bought the land and claimed Ephraim had "unlawfully and forcefully" prevented him from taking possession of it. The district court held for Garlick, and Ephraim appealed. Kingman wrote the unusual opinion that the court could not "determine from the petition" that the land in controversy was part of the land ceded to the Cherokees because "there is no evidence of any kind preserved." Not being able to discover an error, therefore, the district court judgment was affirmed.[41]

Finally, the exemption of Indian lands from state taxation received a significant interpretation in 1874. The question involved the so-called Cherokee Neutral Lands, some of which James F. Jay purchased. After he received title, he sold the lands to a railroad in March 1869. On 2 November 1870 the line paid the balance of purchase money, received patent, and argued that Bourbon County could not tax it for 1870, as the lands were still Indian or national government lands until final patent. In addition, the suit also involved lands the state of Kansas received in Bourbon County from a national land grant to aid in construction of railroads. The state legislature took no action on this gift until March 1871, when it formally accepted the grant. Justice Brewer cited the US Supreme Court decision of *The Kansas Indians* that Indian lands "are withdrawn from the operation of state laws." He determined that, because final title was not obtained until 1871, the title to this area remained in the Cherokee Nation until the state completed its patent. The case was remanded to district court to enter judgment for the railroad, with court costs being divided between the company and Bourbon County.[42]

The construction of railroads played a key role in the economic history of the state and became the subject of endless litigation for decades. The 71 miles of railroad tracks in 1860 in the Sunflower State were expanded to 1,234 miles in 1870. The Panic of 1873 halted this boom temporarily, but the tracks had grown to 3,104 miles by 1880. This expansion assured the future of hundreds of towns, provided farmers with outlets to national markets, led to colorful longhorn cattle drives from Texas and the range cattle industry, and helped produce the "labor problem" that emerged in Kansas during the period of the Horton court.

Before and after the Civil War railroads played a significant role in Kansas history. Construction began in the eastern part of the state before the conflict began and spread rapidly afterward. The Union Pacific, Southern Branch, which became known as the Katy, was the first major line to traverse the state north to south, and the Atchison, Topeka and Santa Fe was the first east–west transcontinental in Kansas. The state chartered a thousand railroads, and perhaps one-fifth of them actually laid track. These lines brought dozens of problems to the Kingman court in terms of land titles, danger of fires, damage to livestock, finances, taxes, and governmental controls.[43]

The national government gave these railroads over 175 million acres (more than the size of Texas) to assist in construction. Kansas donated lands from its federal grants, and local government units contributed money to attract lines to their area. Occasionally railroads squabbled with each other over these millions of acres. The Kansas Pacific, building west out of Junction City, argued with the Katy, then constructing south out of Junction City, over land grants in the Smoky Hill River valley. The lands were reserved from sale, and on 22 January 1867 the president ordered patents for them to be issued. The Katy received patents from the governor for grants the state had received from the national government on 15 January 1873, but the Kansas Pacific claimed paramount title because of federal supremacy and brought suit. Justice Brewer refereed the controversy over the one hundred thousand acres in Davis and Dickinson Counties that subsequently became contested because there had been no "specific designation of the lands granted." The Kansas Pacific grants were generous: alternate sections of odd-numbered ones on each side of the right-of-way within ten miles, or ten sections for each mile constructed, the usual terms for transcontinental lines. The grantee was required to file a map of its general route with the secretary of the interior, who would then withdraw sections within fifteen miles of the right-of-way from the public lands available for purchase or settlement. The railway subsequently changed its route because of topographical features after it reached Fort Riley, east of Junction City, from the Republican to the Smoky Hill Rivers, and on 22 January 1867 the governor granted the lands to the Katy to build from Junction City south through the Neosho River valley. This grant was twice as generous, giving ten alternate sections on each side of the route. Congress approved the Kansas action on 26 July 1866. The company commenced construction and reached Indian Territory on 9 June 1870, and the governor certified this with the secretary of the interior. But the Kansas Pacific grant stated that if its lands were sold or reserved for any purpose, the secretary of the interior would "cause other lands in equal amount to be selected" for the grant. Brewer and the Kansas court determined that the Kansas Pacific lands "were definitely fixed" before the Katy's lands, and the latter would have to accept sections selected by the secretary of the interior as alternate grants.[44]

The court entertained a case that involved land from the Kickapoo Reservation that the Union Pacific had acquired but for which it had not yet completed payment. The railroad sold some of this land to Henry Winsor, who added improvements and sought to restrain Atchison County from collecting taxes. Valentine thought it "ludicrous" for the national government to treat with "a few half naked, half starved savages" as though they were "a great nation," but the government created an even "graver question" over whether it could give this "public domain to a few railroad companies." After expressing these prejudices, Safford concurring, Valentine determined that neither the Winsor land nor his improvements were taxable because final title had not been issued. These decisions appeared to place obstacles in the path of struggling new governmental entities that needed revenues to provide badly needed services to settlers. As long as railroads refused to fulfill their obligations on their huge land grants by receiving title, these sections could not be taxed. In many instances they declined to take title until settlement was quite near their line and pioneers were ready to buy their land. Often the judges supported the railroads because of personal financial involvement. President Grover Cleveland took back some 44 million acres in areas of limited demand because the railroads refused to take title and pay taxes.[45]

The state of Kansas enacted fence laws to protect crops, but this requirement did not extend to railroads. They came under the common law in this category. If livestock wandered onto the tracks, the railroad was not responsible for their injury or death. The defendant in a case brought before the court allowed his cattle to roam at large, and five were killed on an unfenced railroad line. Under common law, as approved by the Kansas legislature, Valentine and the court determined that an owner of real estate was not required to fence it, but unless he does, he is not using "reasonable and ordinary care and diligence" to protect his property. Therefore, he is without remedy if he does not prevent his livestock from wandering or straying.[46]

The emergence of the Industrial Revolution in the nineteenth century produced a "rapid development" in tort reform. A tort is a civil wrong, other than a breach of contract, for which courts provide remedies. Industrial and railroad negligence cases increased, with courts disposed to apply the concept of negligence to carriers and industrialists. On the other hand, when persons cross railroad tracks without stopping, looking, and listening, this "contributory negligence" barred recovery. The "fellow servant" rule protected the employer, but he must also provide reasonably safe machinery or workplace environment. Eventually, the emergence of workmen's compensation served to obviate many of these issues.[47]

Often it meant life or death to a community to attract the services of a railroad, and many local government units mortgaged their future for years to come to bribe a line to build to them. Davis (later Geary) County voters approved $165,000 in bonds to assist the Union Pacific, Southern Branch (Katy), to begin construction at Junction City and build south to Indian Territory. When the company dallied because of financial reasons and litigation over location, the county commissioners reneged on the bonds. Was the original vote a contract? The railroad insisted it was a proposition it had accepted, and it sued for payment. The court's opinion denied the railroad a writ of mandamus because there was no contract but merely an encouragement for the railroad to do what it intended to do anyway. The county was under no legal obligation.[48]

Speaking for the court, Justice Valentine approved government units assisting railroads financially through the power of taxation. A county purchased $250,000 in Union Pacific bonds through the legislative act that gave approval of territorial laws of 1858 and 1859 to provide financial assistance for rail lines. Valentine observed that railroads served the private purpose of making money for their stockholders, but they also served a public purpose and provided benefit to the entire state. Taxes can be levied only for a public purpose, but railroads came under this category.[49]

During the July 1870 term, Kingman's court handed down an important constitutional interpretation. Kansas law required county clerks to assess railroad property within their jurisdiction and send notification of this to the state auditor. A property owner rejected the assessment on railroad land as being too low and appealed directly to the supreme court. The railroad moved to dismiss the case because of lack of jurisdiction. Kingman agreed, because the court had only the original jurisdiction spelled out in the constitution. The legislature could expand appellate jurisdiction of the court, as it had done in this instance, but this gave the court executive as well as judicial power. It was "absurd," Kingman insisted, to give his court "authority to acts purely executive in their charge." He thought it would be "a power as dangerous to good government as it is subversive of the constitution," which distinctly separates executive, legislative, and judicial functions. He dismissed the case, because the power could not be conferred "without a manifest infringement of the constitution" and exercise in judicial review.[50]

Mollie Nash's horse wandered four or five miles from home, and a locomotive hit and killed it at a point where the right-of-way was fenced on both sides of the track. Mollie sued and won $130 from the jury. The jury was out all day, and members prepared to disband for the evening when the judge reminded them that after "sleep and refreshment" they would probably reach a verdict the next morning. But he warned them that they should bring their own dinner with them in case they should be unable to reach a decision, because "the court would not feel like ordering dinner the next day at the county's expense." As a result, they decided in favor of the railroad early the next day. Kingman interpreted the court's remarks as not designed to intimidate the jury. It was reasonable to insist the jury make "all reasonable efforts" to arrive at a verdict.[51]

Texas cattleman T. J. McCoy was a pioneer in driving cattle north to meet Kansas railroads at Abilene for shipment to slaughterhouses in Chicago. Along with these drives came "Texas fever" (a disease fatal to domestic breeding stock in warm weather), and some states, including Kansas and Illinois, enacted laws prohibiting the passage of Texas cattle through their states between "the first days of March and December," when the danger was highest. McCoy accompanied large shipments of cattle to Illinois and spent $4,000 to $5,000 during that winter, with $2,000 of that amount spent to hold the cattle in Springfield, Illinois. The remainder was spent in lobbying the Illinois legislature to repeal its quarantine law. The Kansas Pacific promised to repay him $2.50 per carload for his lobbying activities, and the Abilene depot agent showed a shipment of 2,057 carloads that year. When the railroad refused to compensate him, McCoy sued for $5,127.50, and the jury awarded him $5,042. The railroad sought a writ of error. Brewer wrote the opinion, observing that if McCoy spent the money on the publication of circulars and pamphlets, this was proper. "The use of money to influence legislation," he observed, "is not always wrong." But if it was paid in bribery, it was illegal. McCoy received the award.[52]

Justice Brewer wrote an important decision on uniformity of laws. The legislature had enacted a "fence" law in 1868. It followed this with a "herd" law in 1870 that exempted Saline, Ottawa, Washington, Cloud, Cherokee, and McPherson Counties from the fence law for five years because this was open-range cattle country. Jonathan Darling sued Charles

Rodgers because his horses and mules roamed freely and damaged his crops in Saline County. He won $25 and court costs. Justice Brewer announced that "all laws of a general nature shall have uniform operation." The legislature could enact a fence law or a herd law but could not specify exemptions. If this were permitted, "this valuable constitutional provision are [*sic*] weaker than a rope of sand."[53]

Biographer Michael Brodhead concluded that the Kingman court "showed a general tendency to agree with the public's insistence that the railroads and other large business interests be required to serve the public's best interests." A few years later the Populists would demand this as a matter of course. In fact, the Populists went beyond this to request that the state construct its share of a transcontinental railroad to compete with existing lines.[54]

Clear title to property was an important legal issue in the early court because of carryover from the territorial period and the youth of the state government. Robert Stringfellow became involved in litigation when it was discovered that his house and lot in Atchison lay in section 36, which was reserved for public education by the Northwest Ordinance of 1785. In 1854 part of that section was platted for town sites, and Territorial Governor R. J. Walker patented it into the town company. The state sued Stringfellow to recover his plot because it never recognized this particular territorial action. The district court found for Stringfellow, and the state appealed. Chief Justice Crozier agreed that it was an injustice for Stringfellow to be able to purchase the land at $2.50 per acre under the homestead law when he should have paid four times that amount, but this point was "immaterial." Crozier decided that Stringfellow had legal title to the land caused by an administrative error when the suit was begun, so he affirmed the decision of the lower court for Stringfellow.[55]

When a sheriff sold property for delinquent taxes, the law required him to advertise it carefully. In one case, the sheriff offered property for sale on "July 14." He confused his dates, and when the advertisement was published, it read "June 30," and he sold a different property on July 14. The plaintiff asked the court to set aside the latter sale because it was not advertised as required by law. Justice Safford could not discover "upon what grounds the lower court refused his petition" and held for Terry, the sheriff. The tax deed was prima facie evidence for clear title, and Safford held that the district court judge erred twice in refusing to permit this tax deed to be read in evidence during the trial.[56]

Assessor decisions are often challenged. In an early case a taxpayer listed the value of his property at $1,185. Without notice of hearing as required by law, the county commissioner's board of assessors increased this substantially to $8,000. The taxpayer asked the board to correct its error but was refused. He paid the taxes he believed he justly owed and received an injunction against the board collecting further money. Kingman said the man "stood charged with an unjust and illegal tax," and he had a right to seek remedy. "He was injured, had a remedy, and used it."[57]

The issue of church and state on taxes was questioned. Douglas County treasurer M. S. Beach levied a tax of $218 on a house owned in Lawrence by the Protestant Episcopal Diocese of Kansas. The bishop used this as his official residence and sought an injunction against the collection of the tax. The district court refused the injunction, and the diocese appealed. Chief Justice Kingman cited *Washburn College v. Shawnee County* that it is the use, not the ownership, of property that determined the tax exemption. In this case the house was used only "incidentally" for religious purposes and did not meet the requirement of use "exclusively" for religion.[58]

Females had few rights in nineteenth-century Kansas outside the protection Samuel Kingman gave them in the homestead clause. All the discussions about "free" Kansas involved the question of black slavery, not inherent rights of citizens regardless of gender. Women were given the vote in municipal elections in 1887 and were finally granted the full franchise through a constitutional amendment in 1912, but meanwhile they were sadly lacking in equal status. Kingman and Brewer did what they could to support women in the divorce process, although the law often worked against this, as was true throughout nineteenth-century America. Divorce was quite rare in colonial America and still uncommon in the early twentieth century. New York permitted it only in case of adultery, and other states occasionally allowed it for desertion, fraud, impotence, conviction of a felony, or habitual drunkenness. Many cases of divorce, of course, raised the problem of child custody and support, which influenced judicial decisions. Common law awarded fathers child custody, but this practice gradually declined in the nineteenth century as the concept of "best interest of the child" emerged.[59]

The case of *Harris v. Harris* provided some amusement for the chief justice and slight embarrassment for Justice Brewer. Kaufman and Lotta Harris had three minor children when they divorced. The decree gave Lotta custody of the children two days after a fourth child was born. Kaufman conveyed his property of two stores for their income to support the family until the buildings were destroyed by fire. When Kaufman refused to pay child support later, Lotta maintained the family financially by taking in boarders. She brought suit for support for the intervening three years, but District Court Judge David Brewer instructed the jury, and it awarded her $138 annually only for the fourth child. She sued to reverse that judgment. Her only legal recourse, the supreme court said, was to reopen the divorce case and ask for "such full justice as the case requires, having reference to advances already made." After Brewer left the district court the husband hired him and partner John Pendery to appeal the decision. Kingman later recalled that Brewer "seemed awkward and in half apology" in presenting his brief, and Brewer said "he could not see why he should not complain of his own decision, as everyone else had done so."[60]

A case involved a couple who had a small child, and the wife testified that her husband had asked her to sign a deed transferring a quarter section of land, their homestead, to his brother. She refused to sign, and he struck her with his fist three times and pulled her hair. She was in "poor health," and that evening he brought in an axe and "sharpened a large knife." Upon seeing this she agreed to sign but later divorced him and received alimony. The court was forced to conclude that the law forbade a wife to testify "concerning any communication made by one to the other during the marriage." The court acknowledged that "it seems a peculiar hardship to allow a husband to shield himself under the protection of the law from the consequences of his own outrages." But the law is the law, Kingman insisted, and it was "founded in wisdom" and must be maintained "however much that case may appeal to our sense of justice."[61]

A lower court granted John Brandon a divorce from Mary Ann Brandon because of her "habitual drunkenness" but gave her custody of the two small children. She also received custody of their homestead "during her natural life" and alimony of $25 monthly. The title of the home was in his name and protected by the homestead clause. Brewer held that "upon divorce the court has the power to assign it" to either the husband or the wife. This constitutional grant of power to the district courts also included the power to determine disposition of property and custody of children. If, the court added, after children passed the age that "especially demands a mother's care" and her habits of drunkenness continued, the court could modify its order and give custody to the father. The alimony, the court assumed, was for the benefit of the children, not the wife.[62]

In an interesting early interpretation of the Fifteenth Amendment, Valentine, supported by Kingman, held that this amendment worked to strike the word "white" from the Kansas constitutional qualifications that limited suffrage to "every white male person." In a mayoral election Anthony received 1,406 votes and Haldeman 1,453. In a quo warranto proceeding S. D. Lecompte represented Anthony and argued that 130 people of "African descent" voted because they met all the other constitutional requirements. Kansas politicians, however, ignored this ruling until the civil rights movement of the mid-twentieth century forced them to accommodate to it.[63]

Criminal law received a good vetting and molding by the early court. Joseph W. Reddick killed John Lykens in December 1870. Reddick pleaded insanity, and his doctor testified on his behalf. He had known the defendant for "18–20 years" and knew that when he was "6 or 7" a colt kicked him in the head, "broke his skull and about a teaspoon of his brains lost." Then four years before the murder he was stabbed in the head near the former wound, and "a small fragment of the knife blade remained in his head." The court charged the jury that it must convict him of the crime if he committed it, but the judge did not specify "what degree of the offense if they found the defendant guilty." As a result, the jury voted for the death sentence. Brewer had been one of the counsel involved in the trial, so he did not participate in Kingman's decision. Valentine concurred with the chief justice that the case should be remanded for a new trial with proper jury instructions.[64]

When McCord shot Lorenzo Hilliard three times with a pistol, the crime raised two constitutional questions. This premeditated attack resulted in mortal wounds, and McCord was charged with first-degree murder. The criminal law of 1871 said that no witness should be incompetent solely because of being the husband or wife of the accused. The state called his wife, Sarah, and she testified. The court's decision noted that this exception was not a limitation on competency but on the power of the court to compel such testimony. The jury was instructed to find him guilty of first-degree murder, any one of several kinds of manslaughter, "or of an assault only." The jury found him guilty of third-degree manslaughter, and he immediately moved for a new trial, hoping for a lesser penalty. Kingman held that this was not double jeopardy but placed the defendant in the same situation as if no trial had taken place because of his own legal action. McCord's luck ran out, as the new jury convicted him of the harsher penalty of second-degree murder.[65]

A bizarre case of extensive larceny in Shawnee County was exposed when a family of thirteen squatted in a one-room house, cut prairie hay, and built several hollow haystacks in which to hide their loot. Four of them were arrested for stealing a double set of harness valued at $50. In searching the premises, officials found the harness in a haystack close to the stable. There and in three other stacks they found gunnysacks full of harness, barrels of salt and molasses, carpenter tools, and two wagonloads of stolen goods. Before the trial three of the prisoners escaped, but Leonard was too sick to run. He was convicted of larceny whether or not he was the one who actually stole the harness because he was an "accessory before the fact" of the felony charged. The court refused to interfere with the decision of the lower court.[66]

Thomas Madden was charged with mixing Spanish fly, or cantharis, with water and gin to give to Ann Smith to drink with the intent to "do her an injury" and "have carnal knowledge of her." The jury convicted Madden of having administered the potion to further his intentions when the charge should have been for his mixing the poison first. In addition, the jury was charged with misconduct when the bailiff was absent "and at least one person went into the building and had communication with the jury." Justice Kingman decided that this must be "corrected in the new trial" and reversed the judgment of the lower court.[67]

William W. Jones was charged with having "willfully, unlawfully, and feloniously" defiled a girl under eighteen years of age by carnally knowing her. The parents had allowed Jones's wife to hire her for housework, and the girl was thus confided to his care and protection. Jones was found guilty, sentenced to the county jail for nine months, and fined $500 and costs. Although two previous justices of the peace released him, in part because of the girl's reputation, a third one charged him, and he was brought to trial in district court. Valentine wrote the opinion and agreed that the first preliminary examination did not bar a second one. Also, the indictment did not allege that Jones knew that the girl was under eighteen years of age, but the trial judge said this was not necessary. To Jones's defense that the girl was not "chaste," Valentine responded that because she "lost her virtue by a single act of unchastity," she should not be "wholly abandoned to the insidious wiles of every designing libertine in whose care or custody she may unfortunately be confided." He affirmed the conviction of Jones.[68]

A mob of some fifty persons took George Johnson, who was charged with murder, from the jail in Atchison and hanged him. In a fury of racial prejudice the mob seized the "negro" and "shot him in several places" before dragging him through town with a rope and hanging him on the Fifth Street bridge. Newspaper editor John Martin lamented this violence because the murder "may have been an accident or . . . an act that would have been punished in due course of law." Johnson's widow, Eliza Ann, sued the city to recover damages for his death, but before the trial actually began, the name of William Twine, as executor of the deceased's estate, was substituted as plaintiff, and a change of venue to Doniphan County was approved. Chief Justice Kingman's opinion held that Twine's substitution was in error, and he ordered a new trial.[69]

John Millar was indicted and convicted for shooting George Stegers with intent to kill and was sentenced to two years at hard labor. It was later discovered that the original indictment was lost and a copy was presented during the trial. In one of his rare opinions, Justice Bailey wrote that the prosecutor should have shown that the original bill had been lost or destroyed, but he did not, and this omission was "a technical error or defect" within the meaning of the criminal code and "must be disregarded." He affirmed the lower court's decision. Obviously, many of these cases involved trivial procedural errors, but they reminded district judges to prevent these blunders when possible and instruct jurors correctly.[70]

George S. Smith was the treasurer of Leavenworth County and collected $564,460.66 in several kinds of money, vouchers, and warrants and various types of valuable securities. He "unlawfully, fraudulently, and feloniously" embezzled $67,378.42 "without the assent of the county." Chief Justice Kingman reviewed the pertinent statute of the criminal code, which stated that any clerk "of any private person, or of any co-partnership . . . or . . . of any corporation" convicted of embezzlement would be punished. Smith's counsel rooted his defense in the interpretation that the Leavenworth County government was not a corporation and argued "with great ability and ingenuity" that his client was not guilty. When he gave his bond as a county officer, counsel argued, he became "a special insurer of the public funds that come into his possession, and therefore no criminal liability attached to him for the use he made of such money." He did not state what the defendant wanted to do with the 42 cents. Kingman did not accept this line of reasoning that Smith had no "employer." He also observed that it was not necessary to spell out in the indictment each type of security he embezzled. In "a large community running through a long period of time . . . a description of the funds is impossible." The jury, the chief justice stated, "must find that the accused converted the money to his own use." The court found, though, that the lower court instructed the jury that if the funds were not produced "when properly or legally demanded, the law assumed an illegal conversion," and Kingman could not accept this charge. He ordered a new trial.[71]

George W. White shot James Black with intent to kill, was found guilty, and was sentenced to four years in the penitentiary. He appealed on the basis that the indictment failed to use the required term "on purpose and of malice aforethought." Justice Brewer thought the terminology used was sufficient. In addition, testimony was introduced that White was intoxicated and therefore insane. Brewer said that the intent of White's action was not revealed at the trial, and the court's instructions to the jury must be "assumed" to be "correct and sufficient." Drunkenness, he affirmed, "neither excuses nor extenuates crime."[72]

The firm of Sawyer and Ficklin operated a stagecoach line between Chetopa and Baxter Springs. The driver was drunk on one trip, the horses became "spooked," and they ran away. The plaintiff attempted to escape the coach and in the process broke his leg. He sued for damages and won $3,500. The jury was instructed that if it found that the plaintiff was injured from negligence in hiring "a known drunken driver," it would be justified in giving "exemplary damages." In addition, the jury was instructed to consider negligence on the part of the plaintiff. The court approved the decision of the lower court, noting that the plaintiff had suffered a compound fracture of his tibia, was confined to bed for thirteen weeks, and was on crutches for an additional month, so the judgment was not "excessive."[73]

An indictment was brought in the criminal court of Leavenworth County for larceny committed on the military reservation of Fort Leavenworth. The accused excepted to the court ruling that it had jurisdiction and filed a plea of not guilty, but the jury convicted him. He appealed to the supreme court on the basis that only the United States had jurisdiction over the military reservation by virtue of the original cession of the territory from France in the Louisiana Purchase in 1803.

Justice Bailey decided that the purchase was made without the consent of Kansas, that it was a part of a vast territory, and that it was not acquired for the erection of forts. Congress did not reserve its control over the military reservation, and with the admission of Kansas as an equal state, "this jurisdiction is conclusive." Bailey cited Justice Joseph Story's *Commentaries on the Constitution* that if the control is not ceded, "the state jurisdiction still remains complete and perfect." The state of Kansas could prosecute the case.[74]

The issue of prohibition became a perennial in Kansas history when the state reenacted the territorial dram shop law in 1868, and this received several tests. When the territorial legislature met at Shawnee Methodist Mission in 1855, most of its members chose to board at nearby Westport, Missouri, even though rooms were available in the vicinity. The US government forbade sale of liquor to Indians, the area thus had no open saloons, and the solons enjoyed the stimulus of John Barleycorn in the evenings. In 1855 by "lopsided majorities" these legislators enacted a dram shop law that provided for a local option vote every two years. The seller had to apply for a license, and the law forbade selling on Sundays, to Indians, and to slaves without the owner's consent. In 1859 the legislature amended the law to eliminate the local option vote and exempted towns of one thousand or more population from the petition requirement.[75]

James and Jackson Thompson of Shawnee County were charged with keeping their "grocery, alias dram shop alias tippling house" open on Election Day and selling intoxicating liquors in violation of the law. The accused moved to quash the indictment because the state failed to charge that the offense was not committed in an incorporated city of one thousand inhabitants and the statute was not uniform in operation. Kingman's court sustained the indictment, however, because the exception on incorporated cities was not necessary "to be negatived in the indictment" and the uniformity clause applied to laws passed after the adoption of the constitution. The legislature had approved the territorial statute. Kingman ruled the judgment of the lower court overturned and remanded the case for further trial.[76]

Albert Hagan sold intoxicating liquors in a building in Council Grove without a dram shop license. He was convicted, and he moved to quash on the grounds of a faulty indictment. It referred to selling "in a certain unframed building used by the said Hagan as a store." He argued that the indictment "was not sufficiently certain as to place," and it should have said that the store was "used and occupied by the said Albert Hogan." Justice Safford decided this technicality on the part of the district court of Morris County "was clearly erroneous" and reversed its judgment.[77]

The question of an election for state senator from Doniphan County produced two interesting cases. The board of canvassers counted the votes of persons in military service. Nathaniel Price claimed that these votes were illegal, and he would have won if they were not included. He asked for a writ of mandamus to reconsider the vote minus the military electors. The board of canvassers had found for the election of Price upon recounting, but the secretary of state refused to deliver his certificate of election because he had canvassed the votes and believed F. H. Drenning and J. T. Lane had won the two seats for that county. He certified them instead. Justice Safford determined that the secretary of state is "not responsible for the action of the board—be it right or wrong—but he must be governed by such action," and the writ was granted. The prior issuance of a certification to Lane "was unauthorized, and it does not prevent the issuance now of a certification of election to the relator." The military vote, Safford observed, "was disposed of" before this case began.[78]

Article IV of the US Constitution places four limitations on the states, including the declaration that "no state may impair the obligation of contract." Justice Valentine subjected this guarantee to an interesting interpretation. Anne Nichols and Michael Weaver agreed to marry "as soon as possible" in one year after he had enough time to establish himself financially "so he could place himself in a proper condition to get married." Ten years later she brought suit for breach of contract. Valentine denied her suit because the contract was verbal only and not in writing. The court, he said, always accepts the jury decision "unless such construction clearly appears to be erroneous." He also believed such a contract should have "a reasonable time limit," which he thought should not exceed one year.[79]

Justice Brewer subjected the contract clause to a lengthy interpretation in a railroad bond case. The commissioners of Bourbon County held an election, without proper notification, to issue $150,000 in bonds to a railroad that would build a line east of Fort Scott to connect with the Tebo and Neosho Railroad and make Fort Scott a division point with its machine shops located in that county seat. After elimination of fraudulent votes, that election showed a lack of majority for the project. Two years later, when the railroad asked for the bonds, a proper election was held, and the voters gave their approval to the 1867 proposal. A man named Lewis bought one hundred of the one-thousand-dollar bonds, which paid 7 percent per annum, and he asked the Bourbon County commissioners to pay the interest due him on the bonds, which they declined to do. Justice Brewer quoted his uncle, Justice Stephen Field, in the case of *Floyd Acceptances* (7 Wall. 676) that the investor must keep caveat emptor in mind when purchasing bonds that might have been issued illegally. Brewer decided that the initial election was invalid because no specific railroad was named as the recipient and the vote did not receive a majority number. The second election was also invalid, he declared, because there were two questions involved, not one as the law required, namely, to approve the bonds for an unnamed railroad and to approve $150,000 in bonds for the Tebo and Neosho. This constituted "a fraud upon the people," Brewer insisted, and he supported the decision of the Bourbon County commissioners in declining financial accountability.[80]

The Kingman court assisted the legal transition of Kansas from a territory to a state and established the rudiments of its legal system, which served as a basis of growth and further refinement. The Horton court would continue and expand on this basis.

2. The Chief Justice as Politician

The Political Scene

Various problems beset the state and the court after Kingman retired. Organized labor became a reality, prohibition raised its ugly head, politicians finally began trying to control railroads, and Mother Nature continued to remind Kansans of who was really in charge, resulting in a significant alteration in the production of the state's major crop.

Extreme heat and drought dominated Kansas in the summer of 1874. Temperatures in Junction City that July rose to 110°. One afternoon in August farmers heard a great whirring roar, rushed outdoors to investigate, and were immediately blanketed with awesome waves of grasshoppers. Soon everything was covered with four to six inches of locusts swarming in from the west. They devoured everything edible, from vegetation to tool handles saturated with salt from perspiration. The editor of a local newspaper reported that "they came in cyclones, whirlwinds, and clouds, and nothing escapes their insatiable maws. . . . We have spent fully a week trying to discover something they will not eat."[1]

Governor Thomas Osborn toured the devastation and reported not only economic chaos but widespread hysteria over the type of invasion. Many settlers steeped in biblical lore interpreted the drought, followed by the grasshoppers, as an Old Testament curse on the land. The Panic of 1873 still gripped the nation, and many Kansans decided to seek a more hospitable clime. Some migrated to California, while many moved back east to their parents, with the sign on their wagons of "Kansas or Bust" replaced by "Busted, By Gosh." Easterners again came through with emergency relief, and many Kansans began planting winter wheat, which could be harvested earlier than the traditional spring variety.[2]

Secretary of the Treasury Josiah Hayes made the front page of newspapers that year for embezzlement of state funds, becoming the third person in state history to be impeached. State law required that the state auditor, secretary of state, and governor serve as an ex officio body to examine the treasurer's office monthly. These worthy individuals delegated this task to a Topeka groceryman, who made two reports in 1873. Hayes, president of a bank in Olathe, had received federal funds to compensate for the raids made by Confederate general Sterling Price in 1864 and suppression of hostile Native Americans that year. He had mishandled these funds, and the legislature charged him with appropriating another $10,000 for his own use and for illegally depositing state funds in Kansas banks. Before the impeachment trial, Hayes resigned his office, and the managers of the charges decided not to pursue the issue, as this would only result in making Hayes ineligible to hold public office in the future, a high price with low dividends.[3]

Three years later the "labor problem" arrived in the Sunflower State. Preceding, during, and after the Civil War the Industrial Revolution swept the nation. This sea change from an agrarian to an industrial culture created a massive dichotomy between capitalists and laborers, a gulf that continued to widen over the succeeding decades. Mining and railroading attracted large numbers of unskilled workers as well as the traditional skilled to Kansas. These workers formed trade unions. As the country industrialized, workers increasingly found their skills replaced by machines that divided their tasks into simple steps that could be accomplished by lower-paid unskilled laborers. This forced workers to organize unions in defense of their interests. Soon conflicts arose over labor-management relations, with employers dominating. The labor problem emerged on a national scale when workers arose in rage over their callous treatment by "economic royalists."

This problem created diverse reactions among Kansans. Middle and upper classes in large cities denounced strikes as evil, while citizens in small towns tended to view unions, strikes, and picketing as legitimate tools of laborers who were being exploited by their employers while deploring the violence these labor weapons often produced. Capitalists should be able to protect their property, but workers who were neighbors of these citizens had the right to maintain their employment and express legitimate grievances. Small-town citizens also were venting their own grievances when they supported strikes against railroad lines that ran through the middle of town, with their whistles, which caused runaway horses, and their lack of warnings, which killed children on railroad crossings. When the Great Strike of 1877 rapidly spread westward from the east to Kansas, small-town residents supported their neighbors against their railroad employers. Federal troops suppressed this strike in the East, and local authorities managed to maintain a semblance of order in the West. Governor George Anthony felt compelled to dispatch militia to Emporia to control violence in the Santa Fe strike. This crisis forecast what would come to the Sunflower State less than a decade later.[4]

The following year Republican John P. St. John won the governor's race. He proceeded to press for prohibition and prodded the legislature to initiate legislation to achieve this goal. A proposal for a constitutional amendment easily passed the lower house and lacked only one vote for approval from the senate. At that point Mrs. Greever, an active member of the Women's Christian Temperance Union, urged her husband, George, of Wyandotte County to support the measure. He had been voting with the "wets," but he was "foolish" over his recent bride and succumbed to her wishes. The proposal then went to the people, and they ratified it narrowly by eight thousand votes in 1880. In 1881 the legislature amended the dram shop law to enforce statewide prohibition, becoming the first state in the nation to take this drastic step. One writer analyzed this vote as stemming from the bloody turmoil of Kansas history beginning in 1856 and continuing through the Great Strike of 1877.[5]

Representative Bob Wright of Dodge City moved during the debate to exclude all of Kansas west of the 100th meridian because people in that area required "snakebite medicine" for survival. He further threatened secession for the region but promised that if his territory was exempted, "harmony will again prevail upon the border . . . and future generations of cowboys will arise and call you blessed." All of this was to no avail. No exceptions were made to the new law. For sixty-eight years Kansans fought this dichotomous sumptuary attempt at reform. Part of the problem lay in its reservations: "The manufacture and sale of intoxicating liquors shall be forever prohibited in the state, except for medicinal, scientific, and mechanical purposes." The enabling legislation provided for such sale with a druggist's permit, which could be obtained through posting a bond of $2,500 and presenting an application to the local probate judge signed by twelve male citizens that the druggist was of "good moral character."[6]

The extremely narrow vote on the amendment was 92,302 to 84,304, and the state continued this close division for sixty years until repeal was barely achieved. During these decades it appeared that half of the population enjoyed their alcohol acquired by various means, and the other half were convinced they were doing the Lord's work by stamping out the vineyards. President Ulysses S. Grant, known for enjoyment of his tot of whiskey on occasion, appointed Cassius Gaius Foster as federal district judge for Kansas in 1874. After 1880 Foster quickly developed as a leader of the opposition to prohibition in Kansas, calling it "the craze." Justice Brewer of the federal circuit court, as a result, had to take "care of most of the court's business" while Foster "left much of his judicial work to engage in the advocacy of the saloon and utilized the bench to carry on his cause." He was not the first, nor would he be the last, Kansas judge to mingle politics with judicial duties.[7]

St. John continued to advocate prohibition ardently and became that party's candidate for the presidency in 1884. But in Kansas his support for this hotly contested issue, plus his advocacy for women's suffrage, split his party, and in 1882 Kansans elected their first Democratic governor, George Washington Glick. This Atchisonian subsequently supported a number of progressive measures. One that he had earlier introduced as a member of the legislature in 1881 became law during his tenure and established a three-member bipartisan board of railway commissioners. His first message to the legislature as governor called attention to the vicious plundering of citizens by railroads. They charged "excessive and exorbitant" freight and passenger rates, gave rebates to powerful interests, and used the long and short haul differential as a routine practice by often charging more for a short distance where there was no competition than for a longer haul. The subsequent law set rates, and the commission was charged with supervising these rates and issuing annual reports. Through a long metamorphosis this agency finally emerged in 1933 as the present-day Kansas Corporation Commission.[8]

The Republicans easily healed their breach over John Barleycorn and two years later elected newspaperman John Martin as governor. Martin, a member of the state's typographical union, was an eminently fair man with a tendency to support trade unions. This characteristic proved important in his first year in office. In 1884 shop workers on the Missouri Pacific line received notice of an arbitrary 10 percent reduction in wages. This, coupled with earlier pay cuts and reduction in hours of work, resulted in them being the lowest paid railway workers in the tristate region. Arguing that this new amount was insufficient to support their families and that any unexpected economic emergencies made it impossible for them to survive on their current wages, they made careful plans and initiated a strike in March 1885. The Railway Commission "took their job seriously," and Governor Martin utilized their investigations in refereeing this labor-management conflict.

Martin rushed to Atchison to discuss the problems with the strike committee and convinced them to send representatives to St. Louis to resolve the conflict with railroad officials. After careful investigation, Martin was certain the strikers were right in their demands, and he pleaded with Missouri Pacific officials to "endeavor to arrange terms for amicable settlement with your employes [*sic*]." More importantly, he refused to call out the state militia to break the strike and persuaded Governor John Marmaduke of Missouri to decline sending in his troops in response to the railroad officials' request. Without this vital military support, the railroad owners were forced to capitulate and meet the workers' demand to restore the pay cut. Governor Martin played a crucial role in this enormous labor victory and proved to be the most impartial governor in the nation in a labor dispute during the nineteenth century. The state's leading newspaper expressed the hope that his example "would reach every state in the Union." As a result of this experience, Governor Martin successfully sought to establish boards of arbitration in labor disputes the following year.[9]

The Judges

Justices Brewer and Valentine were joined by Justice Albert H. Horton, a frustrated politician who was elected chief justice in 1876. He was born in Orange County, New York, was educated in the public schools, and attended the University of Michigan law school but was compelled to leave because of "an affliction of his eyes." He studied law in Goshen, New York, and was admitted to the bar in Brooklyn in 1860. Horton soon moved to Atchison, where he was city attorney when Governor Charles Robinson appointed him judge of the second judicial district. He served in both houses of the state legislature until Governor Thomas Osborn appointed him chief justice to complete Kingman's term. Horton was elected to that position in 1878, 1884, and 1890. He greatly enjoyed politics but resigned in 1895 to resume his law practice in Topeka to build his personal finances. In 1890 the University of Michigan conferred the doctor of laws degree on him.[10] During his nearly two decades of service on the court he was not "a technical lawyer or judge but looked rather to the broad principles of the law and equity which are the safer guides to right judgment," according to one memorialist. He possessed "a mind of rare clearness, force, and capacity for study and mental labor and great strength of character."[11]

Justice Valentine, who served on the bench with Horton for sixteen years, described him as "an exceedingly congenial and affable companion." He observed that Horton gave "most careful attention to briefs," and "at every setting, almost every consultation day, it was our privilege and good fortune to draw on the great store of legal wisdom he had accumulated and laid by for us and his legal brethren." Valentine failed to mention Horton's overweening political ambitions and how this of-

Fig. 3. Albert H. Horton. Image from the Kansas State Historical Society.

ten distracted his attention from his legal obligations. Perhaps Horton offended voter sensibilities to the preferred nonpolitical nature of judicial work less than did Justice William Smith in the following century, but he certainly gave vent to his ambitions along these lines more than the modern electorate would tolerate.[12]

Judge Horton was one of the foremost advocates of prohibition both on and off the bench. The First Baptist Church in Topeka sent a letter to the Baptist national convention in Philadelphia in 1892 singing his praises. The local Baptists denied reports that "prohibition has proven a failure in Kansas." On the contrary, they insisted, "the Chief Justice of our State declared but recently that prohibition is as well enforced as any criminal law upon our statutes." High license and low license laws in other states "are violated a thousand times to where the prohibition law is violated once in Kansas."[13]

Horton wanted very much to serve in the United States Senate as Justice Crozier had done briefly in filling out the remainder of Alexander Caldwell's term in 1873. John James Ingalls, also of Atchison, did not discourage this ambition. The two were partners at one time. When John Martin was serving in the Eighth Kansas in the South the pair leased the *Atchison Daily Champion* newspaper from him, hoping to make some money and to further their political careers. When Martin returned from military service, of course, he resumed publication of his paper. Ingalls gave Horton's ego quite a boost when he wrote that Horton's prospects looked good if Samuel Pomeroy was not a candidate for reelection in 1872. His fellow Atchisonian described Horton on different occasions as

> familiar with the necessities of the state, by long residence, in the employment of the mature powers of a keen and noble intellect[.] [T]rained by the discipline of the bar and the exigencies of public life, Judge Horton would enter the arena fully equipped for the conflict.
>
> His reputation is unblemished, his instincts humane, and the state would do less honor to him that [*sic*] to herself by electing him unanimously to the Senate.

Alas, John Ingalls became a candidate for the position and was elected over incumbent Pomeroy, dashing Horton's hopes for the present.[14]

Ingalls was unpopular and had a number of enemies, and they did not have to wait too long to pounce. In 1879 a movement was launched to censure him for bribing legislators to be reelected. An investigating committee "showed conclusively" that a friend of Horton, H. T. Anderson of Ellsworth County, and T. J. Raybill of Greenwood County and one of Ingalls' political managers, in the lower house had accepted "money for their votes" to support Ingalls, but nothing further came of the query.[15]

Ingalls faced the usual political crises attendant to holding high office. Both friend Horton and C. G. Forster wanted the federal district judgeship in Kansas. Ingalls told his wife that Horton could not be appointed because of opposition to him "upon general grounds." President Grant favored Foster, and Ingalls said he was able to bring about this appointment in order "to placate an unnamed, powerful political opponent." Within weeks of his return home at the end of that congressional session, Ingalls had to fight for his political life again over charges of bribery. The exposé again blew over but left its scars on his reputation.[16]

After two major disappointments at the hands of Ingalls, Horton decided to run against him in 1878. The incumbent cleverly supported the free silver issue currently popular among Kansas farmers. The Bland-Allison Act had become law that year, requiring the Treasury Department to buy $2 to $4 million monthly in silver, coin it, and put it in circulation. It took four ballots for Ingalls to defeat Horton by six votes. Charges of bribery again were hurled about, and a letter was sent to the US Senate asking for an investigation. Again nothing came of this, with "Judge Horton" traveling to the nation's capital but failing to press his case successfully.[17]

On 3 March 1880 Ingalls came home to deliver a speech in Atchison, lashing out at his enemies, especially Horton. Banners proclaiming "Atchison Welcomes Ingalls, Vindicated" greeted the four to five thousand people brought in by trains from that corner of the state. Ingalls called Horton the "facile instrument" of the memorialists who asked for the investigation. Horton, he charged, said he was not a candidate for the seat, but "everyone knew that for five years he had trodden every devious path that led to the Capitol, that he took his seat on the bench merely as a stepping stone to the Senate." Horton, he said of his former friend and partner, "became the confidential adviser of the conspirators in their final effort to invalidate my election." "Much has been said of the Ermine," Ingalls lamented, but that "traditional fur was never dragged through a fouler puddle." The *Champion* denounced the *Kansas City Times* for describing the crowd in Atchison as "the loafer element predominates," the editor observing that "this outrageous slander" was in keeping with "the shameless disregard of truth or decency always evinced by that journal." In discussing Kansas people, "it never spoke the truth about anything connected with Kansas in its life, and probably never will." On the other side, one friend wrote Horton that he believed Ingalls was "a lunatic to think that he can make these outrageous assaults upon the private characters of men of prominence," and another wrote that his speech was "a childish folly."[18]

Horton continued to engage in political activities but without success. In 1887 the Irish reform movement was at its height, and the Irish League of Topeka held a number of meetings that year, including speeches by the then-little-known Mary Elizabeth Lease. That November Judge Horton presided over one of these meetings. During the presidential campaign of 1892 he sent weekly reports to President Harrison's secretary on political developments in the Sunflower State, but when Grover Cleveland won the election, this eliminated any prospects for the Kansan to advance to a national position, and he never achieved his political goal. Horton would play a role in the fight against Populism in the Legislative War of the 1890s.[19]

Horton sought election to the Senate in 1894 against Lucien Baker but again was defeated. B. P. Waggener, general attorney for the Missouri Pacific, wrote Horton that he was disappointed over his loss, but he "much preferred Mr. Baker to any of the fellows who were avowed candidates." "I would have gone to Topeka" to work personally for Horton, he said, "but was apprehensive if I did it might injure the very object I had in view. I don't know that you have lost anything particularly, because the position of United States Senator is not what it used to be, and politics have so degenerated that it is not a very desirable profession for a man to follow." With the race out of the way, "I want to see you at an early day and see if I cannot induce you to come to Atchison and resume the practice of your profession." He reminded Horton that his offer would be "profitable" and "less burdensome" than his position on the state court. US Justice Brewer had just visited the Sunflower State, and he wrote Horton that he believed he would have been chosen as senator, except that the Republicans in Kansas "were afraid to run the risk of a Populist Chief Justice at the coming fall elections."[20]

The Union Pacific went into receivership in the mid-1890s under the supervision of Judge Walter Sanborn of the Eighth Circuit Court. When General Solicitor A. T. Thurston expressed his desire to retire from this receivership position, Horton hoped to replace him. Frank Hagerman of the Kansas City, Missouri, law firm of Pratt, Terry and Hagerman wrote Eli Thayer that the Kansas chief justice would be a good replacement. "Personally I know that Judge Horton has for some time felt restive in his position" because of "the small salary he receives," the lawyer wrote Thurston. Horton bragged to Hagerman that "much litigation" concerning the Union Pacific had come before his court, and he knew "as much about the road as anyone in Nebraska" who might be considered for the job. More importantly, Justice Brewer wrote in his support but told Horton that friends in Topeka had asked him to recommend Archie Williams for the job. He also confided that Thayer's replacement "has really been arranged for some time."[21]

Waggener wrote Horton that Brewer was "actively engaged in pressing Archie L. Williams" as Thurston's replacement, which the US Supreme Court justice neglected to tell friend Horton. Sanborn acknowledged Brewer's recommendation and wondered if "it would not be better to appoint someone" from Nebraska who "might know more about the complicated affairs" of the Union Pacific line. When Horton lost this opportunity to move to a federal judgeship and increase his salary, he did not run for reelection to the Kansas court that year and accepted the more lucrative situation offered by Waggener with the Missouri Pacific legal staff. During his eighteen years as chief justice some five dozen cases involving the Missouri Pacific came before his court. Cynics could discern a conflict of interest in this change of occupations.[22]

When Justice Brewer was elevated to a US circuit court, Governor George Glick appointed Theodore Hurd to complete Brewer's term. Hurd was a New Yorker who graduated from Casanova Academy, taught school in Virginia for two years, then returned to Utica to study law. He was admitted to practice and moved to Leavenworth in 1859 to practice with H. Miles Moore until Hurd's nomination to the supreme court. His eight-month stint on the bench was distinguished by "unfailing courtesy," and his "diligence and assiduity were remarkable." As a memorialist wrote, his "ripe attainments and well known character for candor and honest discrimination gave him audience and consideration second to none" on the supreme court.[23]

Hurd was succeeded by William A. Johnston, who was elected in 1884 to complete Brewer's unexpired term. Johnston was born in Ontario, Canada, making him the first Kansas supreme court justice who was not a native-born American. At the end of the Civil War an uncle offered to open his home to Johnston in Rockford, Illinois, where he worked on a fruit farm. He was interested in law and taught in the public schools in Appleton City, Missouri, while he also read law. He filed for citizenship and received his final papers from the US district court in Topeka. Hurd practiced law in Minneapolis, served in the state legislature, and while a senator became a prohibitionist when that amendment was proposed. In 1880 he was elected state attorney general and became the first to be charged with enforcing the new liquor restrictions, serving in that office for two terms. With his elevation to the supreme court he would serve an unparalleled fifty-one years on the bench.[24]

The Cases

The court continued to extend protection to couples under the homestead provision. Josephus Warner settled on a quarter section of land and

Fig. 4. William A. Johnston. Image from the Kansas State Historical Society.

farmed it for twenty years. In the meantime, his older son married and left home, his wife died, and he leased the land to his daughter and son-in-law. As part of the agreement he reserved the home for himself and his minor son, and the second year he again leased the land, with the minor son working for his daughter and her husband. Suffering from failing eyesight and poor health, Warner deeded the land to his daughter and minor son if they would give him a home and take care of him. A creditor tried to take his homestead in settlement of a debt. Speaking for the court, Brewer said this was still Warner's homestead, as he lived on it, although he no longer owned it, and his homestead could not be taken.[25]

Thomas George purchased town lots in Muscotah in the name of his wife for $205, half of the amount down and the remainder due in one year. He put the title in her name to avoid creditors. He built $1,200 in improvements, and he and his wife moved onto the lots as their homestead. When he paid the second half, she received the deed. He owed Hixon and Company $858, and the company received judgment against him. The next year he moved his family to Indian Territory, where he took a temporary job with the US government. Hixon and Company tried to recover the debt, but the jury held for George. Speaking for the court, Justice Valentine said the homestead purchase was made prior to the debt George contracted with Hixon, so no fraud could be imputed to him. The creditor argued that this was not farmland, nor was it located in an incorporated city. Valentine responded that the Georges did not abandon their homestead but left it temporarily and planned to return. Therefore, they retained the rights of homestead. Brewer concurred, and Horton recused himself, as he had been a counsel when the case was tried in the lower court.[26]

A court granted J. W. Blankenship a divorce on the basis of "fault of the wife," Nancy, but gave her $1,325 in alimony at 12 percent interest until Blankenship could pay this off. He remarried and stopped payments. The court sold his homestead to pay this lien because it was in the court's power to set the terms of the lien. In answer to Blankenship's complaint that the alimony awarded was too great, Horton, for the court, said that the amount allowed in every case "is greatly in the discretion of the court." He cited *Brandon v. Brandon* (14 Kan. 342) to justify taking the homestead to satisfy the lien.[27]

Preston Bowen obtained a loan of $1,650 and secured it with a mortgage on the family homestead. Before this loan was executed, he and his wife, Constance, signed a parole contract that the money would go to her for her execution of the mortgage, and he could keep the profits from the investment of the loan. The Citizens Bank of Garnett wanted to foreclose on the homestead for nonpayment of the loan. Chief Justice Horton, for the court, said this money belonged to the wife and was not subject to the demands of creditors. Constance's homestead could not be used to satisfy this debt.[28]

Abijah Wheeler, who owned a quarter-section farm in Atchison County, bought a house and two lots in Doniphan. Because of poor health, he rented his farm and kept one room in the house there to store furniture. He planned to return to the farm when his children completed school, but he died suddenly intestate. His administrator filed the final account, but the Atchison Savings Bank received a judgment for $891.06 and the same judgment of $243.84 for a debt to A. C. Lowe. Ruling for the court, Chief Justice Horton decided that the house in town was the homestead and the farm could be sold to satisfy debts.[29]

Cases involving Native Americans continued to arise. James Grinter of Kentucky migrated to Kansas in 1853. He married a Delaware woman but was never adopted by the tribe, although he established his residence on the reservation in 1854 and the couple lived there. When the Kansas Pacific built its line across his land he asked for $5,675 in damages. Speaking for the court, Horton said that the railroad had no right of eminent domain in regard to the reservation, but the tribe had given the right-of-way, for which the railroad paid compensation. The US government guarantees protection to the railroad and the Indians in this instance, but Grinter was not a Delaware. He was "an intruder on the lands of the tribe" and had no right to claim anything under the treaty of 1860.[30]

The case of John D. Brown brought an interesting interpretation to the field of Indian law. Nancy Bluejacket, or Wah-na-se, a Shawnee, received patent to land under the treaty of 1854 but died unmarried and childless. John Brown was a child of a dead sister, and Mary Rogers was a daughter of a deceased brother. Under Kansas law, Brown and Rogers would share the estate, but Mary was a full-blood and John was a half-breed. In this type of situation, the Shawnee council determined descent, and that body decided that Mary, the full-blood, was the heir. The US government still recognized the existence of the Shawnee as a tribe along with their chief. Thus the treaty and US recognition of it prevailed over Kansas law, which would have divided the inheritance.[31]

In *Franklin County Commissioners v. Sarah Pennock* the chief justice, speaking for the court, resolved a difficult issue. Sarah was a half-breed Sac and Fox Indian. In 1870 the tribe signed a treaty and removed to Indian Territory. Her husband, a white man, was a resident of Kansas and a citizen of the United States. The tribe allotted Sarah land, and she and other Sac and Fox members bought additional reservation land. They were assessed taxes for 1871, but the district court held that these former tribal lands were not taxable, so the county commissioners appealed the decision. Horton said that when the US government conveyed land in fee simple to her it belonged to her and was "subject exclusively to the laws of Kansas." The government did this because the treaty provided that there would be no tribal organization or chiefs or councils of the tribe in Kansas. They were thus subject to Kansas law, and their lands were taxable.[32]

Railroads continued to bring considerable litigation to the supreme court, and during this period the court generally held them to be liable for their negligence, especially under the "attractive nuisance" rule. Boys enjoy adventure, are attracted to dangerous play, and are compulsive in their belief that they are indestructible. This concept was affirmed by the US Supreme Court in 1873 and used in a Minnesota case two years later. The Kansas court began applying it in a case in 1877 concerning a railroad turntable. Peter Karzten calls this a "legal fiction rule," adopted in several states in the early 1870s, and Kansas jurists used this, along with the concept of "comparative negligence," to hold railroads liable for accidents.[33]

In 1874 a case came before a district court involving a twelve-year-old boy. He was playing on a turntable and lost his right leg when his companions turned the table around and it met the exit track, crushing his right leg. The turntable, located on a railroad being built from Leavenworth to the Colorado line, was not locked, guarded, or enclosed. The Washington Improvement Company had completed fifty-six miles of the road, and Chief Justice Horton ruled that the railroad owned the road and thus was responsible according to the attractive nuisance rule, remanding the case accordingly. Valentine concurred, but Justice Brewer dissented on the grounds that no evidence was presented to show that the line had yet attempted to gain possession, and thus the Washington Improvement Company was at fault.[34]

In another turntable case, an eleven-year-old boy was injured while playing on a turntable in Leavenworth and died intestate. His father, "a poor man not owning the house in which he lived," worked as a steam engineer. The jury awarded him $3,000. In Chief Justice Horton's opinion, the boy at that age had no knowledge of the danger the mechanism posed for him, and he found no contributory negligence. He had no objection to the jury failing to itemize the amount of future earnings the child might have brought home, but he did not think the award of $3,000 was excessive.[35]

In a different type of attractive nuisance case, a young boy was killed while playing in a dangerous situation. A nail and barbed wire factory in Lawrence using water power had a shaft housing a turbine that revolved 100–150 turns per minute. The boy, who had been fishing, began playing around the shaft. The turbine caught the back of his coat, pulled him in, and killed him. Soon after the accident, the company put "danger boards" in place around the shaft. The court found "gross negligence" in the company failing to enclose the shaft and approved an award to the administrator of the boy's estate.[36]

The Atchison, Topeka and Santa Fe employed William Haas, a strong twenty-six-year-old, in its east yard in Emporia. When the new west yards opened up, he transferred there because it included a raise in pay. The yard was not yet completed, and, after seventeen days on the job, when he was coupling a boxcar loaded with bridge timbers, he stepped into a ditch with which he was unfamiliar. It had rained recently, and the ground was muddy, although the ditch contained no water. He slipped but recovered his balance and had raised himself up just as the other car hit, crushing his head in the coupling. The administrator of his estate sued. The evidence presented to the jury showed no negligence on Haas's part, but the jury decided for the railroad on the basis of the infamous nineteenth-century concept of the "fellow servant" rule (this rule required the employer to provide reasonably safe machinery or workplace environment). Valentine, writing the court's opinion, reversed the lower court's decision and remanded the case because of negligence on the part of the company for sending men to work in these hazardous conditions.[37]

The same railroad was taken to court later in another negligence suit. Karl Koehler was working with others loading railroad rails on a car. They were using rails as skids to slide the rails from a ten-foot-high pile down to the ground. Some of the men, including Koehler, then lifted the rails onto the car. They finished with one lot, and he stepped aside to wait for the next batch. Without waiting, the men on the pile sent another series down, and Koehler did not see them coming. One hit him "with great force," crushing one leg, and he later died from the wound. His widow sued for negligence. The lower court held that the men should have seen him, and the decision blamed his fellow railroad workers. The railroad appealed, and the court, Johnston speaking, said the negligence law of 1874 provided that the company be held liable for damages done by its employees.[38]

Joseph Peavey was a brakeman and yardman in Armstrong. When he was coupling two cars together, the engineer "carelessly and recklessly" shoved the car against him, and he lost his thumb and the first finger of his right hand. The railroad tried to persuade him to sign a release holding it free of responsibility, but the legislature had recently changed the common law regarding the fellow servant rule to make the company liable for negligence of fellow workers, so he refused to sign. The jury awarded him $6,500, which the company thought was excessive. Speaking for the court, Horton agreed and remanded the case, with Brewer concurring. Valentine concurred with the result but dissented in part because the court had never considered "comparative negligence" before. He believed the lower court erred in referring to "remote negligence," although the court had occasionally held that a plaintiff *might* recover damages even if he failed to exercise ordinary care because the defendant's conduct "might be grossly negligent and wanton."[39]

Frequently the court found for the railroad. In 1880 the aunt of Sue Flinn put her and another young girl on the train at White Cloud to ride to Iowa Point. The other girl, slightly older but the same size as Sue, suffered from Saint Vitus's dance (a form of chorea usually found in children). The aunt failed to contact the conductor about the girls, they did not have tickets or fare money, and they were in no one's custody. The railroad as a rule did not ask for fare for children if they were in the company of an adult. The conductor did not know that these children had no adult with them or that they wanted to get off at Iowa Point, but he did see a man named Painter sit opposite the girls and talk to them, so he assumed he was in charge of them. The train stopped at Iowa Point long enough to get off, but the girls remained onboard. As the train started up, a male adult, F. J. Starr, decided to help the girls off the moving train. The older girl got off all right, but the younger one fell on the platform under the wheels, and both of her legs were crushed, requiring amputation. Speaking for the court, Valentine said the conductor could assume that the girls were in Painter's care. It was not the railroad's fault that the girls had no adult supervision, and the lower court erred in finding against the railroad.[40]

The court ruled similarly on a case involving a railroad handcar. The line built a switch track on its land with a grade of eighty feet to the mile near the village of Farmington and used the track for years. Four-year-old Charles Henigh was playing on the handcar and released the hand brake. The car began moving down the slope, and the boy either jumped or fell off. The car ran over him and killed him. His father sued for $10,000 damages for neglect of the line, and the jury agreed with him. Valentine did not find any facts showing negligence. He noted that the family lived near the tracks and knew of the danger. In this instance the father was not around, and the mother was taking her two boys to visit a neighbor and was unaware that the smaller one stopped to play or was in immediate danger. "The railroad could have exercised more care," Valentine observed, "but so could Mrs. Henigh." There was no culpable negligence on the part of the railroad.[41]

The court arrived at a similar decision in the case of Emma Mason, who was returning home one night and decided to take a shortcut across the railroad tracks instead of keeping on the sidewalk. She crossed the railroad trestle bridge over the Jersey Creek where it empties into the Missouri River. There were steep banks on both sides, and there was no railing on the bridge or the foot walk, so one had to step on the ties. She was hit by a handcar and injured. Evidence was presented that she could have stepped out of the way, and judgment went against her in the lower court. Her husband appealed, but Chief Justice Horton wrote that this was not a public thoroughfare in any sense of that term. It was railroad property, and she was trespassing, so the verdict against her was upheld.[42]

The Stock Killing Act of 1874 made railroads liable for injuries to livestock in unfenced areas. The act's purpose was to obviate the necessity of inquiring into negligence by making the railroads responsible. When a train killed two mules belonging to the state penitentiary, the warden sued. He had sent a herd of mules out to pasture under the supervision of two trustees. The mules went to water at the only place along the track where they could access the creek. A witness testified that he heard no whistle or bell warning. The train was an excursion train for the German Turners' Society of Leavenworth on a Sunday holiday. It came through the area some two-and-a-half hours after the regular passenger train had passed. The train did not have air brakes, but the engineer testified that he blew his whistle, although it might have been too late for the mules. The lower court held that there was no negligence, but Brewer and the court ruled that the mules "were driven across at a place where it is conceded they might rightfully be driven," and the 1874 law made it unnecessary to determine negligence.[43]

The Kansas Constitution required that fines for a breach of penal laws go to a fund for the common schools. Marion Saunders brought action for the state against alleged violations of the railroad for failure to ring a bell or sound a whistle at crossings of public roads. He asked for a judgment of $20 for each of 207 counts, or a total of $4,140; as an informer, Saunders wanted to split the award fifty-fifty. The railroad appealed on the grounds that the law required all the proceeds to go to the common school fund, providing the railroad actually did neglect to signal eighty rods before a crossing. Saunders had no authority to take this action on behalf of the state. The counsel for Saunders argued that the fines were not for criminal action but for civil action. Valentine decided that there was no difference in this instance. The constitution was clear on this: all money goes to common schools, and none goes to informers.[44]

The legislature enacted a statute to enforce the prohibition amendment in 1881. The program was challenged before the ink was scarcely dry. Many of the cases came from the capital city, where the counsel did not have far to travel. The first cases, lumped together and logically labeled the *Prohibition Cases,* received an important interpretation. Brewer expounded at length on this great social issue by noting that, on the one hand, citizens had been told that "it is the crowning effort of a brave and earnest people to free itself from the curse of intoxication; on the other, that it is a departure from the wisdom and experience of the past, a radical change of policy, trespassing upon personal liberty and rights of property." This was a policy made by the legislature, and the courts should determine if it infringed on the constitution. Opponents argued that it should be struck down, because the issue appeared in both house and senate journals as "senate joint resolution #3." "The central idea of Kansas law, as of Kansas history," Brewer intoned, "is that substance of right is grander and more potent than methods and form." Regardless of what the law was called in its journey through the legislature, the voice of the people was heard, and the process was achieved by the usual route, so the end result in this case did not violate the constitution.[45]

Brewer rejected the argument that the amendment contravened the Fourteenth Amendment clause that no person shall be deprived of life, liberty, or property without due process of law. In support, he cited the US Supreme Court decision in *Bartmeyer v. Iowa* (18 Wall. 129) and other national decisions that a state law prohibiting the manufacture and sale of intoxicating liquors was not repugnant to any clause in the US Constitution. The major question, Brewer asserted, was the amendment's effect on the state's dram shop law. "Upon this question," he admitted, "the members of the court are not fully in accord." But they could agree that the amendment "has simply enlarged and increased these restrictions." The right to sell remained, but the amendment limited the purposes for sale.[46]

The justices could agree that the law now classified intoxicating liquors in three categories. Those intended as beverages, such as whiskey, gin, brandy, wine, and beer, were fully covered by the prohibition law. A second group that included liquids not intended as beverages, such as toilet articles, extracts, varnishes, and medical compounds, were not covered. The third category involved the very popular patent medicines, such as tonics, cordials, bitters, and syrups. "Here the court threw up its hands and held that the total factual circumstances as determined by each individual case by a local jury would be binding." This ruling brought innumerable cases before the court in the next six decades.[47]

Leavenworth and Topeka seemed to top the list for infractions by people who wanted to test the law, and soon several cases arrived, lumped together as *Intoxicating Liquor Cases*. S. H. Holmes, a Leavenworth druggist, sold a pint of bay rum for bathing or toilet use without the required permit, a supervisory duty assigned to judges of probate court. Another sold, for medicinal purposes, one-and-a-half-pint bottles of Dr. J. H. McLean's Strengthening Cordial and Blood Purifyer and half-pint bottles of lemon extract and tincture of gentian. In another case, a doctor prescribed rum for consumption. Speaking for the court, Brewer said that the constitution defines the jurisdiction of probate courts, and nowhere could one find a restriction on them holding other offices of profit or trust, as did the ban on district and supreme court judges. The law was also challenged in these cases as being class legislation because it was limited to druggists. Brewer thought this limitation was acceptable and logical because druggists deal with medicines. He affirmed all the decisions except the sale of McLean's Cordial, which consisted of a conglomeration of whiskey, tolu, wild cherry, and prickly ash bitters.[48]

Henry Schweiter sold and bartered spirituous malt, vinous, fermented, and other intoxicating liquors without a license. He insisted on compelling the county attorney to state if he was prosecuting for *selling* or *bartering* liquor, because to charge him with both was duplication. He also said that the prosecutor must specify the kinds of liquor sold and the names of people who bought it. Probate Judge Jewett was acquainted with the defendant personally and knew that he had never issued him a permit to sell. Judge Horton affirmed the lower court's decision for his colleagues that the prosecution could couple these charges together, as the penalty was the same for both. In regard to listing the names of buyers, the enforcement law of 1881 required this, but Horton held that this violated the state constitution's bill of rights on self-incrimination.[49]

In an intriguing case that took place in Salina, Peter Mugler was charged with manufacturing and selling beer without a permit and was fined $200. He argued that his brewing equipment was worth $10,000 for this purpose but probably only $2,500 for any other use, and therefore prohibition took his property without due process of law. Speaking for the court, Valentine distinguished between Mugler's "intangible" property, which prohibition destroyed, and his "enjoyment" or "use of his tangible property." In an interesting dissent, Brewer agreed with the prosecution of Mugler for selling beer, but his "judgment was not satisfied" on the issue of manufacturing. He did not think the legislature could prescribe what a person eats or drinks, and this decision was taking $7,500 in property for public use without compensation in defiance of the Fourteenth Amendment. The court never came to grips with this legal dilemma.[50]

"Wets" tried various schemes to circumvent the law. One was to set up a private club to sell liquor. Nickerson was convicted in Dickinson County for violating the prohibition law. The statute declared that all places that violated the ban were to be declared a public nuisance. Nickerson claimed that it was immaterial who owned or kept the liquor. As a member of the club he could buy liquor for himself but not for a nonmember. The private club approach, Brewer decided, was not a legitimate alternative.[51]

Topeka, a first-class city, exercised a corporate power for two years in licensing "tippling houses" and assessing taxes on them. When the state prosecuted, the court held that the city was not empowered to do this. Horton insisted that the city was "usurping a privilege of a public nature." The only way to control a sovereign city, he said, was to prevent it from exercising a power not given to it.[52]

The city of Topeka then tried another approach. In June 1881 the city council passed an ordinance to grant permission to sell intoxicating beverages for an annual fee of $600. From that time until September 18, 1882, the city collected about $22,000 from this scheme. With adverse publicity from the "drys," the mayor ordered all such places closed, and the council passed an ordinance prohibiting such sales. The city thus made up the lost revenue by fining violators of its ordinance but not closing them down. Valentine called attention to the law that required licenses to be issued only by probate judges. The city was not authorized to issue a license, so it accomplished the same objective through its officials condoning these sales but controlling them through fines and not closing them. These officers, he noted, were required to take an oath to support the state constitution and were violating it through these illegal actions.[53]

Lester Crawford and his partner ran Crawford Opera House in Topeka for several months with a saloon in it that sold intoxicating liquor. Neither man had a druggist's license, and Crawford "purposefully and contemptuously carries on said business," opponents charged. Speaking for the court in a long, rambling opinion, Valentine observed that this is "a novel proceeding" because "such vast numbers of illegal drinking saloons have been openly and publicly operated" since prohibition began. Are they "nuisances," he asked? As far back as the territorial legislature in 1859 they had been held to be such. "Social drinking is the evil of evils," he observed, but courts of equity "never attempted to enjoin past occurrences, or already consummated wrongs." He could find no legal alternative but to support the state in its abatement of the saloon and held that it could be "shut up." Liquor, he intoned, "sold repeatedly, continuously, and persistently in utter violation and defiance of the constitution and statutes" could be abated.[54]

The city of Sedan levied a license fee on druggists of $80 annually to sell liquor within the limits of the law. If they wished to operate a drugstore only, the fee was $5. James K. Tuloss sued to recover his $5, arguing that these fees were illegal because they levied a greater tax on licensed druggists than on businessmen like himself. Speaking for the court, Valentine justified this difference on the basis that "the druggist who sells intoxicating liquors may do a business vastly greater than the druggist who does not sell any such liquors." He further stated that the court had to uphold the tax even if "it may not correspond with our notions of what is wise, or just, or expedient."[55]

John Brown was found drunk in the courthouse in Cottonwood Falls and was fined $10 and costs. He appealed on the grounds that he did not know that the beverage he drank was intoxicating. The normal interpretation held that ignorance was no excuse. In an unusual decision, Judge Valentine accepted Brown's plea. He noted that society would not punish "idiots, insane, children under 7, or babes" because they would not know that a substance was intoxicating. Why should we punish a competent adult who "made an honest mistake" or had an "unavoidable accident"? If while drunk he still possessed the faculties to know what he was doing, he would be found guilty.[56]

In his biography of Justice Brewer, Michael Brodhead notes that in matters of domestic relations, Brewer's "devotion to the family and Christian values burst out of the shell of legalism." He wrote the opinion for the case of a man who married and fathered a child, but his wealthy father disapproved of the marriage. The man disowned the son, who wandered fruitlessly in search of a living for his family until his wife became ill and could no longer take care of the child. The couple finally gave custody of the girl to the wife's sister. Soon after his wife died the man and his father sought to regain the child, but her foster mother regarded her as her own and opposed the writ of habeas corpus to give up the child. According to a strict interpretation of the law, Brewer recognized that the natural parent had prima facie custody of children. But a child, he said, was "not like a horse or other chattel." The best interests of the child should decide. Her father and grandfather had wealth, but Brewer found flaws in the father's character, and, most important, the child looked upon her foster mother as her real mother, so he ruled that she should remain in the home of the one who loved and raised her.[57]

Peter Larson allowed Charles and Sarah Berquist to employ his daughter Tilda for housework that was suitable for her age and strength. She was to receive board and clothing for the first half of the year and be paid $1.25 per week instead of clothing for the second half. Tilda had no mother, and when her menses began she had no one to explain what was happening to her. She was experiencing considerable pain and sickness, so she asked the Berquists what was happening, as she trusted them. They told her that she had "a dangerous and unusual disease" that was very likely to end in insanity and death. The only known remedy was "constant, hard and unremitting work and labor." They placed the girl on a demanding regimen, getting her up at 5:00 a.m. She went to bed at 11:00 p.m. after milking fourteen cows, hauling water up a hill for twenty to forty hogs, digging potatoes, scrubbing floors, and cooking. Speaking for the court, Justice Johnston agreed that her father could recover damages. He not only lost her services, but it cost him $500 in medical bills for the girl to recover her health.[58]

Margaret Powell sued James Powell for a divorce because he was impotent and cruel. He also suffered from insanity, which was growing worse, and he was finally committed to the asylum at Osawatomie. The court gave her custody of the children, and as alimony she received "certain real estate" with the right to sell it. Eleven months later James improved and was discharged from Osawatomie, and he sued to vacate this judgment. Speaking for his brethren, Judge Horton declared that impotence after marriage was not grounds for divorce and that marriage of an insane person was "absolutely void." Margaret could not have a divorce, but if she wanted to nullify the marriage because of insanity, she could amend her petition. Horton noted that she would lose the alimony in either case.[59]

William S. Townsend was riding his horse when he saw Nancy O. Nutt, whom he disliked, and tried to ride her down. She grabbed the bridle and prevented this, but in the process she suffered injuries, paid $25 for medical treatment, and sought $500 damages. Chief Justice Horton agreed that the law provided for a woman to sue whether she was married or unmarried. The plaintiff claimed that the lower court erred in permitting her to testify that she was "with child" and suffered a miscarriage and later had "misery and distress and pains" in her back. Horton decided that this error was not crucial because the questions were not scientific and thus did not require an expert to answer. The lower court erred in forcing the plaintiff to prove "financial ability" over his objections, but the chief justice said that the law permits this in cases of exemplary damages. The defendant was guilty of criminal assault, and he could be compelled to answer in a civil procedure but not in this criminal case.[60]

John Spurgeon leased 125 acres in Lincoln County and planted it to winter wheat. Jenny Horton would supply the land and seed and get the seed back plus ninety-nine bushels. John then handed the lease to his father and said, "This lease is yours." He abandoned his wife and two children and left for Colorado. He later made a written agreement on the lease with his father, who cut 1,800 bushels that cost him $1.50 per acre to head (a form of harvesting). John's wife, Maria Ann, brought suit to recover two-thirds of the wheat. The chief justice, speaking for the court, said there was no evidence that John intended the lease for his wife because he had left the written agreement with his father. Horton could find no evidence that when John abandoned his family he left them "in needy and destitute circumstances." Women had few rights in nineteenth-century Kansas.[61]

In the late nineteenth century, cities in Kansas were modernizing, turning wooden sidewalks into concrete ones and building sewage, water, and power systems. In 1872 Council Grove was a third-class city with about one thousand people. On 29 February the legislature made Osage Mission, Wichita, Council Grove, and Sabetha second-class cities so that their mayors could divide them in two for voting wards. Upon appeal, the supreme court held that this violated Section 1, Article XII of the state constitution, which said: "The legislature shall pass no special act conferring corporate powers." Thus the acting city officials of these towns had to relinquish their offices to those whom they displaced.[62]

When Topeka installed a sewer system, F. G. Hentig fought the application of a special tax on empty lots. Justice Valentine wrote that a sewage system was necessary for "cities of any size" but that taxes should be levied only on property owners who used them. The fees should be apportioned according to the value of the owner, because a sewage system was not like streets or alleys, which are open to the public. Also, advance notice must be given to the owners so that they had time to contest the fee.[63]

C. F. W. Dressler was arrested for refusing to pay a road tax that was sometimes called a poll tax, was fined $5, and was jailed until he paid the tax. Chief Justice Horton noted that these fees are not debts within the meaning of imprisonment for debt, and neither is the required annual work on roads a system of involuntary servitude. Payment of this tax was not a requirement for voting, but the registration list showed who was liable for this category of work. A Leavenworth ordinance required each male resident to contribute two ten-hour days of street work annually or pay $1.50 for each day. Most men paid the fee instead of working.[64]

The state legislature authorized third-class cities to levy license fees for certain activities. D. S. M. Fretwell was an auctioneer who paid the tax of $5 for an auctioneer's license for one year but did not renew it. He was arrested and fined $25 for failure to obtain the permit. He argued that he had no interest in the goods but was only selling "the same for another person." Speaking for the court, Brewer upheld the law, saying that the city made a clear distinction between a license to carry on a business and a license for auctioneering, and both were needed in this instance.[65]

The Winfield Gas Company contracted with that city to provide streetlights. The city would pay $30 per lamp annually, except during moonlit nights, when the lamps would not be needed. The company sued for nonpayment during some hours when the lamps were not on. The court upheld the city of Winfield because it had added the proviso "as a wise protection" for not paying when the lighting was not needed. The city had not broken the contract.[66]

William Baldwin was convicted of first-degree murder on two counts of killing his sister. The first count was for using chloroform, and the second was for holding a pillow over her mouth, nose, and face to smother her. The court sustained his conviction on the grounds that the case had been "well and fairly tried" in the lower court. Justice Johnston observed that the administering of poison presupposes intent or premeditation, and the first-degree conviction was justified.[67]

A detective warned police that a certain saloon would be burglarized. The owner prepared by hiding with two policemen in the coal shed at the rear of the saloon. They shut the rear door but did not bolt it as usual. Two burglars, Wiles and Jansen, entered the building. The policemen arrested them and confiscated their burglar tools. Counsel for the defense of Jansen argued that Wiles was a decoy, and when they arrived at the police station, he was freed, and the police fired shots in the air as though he had escaped. In addition, leaving the door unbolted invited entry. Speaking for the court, Brewer said that even if Wiles was a detective, this would not excuse Jansen for illegal entry. At 2:00 a.m. the storekeeper was not inviting entry but facilitating "the arrest of an expected criminal."[68]

James Adams was convicted of burglary and appealed his sentence on a writ of error, asking for a change in venue. Adams's attorney filed affidavits of seventeen people saying they had heard threats against Adams, and the jury was thus prejudiced against him. The prosecution also filed seventeen affidavits insisting there was no prejudice involved. Adams and three other men were part of a ring of burglars who met two nights before to plan the burglary. One of them was used as a witness against Adams. In addition, the court dispatched the jury under the supervision of an officer to investigate the place where the burglary occurred. When the jury retired to discuss the case, one of the jurors was wanted as a witness in another case, so the sheriff retrieved him and then returned him after he gave his testimony. Finally, Adams argued that the jury was given a questionable charge, and during the testimony witnesses admitted information showing that Adams committed another, different burglary. The court found that there were three informations filed against Adams, so it was not surprising that there was considerable talk about the trial, especially when the jury failed to come to an agreement on the first one. During the charge to the jury the court neglected to specify which of three degrees was asked of the jury, so the verdict of second degree was proper. There were no errors committed that were sufficient to require a new trial.[69]

Lena McNeil asked Charles Payson to draft a deed conveying a piece of real estate to her mother. Instead, he drafted it to himself and "by false pretenses" got her signature on it and had it recorded. He was sentenced to prison for fraud, held by the sheriff, and petitioned for a writ of habeas corpus. He argued that a signature could not be stolen, and thus his sentence was void. Justice Valentine thought this was not just a plain signature but one on "a written instrument," so it became "a valuable thing." Payson was remanded to the Cowley County sheriff. This appears to be such an obvious decision that one questions why the court wasted its time in accepting the appeal.[70]

In 1872 Margaret, wife of George Roberts, applied for a two-thousand-dollar life insurance policy on him. The couple paid the first half of the premium with a note for $37.96, and the agent executed a receipt with the policy to follow in fifteen days if approved by the company. The company agreed and remitted the policy on 23 September. George died on 17 October, and Margaret later remarried. On 28 February 1873 the insurance company sent her agent a draft for the amount less payment of the second premium. Agent Reuben Partridge of Leavenworth told Margaret the policy was void because she failed to make the second premium payment. He persuaded her to employ George English, a Leavenworth attorney and also Partridge's cohort, to sue the company, and he would keep any amount he won over $500. English gave her $500 after Partridge endorsed the check and split the proceeds with him. A year later Margaret read an "insurance almanac" in which it stated that she had brought suit and recovered $1,957.04 with interest. She thought it was strange that she had signed a receipt for almost $2,000 but only received $500, and she sued the insurance company. Chief Justice Horton wrote that it was an established precedent that a company was responsible for deceit practiced by its factors and held that Margaret should receive the difference between the amount due her and the $500.[71]

A man named William Gross bought a yoke of oxen in 1875 and loaned them to a man named Wilson to break virgin prairie sod. When he asked for their return, he found that a Mrs. Knight had brought suit against Wilson and received the oxen as a judgment. The constable seized the oxen but left them in the care of Wilson temporarily. Gross brought suit for a writ of replevin to regain them. Brewer called attention to the common-law doctrine that property in the hands of an officer of the law cannot be taken by another writ. When accepting the common law, the legislature had acted clearly and with intended distinction for "any other mesne or final process, issued against said plaintiff." The jurist noted that Gross did not have his oxen taken from him by any writs, so they remained his. The comma inserted before "issued against said plaintiff" meant that the legislature intended the oxen to be separate. Placement of a comma sometimes becomes very important![72]

A man was accused of rape and the jury in the district court decided that threatening a female with violence or death is as much "a forceful ravishing" when she finally submits as it would be if he used physical force. The accused admitted to intercourse but insisted it was voluntary on the woman's part. She claimed "forceful ravishing" by him and the jury accepted her version so the judgment of the lower court was affirmed. Females were beginning to acquire some rights in some categories by the late nineteenth century.[73]

John Mulkins was charged with defiling a young girl under ten when she was under his care and was sentenced to three years and six months in prison. Between 6:00 p.m. and 8:30 a.m. the jury was separated for the night, but the court failed to admonish jurors as required by section 235 of the criminal code to "not converse among themselves or others" about the case. Valentine, for the court, remanded the case for retrial because the nature of the offense was "well calculated to arouse the feelings, and even the indignation of the public." The court's failure to admonish the jurors thus opened the door to prejudice, he noted, leading one juror to say, "We do not know that any case like this has ever before been decided." A part of the court's work continued to be reminding judges of the proper procedure in instructing juries.[74]

In redistricting the state in 1873, the legislature's membership was changed from the original 75 to 129 maximum in the house and from 25 to 40 in the senate, the current number. Because of population shifts, the elections of 1878 brought 129 members of the house in 1879 without action of the senate or a new law approving that number. Six new members from Edwards, Barbour, Rooks, Rush, Harper, and Kingman Counties voted with the majority for a bill paying the state fish commissioner $500. Without the vote of three of these six members, the bill would have failed. The court held that the law was illegal and supported a restraining order by the attorney general not to pay the members' salary.[75]

John S. Gilmore was elected to the lower house in 1876. Action was brought to remove him from office for being "guilty of being in a state of intoxication produced by strong drink voluntarily taken." This action was brought under the law of 1875 providing for removal of state, district, county, city, and township officials who were not subject to impeachment by this means, as the law provided for no other way of eviction. Brewer held that the constitution provided that each house was responsible or the judge of "elections, returns, and qualifications of its members," and this law violated that section as it pertained to the legislature.[76]

C. A. Saunders, an agent of the Adams Express Company, shipped four prairie chickens, legally killed as game, from Columbus to Chicago. Kansas law forbade shipment of "animals, wild fowl, or birds" in or out of the state. He was fined $10 and costs and appealed the fine. Justice Valentine decided that the birds were taken legally. The defendant claimed that the law violated the US Constitution, which gave Congress power over interstate commerce. The US Supreme Court was still groping over interpretations of this clause, but it was fairly well decided that a state could not act to interfere with the interstate commerce power whether or not Congress had legislated on a specific issue. Therefore, Valentine asserted, a law that "allows the catching and killing and thereby to become the subject of traffic and commerce and at the same time directly prohibits their transportation from the state to any other state, is unconstitutional and void." The court ordered the case reversed and remanded. This would become an important question a century later, when the sport of hunting game involved in interstate commerce became popular.[77]

Kansas poor laws provided for county commissioners to have jurisdiction over destitute people, and each county handled this in different ways. But Kansas law further required overseers to grant "temporary relief" to indigents, and if they died under the overseers' care, they had to bury them, and the commissioners had to pay the bills if they deemed them "reasonable." The courts had to interpret "reasonable." Physician Albert Morrall of Potawatomie County was employed as overseer of the poor. He took care of George Allen for eight weeks, during which time Morrall amputated "one of his limbs" and "part of the foot on the other limb." Allen was not an inhabitant of the county and had neither money nor friends. Morrall filed a bill for $100, and the commissioners refused to pay on the grounds that it was "unreasonable." The overseer had to play the role of the Levite, Chief Justice Horton observed: "The laborer is worthy of his hire." The statute did not "deprive parties of an appeal from an arbitrary and perhaps an unjust decision." The court permitted the good doctor his appeal.[78]

H. M. Mayberry was driving home in his horse and buggy when he saw his neighbor Sivey walking the four miles to his farm and invited him to ride. About half a mile from Fort Scott they overtook Clark driving a span with a wagon. Mayberry "whipped up his horse to pass" and challenged Clark, who then "whipped up his team." Sivey repeatedly begged Mayberry to let him out, but he continued "to race recklessly, carelessly, and negligently" until they hit a stone fence. Sivey was "severely wounded and bruised" and was bedridden for six weeks. The jury awarded him $400. His doctor testified that he had dislocated a shoulder and that there was nerve damage to one hand. The doctor refused to swear an oath as the law required witnesses to do, but he promised to "tell the truth." The lower court erred in not insisting on an oath, so Horton ordered a new trial.[79]

On 10 February 1859 the territorial legislature chartered the Kansas Medical Society. Twenty years later the legislature authorized the association to exercise the duties of medical examiners. When this was challenged, Chief Justice Horton said that the legislature had the power to incorporate these examiners "by a special act" making them "a legally incorporated body." The state constitution bars conferring extraordinary powers by a special act. Was the law in 1879 a special act, or was their acting as examiners something unusual? The state legislature had stated that all territorial laws "shall continue" until they expired or were repealed unless they conflicted with the constitution. Horton held that the board's power came from the statute of 1879, and if this power were stricken down, the same would apply to the powers of the Eclectic Medical Society and the Homeopathic Society. The Medical Society could exercise the duties of medical examiners.[80]

Kansas law prohibited racial discrimination in public schools, except that first-class cities were empowered, but not required, to segregate their elementary schools. School boards could *grade* students but could not *separate* them on the basis of color. Elijah Tinnon asked for a writ of mandamus for his son, Leslie, "a colored boy of school age," to compel the school board of Ottawa to admit him to one of their public schools. This raised the question of boards of a second-class city establishing separate schools without violating the Fourteenth Amendment. The court split on this one. Valentine cited *Strauder v. West Virginia* (100 U.S. 307) that this action violated the equal protection clause. Horton concurred, but Brewer dissented in what his biographer said cast him "in an unfavorable light historically." His dissent was "not overtly racist," but he insisted that school boards must have the power to "classify" students as they wished. But whose judgment controls in this classification? He believed that the court should sustain the precedent that local control rules public schools, and he could find nothing in the Fourteenth Amendment to the contrary. Ten years later the court applied this precedent to the city of Independence. This would become a highly charged national issue seven decades later.[81]

Fletcher P. Privett claimed that he was legally elected sheriff of Harper County and asked for a writ of mandamus, as the county commissioners refused to approve him on the basis that he was ineligible for the office because he had served in the Confederate army. Valentine approved the writ because Privett claimed that his service was involuntary, and the court said that he did not voluntarily "aid and abet" the rebellion. The county commissioners, acting as a board of canvassers, made this decision as "ministerial officers," and the decision on the plaintiff's eligibility would be determined by some other tribunal. If he was found ineligible, "it will be time enough to consider that" when he attempted to claim the office.[82]

Privett won 607 votes to his opponent's 401, but when he claimed the office, the sheriff refused to surrender it. Evidence was produced to show that Privett voluntarily served the Confederacy, so Sheriff Bickford insisted on retaining the office until someone eligible was elected. The state legislature had removed this disability during the 1881 session. Upon appeal, Horton ruled that the restriction applied to Privett's capacity to occupy the office, not his eligibility to be elected to it. Because the legislature made him eligible, he could take possession of the office, and defendant Bickford had to pay the court costs.[83]

Atchison Savings Bank received judgment on John Costello and M. M. Harrington for $277 and costs. The sheriff received a writ of execution but failed to obtain sufficient money to cover it, so the bank moved to amerce him for negligence of duty. A stock of goods was sold for $1,400, several times the amount of the judgment, and the sheriff tried to amend his return. Brewer held that his first return was "prima facie correct" and he could not amend. The lower court was correct in holding the sheriff liable. Brewer said that "the law placed the power of amercement in the hands of the court, so that every sheriff in the state may remember that there is no safety in any departure from the strict letter of the law."[84]

The Horton court managed to continue the vital work begun by the Kingman court, despite the political ambitions and distractions of its chief. This was mainly because of the ability and dedication of Justices Valentine and Brewer. In a short time the court and state would be faced with a movement of protest brought by agrarians that would constitute a temporary revolution and a permanent change in government and society. As a congressman noted, "The farmers of Western Kansas are burning corn for fuel, while coal miners and their families in another section of our land are famishing for food." Farmers and laborers sought to rectify this topsy-turvy situation.[85]

3. The Populist Interlude

The Political Scene

The Industrial Revolution and its new social order brought sea-changes to the farmer's world as it did to that of the wage earner. From the Civil War to 1894 America moved from number four in world industrial production to number one, metamorphosing a rural culture to an urban nation dominated by capitalists. This small class appropriated the nation's wealth through the assistance of national, state, and local governments, which the capitalists controlled. A Jacksonian democratic economic system was replaced by a Hamiltonian centralized laissez-faire economy that the capitalist class could control. The Populist movement that sought to change this system at the end of the nineteenth century had a major impact on Kansas history and its legal organization. The reform efforts of the Populists also had a long-range positive effect on later Progressive reforms.[1]

Farmers and laborers of a more primitive agrarian culture still thought of themselves as "producers," but in reality they now found themselves as replaceable cogs in a new mechanized world that they considered controlled by nonproducing parasites living off the labor of others. Workers, both urban and rural, began demanding a return to a truly republican society where there would be "equal rights to all, special privileges to none." Agrarian reformers emerged to celebrate these ideas of a simpler age that had been irretrievably lost.[2]

These prophets were assisted in their quest by the writing of Edward Bellamy, whose *Looking Backward* of 1888 proclaimed a new Utopia in the future. This novel projected a socialist economy into the twenty-first century operated by a powerful central government and dominated by the technological elite. Everyone worked, and everyone shared in the production. *Looking Backward* remained a best seller for years and was widely read on the farms and in the cities, giving succor to the downtrodden during their tribulations of searching for their niche in the new system.

The new order included great changes in money and banking. To help finance the Civil War the National Banking Act of 1864 established a new system of banks and currency. The statute required banks receiving a national charter to invest at least one-third of their capital in national securities. In turn, they were authorized to issue a new type of currency, called United States Notes, up to 90 percent of the value of these bond holdings. The law further taxed state currency out of existence, thus creating a system of uniform national currency that proved to be of inestimable value to capitalists. The US Supreme Court approved this unique use of the taxing power on the basis that the judiciary could not question the purpose of a tax. But this sound or "dear" money plan significantly hurt the debtor classes, who wanted a cheap system of money to help pay their obligations.[3]

Financiers and speculators created a national system of transportation. While railroads provided a national market for their goods, the lines posed problems of monopoly for reaching those markets. The elevators that purchased farm produce often were controlled by the railroads, but in any case they constituted a monopoly that determined the price farmers would receive for crops. While a railroad was a vital necessity to a community in the new order and often resulted in the death of a town that did not attract a line, it could, and did, charge monopolistic prices for services.

Farmers also mechanized in this new age of machines in order to compete with other producers, thus adding another cost to the agrarian mix. Farmers considered International Harvester to be a trust that could charge unreasonable prices for its products. The term "trust" took on such evil connotations in the minds of farmers that they often believed there was a trust when none existed, except in the minds of hard-pressed farmers who saw economic forces combining to deprive them further of a meager livelihood they were extracting from their hard-scrabble farms. Interestingly, though, the farmers hardest hit during the 1880s were not the poorest nor the richest but those in the middle who had daringly acquired debts to buy more land and more machinery in the increasingly competitive system.[4]

When farmers in the Gilded Age switched to commercial farming with machinery and began specializing in cash crops, they raised their standard of living but increased their dependence on money and "on decisions and policies originating primarily from remote urban centers." To buy land and machinery for expansion, "farmers generally found it necessary to go into debt." This meant paying exorbitant interest rates, which often resulted in a situation where adverse weather conditions or competition from other countries could make or break a farmer in any given year or vicinity. A farmer on the Great Plains had to become a jack-of-all-trades and businessman, dependent upon money, to survive in the new order.[5]

When confronted with these complicated problems, farmers for the first time sought to organize to solve them. They enjoyed their earliest success in creating the Patrons of Husbandry, or Grange, in 1867 to fight the railroads. The Grangers made two major breakthroughs that reformers used later to build upon. They established cooperatives to market and purchase products collectively. These failed because the farmers who managed them often proved to be poor businessmen, but during the Populist period the cooperatives developed some good managers who operated co-ops successfully during the Alliance period. Second, the Granger laws established a system for regulating railroad and warehouse practices to curb their worst abuses. The US Supreme Court sustained these regulations with the significant precedent that the public could regulate private companies when they served the public. The Court modified this significantly, though, in the *Wabash* decision in 1886 in drawing a line on what states could regulate without infringing on the interstate commerce power.[6]

As agrarian conditions worsened during the mid-1880s, reformers began establishing alliances that sought to relieve farm distress by providing a means of cooperative buying and selling. Alonzo Wardall of South Dakota proved to be quite adept in this financial world and moved to Topeka in 1895 as head of the Alliance Aid Association until he left this work in 1899 following the collapse of the People's Party. The Alliance economic movement was as important as the Populist political activities in attempting to resolve agrarian problems in the last decade of the nineteenth century. The Alliance organized farmers for the economic purpose of establishing cooperatives, and the politicians found they could utilize this organization to further their purposes. In addition, the Alliance had its own set of lecturers, and this helped develop speakers and organizers for later political activities.[7]

As the Alliances spread across Kansas, like the previous Grangers, the aggrieved farmers began realizing the political potential of their great numbers. If they could organize politically and especially attract the support of their fellow sufferers, the national wage earners, they had great potential for success in their reform efforts. They wanted to revamp the currency system by expanding the per capita of $10 to at least $50; they wanted to control railroads and grain elevators to mitigate what they considered to be their outrageous exploitive practices; they sought to curb the powers of the great trusts and to break their monopolies. One of their greatest dreams was to establish a subtreasury system whereby the national government would set up a series of warehouses across the farming regions in which to store perishable crops. The farmer would receive negotiable receipts at storage time and claim his crop later when the prices rose by paying off the receipts he had spent during the interim in order to support his family.[8]

Agrarian reformers were deeply religious, of course, and were convinced that God supported their cause. Peter Argersinger described this crusade as "not only a movement of religious people but a religious movement of people." As Kansas congressman John Davis observed, "The battle is between God's people and the worshippers of the Golden Calf." One of their principal goals was the destruction of the parasitic capitalists who contributed nothing to production but bled off the just rewards of the working people, as outlined in Bellamy's book. While Kansas Populists insisted on aligning the government with the teachings of Christ, Republican opponents denounced their efforts as "anarchy" and "communism." The Reverend Richard Wheatley of Topeka was one of the few "better people" who recognized the Populists' aim not as anarchy but as "Christian Socialism."[9]

Politically active agrarians held a momentous meeting in Topeka on 12 June 1890 and formed the People's Party, more commonly called the Populists, in Kansas. They nominated a slate of candidates, including John F. Willits for governor and William F. Rightmire for the supreme court. In the election of 1890 these "hayseed Socialists" frightened the long-dominant Republicans, who labeled them "anarchists, misfits, loafers, cranks, idiots, jays, harpies, communists, or demagogues" and even refused to capitalize the word Populist in their conservative newspapers. The "Pops" had little or no success in these off-year elections but looked forward eagerly to the national election of 1892.[10]

The Populists did achieve the goal of ousting "Mr. Republican" from the US Senate. This was a strange victory, as John J. Ingalls had not opposed any Populist programs, yet they presented him as the "anti-Christ." Ingalls had always endured criticism as a senator, partially out of jealousy of his office and especially because of his offensive tongue. He just could not resist sarcasm, and many Kansans had felt the sting of it. Populist success in 1890, although meager, provided Mary Elizabeth Lease, Lorenzo Lewelling, and other party leaders the opportunity they were looking for, and they combined with Democrats to replace Ingalls in the spring of 1891 with the capable Populist William A. Peffer, noted especially for his luxuriant beard.[11]

The Judges

By 1892 the Populists were far better organized than they had been two years previously, and they won significant victories. Stephen Haley Allen narrowly defeated Justice Valentine 162,000 to 158,000 for his seat on the supreme court. One of nine siblings, Allen was largely self-taught, as his formal education in New York ended in 1862 when he reached age fifteen. He worked in a variety of occupations, mastered the Latin classics in the original through his own efforts, taught school, became a civil engineer, and studied law in his brother-in-law's office. He migrated to Missouri and thence in 1870 to Pleasanton, Kansas, where he practiced law for two decades, meanwhile joining the Democratic Party. In 1892 the Populists endorsed him for the supreme court. Republicans were frightened by the prospect of having "this ignorant, rustic lawyer" on the bench, but they were soon surprised by his objectivity and knowledge of the law. He made no overt effort to mold the law to fit the Populist platform, and in his first four years there was "considerable unanimity" in the decisions of Allen, Johnston, and Horton. During his last two years he and Chief Justice Frank Doster constituted a Populist majority on the supreme court, but the quiet Allen "seldom drew attention to himself or his views" except for the "legislative war" in 1893. With the decline in Populist strength, William R. Smith defeated Allen for his position on the bench in the election of 1898. This followed a significant political downturn in membership in the Populist Party after the election of 1896.[12]

In the election of 1892 the Republicans emerged with sixty-five certifications of election, the Populists fifty-eight, and the Democrats only three. The two major winners challenged each other's victories in a number of elections, and the supreme court refused to intervene on the basis of its previous interpretations that the two houses of the legislature were the final judges of elections. The Populists had no trouble organizing the senate, but they also insisted that the house was theirs to control. The parties elected a dual set of officers for "their" house and informed the senate and the governor that they were prepared to do business. The Douglass House (Republican) and the Dunsmore House (Populist), with a majority of sixty-eight, counting ten contested seats, for the next month used their legislative hall alternately, ignoring each other as much as possible, making speeches, and passing their own bills. The press, both nationally and locally, had a field day reporting on this "legislative war," with the Republicans winning because of the Populists' lack of a viable press. The Republicans took advantage of the situation to insist this was the inevitable result if they allowed the "anarchists and Jacobins" to take control.[13]

The Pops managed to agree with the minority Democrats in the election of Democrat John Martin, who had promoted his party's endorsement of the Populist ticket, to replace Senator Preston B. Plumb, but from then to the end of the session it was chaos in the lower house, with the dominant press labeling the situation "anarchy." Both factions recruited armed guards to protect their positions, and the Republicans ruled that if the "duly elected" Populists did not join them, their seats would be declared vacant. This stalemate created a problem for the GOP, however, as it could not acquire a quorum without the presence of some Populists. The Populists finally seized control of Representation Hall and posted guards there, while the Republicans met in a Topeka hotel until they marched on the house of representatives, battered down the door (injuring G. C. Clemens and another Populist during the melee), and barricaded themselves in the hall. When Governor Lewelling ordered the militia to clear the room, the Republican commander refused. He was court-martialed, but no further attempt was made to oust the Republicans. As a result of this sorry situation the people's representatives managed to enact only the Australian ballot provision and an act prohibiting corrupt practices in elections; they deadlocked on a measure to regulate railroads.[14]

The opposition rushed this "war" issue to the supreme court that February despite the legal precedents that the houses were the judges of their own membership. George L. Douglass, Republican speaker of the house, had his sergeant-at-arms arrest Populist L. C. Gunn and take him into custody at Parsons because he refused to answer roll call for a quorum (there were fifty-four Populists the Republicans recognized as legally elected). Gunn sued for a writ of habeas corpus, and the supreme court agreed to take the case, the majority said, because it had original jurisdiction to hear habeas corpus. In a sixty-page opinion in which Horton spoke also for Judge Johnston, he cited the "Reed Rule" established by Speaker "Czar" Reed of the US House of Representatives, who ruled that if a member of Congress is present but does not answer roll call, he will be counted present. The Populists who were duly elected to their seats in the house, Horton said, could be counted by Speaker Douglass if they were physically present. He grounded his decision in Kingman's ruling in *State v. Hillyer* (2 Kan. 17) in 1863 that there was no constitutional inhibition on the session of one legislative house if the other was not in session. He also cited Chief Justice John Marshall that the court cannot take jurisdiction "if it should not but it is equally true that it must take jurisdiction if it should." The house is only part of the legislature, the majority ruled, and after reading the documents prepared by the house Republicans to support their case, the court decided it would exercise jurisdiction despite its long-standing rule that each house judges its own membership. The Republicans, therefore, constituted a majority in the lower house and had authority to arrest Gunn.

In an equally long dissent, Justice Allen agreed that the court had jurisdiction in this instance, but he differed from the majority on "the legal scope" of its inquiry. To justify his dissent, Allen cited *Luther v. Borden* (17 How. 1), arising out of the Dorr Rebellion to democratize Rhode Island, in which Chief Justice Taney ruled on the basis of the national guarantee of a republican form of government for the states. This important decision established the judicial principle that the court would refrain from entering a "political thicket" of ruling on legislative political questions. The illegal side of the controversy could not interfere with the legal government. Allen was determined that the constitution gave each house jurisdiction over its elections and that the Republican house was illegally organized without Populist representation. Speaker Douglass had no authority to arrest Gunn, he concluded.[15]

Justice Brewer in Washington hastened to write Horton, congratulating him on his opinion. He expressed disappointment that Allen decided to dissent. He had the chance of "establishing himself as a judge in the eyes of the country," but he "preferred to remain a partisan." One lawyer "of prominence" told Brewer that Allen "seemed in a hurry to say to history, write me down an ass." B. P. Waggener of the Missouri Pacific line wrote Horton that he was "surprised and grieved at the attitude of the Populists toward you" but assured him that his opinion for the court "meets with the approval and commendation of all decent citizens of this state." He called attention to the fact that "these anarchists are so bitter, that it would be well for you and Judge Johnston to look out for your own personal safety. I hope it is not true but I fully believe that there are some men in the Populist organization who would not hesitate at assassination, if necessary to accomplish their nefarious ends and designs." Members of both major parties and the press were so fearful of Populists that they had grave concerns about Populist jurists' ability to render objective legal decisions. As the authority on Kansas Populism, O. Gene Clanton, observed, it would be impossible for anyone to search the ranks of Kansas Populists and find an anarchist and certainly not a Jacobin, but Waggener's opinion reflects the fear of conservatives for the liberal Populists.[16]

Crushed by the Populist success in 1892, the Republicans regrouped in 1894 and threw many Populists out of power, including the hapless Governor Lewelling, who had achieved little during the "war." Republican Edmond Morrill was elected governor, and the GOP easily recaptured the legislature. Women's suffrage was an issue dividing the Populists, with Frank Doster leading the supporters and House Speaker Peter Elder an opponent. Elder and liberal Annie Diggs staged a heated debate on this question before the Republican convention. This issue made a difference in the size of the Republican victory. The GOP presented "an elaborate funeral in Topeka to celebrate the death of Populism" after the election, but the Populists refused to roll over and die so easily.[17]

By 1896 the Populists had added another burning issue to their campaign, the plank of free and unlimited coinage of silver at the ratio of 16 to 1, brought on, in part, by the devastating Panic of 1893. This plank urged the coinage of silver at a ratio of sixteen ounces of silver to one of gold when the Treasury Department purchased such bullion. The Populists also followed the questionable advice of those who sought political office over maintenance of party principle by seeking fusion with the Democrats. They endorsed the Democratic candidate for president, William Jennings Bryan, out of fear of splitting the proinflation vote if they nominated their own choice. The Populists named John Leedy for governor and Frank Doster for chief justice. The Populists and Democrats agreed to split state offices and support each other, although the Doster choice was "a bitter pill" for the Democrats because of his support for women's suffrage, which they opposed. It was during this campaign that the young editor from Emporia, William Allen White, wrote his vitriolic diatribe against Populists entitled "What's the Matter with Kansas," calling them "clodhoppers" and "gibbering idiots." The clodhoppers won, though, with the Republicans losing all three branches of state government for the first time in Kansas history. Doster joined Stephen Allen to constitute a Populist majority on the supreme court.[18]

Frank Doster was born in West Virginia in 1847. His agrarian parents moved to Indiana, where he falsified his age to join the Eleventh Indiana Cavalry. He saw considerable action in Tennessee and Mississippi before being transferred to Kansas to patrol the Santa Fe Trail. After the war he attended the state university and Benton Law Institute in Indiana but failed to take a degree from either school. After marriage in 1870 he and his wife moved to Kansas, which attracted him during his military service, and he practiced law in Marion, then labeled Marion Center. The couple also invested in local real estate, both farms and town lots. He was elected to the state legislature as a Republican but was attracted to third parties, first to the Greenbackers, then to Union Labor. Republican governor John Martin appointed Doster district judge in 1887, and he was subsequently elected to a full term. When he ran for reelection in 1891 he was a full-fledged Populist, and a combination of Democrats and Republicans defeated him. William Allen White labeled Doster "a shabby, wild-eyed, rattled-brain fanatic" in his infamous anti-Populist editorial, for which White later apologized to Doster. The chief justice spoke out strongly for women's suffrage during this period "and in opposition to bigotry and prohibition." According to Republicans, this election of a purported communist to the state supreme court posed a great evil because he had promised to "find some law" to benefit the common people, and they took this to mean that he would invent laws to achieve his radical purposes.[19]

Fig. 5. Frank Doster. Image from the Kansas State Historical Society.

Doster published an article in 1874 rejecting the idea of a constitutional amendment to establish Christianity as America's official religion. He grounded his argument in the 1796 treaty with Tripoli in which Americans stated that their government "was not in any sense founded on the Christian religion." The article was published by sisters Victoria Woodhull and Tennie C. Claflin, notorious advocates of free love. Doster was not a free lover, but during his early Populist career he observed that "the rights of the user are paramount to the owner," rightly explaining that this was a summation of the famous *Munn v. Illinois* decision of 1877 that sustained the Granger laws, but it was an opinion that horrified conservatives, especially when taken out of context.[20]

Justice Johnston joined Allen and Doster to appoint G. C. Clemens as court reporter. A lawyer who began his career in Topeka, Clemens had gained the reputation of a radical or even an anarchist with his written defense of the Haymarket Square radicals, a group of Chicago anarchists who were wrongly convicted of killing several people with a bomb during an outdoor political gathering. He was a good lawyer and represented Populist governor Lewelling in his varied litigations during his term in office. While he served as the court reporter, one memorialist recorded of Clemens, his work was always well done, and he adopted some new features in indexing the *Reports* that many regarded as a substantial improvement. When the Populists lost their majority on the supreme court in 1898, Clemens was jobless, and he eagerly turned his attention to organizing a new political party in Kansas, the Socialists, that attracted many Populists who had become disenchanted, as had Clemens, with the failure of fusion and the subsequent rapid decline of the Populist Party after 1896.[21]

When Horton resigned on 30 April 1895, Governor Edmond Morrill appointed David Martin as chief justice, and in the election of 1896 Martin was chosen to complete Horton's six-year term. Martin was another average judge who received his appointment for political reasons, and friends found it difficult to sing his praises very highly. He was referred to as "a very thorough lawyer," a "scholar of wide general information," and "utterly devoid of ostentation." A biographer managed to laud him because he "did not hesitate vigorously to denounce whatever he deemed wrong in public affairs," a damning with faint praise.[22]

R. A. Burch defeated Doster 158,000 to 117,000 in his reelection bid in 1902. According to his biographer, "certain prominent Republicans and Cleveland Democrats showed more enthusiasm for seeing Doster returned to the bench than many Populists." A lawyer who called himself a Cleveland Democrat asserted that Doster was "one of the fairest men and one of the best judges I have ever found on a supreme bench. . . . He is a credit to the state, a credit to the bench, and a credit to his profession."[23]

Doster continued to contribute to Kansas legal history with his activities and writing after he left the court. Many were astonished when he succeeded Albert Horton on the legal staff of the Missouri Pacific. "The arrangement was believed to have been engineered by the dying Horton and . . . Bailie Waggener." In this instance, two dozen cases involving the Missouri Pacific appeared before Doster's court, again a possibility of conflict of interest by modern standards. His achievement of public respectability was soon shown when Washburn University invited him to deliver its commencement address in 1903, and he lectured to its law students on wills and administration of estates from 1903 to 1905. During the debate in 1912 over women's suffrage, the Doster family "turned their home into a factory for making buttons, badges, and pennants for the cause." He believed supreme court justices were attempting "to unfetter themselves from the hard and fast, though plain and fundamental rules of law, in order to do what they conceive to be the justice of the case." He urged them to return to the law of "the venerable masters."[24]

In 1923 Doster gave an address entitled "Some Bad Decisions." After the great flood of 1903, the legislature established an organization for drainage districts with power to elect officials and impose taxes for the work. Only the "freeholders," or landowners, could vote in these elections. When the supreme court upheld this statute, Doster insisted that the statute violated the state constitutional clause prohibiting property qualifications for voting. The supreme court erred, he asserted, when the judges held that the constitutional prohibition applied "only to those elections and those officers" provided for by the constitution. "The largely preponderating numbers of offices are statutory in their creation," he asserted, and the framers of the state constitution certainly intended to cover them, whether appointed or elected. With this dangerous line of reasoning, the legislature "could create new agencies and require their officers to be Roman Catholic, or Episcopalian, or Holy Roller."[25]

In January 1899 Doster was joined by William Redwood Smith, who had defeated Allen in his reelection bid in 1898 by 148,000 votes to 131,000. Smith was born in Illinois and was brought to Kansas by his farming family in 1858 when still a child. They farmed in Jefferson County until he went to college. He graduated from Kenyon College and the University of Michigan Law School in 1874. Smith returned to Kansas and practiced law in Atchison. Friends labeled him "competent," a "well read lawyer," and "a gentleman who makes and holds friends." He was introduced at a rally as "a representative of the tough-fisted hand yeomanry," and he responded that he thought a lawyer could be a farmer and vice versa. He was reelected in 1904 and the following year resigned from the bench to become solicitor general for the Atchison, Topeka and Santa Fe Railroad, making him the third retired supreme court justice in less than a decade to join the legal firm of the two largest railroads in Kansas.[26]

Rosseau A. Burch was born in Warren County, Indiana, in 1862. Seven years later his family moved to Salina, where he eventually became a prominent lawyer. He was described as a gentleman scholar who rose from humble beginnings and was "rather elusive." He attended Valparaiso College in Indiana for a while and graduated from the University of Michigan Law School in 1885. He was one of several whom Governor Stanley appointed to the supreme court in 1902. When Justice Johnston retired in 1937, Burch was elevated to chief justice and held the second longest tenure on the court, after Johnston. During his service he wrote 1,900 opinions.[27]

John C. Pollock was born in Belmont County, Ohio, in 1857. He attended country schools and graduated from Franklin College in 1882. He taught school, read law, was admitted to the Iowa bar, and moved to Winfield in 1887. Governor Stanley appointed him to the supreme court in 1901, and he resigned two years later upon elevation to the US District Court of Kansas. He wrote 110 "short and pungent" decisions while on the court. One writer believed that Pollock's opinion in the Grain Dealers Association was "one of the greatest opinions of his long judicial career."[28]

The Populists sought to modernize the state's agricultural college when they came to power in 1896. They insisted that current monetary and economic policies were not being taught these agrarian students properly, and in 1897 they revised the college curricula and faculty. First the Populist legislature changed regential terms of office to four years and added another member to ensure the Populist majority. This allowed Governor John Leedy to appoint five new Populists, including Christian Hoffman, the radical wheat miller from Enterprise whose two sons had been ejected from the college, attracting his interest in its activities. President George T. Fairchild, whom Populists regarded as an old mossback, was isolated from this college revolution. He had resisted offering courses in the new "political economy" emanating from the University of Wisconsin and other progressive schools. A motion by Regent Hoffman led to his firing as well as many of the older faculty. The regents chose Thomas E. Will of Boston to replace him, and Will began a series of weekly lectures on agrarian economics by experts such as Mary Elizabeth Lease and Jerry Simpson for $25 and expenses.[29]

One critic charged that Hoffman led the revolution because of the treatment of his two boys, which might have been one motive for him. Hoffman was elected treasurer of the board of regents, and the college administrators created a college bookstore and a dining hall, modern innovations that were greeted with hostility by local merchants who enjoyed selling to captive student customers. Under Will's leadership the administrators also built a new hall to house the domestic science department, the first such in the nation, and eradicated tuberculosis from the state herd of experimental cattle. When the Republicans ousted the Populists two years later, they retained all these innovations except the dining hall and the bookstore, where they yielded to community pressures. Under President Fairchild the college was constantly underfunded until the annual federal bounty of $38,000 for land-grant colleges arrived each July. Populists changed these budgetary arrangements by adequately funding the college, and Republicans continued this desirable practice.[30]

The Cases

The Republican legislature charged regent Hoffman and J. M. Limbocher with mismanagement of state funds, specifically that Limbocher billed the state $15 monthly for his dining room services, and Hoffman abetted him in this. They also accused President Will of doctoring the books so that they appeared to show that everything had been done legally. The Populists enlisted G. C. Clemens to defend the two. He won a stay of execution until the supreme court could hear an appeal of the investigation. In *Yoe v. Hoffman*, to the surprise of no one, the two Republican justices supported the new Republican regents, while Justice Doster dissented. Smith, writing for himself and Johnston, justified the removal of Hoffman and Limbocher for malfeasance of office in approving illegal expenditures to Manhattan citizen Limbocher for his dining hall. Doster correctly argued that the Republicans never demonstrated that Limbocher made a profit on the dining hall he operated, and, second, they failed to show "a wrongful intent." Someone had to pay for the meals the students consumed. The charges against the Populist regents were "trivial," he insisted correctly, and were brought in order to gain a majority on the board of regents.[31]

In the nineteenth century each political party was responsible for preparing ballots for elections. They used various brightly colored ones, and it was easy to tell whom voters supported by looking at the color of the ballot they were marking. The Australian ballot, or secret ballot, was a major goal of Populists, and they required it when they first came to power in 1892. It placed the burden on the state to issue white ballots with the various candidates and parties listed on it. The voter could enter a booth and cast his ballot in secret. The law was soon litigated.

Two contenders for the same office challenged a provision in the law. Enough ballots were marked with the X outside the box to change the election results. Horton wrote the opinion that stated that the statute was taken "almost bodily from the Iowa law" and was enacted "to prevent intimidation, fraud, bribery, or other corrupt practices." If the voter did not put his X in the exact box, his vote would not be counted. If this seems strict, Horton said, the remedy lies with the legislature. Populist justice Allen and Populist-endorsed chief justice Martin agreed.[32]

William Thomson of Burlingame was nominated on the "miners and laboring men's party" ticket and also ran for the office as a Republican. Populist Justice Allen wrote the opinion that the purpose of the reform was to allow voters to make their choice "freed from all influences which might tend to corrupt or intimidate them." Allen thought the change "wise and beneficial," and he saw no serious harm in printing Thomson's name on the ballot twice, even though "the certificate of his nomination be informal" for the second one. The law did not require that "his name should appear under separate headings," and there was nothing to prevent "two or more parties" from selecting the same candidate.[33]

A man claimed the Republican nomination for probate judge in Wyandotte County and demanded that the county clerk put him on the ballot. The clerk insisted that this could be done only with the usual procedure of following the request of the Republican State Central Committee. But the Wyandotte County Committee proceeded to split in principle, so they agreed to use the primary to decide their nominees. John T. Sims and his supporters declined to accept this decision and took the question to the district court. But the Republican State Central Committee ultimately recognized the ticket supported by Sims's opponent, Leonard Daniels. Allen agreed with Sims that he should be on the ballot. Johnston dissented. The disagreement was resolved, Allen said, so there was no fraud involved.[34]

H. H. Hamilton defeated A. D. Rathburn 445 to 354 for a county commissioner's seat. He was nominated by the Populists, and party officials took their sworn certificates of nomination to the county clerk, but these were lost. Rathburn contended that Hamilton's nomination was invalid or insufficient, and Justice Johnston, speaking for the court, decided that this lost paper was "a mere memorandum of the time of filing" and was not "the filing itself." The court overruled the plaintiff's demurer and sustained Hamilton's election.[35]

The Populists had high expectations that the Railroad Commission would control railway rates. Snyder Grocery of Atchison was a jobbing company for sugar, coffee, beans, and canned goods in Kansas. In March 1892 the Railroad Commission issued an order reducing rates on car lots of these commodities to 15 cents per hundredweight in eastern Kansas and from there 22 cents to Salina, 25 cents to Hutchinson and Wichita, and 28 cents to Arkansas City. Less than car lots would be 34 cents, 41 cents, and 49 cents, respectively. The company, supported by the Atchison, Topeka and Santa Fe, Missouri Pacific, Rock Island, Katy, and Union Pacific Railroads, protested this reduction. Writing for the court, Johnston sustained the commission's action. A distinction like this could be made and still be "reasonable," as the law required. If it was found that the rates were discriminatory, the Railroad Commission was "a continuous body," and upon appeal, it would correct its decision.[36]

In 1898 the Populist-dominated legislature sought to regulate railroads more strictly by creating the Court of Visitation. Justice Allen assisted the solons in developing the measure that would control discriminatory and other unreasonable rates on the railroads and other corporations. The constitutionality of this court came up for review in 1900, when the Republicans constituted a majority on the bench. The two justices ruled that the statute commingled legislative, executive, and judicial powers to an extent that rendered it unconstitutional by violating the separation of powers concept. Chief Justice Doster dissented on the grounds that a complete separation of powers could never be achieved, adding that his colleagues based their opinion "on the assumption that the power to declare a schedule of railroad traffic is a legislative power" when this authority "may be committed to an inferior tribunal."[37]

When the Populists came to power and appointed their supporters to office, this created a series of litigations. Prior to the Populists assuming power in 1893, the legislature passed a bill to establish the Bank Commission. Late in that session Governor Lyman U. Humphrey appointed Charles F. Johnson as commissioner for four years. The legislature adjourned before he could receive senate approval, so he assumed office anyway. In 1893 Populist governor Lorenzo Lewelling appointed John Breidenthal to the position, and the Populist-controlled senate confirmed him. The Republicans regained control of the government, and four years from the time Johnson was appointed, Republican governor E. N. Morrill appointed C. S. Jobes to the office. Breidenthal insisted that he was duly selected and confirmed, Johnson was not, and therefore his term did not expire until February 1897. Speaking for the court, Johnston decided that Johnson was properly appointed, and his term began in March 1891. He should hold office until the senate confirmed him. But the governor failed to reappoint him and seek senate confirmation, and therefore Breidenthal was merely completing Johnson's term, which would end on 21 March 1895. This case had an interesting display of talented counsel, with Valentine representing the state and Clemens appearing for the Populists. Breidenthal would soon thereafter assume his influential position as state secretary to the Populist Party in Kansas.[38]

The Populist governor appointed M. A. Householder as a member of the board of regents. He was confirmed by the senate and given his commission. When the Republicans returned to power the legislature began an investigation of him on charges of corruption. Republican governor Morrill suspended him from office, and Householder sued for a mandamus to retrieve his position. Populist justice Allen wrote this important decision. The court ruled that it could compel a mandamus for a ministerial duty, but in this case the governor was acting as the head of the executive branch, "not as a mere ministerial officer," and the judicial branch could not issue a mandamus to order the governor to perform a duty, as he represented a coequal branch of government.[39]

Regent William Rogers was removed from office for "excessive use of intoxicating liquors," and the governor appointed O. L. Moore to replace him. A legislative committee of two senators and three representatives investigated and brought official charges against Rogers. The new chief justice, Martin, who replaced the retiring Horton, wrote the opinion. There was no misconduct in office, he wrote, but public drunkenness is a misdemeanor, and Rogers should not hold a public office because of this weakness. Populist Justice Allen dissented because the investigation must be for "a clearly expressed" purpose. Neither the Kansas Constitution, Allen averred, nor any other state constitution gives a legislative committee the power to try and to condemn a state official. Allen insisted that the legislature had to demonstrate that the person's conduct affected his official conduct of office, and the committee produced no evidence that Rogers was under the influence while he was performing his public duties.[40]

The famous Populist speaker Mary Elizabeth Lease challenged her party over the office to which she had been appointed as a reward for party service. Lewelling named her to the state board of charities, but they soon had a falling out. He removed her from office, declaring that she was completing an unexpired term that ended 1 March 1895. She brought a quo warranto suit insisting that she had been appointed for a term ending on 1 March 1896. The court upheld Lease on the basis that she could not be terminated "without cause and without notice." Lewelling's recourse was to bring charges against her, and he wisely dropped the matter.[41]

In 1896 Kansas Populists tried the fusion approach to win offices and share them with the Democrats. When the Democrats nominated William Jennings Bryan for president, the Populists endorsed him. They could not accept his running mate, wealthy Maine banker Arthur Sewell, however, and nominated Tom Watson for the vice presidency. Watson sought to have his name removed in Kansas because he said this was a deception to entice voters to select the Democratic ticket. John Breidenthal, now secretary of the Populist Party in Kansas, brought suit for a mandamus to compel the secretary of state to place Watson's name on the ballot with Bryan. Chief Justice Martin said the Australian ballot would be "unintelligible" to the voters without this addition and granted the mandamus. Allen concurred with Martin, but Johnston dissented, saying that Watson's name along with Bryan would be "a deception." The purpose of the Australian ballot, he averred, was to prevent this type of fraud.[42]

Following their victory in the election of 1896, the Republican legislature investigated charges of bribery brought by "reputable citizens." Thomas Davis was testifying "at some length" to a congressional committee but refused to answer certain questions. Four of the five investigating members signed a warrant to imprison him until he agreed to answer. Justice Allen spoke for the court, asking two questions. First, could the committee continue investigating after the legislature adjourned? The resolution creating the committee appropriated $3,000 for its expenses, so Allen concluded that with this large sum of money the intent was clearly for the committee to continue its work. Second, could the committee punish Davis for refusing to answer its questions? The state constitution does not grant legislative power to punish, and thus the court could not say that an agent of the legislature could do something the entire legislature could not do. Only the judicial branch can punish, said Allen. Justice Doster penned a significant dissent to his political colleagues, observing that the judges had yielded too often to those who "want to minimize the power of the legislative branch and maximize the power of the judicial branch." Only four years ago the court "gravely assumed the right" to decide on the "legislative war." In urging judicial self-restraint here, Doster said that the courts are only "instrumentalities of the executive power," and the framers of the state constitution had no intention "to invert the order of nature" by magnifying the judicial branch over the legislature.[43]

The supreme court interpreted the scope of the decision-making power of educators in two cases. Former justice Valentine represented the University of Kansas in its defense of charging a five-dollar fee to use the library. The attorney general sought a quo warranto opinion, and Allen, speaking for the court, held that this fee was not a tax. A law of 1889 granted free admission to the university except for out-of-state students. In this case the university could collect the fee or deny use of the library to those who refused to pay. In addition, a Populist law of 1897 established the principle of uniformity of public school textbooks by giving the state textbook commission the power to make these selections. Before this law was enacted, the school board of Topeka entered into a five-year contract with the publisher Scott, Foresman and refused to accept the state adoption. The court held that the school board must conform to the commission's decisions.[44]

Finally, two cases on monopoly came to the supreme court during this period. The state sued for a writ of mandamus to insist that the Court of Visitation assume jurisdiction on a case involving the Atchison, Topeka and Santa Fe. Prior to December 1899 the railroad charged $36.20 to ship a carload of cattle from El Dorado to the stockyards in Kansas City, Kansas. At that time the line raised its rates to $42, which the Populists thought to be unreasonable. The court decided that it was unconstitutional to mix judicial and executive powers in this way. The Court of Visitation could not use this power because determining rates was a legislative function, and this power could not be delegated to a commission. "Despotism begins," the court opinion intoned, when the three branches of government cease to be independent from each other. Doster dissented, expressing the belief that a commission could adjudicate freight rates for the legislature that created it for this purpose.[45]

In a twentieth-century case, the Kansas State Grain Dealers Association violated the Populist-inspired antitrust law of 1897 and initiated a case testing its constitutionality. In a forceful opinion, Chief Justice Doster wrote that it had always been the intent of the common law to encourage competitive trade. "A state possesses all power not expressly withheld," Doster asserted, and this antitrust law was fulfilling this precedent. The other justices (the court had expanded by this time) concurred, but Justice Pollock dissented in a twenty-two-page opinion. The law was too drastic, he observed, because it "makes criminal otherwise innocent, every-day affairs of life." Upon appeal to the US Supreme Court, Justice Brewer upheld Doster's opinion and sustained the antimonopoly law.[46]

The Populists also created a significant body of laws to help laborers. Many protections were needed because judges had to keep up with rapidly developing technology. Richard Wilson sued a mining company on behalf of the estate of James Wilson, who was killed in a mine explosion caused by company negligence in allowing gases to accumulate. The company insisted that the accident was caused by negligence on the part of "fellow servants," the common law rule that allowed companies for centuries to escape payment for injuries or death brought on by dangerous work. But the jury awarded the estate $5,000. This bituminous coal was mined by blasting seams loose, and the company blamed miners for careless use of dynamite. The coal company had its engineers testify that the mine was safe, but much of the testimony was disallowed by the lower court, including the company's insistence that coal dust is not flammable. Johnston wrote the opinion that the district court erred in not allowing this testimony from experts. Gases from coal dust were not flammable, he incorrectly asserted, so the decision was reversed and remanded.[47]

Morbach v. Home Mining Co. involved the Leavenworth company sinking a vertical shaft into a coal mine. It worked men three shifts for twenty-four hours daily, and the mine superintendent was responsible for the shaft being properly cased or cribbed as workers sank it. He was a newcomer to the company, although he was experienced in coal mining in Ohio. Evidence was presented to show that the superintendent wrongly told the men the shaft was safe. John Morbach was subsequently injured in a cave-in but later returned to work. He knew how unsafe the timbering was because he worked on it. Horton wrote the court's opinion that if Morbach thought the work was unsafe, he should have left the mine "in a reasonable time." When he was injured the second time and brought suit against the company, Horton said it was Morbach's negligence that caused his accident, and he could not recover damages. It was decisions like this in both state and national courts that forced men to unionize to seek collectively the protection the judicial system denied them.[48]

Kansas established an eight-hour day in 1891 for all workers in state government except for cases of "extraordinary emergency," including workers furnishing supplies to government employees. When a Fort Scott employer refused to obey a city ordinance requiring male inhabitants between ages twenty-one and forty-five to donate two ten-hour days of work on city streets annually or pay $3 instead, the city decided to test the law. Justices Allen and Doster held that the eight-hour statute applied to the public streets of a city just as it did in state governments. Populists and laborers alike were pleased with the decision.[49]

The same law was challenged in a Geary County case. J. T. Ralton and his partner were contractors building a county courthouse and jail, and they worked their men ten hours daily. Smith wrote the court's opinion that when one works for the state, the eight-hour day applies. There was no compulsion to make either the contractor or worker comply if he disagreed, and this was no infringement on his constitutional rights. If workers disagreed with the terms of the law, they should not take a job with the state or its agent, the county. This was merely a constitutional directive of the state to its agents.[50]

The Populists also enacted laws to protect the dangerous work of coal mining and the deplorable wages paid for that labor. Mine owners shamelessly cheated their workers in weighing their coal output. The Populists enacted a law in 1893 that forbade screening before weighing. Obviously, the process screened out much of the miner's production. Smith wrote the court's decision that this was a legitimate exercise of the state's police power, and it was intended to make certain that the miner received the gross weight that he had mined that day. Johnston dissented on the basis that the law was designed to restrict the right to contract. This was unfair and came about because "we know" the law "was based on the claim that coal miners were not paid enough." For decades the national and state courts struck down minimum wage laws and other attempts to procure a living wage for working men on the basis of the "liberty of contract" concept, a doctrine not found in the

US Constitution, that if a man wishes to contract to work for starvation wages, that was his choice.[51]

Mine owners also cheated their workers in requiring them to buy everything in the company store, where goods were highly overpriced. They often paid the men in company scrip, or what the mining families called "clacker," good only at the company store. The Populists enacted a statute in 1897 requiring companies employing ten or more men to pay in lawful US dollars. Smith wrote the Republican majority opinion for the court, stating that, while the act was designed to benefit the laborer, it was a violation of the freedom of contract, and it discriminated on the basis of class legislation for companies of ten or more employees. Doster wrote a stinging dissent in which he insisted that the law was not class legislation, and it did not deny property without due process of law for the employer. He pointedly observed that "I do not put my brethren in a false position by disagreeing with them. . . . I but unmask the position they already occupy."[52]

Prohibition continued to rear its ugly head as Kansans used their imagination to find various ways to test the law and the patience of the "better classes." The Saloon and Druggists Protective Association of Newton was selling liquor illegally in 1883. The group decided to "frustrate the law to the extent of evading all punishment for its violation" by retaining the law firm of Bowman and Bucher and paying the firm $80 monthly as a fee to defend them in all cases. They paid $720 before deciding the counsel was not needed, and ceased payments. The law firm brought suit to collect the remaining $240 for the year. Valentine, speaking for the court, held this contract to be a violation of public policy to contract for contemplated violations. This merely encouraged violating the law. Lawyers were supposed to do everything possible to prevent violations of the law, and thus they could not collect the remainder of their retainer.[53]

F. W. Fulker sold "prize packages" of a box containing a jug of whiskey shipped from Nebraska to Oheto in Marshall County in its original container. As early as 1827 Chief Justice John Marshall had developed the "original package" doctrine, which stated that as long as that commodity remained in its original package, states could not tax or regulate that commodity in interstate commerce (*Brown v. Maryland*, 12 Wheat. 419). This had to be modified later in the century when some areas, such as Kansas, enacted prohibition. In 1890, in *Leisy v. Hardin* (133 U.S. 100), the Supreme Court tempered the *Brown* rule to allow the sale of products after they arrived in the state of Iowa. Balie P. Waggener, general counsel for the Missouri Pacific Railroad, decided this decision permitted his out-of-state client, J. J. Douglas Company, to ship liquor to an unauthorized seller, and the company could then dispose of it in the original package. Attorney General Simeon Bradford was surprised at this theory and insisted that, no matter how the liquor came into Kansas, the state police power would prohibit its sale. Bradford was correct.[54]

Fulker believed his product was free from this type of control. Justice Johnston, however, refused to accept Fulker's interpretation. He insisted that the Supreme Court had upheld Kansas prohibition in *Mugler v. Kansas* (123 U.S. 623) because it did not contravene the interstate commerce power. Kansas law did not absolutely forbid intoxicating liquor but allowed it for medicinal, scientific, and mechanical purposes. A Kansas citizen could bring in liquor, but he could not sell it except for those uses.[55]

James Nash asked A. B. Smith if he could find some whiskey for him and a friend. Smith had just left Bob Durant's house, where Smith was told that if anyone wanted whiskey, Durant had it. Nash asked Smith its cost, and he replied that is was $1 per pint. The two men each gave Smith $1, and it took about fifteen minutes to obtain the whiskey. Nash and his friend watched Smith put it in an outhouse for them. Smith had no permit to sell. Horton said the jurors were misinstructed when told that the exchange of whiskey was "transmutation" instead of "exchange," and they could not find Smith guilty unless he sold on his own account or as an agent for Nash. The jury held him innocent because he simply purchased from Durant as an agent for Nash. Chief Justice Horton affirmed the jury's decision because "the instructions were sufficient and not misleading."[56]

The Allen County sheriff jailed Sims because he refused to swear as a witness in a prohibition prosecution. The county attorney asked Sims a question, and when he refused to respond, the attorney "immediately passed on his own right to ask the question" and judicially determined he had posed the proper question. Populist Justice Allen spoke for his colleagues when he said that the court must maintain the principles of separation of powers. Can the state legislature confer power to punish for contempt? The legislature can confer judicial power, but this was a criminal case, and the power the attorney claimed here was to jail Sims in order to carry out the prosecution. The power to punish for contempt, Allen said, should never be exercised except by legislative or judicial officers.[57]

L. R. Yates pleaded guilty to illegal sales of intoxicating liquor. The court levied a three-hundred-dollar fine and costs, and Yates was to remain in jail until he paid the fine. The following day Yates filed two motions: he alleged that the county attorney promised him a fine not to exceed $100 if he pleaded guilty, and he believed his fine was excessive and higher than normal. Chief Justice Horton said the rule provided that a guilty plea could be withdrawn and a plea of not guilty substituted. Two of the defendant's friends had talked to the county attorney, who told them the fine would be no higher than $100, which they passed on to Yates. Horton insisted that "no definite promise was made." The county attorney had not acted in bad faith because he could not know what the judge would decide was proper punishment, nor was the judge bound to impose the lowest fine possible. Yates would have to accept his punishment.[58]

On 17 February 1901 Balfe H. Stark, with Carrie Nation and six others, "did willfully, unlawfully, and maliciously break, destroy and injure the doors and windows" of a cigar store and billiard hall at 111 East 6th in Topeka. They asked for a change of venue because the judge told the leader that, "having broken the law[,] you have no more rights than the jointist [beer joint or liquor sales]. Your contempt of the law is as great as his. . . . This unwarranted destruction of property must stop." Justice Smith ruled that the above language was directed at Carrie Nation and not at Stark and denied him the change of venue. The group had committed trespass for the purpose of destroying property and must serve their sentence.[59]

Julia Smith owned farmland adjacent to the city and subdivided an acre for sale as city lots. When the city annexed the land, she brought suit because her homestead would be diminished by one acre. She won her demand to prohibit the city from collecting taxes after annexation. Upon appeal, the supreme court affirmed that the annexation was constitutional because she subdivided her homestead and voluntarily plotted the acre for homesites; thus, her homestead rights were not infringed.[60]

The second-class city of Hiawatha called for an election in 1886 to issue $50,000 in bonds for thirty years at 6 percent to build a water works. A majority of voters supported this, but, subsequently, there were no acceptable sealed bids for the bonds. The city council then sold them at public auction. S. D. Smalley bid $49,169.50, and this was the highest bid, so it was accepted. The council later received another bid from Spitzer and Company for $52,906.85 and approved it. Chief Justice Horton ruled that the city could not change its first decision. It could decide how to sell the bonds when the sealed bids were unacceptable but could not arbitrarily void Smalley's highest bid on the second offering.[61]

Plaintiff sought to prevent his city from annexing thirty acres that were adjacent to the town boundary and to halt the county treasurer from levying taxes on it. The court unanimously held that a city can annex land adjacent to its boundaries and can tax it. This land was legally annexed and taxed.[62]

A large dry goods store in Ottawa displayed a box in its front window that contained $25. Anyone buying 50 cents or more in merchandise was given one of several keys, and one of them would open the box. Owner Davenport was arrested and fined $5 on each of two counts of gambling in violation of a city ordinance. Justice Allen ruled that the main purpose of the box was to increase business and attract attention, but the chance on which key would open it was a lottery and thus illegal.[63]

W. C. Long sued the city of Emporia because it constructed a sewer emptying into the Cottonwood River. His land was adjacent to the river, and the construction was done without his consent. The project received the necessary approval of the mayor and city council, and a board of taxpayers was established to assess damages to landowners. Notice of the sewer line was published in the local newspaper, and signs for it were posted at the river. There was no damage to Long's land: he had only riparian rights, the river continued to flow, and his property was left intact. The supreme court held that the river water was contaminated by the sewage "as to render it unfit for use." Long was an involved landowner, and no warning notice was given to him. Landowners should be protected in this type of city improvement, the court decided. The judgment of the lower court was reversed, and the case was remanded.[64]

Justice Doster continued the application of "attractive nuisance" to liability cases. A city had allowed its power and light company to string its wires along a viaduct. The viaduct had a railing or balustrade where boys liked to climb and play. Over the years the insulation on the wires rotted away and presented a danger. Ten-year-old Holly Healy was playing on the viaduct when he touched the wires and was electrocuted. Doster's opinion acknowledged that the company was aware that boys were climbing there and did nothing to prevent the danger. The chief justice affirmed the lower court's damage award on the basis that this presented an attractive nuisance to the public.[65]

In a different type of litigation, Doster continued this concept. The Atchison Water Company maintained three acres of "deep reservoirs of water" that were fatally attractive to young boys for fishing and swimming. The pools were ten feet at their deepest, and the area was enclosed with a barbed-wire fence. There were sheds, or "large boxes," nailed to nearby trees, so it was a simple matter for boys to climb them and have access to the pools. An eleven-year-old drowned, and his parent sued. The parents had warned him about going there, and his friends had alerted him that he was getting too close to the deepest end. For Chief Justice Doster, it was a question of whether "a bright, intelligent boy" could accurately determine the danger. He concluded that this case was similar to the turntable cases. The boy had followed the instincts common to all young boys, and the pools presented an attractive nuisance. This was a case for the jury to decide, and they supported the appellants.[66]

In a different type of situation, the city of Leavenworth had a caretaker for its dump, and the city insisted that the dump was not an attractive nuisance. Some boys were searching for "valuables" when one of them fell into a smoldering fire and was badly burned. The caretaker had seen them moving through the trash but did not warn them, as he believed it unnecessary because he could see no danger. The court held for the boy, saying that the city had an obligation to use "reasonable care" and had failed to do so.[67]

The Union Pacific had property along a steep bluff that was between forty and one hundred feet high. Boys had tunneled "caves" at the bottom, and a thirteen-year-old was playing in one when it caved in. He suffered a fractured vertebra that left him paralyzed. The parents sued for $50,000. Justice Hopkins, writing the opinion, cited the turntable cases but held that they did not apply here. He distinguished between an "artificial instrument," such as a railroad turntable, and a natural feature, such as a bluff, and held that the artificial instrument did not apply.[68]

Railroads were well aware of the importance of political support for their well-being and made certain that public officials received annual passes to ride their rails free of charge. This was a sought-after privilege but also a sore spot for Populists, who resented this courting of favors from public officials, who Populists insisted were subject to public regulation. N. A. and Ossie English gave the Wichita and Southwestern Railroad easement for construction of a depot and side tracks on their land in return for a lifetime pass on the line. The railroad rejected this agreement, insisting that Agent T. J. Peter had no authority to issue such a pass and that the claimed promise of it was not in writing. The jury found that the Englishes were correct in their interpretation that an agent can act for his employer, and the pass was legal.[69]

A train derailed in Johnson County, and two or three carloads of cattle had to be released to prevent their death. Some of them subsequently escaped, and the railroad claim agent told section foreman Joe Landry to employ some men to help in the roundup. He hired Samuel

Randall, son of J. D. Randall, and the boy obtained his father's horse to ride in the work. He did not have his father's consent, and the mare was gored by one of the animals. The father brought suit against the railroad, and the jury awarded him $325, or $75 for veterinary medicine and $250 for the mare's "deterioration." The railroad appealed, and Justice Valentine concluded that young Randall was in the railroad's employ, along with Landry, so the company was responsible for the damage.[70]

An election was legally called for a vote on railroad bonds of $18,000. Three days before the date, both citizens and the railroad decided that public opinion would not support that amount, but if it were lowered to $10,000, it would pass. On this basis a majority voted for this promised reduced amount. A taxpayer sued on the grounds that reducing the amount constituted a bribe, and both sides enjoined further action until a decision was reached. Justice Valentine rejected the taxpayer's view, saying that the object was to aid the railroad in its construction, and if the line was satisfied with the sum, the vote was acceptable. This informal agreement did not invalidate the election for approval.[71]

Harriet Howard and her husband were a sixty-year-old couple walking home one night when a train blocked the major street in LaCygne. They asked the trainman how long the train would remain there, and he replied, "A good while." The trainman then recommended that they climb over the train if they were in a hurry. They climbed over a coal car, and Harriet broke a bone in her foot after slipping on a tie. The couple asked for $5,000 in damages. Justice Johnston wrote the decision that Harriet knew the train could move at any moment. She was not in danger but merely did not want to wait. This was insufficient, Johnston concluded, to risk this "great peril." She was mature enough not to make such a rash decision, and her accident would not have happened if not for "her reckless act."[72]

When the Union Pacific changed its route at Junction City and received its land grants to build west, the Katy then received its grants as the secondary line to build south. The state gave the line a two-hundred-foot right-of-way through Osage lands. The railroad later changed its route in 1869 from the one it had selected two years earlier. Meanwhile,

J. B. Cook bought land from the state that ended up along the new right-of-way. The Katy brought suit to reclaim the land, and the district court supported Cook's claim. The supreme court refused to look into the statute of limitations, as the case arrived over twenty years after the fact. The supreme court affirmed the district court's decision that Cook bought his land legally and should retain title to it.[73]

A minor child, Chester Long, bought a railroad ticket in Anness. Station agent Clayton had smallpox and transmitted it to the boy during the transaction. Suit was brought for $20,000 in damages. The court held that Clayton's disease was unknown to railroad officials, so the line was not liable. Counsel had made no references to precedents, the court noted, "and we cannot find in the books where a master or railroad company has been held liable in a case like this." The court, therefore, had no alternative but to rule against the boy.[74]

In 1881, 1883, and 1884 the legislature enacted laws to protect domestic cattle from those coming from Texas that carried splenic, or Spanish, fever. Texas cattle were carriers that were immune to the disease, but domestic ones were quite vulnerable. The Missouri Pacific sent a train with fifteen cars of diseased cattle into Brown County en route to the Omaha stockyards. The train wrecked, and some one hundred of these cattle had to be unloaded or they would die. When the trainmen released them, the owner warned that they were diseased, and he drove them to Hiawatha to be loaded on another train. Leander Finley's cattle caught the disease, and one hundred head, worth $900, died. He spent two months and $50 in medicine to halt the spread of the disease, and he sued for $1,050 in damages. Writing for the court, Horton decided that the corporation is a fictitious entity and can act only through people. But the owner of the diseased cattle took charge, and this relieved the railroad of responsibility because it had no control over the cattle after that. The Texas cattle company was responsible for the disease and for violating state quarantine law.[75]

A law of 1884 established a bureau of animal husbandry to control diseases in livestock, but this law specified that it could not conflict with or replace the law controlling what was commonly called Texas fever. Any railroad that brought diseased animals into Kansas would be held liable. The Katy brought in cattle from Texas, unloaded them, and drove them from Lyon to Chase County. As a result, Charles Huber lost $2,500 in cattle exposed to these diseased animals. The railroad said it had complied with federal law because this was an interstate shipment. Populist Justice Allen responded that this violated Kansas law, which did not conflict with the interstate power, and he affirmed the district court judgment against the Katy.[76]

Ten-year-old Asa Kinchlow was playing on elevator land with railroad tracks on either side. The elevator engine house had a boxed-in shaft to transmit steam power from there to the elevator. The company placed many Danger, Keep Away signs around this and the storage barrel. John McQuillan's job was to sweep out the boxcars when emptied, and he hired two or three boys to help him. Asa was staying with McQuillan, and he helped with the job, so he was familiar with the surroundings. McQuillan forbade the boys to go into the office or engine house. On this cold evening a little girl told Asa the steam barrel was a good place to warm cold feet. Asa stepped onto the cover and fell into the steam barrel. He was badly scalded, and the skin came off both of his feet and legs from the knees down, resulting in his requiring skin grafting. The jury, Chief Justice Martin ruled, would have to decide if the company was negligent in covering the barrel properly or if the boy was negligent, and he remanded the case for a new trial.[77]

George Wiley was approaching a railroad crossing where the view was obstructed by a grove of trees and a line of hedges. The locomotive did not whistle, he did not see it, and the train hit him. He suffered a broken leg and an arm and "large contused wounds and gashes on his head." There was no mention in the petition of him suffering mental impairment, but the court instructed the jury on this possibility. Populist Doster held that negligence in this case had to be determined by a jury, not by the court. He raised the point that if there was an obstructed view, Wiley should have assured himself of his safety in crossing the tracks. In this, and in many of his opinions, Doster expressed his emphasis on judicial restraint.[78]

In 1892 Charles Lewin was sentenced to six years in Leavenworth prison for burglary and larceny. He escaped and was captured, bringing into operation a law of 1891 that required a convict who escaped, or attempted to escape, or committed mutiny, or made an attempt at mutiny would serve all of his original term plus extra time for escaping. Justice Allen wrote the court's opinion. He held the law to be unconstitutional because it did not mention trial by jury on escapes. It also "violates our sense of justice," he wrote, as punishment was not defined by the degree of offense but on the date of the original sentence. The law required the lower court to reimpose Lewin's original sentence whether he had served one day or twenty years of it. The court declared this section of the statute void.[79]

The county of Labette witnessed a sensational murder in 1898. Marion Ashbell and his wife had been married for two years when their domestic relations deteriorated. Both had been married and had children by these previous marriages. Mrs. Ashbell believed her husband was having "illicit relations" with her daughter, Maggie Whiteside, and she tried the divorce route, but these attempts "were abandoned." One day her body was found in the cellar with a bullet in her head and a pistol lying nearby. Her husband's trial was "one of the most sensational and bitterly contested in the criminal annals of Labette County," and public sentiment was strongly against Ashbell. The jury found him guilty and sentenced him to life imprisonment. Justice Johnston, speaking for a unanimous court, affirmed his conviction. The relations of the defendant and Maggie, Johnston wrote, "as well as between him and the deceased, furnishes a motive for the commission of the offense." The testimony during the trial "makes it very improbable" that the case was a suicide. Ashbell's conduct before the death of his wife and that subsequent to her body being discovered "tends to support the finding of the jury."[80]

Ashbell petitioned for a new trial on what he insisted was new evidence, but the district court decided that the sovereign state of Kansas could not be sued in this situation. Doster, writing for the court this time, agreed with the district judge and stated that the summons to trial for the state was invalid. The defense cited the case of *State v. Calhoun* (50 Kan. 523) as a precedent, but Doster responded that in that instance the state won its case; however, Calhoun did not initiate a new suit to appeal the decision, as Ashbell was attempting to do.[81]

The second-class city of Arkansas City was entitled to two justices of the peace. Isaac H. Bonsall and William S. Cline won these positions in the election of 1893. Their victory was challenged on the grounds that it was based on the votes of several women who could vote in municipal elections, but petitioners raised the question, Was a justice of the peace a city official? The women's votes were easily determined because the ballot boxes were separated, and officials "entered their votes on a tally sheet so they could be distinguished according to sex." Chief Justice Horton wrote the unanimous opinion that women could vote in municipal elections, but a justice of the peace was a township office, not a municipal one, and their vote here was illegal, thus helping "limit women's participation in the political process."[82]

Taking a lesson from Native Americans, white settlers on the prairie found it beneficial to burn the native grasses periodically. The Cattle Company set such a fire, but a "violent and unanticipated gale and whirlwind" carried "burning trash and cattle chips" across the company's fire guards. The pasture was one and a half sections in size, and the guards were six furrows wide, plowed with a sixteen-inch plow. The fire burned out of control and scorched some of Joseph Kline's land. A jury awarded him $437.77 in damages, and the company appealed on the basis that its fenced-in land was still prairie in the meaning of the law. A Kansas statute required the plaintiff to prove negligence, and its purpose was to punish "disastrous" prairie fires set deliberately. In one of his earliest (actually the tenth) decisions, Allen supported the company's position that this was prairie within the meaning of the law.[83]

Anthony Kimmie purchased a Champion Harvester with a cord binder from implement dealer Alvin Acker of Leona for $250 plus freight. The machine carried a manufacturer's warranty that warned it was insufficient for cutting hemp or extra tall rye. When the machine arrived, it would not work. Kimmie told Acker he should inform the manufacturer, and the dealer telegraphed three times for an expert to come and service it. Kimmie failed to notify the manufacturer to initiate his warranty, but he insisted that he bought the machine from Acker, not Champion Harvester. Kimmie brought suit to recover his purchase price, but the district court said it was his duty, not the dealer's duty, to contact the company. The supreme court affirmed this decision, confirming the belief of many farmers that this was a good example of the capitalist system being opposed to their well-being.[84]

Widow Mary Brophy was a Roman Catholic who left her estate to her children and grandchildren. She also designated a subsidiary sum for her grandson, Rev. James Collins, to say masses for her and her husband. The heirs contested this designation, and the district court sustained the bequest. Upon appeal, Chief Justice Doster said the gift could not be voided because Mary could have left this gift without insisting on the ceremony. He further held that this was not repugnant to the law against leaving bequests for "superstitious uses." His opinion was a reminder of the Roman Catholic doctrine of Purgatory, and he affirmed the district court decision on the basis of "our religious toleration."[85]

Nellie MacDonald's husband was a member of the city fire department who drove a team with a hook-and-ladder wagon. Answering an alarm one night, he drove to the fire "at a high rate of speed." He hit a long pile of rocks in the street, was thrown out of the wagon, and was killed. There were no lights or warnings about the danger, and city ordinance permitted builders of houses to store their materials in the streets. In its defense, the city cited an ordinance against driving horses faster than "an ordinary traveling gait." This was "an unreasonable restriction" to apply to a fire department, Justice Smith said, because speed was often of utmost importance in the case of fires. The fire department had an accident policy covering its employees, and Nellie received $2,000 from this, but she sued the city of Kansas City because the rock pile was a hazard that was the cause of her husband's death. The lower court held the city to blame for not marking this obstruction in its streets, and the jury awarded her an extra $7,500, which the supreme court sustained.[86]

The Fourteenth Amendment was directed at making the freedmen citizens of the United States and of the state they lived in, declaring that no state "may deprive any person of life, liberty, or property without due process of law." This was to counteract the Black Codes of Reconstruction, which put various restrictions on freedmen to keep them in a state of bondage in the South. Corporation lawyers soon persuaded the US Supreme Court to interpret railroads as "persons" within the meaning of the amendment and forbid states to deprive them of "property by regulating their activities." This concept was soon widened to include all corporations as "persons." The Kansas Supreme Court had an opportunity to interpret and to apply this unusual concept to Kansas law.

A statute of 1897 repealed the law creating the eleventh district and removing obsolete sections of an 1889 measure. This was challenged on the precedent that if a statute contained more than one subject and also the subject was not stated in the title, either or both constituted a violation of the state constitution. Allen wrote the court's opinion, with Johnston concurring, that if the legislature changed many subjects by a repealing law, this would obviously contain many subjects in one measure. Justice Doster concurred but also believed that the repealer violated not only the state constitution but also the Fourteenth Amendment by denying equal protection in absorbing the district court into another one. Doster admitted he was not "a believer in the exaggerated extent to which the supremacy of the Federal constitution and laws in the affairs of the state have been carried." "Many refinements" of the state constitution "have been placed upon the Fourteenth Amendment to adapt it to purposes not within its original intent." The statute in question, he affirmed, was a denial of equal protection, but he was absolutely correct in his denunciation of the abuses created by defining a corporation as a "person" in the eyes of the law.[87]

The Kansas Constitution stipulated that counties were responsible for what would be called "welfare," and most delegated this duty to the county commissioners. Many decided to establish the degrading "poor farm," provided for in the constitution, in which the poverty-stricken were removed from the sight of society to work for their living in agricultural pursuits. The Pratt County commissioners decided to buy a farm, but the county clerk failed to record the calling of an election for the voters to ratify it. No one questioned this oversight, so the election was valid. In calling for the election, though, the commissioners failed to specify the amount to be approved. Speaking for the court, Valentine held this omission to be acceptable as long as the sum did not exceed what a levy of eight mills, the statutory limit, could raise. The county clerk also was negligent in failing to have the board of canvassers sign their returns, but this omission was not sufficient to invalidate the purchase.[88]

In 1899 the legislature appropriated $100,000 to acquire land and to build a state insane asylum, and it established a committee to select the site. After investigation, the committee chose 640 acres outside Parsons and agreed to pay $28,000 for the land. Upon appeal, Justice Smith decided the committee had authority to locate the site, but it was within the authority of the trustees of charitable institutions to negotiate the purchase and the superintendent to oversee the construction of the building. The site committee had exceeded its instructions.[89]

The Marion Water Supply, Electric Light and Power Company owned land on which its generator was located and it had a franchise from the city to erect lines to distribute the power. The company bought seventy cedar poles from the Badger Lumber Company, the largest lumber dealer in the country at the time, but failed to pay for them. Badger received a mechanic's lien on the poles for $227.50. Upon appeal, Justice Johnston determined that the power lines were an extension of the company's premises, and the company was not exempt from a lien. The court sustained the Badger Lumber Company.[90]

During the exciting Populist years many changes were developing in the legal system of Kansas. These came during the Horton, Doster, and Johnston years and did much to modernize the legal process and those who functioned under it. The opening of the twentieth century would also bring great changes in the legal system.

4. The Grand Old Man's Court

The Political Scene

At the opening of the twentieth century the nation and the state were poised for great changes. The ideas of the Populists, who died a rather quiet death after their effort at fusion with the Democrats failed in 1896, were taken up by various progressive groups, including many old Populists, and enacted into law. The Progressive movement, beginning at the turn of the century and lasting until World War I, brought many Populist goals into fruition. Kansas was in the van of this reform legislation.

The great legal jurist of the nineteenth century, Thomas Cooley of Michigan, wrote his famous *Treatise on Constitutional Limitations* in 1868, and it remained the authoritative source on constitutional law for five decades. Cooley argued for constitutional limits on governmental actions and encouraged state courts to compare their laws with the jurisdictions of other state courts. He insisted on reliance on the courts to protect the nation against ill-advised reformers attempting to meddle with the natural social and economic order. This laissez-faire rationality culminated in Cooley's listing of the liberty of contract as a great natural right. If a man could not contract to use his property within the permissible bounds of others, he would thus be deprived of his liberty without due process of law. Cooley's writings equipped judges "with a firm rationale on which to limit legislative action."[1]

Cooley's legal work supported the laissez-faire economics of Herbert Spencer's social Darwinism. His work *Social Statics* was published in England in 1851 and found a receptive audience in the United States following the Civil War. Spencer applied Darwin's theory of evolution to society and concluded that the "survival of the fittest" resulted when natural selection was left alone. Leave society unregulated, and it will eliminate the weak. The strongest will survive and perpetuate themselves. Edward Youmans founded the magazine *Popular Science Monthly*, which published articles such as "Law as a Disturber of the Social Order" to support laissez-faire as governmental policy and to denounce legislative efforts to improve society through regulations.[2]

Expanding on this legal concept, in 1897 Justice Rufus Peckham of the US Supreme Court insisted that the due process clause of the Fourteenth Amendment applied to substantive as well as procedural due process of law. That is, in contrast to the procedures by which due process is maintained, the amendment also includes protection of things of substance such as property and jobs. In *Allgeyer v. Louisiana* (165 U.S. 578), he noted that the freedom to pursue a livelihood included the right to enter into contracts that "may be proper, necessary, and essential" to that end. As liberals interpreted this concept, it meant legally that man had the right to contract to work for starvation wages if that was his choice—it did not matter that he might not have a choice but had to agree to this wage or nothing. State legislatures were to avoid regulating, and when they did act, courts were bound to strike down these efforts as unconstitutional invasions of "liberty" or the free use of property. The Populist law on regulating air in coal mines was struck down on this basis, as noted in the previous chapter. On the other hand, this principle was not absolute, as recorded earlier when the Kansas court sustained the Populist eight-hour-day statute of 1891.[3]

First the Populists, then the Progressives, however, began successfully challenging this doctrine by promoting the use of the state's police power to regulate the new industrial order. The state inherently possessed the power to regulate the health, safety, morals, and welfare of its citizens as part of its sovereign powers, a right to override both individual and property rights for the good of the public. Justice Oliver Wendell Holmes, Jr., sustained the police power in 1911 in *Noble State Bank v. Haskell* (219 U.S. 104) "in aid of what is sanctioned by usage, or held by prevailing morality, or strong and preponderant opinion to be greatly and immediately necessary to the public welfare." According to this, the police power could extend to "almost anything the legislature wished to regulate," except, of course, what the judiciary would not tolerate. Merely declaring the law to promote the public good was insufficient; it had to be shown clearly to judges to relate to the objective as seen by "men of ordinary prudence."[4]

Legislative use of the police power took various forms and directions. One was to alter the inherited common-law precedents of an earlier age and more primitive society by which employers could escape the obligations of responsibility for injury or death in the workplace. The first of these was the fellow servant rule for claiming that an accident occurred because of the negligence of a fellow worker. This stemmed from the logical rule that workers should familiarize themselves with the work habits of their comrades in order to avoid being hurt. The second concept was contributory negligence, whereby workers should take all necessary precautions to assure their own safety; otherwise, this would relieve the employer of responsibility. Finally, the assumption of risk held workers liable for accidents caused by the dangers of certain types of employment that they assumed upon accepting such work assignments. All three of these rules mitigated against the employee.[5]

Immediately after the collapse of the Populist political movement, a period of intense factional fighting began among the dominant Republicans in Kansas called "boss busting." Progressive Republicans began their political careers as anti-Populists. Because the national political climate changed at the turn of the century under the leadership of Theodore Roosevelt, William Jennings Bryan, and Robert LaFollette, Kansas Republicans began to realize the needs espoused by those they had derided in an earlier period as "radicals." They began to see the correctness of the radical agrarian views that plutocracy threatened popular government, that farmers were being cheated by the industrialists and railroads, and that Prohibition was being violated on a large scale. William Allen White epitomized what happened. Theodore Roosevelt converted him to the new order of progressivism when "he sounded in my heart the first trumpet call of the new time that was to be."[6]

Kansas Progressives drew their major support from the most agrarian regions of the state, the western two-thirds, while the mining and manufacturing areas of the eastern part of the state were more prone to vote Socialist or Reform Democratic until 1910, when the progressive element of the Republican Party began offering programs that appealed to the working classes. Theirs was more of a moderate reform movement, in contrast to the Socialist and Populist social upheaval program, although many of their goals were rooted in Populism. They pressed for temporary experimentation in use of the police power. As Chief Justice Johnston noted in an address to Grangers, Kansans would keep pace with Progressive reforms, but "no one need fear that Kansas law-makers will imperil property rights, arrest progress, or injure the institutions of our state. . . . The people are naturally fair-minded and will rebel at once if any man or legislature should by statute or otherwise undertake to do that which would cripple business, sacrifice property rights or liberties of any one." His court stood ready to ensure the success of this philosophy.[7]

The Progressive movement in Kansas took place during a period of abundance when even the national depression of 1907 had little impact on the agrarian Sunflower State. Reform came about through rising economic expectations, "party factionalism, ambition for office, and a sincere interest in furthering democratic idealism." As Progressive governor Walter Stubbs observed in 1905, "It is now for our people to determine whether to be a Kansan shall be greater than to be a resident of any other state in the Union." Kansans would be proud to be on the cutting edge of progressivism on the national level until entry into World War I created a hysteria that resulted in a serious lapse into reactionary policies.[8]

On the other hand, contemporary politicians questioned William Allen White's insistence that these reformers were "the highest caliber of leadership." Arthur Capper tried twice to carve a niche in the state printing "graft," as his newspaper later described it, but was outmatched by Wichita publisher Henry Allen. White shared in this printing "boodle" after he gained a national reputation among conservatives with his

"What's the Matter with Kansas" editorial. The Roosevelt administration shipped its printing job for pension vouchers to Emporia until Old Guard Republican boss Cyrus Leland became pension commissioner and stopped this expensive and impractical arrangement. Leland gave it instead to party regular Arthur Capper, publisher of *Capper's Farmer,* in return for his political support among farmers.[9]

Governor William Stanley was a conservative who bridged the gap at the turn of the century between the Populists and the new progressive Republican leadership emerging under Walter Stubbs, Edward Hoch, William Allen White, and Joseph Bristow, who were ardent Roosevelt supporters. When Roosevelt ran for the presidency in 1904, Kansans gave him 66 percent of their votes. His supporters, the "boss busters," eventually, if only temporarily, took control of state government and policies. The new progressives, arising from the ranks of boss busters, gradually assumed control of Kansas politics and enacted an extensive program of liberal legislation. Under Hoch the legislature enacted a child labor law, established a juvenile court system, regulated hours of railroad employees, created a state printing plant, enacted a maximum freight rate bill, established a new provision for assessing railroad property and an antipass bill, and created a new primary election system, all Populists ideas that had failed earlier.[10]

Led by the Progressive governor Walter Stubbs, in 1911 the legislature wrote a workmen's compensation bill that provided for employer liability for accidents or industrial deaths. In 1912 the state added a constitutional amendment to grant full suffrage to women. In 1913 the legislature consolidated several agencies into the Bureau of Labor and Industry to provide for, among other duties, the inspection of mines and industries. In 1915 the initiative, referendum, and recall were added to the democratic arsenal. In that same year the legislature pioneered in creating a small claims court to eliminate the expense of legal representation regarding the settlement of debts under $20. The disgrace of child labor was finally addressed and involved a long history of regulations, culminating in 1917 with a statute conforming to national standards enacted the previous year. Not only were maximum hours mandated, but the problem also was attacked through school attendance requirements. In many of these reforms, Kansas led the nation, or at least was in the forefront, and the supreme court was in the vanguard in sustaining them.[11]

During these years Kansas was on the cutting edge of public health reform under the leadership of Dr. Samuel Crumbine in the state Department of Health. He campaigned against unclean water, spitting on sidewalks, and adulterated foods. He also promoted a "swat the fly" campaign to combat this notorious carrier of diseases and fought the use of common drinking cups and roller towels. Crumbine promoted improved medical treatment of consumptives, babies, and prostitutes working near military camps. He fought for educational programs on social diseases and promoted sex education and vaccinations in public schools. He fought mightily, and somewhat successfully, against the great flu pandemic at the end of World War I. These were exciting years in Kansas as the nation geared up to fight the Great Crusade.[12]

Women's rights were a growing concern. In addition to the suffrage issue, the state Federation of Women's Clubs fought for equality of the sexes in other areas. In 1914 there were twenty-three women in appointive governmental offices, and two years later the state boasted nineteen female lawyers. They supported Dr. Crumbine in his crusade for pure milk and the creation of the Division of Child Hygiene in his Department of Health. They were also in favor of spending as much money on registering child births as on listing hogs and cattle, as the farmer-dominated legislature was wont to do, and for cleaning up city streets and disease-infested alleyways. Women took the lead in historic preservation in the state. In 1919 the Menningers founded their clinic in Topeka and soon became world famous for their work in mental health.[13]

Rapid settlement of the western counties posed judicial problems. In 1889 the legislature created six new judicial districts to accommodate this expansion, bringing the total number of districts to thirty-five. This, of course, led to a disparity in caseloads between the east and the west that needed to be addressed, and the legislature acted in 1895 by redistricting the state to equalize the system. Two years previously the state bar association had created a judiciary committee to study the judiciary and make recommendations for reform. Judge John Guthrie of Topeka was named chairman and reported for the committee, recommending a general constitutional convention to revise the constitution, or at least Article III, to update the entire judicial system.[14]

The three supreme court justices were hopelessly overworked, and a commission of three judges was created "to aid the court in catching up." They heard and decided cases, and, "upon request," these could be "reheard" by the supreme court. They reported their recommendations to the supreme court, and the justices ordered the recommendations accordingly, unless the judges "entered a contrary judgment." This failed to relieve "the delay in the docket," so two intermediate appellate courts of three judges each were created in 1892 with jurisdiction over cases under $2,000. These also proved inadequate to relieve the overloaded system. Their decisions appear in a separate set of ten volumes of the *Kansas Appeals Reports*. Defeated parties were taking advantage of the delays "simply for the benefit of time," and corrective action was needed immediately. Still the state legislature procrastinated.[15]

As early as 1889 Chief Justice William A. Johnston, in delivering his presidential address to the state bar association, urged "a reorganization of the entire judicial system by revision or amendment, or both [because it] is so imperative that delay is not only a blunder but will work positive injustice and irreparable injury to many people and interests." Justice delayed is justice denied, the saying went. Finally, in 1899 the bar's judicial committee recommended a special body be appointed to "urge upon the legislature" the necessity "of increasing the number of justices from three to seven." The proposition was submitted to the general election in 1900 and was approved by a substantial majority. It also provided that the justice with the greatest seniority would serve as chief justice, this being added for the benefit of William Johnston. The position of chief justice per se would no longer be elective but be based on seniority.[16]

Action on a bar association committee recommendation led to a change in judicial procedures in 1914. To overcome inaccuracies of statements of facts in supreme court decisions, six justices thenceforth would visit the chambers of the remaining judge in rotation and hear the report of that justice on the cases assigned to him. They would compare the views that were obtained from the oral and printed arguments and abstracts "and agree upon the decision to be made." The justices, in other words, "have only a limited knowledge of the cases assigned to their colleagues when they consult with [them]." This would address that weakness. Continuing consultation on any given case, therefore, tended to eliminate errors of the "one-man opinion" variety. During the period from enlargement of the court through the next fourteen years, thirty volumes of more than a thousand pages each cover 4,256 cases, still leaving the court "at least eleven months behind its docket."[17]

The session laws of 1913 experimented successfully with elections to the court. Party nominations were banned, and ballots for nomination were used in the primary election. Persons desiring to be nominated as a judge would file such intent within one hundred days and not less than forty days before the election with the secretary of state with a petition signed by not less than one-fourth of 1 percent of the total vote cast for the secretary of state in the preceding general election. The two candidates with the highest number of votes would be nominated. Where two justices were to be elected, the words "Vote for Two" would be printed over the four nominated or "Vote for Three" over the six named. This was intended to secure a nonpartisan selection of judges, a goal that was never realized. The voters were forced to continue to rely on the character of the judges elected to follow a nonpartisan philosophy in making their decisions on the bench. This process was repealed in 1915 due to the difficulty of voters in identifying good and bad judicial characteristics, especially before the candidate had seen service on a court.[18]

The Judges

The significant expansion of the court in 1900 permitted Governor William Stanley to appoint several new justices. His first, Abraham Halstead Ellis, was born in New York in 1847. The Ellis family moved to Michigan, where he was educated in Battle Creek. Lying about his age, he enlisted in the Seventh Michigan Cavalry and saw action in the last two years of the Civil War. He was admitted to the Michigan bar in 1872 and practiced in that state until 1878, when he moved to Beloit. He served a term as county attorney and as delegate to the Republican National Convention in 1892. During this period "he was the leading lawyer in Northeast Kansas." Governor Stanley appointed him as justice, and he served only eighteen months before his premature death in 1902. He became the first justice to die while sitting on the bench.[19]

Edwin W. Cunningham was born in Ohio in 1842 and lived there until after the Civil War. He was educated in the common schools, at Baldwin University in Berea, Ohio, and at Hillsdale College in Michigan, where he graduated in 1864. He served as administrator of public schools in Ohio and Illinois, then relocated to Emporia, and was admitted to the bar in 1869. With the enlargement of the supreme court, Governor Stanley nominated him, and he was elected to a two-year term in 1902 and reelected for a six-year term in 1904. His "learning, integrity, and fairness . . . gained for him . . . the respect of his opponents and the esteem of all."[20]

Charles Burleigh Graves was born in Wayne County, Indiana, in 1841. His family moved to Illinois in 1851 and to Woodson County, Kansas, in 1859. He served in the Civil War for three years. At the end of hostilities he engaged in farming and then the milling and lumber business while reading law. He was admitted to practice in 1869 at Neosho Falls, then moved to Burlington. Graves served two terms as county attorney and was elected district judge for three terms. When Justice Ellis died, Governor Edward Hoch appointed Graves as replacement. He was elected to a regular term on the supreme court in 1906. To him, a lawsuit was "a search for truth." "His words were few because he weighed them well and they carried force accordingly." His opinions on the bench were "terse, crisp, pointed."[21]

Adrian L. Greene was born in Missouri in 1848 and received a common school education in a farming community. He studied law, was admitted to the bar, and practiced in Miami, Missouri, before moving to Newton in 1871. Governor Stanley appointed him to a one-year term on the court, and in 1902 he was elected to a full term. His opinions for the court were noted for their "precision, reserve of statement and the weighing of words." He was a promoter of community interests, "a genial companion, a true friend and a fair opponent" with "a sense of humor . . . and kindly banter." He died in 1907, becoming the third of Stanley's appointments and the third member to die while serving on the court.[22]

Alfred Washburn Benson was born at Jamestown, New York, in 1843. He enlisted as a private in the Union army in 1862 and was discharged as a major at the conclusion of hostilities. He was educated at Randolph Academy in New York, studied law, and was admitted to the bar in 1866. In 1869 Benson moved to Ottawa, Kansas, where he was elected mayor and then county attorney of Franklin County. He was elected district judge three times. He was serving in the lower house when Senator Ralph Burton resigned, and he replaced that unfortunate person in the US Senate in June 1905. Following this experience he was elected to the supreme court. When asked to compare the two positions, he said he "enjoyed life in Washington" but felt he was "in a place where I was not most useful," in Kansas, and he enjoyed the life of a judge much more.[23]

Henry F. Mason was born in Racine, Wisconsin, in 1860. He was educated at Madison High School and then the state university and its law school. He worked for a newspaper for four years and in 1886 moved to Garden City, where he practiced law. He was city attorney and attorney for Finney County for two terms each. Mason became grand master of the Masonic Lodge in Kansas and was well known in the state. "He was one of the most popular men in Kansas," and his nominating petition was signed by people throughout the state, including "more than 100 in the Topeka area."[24]

Governor Bailey appointed William D. Atkinson to fill the vacancy left by John C. Pollock's promotion to the US District Court of Kansas. Atkinson was born in Dubuque, Iowa, in 1865 and graduated from Iowa State College in 1882. After serving as superintendent of schools in the Neosho County system, he read law and began practicing in Parsons. He served as city attorney for fifteen years. Atkinson's opinions "reflect industry, thoroughness, and clarity of mind." In 1904 Clark Smith won the position.[25]

Clark A. Smith was a farm boy from Rock County, Wisconsin. He alternately taught school and attended the University of Wisconsin, where he graduated from "the arts and law courses" in 1871. He immediately moved to Cawker City. He served as district judge for four terms until the Populists defeated him in 1890 by one hundred votes. He was elected to the supreme court in 1904.[26]

Silas Wright Porter was born in 1857 in Warren County, Illinois, where his father was a judge. He graduated from Monmouth College in 1879 and received a doctor of laws in 1906. Moving to Ness City in 1886 and then to Kansas City, Kansas, he joined the firm of Buchan, Freeman and Porter. Governor Hoch appointed him to the supreme court to replace William R. Smith, a promotion that Porter did not know about until he read it in a newspaper. He served on the court until 1923, when he retired after Judge Pollock named him a referee in bankruptcy for the federal court. He lectured in law at various times for the University of Kansas, Washburn, and Kansas City Law School. Porter had "an insatiable interest" in literature and was a good after-dinner speaker. He "held his own" on the supreme court with his colleagues Johnston, Mason, and Benson. His 1,023 opinions were trenchant and laden with quotes from the great authors of literature.[27]

Judson S. West was born in Michigan in 1855 and moved to Kansas as a boy. He was educated at Fort Scott, became a teacher, and attended law school at the University of Kansas. He practiced law in Bourbon County, served as assistant attorney general and then district judge, and resigned to practice law in Kansas City. He was elected to the supreme court in 1910 and served until 1922, when he retired. West was "industrious in research, tolerant in conferences, honest judgment and gave to the state his best years. . . . He sacrificed his health to duty" on the bench.[28]

John S. Dawson was born in Scotland in 1869 in a village one hundred miles north of Edinburgh, the second on the supreme court not to be native born. He attended public schools and then Robert Gordon's College in Aberdeen. He moved to Illinois to be near relatives. He worked on a farm until 1887, when he relocated to Hill City, where he taught school while attending normal school in Salina and studying law. After admission to the bar in 1898, he practiced law in Wakeeney. He attended law school at Washburn while serving as assistant attorney general from 1904 to 1908 and was Governor Stubbs's private secretary until his appointment as attorney for the state Railroad Commission. From 1910 to 1914 he was attorney general, and he was elected in 1914 to the supreme court, serving there fifty years. He became chief justice a few years after William Johnston resigned. He wrote 1,651 opinions, many of them on railroad cases, and served with "humor and wit." He provided "a good Scots mixture of kindliness and simplicity." Being fearful of deciding unjustly, he continued to read his cases until he was convinced he could render an impartial verdict.[29]

John Marshall was born in Carroll County, Indiana, in 1858. The following year the family moved to Elk County, Kansas, where he was educated in the public schools. He taught school and between school terms studied law at the University of Kansas. He furthered his legal education by studying law while serving as clerk of a district court. In 1904 he moved to Winfield and served as county attorney and later as attorney for the old railroad commission. He was elected to the supreme court in 1914 and served sixteen years, writing 1,056 opinions. Marshall became famous for his use of the injunction and padlock for abating liquor nuisances. He was kind and sympathetic, but it was difficult for people to become acquainted with him. For him, writing was "a laborious even painful task." He gave "thorough and conscientious consideration" to his cases and was a "profoundly religious" Methodist who was "sound and studious but not a brilliant lawyer."[30]

Chief Justice Johnston, the "grand old man," as he was popularly known, presided over these judges and continued on the bench for thirty-five years. In 1934 he celebrated fifty years as a judge and served another two years, one month, and twelve days, a national and international record for jurists in his category, at the same time that he celebrated his sixty-ninth wedding anniversary. He personally knew every governor in the Sunflower State, from territorial governor Robinson to the incumbent, Alf Landon. He served with thirty-two associates and wrote almost three thousand opinions. He was an advisor or counsel for many Republican candidates for office and wrote recommendations for prospective district, supreme, and federal court justices. He administered the oath of office to justices whom he had sworn in as fledgling lawyers.[31]

Born in Canada, Johnston settled in Minneapolis, Kansas, meanwhile becoming an avid baseball fan. The Republican county convention met there in 1875 and failed to agree on a candidate for the state legislature. They adjourned until the evening. Johnston had won a victory pitching for the local baseball team, and the team was carrying him on their shoulders when one of the delegates suggested him as a candidate. He was nominated by acclamation, won the election, and was elevated to the senate two years later. While Johnston was in the senate, the legislature submitted the prohibition amendment to the people. In 1880 Johnston campaigned for prohibition and for the office of attorney general. When he won, it fell to him to enforce the law. Following two terms there, he was elected to the supreme court in 1884.[32]

In writing his opinions, Johnston's prose was "smooth, semi-flowing, well constructed from a literary viewpoint, clothed in language a layman could understand; the facts were stated in appropriate sequence, the legal question to be determined clearly set out, the conclusions and the reasons for them, with sustaining authorities, were logically arranged and forcefully stated." Nothing was said about his declining years. Born in 1848, he was in his eighties when he began thinking of retirement, and, while slowing down, he appeared as capable as ever in composing his succinct opinions.[33]

A Wichita lawyer paid a great tribute to the preeminent man: "In his high position the power of restraint and the restraint of power were one and the same; yet novice and Nestor of the bar alike, have felt the balm and healing of his gentle tact, scholarship without pedantry, courage without bravado, popularity without conceit, have marked his character and career."[34]

The Cases

The prohibition amendment was not two decades old when it became necessary in 1898 for the legislature to provide for an additional attorney in the attorney general's office to press prosecutions. The caseload grew heavier because at the turn of the century communities followed the example of Topeka and indirectly licensed illegal bars or saloons by taxing them and making regular, scheduled arrests. After paying their fines, the bootleggers went right back to their business. Attorney General C. C. Coleman, for example, brought quo warranto proceedings against the counties of Crawford, Geary, Leavenworth, and Sedgwick to halt this "flagrant, offensive and revolting practice." Immigrant miners in the tristate area were especially notorious for manufacturing their own "moonshine," or "deep shaft," as it was called.[35]

One group figured out the system. A. L. Hickox, a Missourian, was a salesman for Bernard Holzmark, a Kansas City, Missouri, liquor merchant. In October 1900 Hickox traveled to Elk County and took orders from W. A. Kendall and George Buel, neither of whom had a license to sell. They were regular customers of Holzmark and bought the liquor for personal use, and Holzmark expressly reserved the right to reject any order. Hickox never delivered the merchandise, but it was shipped by rail, going through interstate commerce. Chief Justice Johnston ruled for the court that intoxicating liquor is a legitimate article of interstate commerce and cited *Leisy v. Hardon* (135 U.S. 110) and *In re Bergen*, an identical case in circuit court (115 Fed. 339), for precedents. Hickox was released from charges.[36]

The Kansas Utopia Association of Everest kept a stock of liquor on hand for the exclusive use of its members. Membership cost $2, and members had to pay for any drink they ordered. They could pay cash or deposit a sum of money and draw from it if the drink was less than $2. The liquor was kept in bulk, and no effort was made to separate it until a drink was ordered. "Stripped of its subterfuges and pretenses," Judge Green declared, "it is a whisky saloon." "Courts," he added, "look with disfavor upon cunning devices to evade the law. This device does not possess the charm of novelty."[37]

Miss Blanche Boies, Mrs. Henry Howard, and others of "a praying band" entered rooms at 402 Quincy in Topeka and found "a flourishing beer saloon." Fritz Durein informed the ladies that it belonged to him and he intended to continue operating it. When notified of this, the assistant attorney general filed charges against him, and within twenty minutes the Shawnee County sheriff had entered and discovered a well-stocked saloon. Ten or twelve people were drinking, and as Durein had no permit to sell, he was arrested, tried, and convicted. Counsel for the defense, G. C. Clemens, demanded a rehearing. Justice Burch declared that the legislature has the power to determine what men will eat or drink or wear. He observed that "man cannot be left to define his own sphere of liberty in all cases," and the state can impose its police power to set conditions. All the current prohibition laws were constitutional, he declared.[38]

Rosina Ziebold and Emma Haegelin manufactured and sold intoxicating liquors, mostly beer. They sold quantities of beer to William Renier and others who became intoxicated and belligerent. Renier shot and killed J. Burchart and C. T. Oathout, fellow drinkers. Ruth Renier depended on her husband for support, and she brought suit because the two women sold him intoxicants that caused him to kill. Justice Green held Ziebold and Haegelin responsible for the illegal sale and subsequent death of William Renier.[39]

The state brought action to stop the city of Pittsburg in its illegal practice of licensing the sale of intoxicating liquor "under the guise of collecting at regular intervals fines for infractions of the prohibitory law." A judgment was issued against the city, and the council was reported as changing its policy. The city decided not to appropriate any money for salaries of policemen and firemen from June to November 1907. The city saloon keepers raised a sum of money and gave it to Frank Lasinski, a Pittsburg resident who was a liquor dealer in Missouri. He was honest with the funds and paid the salaries of the police and firemen. This was an organized attempt to evade the law, and Justice Mason held that Lasinski bore the "chief responsibility" for the fraud. Mason supported the fine of $1,000. In addition, fines of $500 were levied against the other "worst offenders," along with fines of $50 for the police and $25 for the firemen.[40]

It was reported that "the use of ginger as a substitute for whisky has become quite extensive in Junction City." Druggists manufactured and sold Jamaica ginger by diluting it with water and making it a potable, if not delicious, intoxicating beverage. The practice became so widespread that authorities "circulated a blacklist of persons using it too freely." The supreme court affirmed the conviction of the violators on the basis that the prohibitory laws listed bay rum, extract of lemon, Jamaica ginger, "or other tinctures with a large percentage of alcohol" as being illegal for sale as beverages.[41]

Prohibitionists won a signal victory in 1913 when Congress passed the Webb-Kenyon Act, which closed the interstate commerce channels to states that prohibited intoxicating beverages. This failed to stem the flow of liquor into the Sunflower State. In 1915 the Missouri Pacific was convicted on twelve counts of violating this act and Kansas prohibition laws. This carrier, the court observed, delivered from ten thousand to thirty thousand pounds of liquor yearly to known violators. The railroad, the court said, "must be plethorically overstocked with ignorance not to know that such consignments are for other than personal use of those receiving them."[42]

When the US Supreme Court upheld the Webb-Kenyon Act in *Clark Distilling Co. v. Western Maryland Railway* in 1917, the drys stepped up their campaign in Congress. In debates on a post office bill, "wet curmudgeon" Senator James Reed of Missouri threw in a rider to ban all transportation of liquor into dry states. This, he assumed, "would shame the hypocrites." To Reed's shock, the harsh bill sailed right through Congress. The Kansas legislature passed the "bone dry" statute, which Governor Arthur Capper described as "the most drastic anti-liquor enactment written in this nation." The law was challenged in Crawford County, fittingly enough, when John Macek, who was "a persistent violator" of the liquor laws, was acquitted of another violation. He permitted another person, however, to keep liquor in his boardinghouse, and Macek was convicted of owning a nuisance. The court sustained this as not constituting a double jeopardy because this conviction was for a different violation.[43]

Prohibitionists also used the crusading spirit of the Great War to further their cause. To conserve foodstuffs for the war effort, Congress enacted the Wartime Prohibition Act ten days after the Armistice. The legislative body had already approved the Eighteenth Amendment, which established prohibition nationwide, prohibiting the manufacture, transportation, or sale of intoxicating beverages. When this was ratified in 1919 to go into effect 1 January 1920, Congress enacted the Volstead Act to define "intoxicating" as 0.5 percent alcohol by volume. At this point several states abandoned their enforcement machinery and turned this duty over to the federal government. Not so Kansans, who did not trust federal officials to keep their state dry.

John E. Bancord worked at the Atchison, Topeka and Santa Fe Railroad scrap shop in Topeka. He and other workers used a turntable to move defective cars for repairs. The table rails and ground rails were worn and needed replacing. The plank they were using to move an engine was badly worn, and it slipped. The signal to stop the movement came too late, and Bancord was crushed to death. The railroad argued that Bancord and his coworkers knew the equipment was worn, and so this was a case of assumption of risk. The jury decided that Bancord was experienced in such work on moving cars but not on this particular turntable, and jurors held against the company. Judge Pollock agreed that assumption of risk was more than "a knowledge of conditions," and it could not be said that the worker should have known of the risks involved. It was a case of employer negligence.[44]

The Atchison, Topeka and Santa Fe sought to enjoin a Kansas City railroad from appropriating a right-of-way on its land. The law of 1868 followed the "golden rule" in this type of case. The law was changed in 1901 to provide for the Railroad Commission to decide on permission to cross another line or to unite track of one line with another. If another railroad owned the needed land, this did not forbid acquisition of the land by the company using right of eminent domain. The majority of the court held that this kind of dispute did not need to go to the Railroad Commission and approved the transfer if the ATSF was not using the land. If the judges did not rule this way, then a railroad "by skillful extension" of its land could exclude other lines from access to a city. With a rehearing it was revealed that the ATSF was planning to use that particular piece of land for access to its turntable. The court also held this rule to be subject to some limits. The company, for instance, might need the land for later expansion.[45]

A freight locomotive started a fire on L. E. League's farm. The League family fought the fire and believed it to be extinguished. The League boys plowed a fire wall and then went to bed late that night. The fire left coals that recaught, and it spread to a straw stack and then to buildings. The jury awarded Mrs. League $438 and Mr. League $1,510. The railroad claimed the Leagues were responsible, but Chief Justice Johnston, speaking for the court, decided that the arrest of the fire did not produce the next one, and the railroad should have anticipated that the fire might start anew. The Leagues exercised "all reasonable and practical means" to extinguish it, and the jury had to make the decision. The Leagues won the award, and Johnston supported that conclusion.[46]

Alexander Coliati was killed while helping engine hostler Swan. The hostler moved engines over the ash pit to clean them, and the helper went under the engine to hoe ashes out of the bin. One night they took an engine over the pit, and Coliati signaled that it was not placed correctly and to back it up two feet. Swan moved it and then waited. When nothing happened, he investigated and found Coliati pinned between a drive rod and a step on the engine, caught there by the movement. Instead of trying to release him, Swan ran to the roundhouse for help. This took about five to seven minutes, and on his return he found Coliati dead. Experts testified that a man caught like this would live three to five minutes. Swan said that if he had backed the engine, no one would have been there to catch Coliati. He would have fallen on the tracks, and the wheels would have crushed him, so Swan had no choice but to go for help. Juries had to decide issues such as this one, and this jury determined that it was an accidental death, with no one negligent. Railroading was dangerous work in the best of circumstances.[47]

Charles Roebuck, a section foreman for the Santa Fe, supervised a crew that included Mexican section hand José Negreta. The two did not get along, and when Negreta cursed him, Roebuck ordered him to go home. Roebuck feared Negreta because he had "killed one or two men," so he notified his supervisor that he could not manage Negreta. He received the response to continue working the man, and the railroad would protect him. One day, without warning and without provocation, Negreta stabbed and killed Roebuck. The widow brought suit, and the court held that her husband was at fault for "assumption of risk." The railroad was not responsible, although the supervisors had assured Roebuck of his safety. Justices Johnston and West disagreed because Roebuck had reported his fears and was ignored.[48]

After a regular hearing on 7 December 1905 the Railroad Commission ordered the Missouri Pacific to operate a passenger service from the state line to Madison. The railroad attacked the commission for being unconstitutional because the law delegated legislative authority to it. Justice Porter affirmed the law to be constitutional because there was no violation of the concept of separation of powers in the creation of the commission. As a favor, the commission offered to permit the line to run a motorcar service instead as long as it met the needs of passengers.[49]

The weather often makes the wheat harvest uncertain in Kansas. When the wheat is ripe, the farmer must reap it at the opportune time, and adequate transportation is essential in this process. A law of 1905 required railroads to deliver freight cars when demanded or pay $1 per day per car ordered for each delay, except for "strikes, unavoidable accidents, or other public calamity." William Patterson sued the Missouri Pacific for $6,336 for damages for delay because he had ordered nine cars "at once." This particular line ran from Rose to Kansas City through the state of Missouri and then returned, so the company argued that this road was thus in interstate commerce. Justice Smith spoke for the court in sustaining the law because this was a reasonable exercise of the state police power.[50]

When the railroad failed to furnish cars on time, a plaintiff sued for $100 per day for seventeen days because his company could not grind corn and market products for lack of supply of cars. The Railroad Commission insisted that the company based its estimated loss on a full production schedule, and, in addition, the milling company could have compelled the railroad to furnish sufficient cars. The court also admitted that it could not determine from the evidence how much profit was lost. The railroad argued that the company was part of the Southern Kansas Millers Commercial Club, whose purpose was to control the price of wheat and flour to prevent competition and thus violated the Kansas antitrust laws. The supreme court sustained the Railroad Commission in its findings.[51]

In one of those rather rare instances, the court interpreted a state law, and the US Supreme Court reversed it. In response to agrarian demands dating back to the Populist insurgence, in 1909 the legislature enacted a demurrage law, which required railroads to provide cars upon proper notice. If they failed to do so, they had to pay the shipper $5 daily per car and refund attorney fees. The Santa Fe protested this, and the Court held this not to violate the equal protection clause of the Fourteenth Amendment. The court sustained the law under the police power. The railroad appealed, and Justice Mahlon Pitney, speaking for the Supreme Court, noted that the law punished shippers who failed to use cars when they called for them, and they had to pay for the cars but not the attorney fees. If the railroads failed to supply cars, they were liable for the $5 daily penalty plus attorney fees. Pitney reversed the trial court and held this to violate the equal protection clause.[52]

Thomas Gorman had shipped over rail lines many times and knew a written contract was necessary for this service. No contract form was available when he needed one, so he made a verbal one with the station agent to ship cattle. When the train arrived in Fort Scott, the agent cut the cars out of the train because there was no contract. It was a hot, sultry day, and the cars were switched and bumped about over the yards for some time. Gorman tried to follow the cars' progress, and he forced fallen cattle to get up. He finally found an agent who had a contract form. Gorman did not read the contract because he thought that all contracts were the same. This one had no option on the condition of his cattle. When the cattle arrived at the auction, Gorman was forced by the contract to unload the cattle by himself. He found one so badly hurt that it could not be sold; five others were "weighed back" after the sale because of broken ribs. He sued for damages. The court decided that the law required the railroad to transport the cattle, and the company could not enforce a contract that "he was forced to accept to save his cattle."[53]

W. A. Burke was a freight train conductor who was killed while switching cars. The cars were equipped with automatic couplers. When this device failed, workers had to couple cars by hand. On this occasion, when he stepped between the cars to do this, Burke slipped on a chunk of coal or a rock about the size of his head and was crushed to death instantly. Evidence was presented to show that the track was not kept up in the yards, and they were overgrown with weeds and covered with trash. Testimony demonstrated to the jury that Burke was "an unusually careful and prudent man," and the accident could not have been caused by his negligence. The jury found for his widow. Upon review, the supreme court held that no incontrovertible evidence was presented to show that the railroad was at fault, and the decision of the trial court was overruled.[54]

Following the enactment of Populist laws, labor issues increasingly came to the court for answers. The law of 1891 establishing an eight-hour day for state employees was still being tested after the turn of the century. James Wilson was constructing a schoolhouse for Iola and violated the law. Justice Smith, speaking for the court, decided that the intent of the law was to apply to school districts, an agent of government, when the legislature used the word "municipality" in the statute.[55]

W. W. Atkin contracted with Kansas City, Kansas, to pave Quindaro Boulevard and worked his men over eight hours daily. He contended that he was exercising quasi-private powers, but the court said that he must obey the state law when working on state projects because the city was exercising its authority, delegated from the state. Justice Doster dissented because he thought the opinion was too narrow. He believed it suggested that if the project was "a case of purely municipal improvement," such as a waterworks, it might not receive the same interpretation. He believed that the maximum hours law should apply in all city cases, as municipalities were agents of the state.[56]

The case was sustained by the US Supreme Court in *Atkin v. Kansas* (1903), where the opinion established an important precedent for states regulating hours of work on their projects. Justice John Marshall Harlan gave the state almost unlimited scope in establishing work rules for work performed under its auspices. He noted that the Court had sustained Utah's establishment of the eight-hour day for miners in *Holden v. Hardy* in 1898. Paving a road was not dangerous work like mining, but Harlan noted that municipalities are "creatures, mere political subdivisions of the State for the purpose of exercising a part of its powers." Harlan gave states almost unlimited control over establishing rules for work done under a state's control. Chief Justice Melville Fuller and Justices David Brewer and Rufus Peckham dissented, refusing to abandon the liberty of contract doctrine.[57]

In *State v. Ottawa* the court held that policemen and firemen came under the maximum hour regulation. Engineers worked manually for an average of five hours and firemen four hours daily. In all their labors, the court determined, one-half or more of this manual work was of the "heavy" nature. To the argument that these men were paid monthly, the justices responded that the law dealt with hours, not pay, and it made no difference how often state employees were paid.[58]

The law of 1907 required selling black powder to miners in original packages of 12.5 pounds because the legislature concluded that this was the safest way to handle the explosive. J. H. Williams was convicted of selling 25 pounds of powder not in the original container. He was fined $50, and when he failed to pay he went to jail. He sought a writ of habeas corpus because the law, he claimed, violated the state bill of rights and the Fourteenth Amendment by taking property without due process of law. It also was not uniform because it applied only to coal and not to lead and zinc mining. Justice Benson traced the history of Kansas mining laws and found that each of them was progressive and sought to promote safeguards for workers. Coal mining is hazardous, and he justified the black powder law on the basis of the state police power to protect the workers and the sellers.[59]

The factory law of 1903 that required safeguards on machinery came into play when Tony Caspar was killed while working for a scrap metal company. The cutting machine used "alligator shears" to cut up metal to a certain size. It had no device for throwing the driving belt on its pulley, and workers sometimes used a stick or their hand to replace it when it fell off. There was a loose and a tight pulley operating three pairs of shears, and when the faulty equipment broke, Tony climbed a ladder to replace the belt. When he climbed the ladder to reach the belt, it broke, and he was killed. The court held this safety law to come within the state's police power to require safety equipment.[60]

J. E. Drake contracted to operate the mine for a gypsum company that processed the gypsum ore. He was familiar with this type of mining, as he had been working with it for many years. Minnie Laffery's husband was killed by a rock falling from the roof. She sued on the basis of company negligence, and the company pleaded assumption of risk and contributory negligence. The jury found the Drake company to be negligent because it failed to inspect the roof for safety. Judge Benson agreed that the Drake company, not the gypsum company, was negligent. Johnston, joined by Graves, dissented because "mining is intrinsically dangerous," so it devolves on the mine owner to take safety precautions. The owner cannot escape this by blaming the contractor.[61]

Henderson was a switchman on the railroad tracks with twelve years' experience in the mining of gypsum. A miner named Beasley asked him to look at the roof of the mine shaft where he was working. Henderson tapped the roof with a sledgehammer and found that half of it was solid and half was loose. Beasley informed his supervisor, who replied that he needed the ore and that Beasley should take down the loose part. If Beasley declined, he should ask Henderson to do it, as he was experienced. Henderson agreed, but an hour had lapsed since he had tested it, and a shot of dynamite had been discharged. When Henderson hit the roof it collapsed, and he was injured. The jury decided that Henderson was not assigned to this job, and he voluntarily assumed the risk. Judgment of the lower court was affirmed.[62]

The child labor laws of 1905 and 1909 prohibited using boys under sixteen years of age in dangerous occupations. Jesse Casteel drove a horse car on a track that dumped the ore into a hoist on an incline and then rode the car back to the pile of ore. There were loose chains on both sides of the car used for dumping, and they allowed some play on the box. Jesse constantly had to shift his weight to balance the car. On one trip it swerved too close to the shale pile, and, with no brake on the car, it was thrown off the track, and Jesse broke his arm. He sued on the grounds that he was only fifteen and this was dangerous work. The law provided for penalties but no right of action by the injured. Justice Mason decided this was indeed dangerous work, and Jesse should have compensation for the neglect of the company in keeping its machinery in repair.[63]

William Sibley worked in the card room of a mill with forty-eight machines in his area. They were placed in rows, leaving a three-and-a-half-foot aisle between rows. The machines were driven by a belt with a pulley on one side. A stripper belt fell off, and he pulled it into the aisle with his foot and tried to put it on the pulley. His hand slipped, and the mat with sharp teeth to tear the cotton ripped his hand to the extent of requiring amputation. Sibley alleged poor lighting, no guards for the mat, failure to provide a thrower for the belt, and machines that were placed too close together. All this violated the law of 1903 requiring safeguards. The jury found that he had assumed these risks, so there was no claim for damages. The supreme court sustained the verdict.[64]

The small town of St. Marys had a waterworks system, including a well, a windmill, and a pump. Mary Roberts's husband climbed on a faulty ladder to oil the windmill and fell to his death. Employees knew the ladder needed repair, and a worker had driven loose nails back in rather than really repairing the ladder. The court held that cities are responsible for the safety of employees as well as private employers and have to provide a safe work environment. This requirement included all cities, no matter the size.[65]

Brakeman Jay Lupier worked for the Santa Fe. He was riding the engine to Chanute, and his job included jumping down at the proper time and throwing the switch for the siding in order not to lose speed for the incline on the switch track. The siding track had an irregular surface, and it was muddy. He slipped, and the engine ran over his leg, requiring amputation between the knee and hip. The jury awarded him $17,000, and the court sustained the decision based on company negligence.[66]

A 1912 case tested the important law of 1909 that outlawed the "yellow dog" contract in Kansas. This device forced the employee to sign a statement that he would never join a union; thus its pejorative term for an employee giving up his rights. A. R. Hedges was employed as a switchman on the St. Louis and San Francisco Railroad running out of Fort Scott. He was a member of the Switchmen's Union of North America. Superintendent T. B. Coppage informed Hedges that he had to sign a withdrawal from the union or be terminated. He refused and was fired. The state took the case to prove the law's constitutionality. Justice Smith spoke for the court, saying that no right of the employee to contract was taken away or impaired. The employer had no right to compel an employee to make any contract "he does not wish to make." Justices West and Porter dissented, saying that the law was passed to promote the delusion that the state was shielding employees with this useless provision and cited earlier cases that the employer can fire anyone at any time for any reason or no reason.[67]

The decision was appealed to the US Supreme Court in *Coppage v. Kansas*. The high court split badly, with six rejecting the law in a lengthy opinion. The majority cited *Lochner v. New* York (1905), striking down a maximum work law for bakers, and *Adair v. United States* (1908), declaring a yellow dog contract on railroads to be unconstitutional, two reactionary decisions that crippled the progressive labor legislation effort of several states. In an equally long dissent, Justices Oliver Wendell Holmes, Jr., Charles Evans Hughes, and William Rufus Day observed that this decision would strike down similar laws in thirteen other states and that the obnoxious *Lochner* and *Adair* decisions should be reversed.[68]

In 1911 the state legislature enacted a primitive law in this area that would require later clarification of certain clauses for it to be effective. It included the significant provision that if either the employer or the employee did not wish to be covered, he must file a written statement of nonelection, rendering it basically a worthless protection. In the law's first test, Frank Shade was injured on 12 March 1913. On 17 March the company filed for nonelection, but Frank did not; thus, both were covered when the accident occurred. The supreme court had sustained the law that year in *A. E. Hess v. E. S. Conway* (93 Kan. 246), and the justices remanded the case for further action based on that decision.[69]

The automobile was being developed before the turn of the century, and it became popular quite rapidly. Laws were required to regulate this new method of transportation, but they were more of a reaction to the vehicle than an anticipation of what was needed for control. As usual with this type of regulation, legislators followed a trial-and-error approach. Automobile cases were not indexed separately in the *Reports* until volume 87 in 1912. Cities usually enacted rules to govern automobiles' speed or to protect pedestrians or horses from the noisy, dangerous contraptions.

The first automobile case to come before the court involved Calista Brock, who sued the Francis brothers for damages from injuries. Brock was on her way to Cherryvale in her horse and buggy with a load of farm products for sale. George and Will Francis had just left town in their steam-powered automobile. As they approached Brock, she drove her horse over near a hedge, as the noise was frightening her animal. When the car came even with her, its hissing and clanking caused her horse to bolt, and the buggy struck a telephone guy wire, throwing Brock to the ground. The jury allowed her $2,000 for injuries plus $100 but, due to poor instructions, turned in a verdict of $5,000. The supreme court concluded that she should have been awarded $2,100 in addition to $500 for mental and physical pain. She could accept $2,600, but if she refused, the court would offer her a new trial.[70]

It was fair time in Concordia, and Peter Benson was driving his automobile down the street next to the fairgrounds. He hit Margaret

Williams, and she recovered damages of $3,000 actual and $250 punitive. As Margaret lay on the street unconscious, people asked Benson why he did not swerve and avoid her. He arrogantly "complained that she had no right to be in the road and that she had broken the lamps on his car." The city ordinance required auto drivers to exercise the same care as a driver of horses and avoid if at all possible hitting pedestrians. The justices agreed with this admonition but noted that the higher speeds of automobiles "greatly increases the danger of injury to travelers and naturally calls for more constant watchfulness on the part of the driver."[71]

A man named Corley was riding in an automobile as a guest. As the driver crossed the railroad at an intersection, a train struck and killed them. His widow claimed negligence of the railroad for allowing overgrowth on the embankments, hedges, weeds, and foliage that restricted the view. The railroad countered that the guest should have helped watch for danger. The jury held for the widow. Upon appeal, the justices decided that the guest could not be held responsible and remanded for a new trial that would be confined to the issue of unsafe obstructions.[72]

An ordinance in 1909 required automobile drivers to exercise "every reasonable precaution" to prevent frightening horses. If the animals appeared restive, the driver must cut his speed. In this case, the owner had control of his horses, but the automobile approached "practically alongside the restive horses and then stopping it there and leaving the engine in production of the noises described in the petition." The jury agreed that the driver should have turned off the engine if he decided to stop, and the court supported its decision.[73]

L. C. Fisher was driving a spring wagon when he was hit by W. H. O'Brien's automobile. It was a dark night, and soon after O'Brien left town his headlights went out. He stopped at a friend's house and borrowed a lantern to hang on the front of his auto as a warning. He was charged with being intoxicated and running "at too high a rate of speed." The jury did not find him to be drunk, but the court held it proper to instruct the jury that it was negligence to run an automobile along the highway at such a speed that the driver could not stop his machine within the distance he could see objects ahead of him. This is approximately what driving rules would require one hundred years later.[74]

One case involved both an automobile and railroad liability. At the Santa Fe crossing in Valley Center the railroad maintained a bell that warned of approaching trains. On this occasion the bell failed to ring, and John Jacobs crossed the rails without looking or listening for an approaching train. One came and struck his automobile. The court held that if a traveler crosses a railroad track without taking precautions, "he does so at his peril." If a bell does not ring or a whistle sound, this was not "an invitation to cross railroad tracks without taking the ordinary precautions." The justices cited the long-held rule that "it is the positive duty of the driver of an automobile to stop, look and listen before crossing the railroad tracks." In this instance, even though the bell failed to ring, the railroad and enginemen "were not guilty of wantonness" and should not be held negligent.[75]

Pool halls and bowling alleys were becoming popular forms of entertainment. The legislature enacted a law in 1909 that authorized cities to license "billiard halls, pool halls, and bowling alleys." The town of Langdon in Reno County took advantage of this and issued a license. Speaking for the court, Justice Porter upheld this statute as a "proper subject of police regulation." The court, Porter declared, always tried "to interpret acts of the legislature with the utmost liberality and to uphold them unless beyond reasonable doubt they are found to conflict with some provision of the higher law."[76]

In a reversal of this, Burlingame forbade a pool hall or bowling alley in town in 1905. Oscar Thomson had opened his pool hall in 1902, and city officials admitted that he had always conducted it "in a quiet and orderly manner," but they argued that there was always a "constant tendency to become disorderly" in this type of recreation. The court supported the city ban by quoting a Nebraska opinion that "a pool hall in a village is apt to degenerate into a trysting place for idlers and a nidus for vice."[77]

Roy Crawford operated a theater for burlesque, minstrel, and vaudeville shows. A Topeka city ordinance forbade work on Sundays. This ordinance affected his ticket sellers, and, in addition, he required workers to move scenery and to handle the baggage of traveling troupes. The court affirmed this Sunday work law, holding that it applied to theaters as well as merchants.[78]

On a Thursday a telephone line fell across an electric railway line in Kansas City. On the following Saturday morning a policeman found it and coiled it at the foot of a telephone pole; he then reported it. Apparently he received no shock when he handled it (or he did not report it if he did), but when he moved it, the line became electrified. When Edward Gilbert touched it he received a severe shock. The court found negligence on the part of the city, noting that the policeman should have remained with the wire until someone came to fix it. "If one puts a dangerous mechanical contrivance in the public highway," the court held, the city is liable. The court failed to note how the policeman could guard the line and still go somewhere to report the danger.[79]

Kansas enacted a "huckstering" ordinance that required peddlers to buy a six-month license for $35 and another for their helpers for $15, and the purchase of the license had to be properly publicized in the *Kansas City News*. George Overton was arrested for huckstering without a license. The court held that the original objective of the law was the single one of licensing, but it also raised revenue. The fee was comparatively large but not unreasonable, considering the costs of administering it plus the city costs of operations. The ordinance made exceptions for sales of products on land that the seller owned or leased. This was a tax on itinerants, and Overton fit this category.[80]

The Topeka board of education approved a program of opening exercises for public schools that included reciting the Lord's Prayer, reading the Twenty-Third Psalm and a selection from natural history, and singing a song. This fifteen-minute interlude was designed to quiet the students before classes opened and was not required, but students who did not participate had to refrain from regular studies and "preserve order." J. W. Billiard asked permission for his son Philip to enter school when classes began. When the school refused, Philip refrained from coming to school until classes started. He was expelled for "persistent violation" of the rules, and the father appealed. Justice Greene spoke for the court, noting that the state constitution and statutes forbade compelling students to worship and prohibited schools from teaching sectarian or religious doctrine, but there was nothing that would exclude the Bible from schools. A teacher of the Quincy school testified that the opening exercises were necessary "to quiet them down" after being on the playground, and it was a religious exercise for those who were religious and "to the others it was not." The justices affirmed the decision to allow the exercises.[81]

A law of 1879 permitted first-class cities to segregate their schools, and Topeka proceeded to do so. William Reynolds, "a colored man," asked the board to admit his son to a white school and was refused. G. C. Clemens, arguing for the Reynolds boy, believed that integrated schools would "encourage the promotion of intellectual, moral, scientific and agricultural improvement, by establishing a uniform system of common schools" as the laws on public education required. Justice Burch rejected this interpretation, saying that segregation was uniform as to requirements, and to argue that segregation violated the Fourteenth Amendment equal protection clause could not be defended. The plaintiff's evidence presented no "substantial discrimination." Schools, he noted, cannot be "identical in every respect," and thus "no substantial right" was violated.[82]

It was black administrators and teachers who often quietly opposed integration. For black women, especially, teaching offered decent pay, security, and prestige, and it was a high-status profession for them. In addition, they believed their students would be best served by having their own teachers who understood them. If their schools were integrated, they would probably lose their positions, because white school administrators seldom integrated their staffs. As a result black teachers deplored their facilities and equipment and centered their demands on those issues rather than on the dubious technique of working for integration.[83]

The town of Parsons was cut into quadrants by the Katy Railroad tracks running north and south and by Main Street running east to west.

D. A. Williams's four children attended Lincoln school in the northeast quadrant where they lived. In September 1908 they were ordered to attend the school in the southwest ward. This would force them to walk one-and-a-half miles to school across several Katy tracks. Justice Benson, speaking for the court, said that boards of education, not judges, should make these decisions about school attendance and the location of school buildings. In this case, however, the board had exercised an abuse of discretion because the Williams children would have to cross thirteen tracks of the railroad, with switching and passage of trains constantly in all kinds of weather. This could cause unavoidable delays in them reaching school. The court believed the board should admit the children to a school less dangerous to reach. That school was not necessarily Lincoln, but it should be one to which they could have a safe daily journey.[84]

Two years later this case was back in court because a commission that the board of education appointed concluded that there were actually fewer railroad tracks to cross than reported earlier, and the crossings were "reasonably safe." The justices again held that the decisions of boards of education are final, "except when its action is capricious or arbitrary." In this case, the decision to send the Williams children to the southwest school was permissible.[85]

The legislature enacted a special law in 1889, "probably at the instigation of representatives of the city," that allowed Wichita to build a high school, "provided no discrimination shall be made on account of race or color," and applied the law to that city only. In 1905 the legislature made a similar exception for Kansas City, Kansas, and affirmed that in any case there would be no authorization to maintain any grade in its schools for separate education. Fannie Rawles was a seventh grader in Wichita and attended Park School for blacks. Her mother asked for a writ of mandamus to enroll her in Emerson School for whites, and the court approved the writ, applying the ban on segregation of the Kansas City schools to Wichita.[86]

Charivaris were popular celebrations of newlyweds and were intended for good-natured fun and sometimes embarrassing situations. During one of these celebrations in Cherryvale, the celebrants put the couple in a wagon and drove up and down the main street, introducing them to bystanders "in burlesque speeches." The wagon ran over nine-year-old Frank Hawman and broke his leg. His mother sued the city for allowing this "mob violence." The justices agreed that the people were intending only "to subject the victims to embarrassment, annoyance and humiliation" to provide amusement for the crowd. But they constituted a mob in this instance, and however good their intentions, this did not absolve the city from the responsibility of protecting its citizens.[87]

The town of Goodland provided its citizens with water without measuring the amount used. In 1909 the mayor and council enacted an ordinance requiring water meters and requiring the users to pay for the meters and connections. If the city had to connect the meters, the city would charge each user $17 for the service. Citizen Cooper insisted that this was done solely for the benefit of the water company, but the court sustained this action because the meters were "the only fair basis" for determining how much the consumer should pay.[88]

By the turn of the century certain areas of Kansas were beginning to enjoy a boom in the production of petroleum. This benefit, though, brought with it the problem of oil leases. The Chanute Prospecting Company leased land from F. H. and Mary Chapple in Neosho County for ten years. The couple argued that the company broke the lease by not drilling for two years, and they had not received any lease money. The company responded that it had left a check in their bank, and they need only to sign a voucher to have it deposited in their account. The court held for the Chapples, agreeing that this method was not the same as placing the money in their hands or depositing it directly. The lease contract did not have a clause that notified them to accept a check or sign a voucher, and they were unaware of this practice.[89]

There were no standard lease forms used, and one was signed to lease natural gas rights for $1 for ten years. The lessor agreed to give the lessee one-tenth of gas found or cash. He promised to locate the wells without interference with cultivation of the land, or at least as little as possible. County officials decided to tax the mineral rights under a law of 1897. The company appealed this decision, and the court agreed with the lessor because one must interpret each lease "in the light of its own peculiar provisions." No natural gas had been produced yet, and the county could not tax it until it reached the surface.[90]

The inheritance tax law of 1909 was challenged because it did not have a uniform operation, and there were graduated rates based on the relation of people to the deceased. Husband and wife of lineal descent had one rate; brother, sister, nephew, and niece had another; and there was a third classification of "other." The court held that uniformity was not necessary because it was an excise on transfer, not a property tax that required uniformity. The justices cited other state decisions that upheld exemptions for different levels of relationship, so the statute was valid.[91]

Three brothers attempted to settle the estate of their intestate father. James claimed an equal share, but his brothers argued that he had previously received a deed to another tract of land from his father. He claimed that the gift was for services rendered to his father, but his brothers insisted that it was an advancement from the estate. The court applied the common-law rule of "hotchpot": he must bring his property into the estate to claim any portion of it. If the value of his tract was less than one-third of its current value, he could claim the difference.[92]

A law in 1901 created the Board of Medical Registration and Examination to regulate the fields of medicine, surgery, and osteopathy. P. W. Johnson was a graduate of the relatively new field of chiropracty and insisted that he did not fit these categories but needed a license to practice. The court cited *Webster's New International Dictionary* as defining this field as "a system of healing that treats disease by manipulation of the spinal column." The justices also used cases from other states that sustained chiropracty and osteopathy as fields of medicine. But the court majority was unfamiliar with new approaches to medicine. They held that the legislature made provision for osteopathy but not chiropracty and denied his appeal. Justice West dissented because the language creating the Board of Medicine "could not show more clearly an intention to distinguish between osteopathy and the practice of medicine and surgery." The legislature had not yet caught up with the developments in chiropracty and did not provide for it.[93]

Three children in Dodge City were denied admission to the public school because they did not have a vaccination for smallpox. The school board insisted that Dodge City was in imminent danger of an outbreak because the city was a division point on the Santa Fe, and it had many outside contacts for exposure to diseases. The railroad immunization was a requirement of the state board of health, but the mayor and council passed their ordinance "subsequent to the bringing of this action." The state legislature had ruled that no student infected with a contagious disease could attend public schools, so the board of health had overextended its powers in the absence of legislative authority by interpreting the legislative statement to require a vaccination. The court insisted that the board of education had no power to exclude students if they met the state requirements of age and residence.[94]

Increasingly, boys were attending high school after the turn of the century, and this added a burden to the local taxpayers to provide this level of education. One answer was to build a rural school in a county and let the county taxpayers share the costs. A law of 1915 authorized such a school. Ozawkie wanted one, but the village was too small to pay such a tax requirement. Citizens decided on joining two townships to build one school and held an election to vote bonds to build it. A taxpayer brought suit on the basis that this was an illegal tax. The court decided against him, ruling that the law was constitutional. The election for bonds was also constitutional, as it was held under the auspices of the state authorization.[95]

Protecting migratory wildlife became an increasing concern after the turn of the century. The Kansas legislature acted on this problem in March 1913 by passing a law regulating the sport of hunting them. George McCullough and H. B. Savage were charged with violating the law by shooting wild ducks from a motor boat on 12 April 1914. The court held that all migratory birds fall "within the custody and protection of the United States, and shall not be destroyed or taken contrary" to its regulations. The national government had set hunting regulations for a closed season from 1 February to 15 September each year. The conviction of the hunters was upheld because they violated the season rules and the Kansas law against shooting them from a powerboat. The court sustained the state law as it was not in conflict with the national law. This issue would become important later when the United States signed a treaty with Canada to protect these birds. Missouri would challenge these regulations by claiming that the wildlife was under its jurisdiction when the birds landed in Missouri. In *Missouri v. Holland* in 1920 the US Supreme Court sustained these federal regulations with the highly significant decision that held a treaty to be the "supreme law" of the land, and this took precedence over state sovereignty.[96]

An action was brought by Wah-me-go against Nah-can-be, alias Henry Bear Claw, in Jackson County to partition the property of Shough-ne-gish-go-quah. Wah-me-go was part of the Prairie Band of Potawatomie. Shough and Wah-me-go were married and had two sons. According to the Indian custom of dissolving marriage when it became tiresome or for whatever reason, they left each other and married someone else. They had received lands allotted in severalty, and these lands were in question when Shough died. Justice Graves spoke for the court in deciding the marriage was valid, and after allotment the two became citizens. Marriage by the state cannot be annulled except by state law. At the time of Shough's death Wah-me-go was Shough's legal husband, so he should have half of her estate, not Henry Bear Claw, the other half going to their sons.[97]

In 1898 Nellie Bales instituted a bastardy proceeding against Albert Baker in Sedgwick County. He appeared and paid $80, and she accepted the sum as satisfactory. A second action was brought because the county attorney did not participate in the first as required by law. The court concluded that bastardy is both a civil and a criminal proceeding. The girl was a minor, but the law does not distinguish between adults and minors in this type of action. There being no fraud or deception in the proceedings, the presence of the county attorney was not necessary.[98]

In a similar case, bastardy proceedings were brought by the county attorney on behalf of Anna Yilek, "an imbecile," against Jacob Jehlik, who subsequently was termed mentally unsound and under guardianship. Jacob was arrested and found to be the father of Yilek's child.

A motion was made to set aside the decision because only the mother can be sworn or make a complaint in this type of action, and she was incompetent to do this. Chief Justice Johnston wrote the opinion that the county attorney cannot originate this action but only assist the girl. Can one "without intelligence or understanding" of the statute do this, he asked rhetorically? The fact that Jehlik was unsound was discovered during these proceedings, and the court observed that the arrest and prosecution of "one mentally irresponsible is beyond reason." The court had not only the right but the duty to set aside this verdict.[99]

Not only did World War I halt the Progressive movement, but this martial crusade with religious overtones also ushered in a period of political reaction in Kansans. The Progressive movement never recovered from this conservatism, and it can be stated that the Sunflower State had only temporary bursts of liberalism from the Great Crusade to the present. How this important result came about is necessary for an understanding of Kansas history in the twentieth century.

5. Reaction in the Roaring Twenties

The Political Scene

Kansas entered a period of decided political reaction in the decade of the twenties prompted by a public hysteria that was a carryover from World War I. President Woodrow Wilson once warned that if this proud nation were led into war, the American people would "forget there ever was such a thing as tolerance." This was a self-fulfilling prophecy, as the president established the Committee on Public Information (CPI) immediately after Congress declared war. To mobilize the public mind for support of the war, Wilson appointed Denver journalist George Creel to head the CPI. Creel subsequently transformed the war into a Great Crusade "to make the world safe for democracy" and "the war to end all wars" through a barrage of relentless propaganda, oral and written. He mobilized seventy-five thousand "Four Minute Men" across the nation, local patriots who presented short speeches on "why we fight," war atrocity stories, and similar topics at public gatherings. There was also a good deal of pamphleteering, including the Why We Fight series. These activities created a frenzy in the public mind against new ideas or liberal thinking, a rejection of Progressive programs, and a retreat to what the public considered the "good old days," which had permitted industrialists to crush labor demands with the charge of "disloyalty" and "communism."

The public applauded spectacular raids on Industrial Workers of the World (IWW) headquarters and the conviction of some two hundred persons in mass trials for sedition in connection with their struggles to improve their working conditions. A mob seized pacifist clergyman Herbert S. Bigelow, bound and gagged him, stripped him to the waist, and lashed his back to ribbons "in the name of the poor women and children of Belgium." (When Germany invaded and "raped" neutral Belgium by invading in 1914, many across the United States reacted with horror to this atrocity.)[1]

The IWW, a radical branch of socialism, opposed war in any form. It became highly unpopular in Kansas because of its importance to and alleged interference with the wheat harvest, which was vital to the war effort. Congress sought to enforce conformity in support of the war with the Espionage Act of 1917, which penalized, in broad language, anyone who aided the enemy or who interfered with the draft or operations of the military services. The IWW headquarters in Augusta was raided, and evidence was illegally seized to prosecute the leaders. The twenty-six IWWs arrested in Kansas suffered terribly in antiquated jails for two years, a violation of the speedy trial guarantee, while federal indictments were drawn up charging them with violating the Espionage Act. They were imprisoned along with consumptives and mental defectives in physical conditions that horrified both state and federal inspectors. Tried by federal district judge John Pollock in Kansas City, the IWWs received various sentences to Leavenworth federal prison, and the organization never recovered financially from this assault.[2]

This experience prompted the state legislature to enact a significant criminal syndicalist law in 1920. Three years later Harold B. Fiske was organizing for the Agricultural Workers Industrial Union, a branch of the IWW, in the wheat fields of Kansas. He was arrested in July with IWW literature in his possession and charged with violating this statute. The jury found him guilty, and he was sentenced to Lansing state prison. The state supreme court affirmed his conviction, holding that Fiske's freedom of speech was not violated by the law and that he was properly found guilty because the preamble to the IWW constitution, found in his possession, could have been interpreted by Fiske to promote violence when he explained it to recruits. The decision was appealed to the US Supreme Court in *Fiske v. Kansas* in 1924, and the justices unanimously reversed his conviction. The law had been applied to Fiske without any evidence that he or the IWW had advocated violence, and this constituted "an arbitrary and unreasonable exercise of the state's police power." The justices did not rule the law invalid but insisted that its application in this instance violated Fiske's Fourteenth Amendment rights.[3]

Late in the war and afterward, Kansas and the world suffered a terrible pandemic of Spanish influenza. Because of troop mobilization and transportation across the state with the location of Fort Riley in the center, this massing of diverse people was conducive to the spread of diseases. It is difficult to determine, accurately, where the plague began. In late 1917 cases were reported in New England ports, and it soon spread to Forts Leavenworth and Riley and Camp Funston. In Kansas the US Public Health Service and the Kansas Department of Health greatly expanded their work to meet this crisis. Public schools, churches, theaters, and other meeting places were closed. Kansas health secretary Samuel J. Crumbine closed the Kansas-Missouri border in some areas. The disease claimed over five thousand lives in the Sunflower State, or more than the Kansas military deaths during the war, and between twenty and thirty million people died worldwide before it finally ran its course in 1919. No legal questions were raised during this period over the arbitrary actions taken by Crumbine and Governor Arthur Capper to combat this epidemic. They were considered vital to meet the health crisis.[4]

Three pimps infected with venereal disease during the war did, however, protest their incarceration with prostitutes at the State Industrial Farm for Women in Lansing by Crumbine and the department of health. The supreme court sustained the power of the state to quarantine these infected people but suggested that it was unfortunate the authorities used the term "penitentiary" when they should have said "detention" in the order detaining these men.[5]

Near the end of the war, the court enjoyed a precedent for the justices when the first female lawyer appeared before them to argue a case. Nellie Cline of Larned was associated with her father's law firm; and G. Polk Cline was recognized as "one of the most widely known trial lawyers in western Kansas." A number of young women were in law practice at that time, but they tended to confine their work to "office service." Ms. Cline spoke "calmly and without hesitation" for fifteen minutes in presenting her client's case, appealed from the Pawnee County district court.[6]

The militant hysteria created by the Creel Committee, which was difficult to contain during the war and to subdue afterward, carried over into the postwar era in what was labeled "The Big Red Scare," in which the public tended to label anything different or threatening to their values as "communistic." Wartime inflation of 100 percent, with wages lagging far behind, produced labor unrest, and this, too, created strife in the postwar period. Capitalists used a general strike in Seattle, a massive steel strike, and the Boston police strike in the first postwar year to fire the nation's indignation against organized labor. The state's bituminous coal industry, centered in the tristate region, became the focus of labor strife in Kansas. A speaker at the annual Kansas State Federation of Labor in 1919 encapsulated the mood in the Sunflower State perfectly when he observed that "super patriots" frightened the state legislature by "howling IWW, NonPartisan League, and Bolshiviki. It proved to be one of the, if not THE, most irrational legislature that ever met in the state house in Topeka." This legislature, prompted by the governor, produced a shocking piece of legislation to cure the postwar problems in collective bargaining that were engulfing the nation.[7]

The coal strike in 1919 brought two strong protagonists to the limelight. Alexander Howat, president of District 14 of the United Mine Workers of America (UMW), was a powerful, ruggedly handsome Scotsman whose union members worshiped him and would obey his orders without question. His miners had 100 percent union membership, and his combative nature strongly suggested that he would clash sooner or later with the equally bellicose governor, Henry J. Allen of Wichita. Howat often said he would accept jail rather than give up his constitutional rights, and Governor Allen stood ready to accommodate him. Allen, along with William Allen White and Walter Stubbs, broke with the Old Guard Republicans and became strong supporters of Theodore Roosevelt in the Progressive-Republican split of 1912. During the war, Allen and White investigated Red Cross activities in Europe, and the former became the only man elected governor of Kansas while on a European junket. Governor Allen did not understand the labor movement or the principles of collective bargaining, and he was destined to clash with the UMW leader.[8]

When the UMW struck, Governor Allen immediately involved his office in the dispute. First, he tried to bring the two sides together, and, failing this, he seized the mines and called for volunteers to mine coal for the coming winter. Howat, a national officer of the UMW, was busy in Indianapolis helping coordinate the national strike and left the explosive Kansas situation in the hands of his capable lieutenant, August Dorchy, who kept the men on strike. Volunteer miners answered the governor's call and came to the tristate area from the University of Kansas, army regulars in Fort Riley, and the Kansas National Guard. For twelve long, cold days the men tried their best to become miners at great expense to the state, proving the old adage, "you can't mine coal with bayonets." In late December the governor returned the mines to their owners. Allen's frustrations in this situation led him to believe that he had the correct solution for handling difficult labor-management relations.[9]

In January 1920 Allen called the legislature into special session. Allen believed in the concepts that labor leaders were "dangerous radicals" who needed to be controlled and that employers' actions in dealing with their employees were arbitrary. Free-market forces were not operating in this situation, so the relations between labor leaders and employers needed to be strictly controlled. The legislature was eager to act against anyone it considered radical and quickly passed the criminal syndicalist law. More importantly, it enacted a program for an industrial court to govern labor-management relations. The law specified five areas of public interest—food, clothing, fuel, transportation, and utilities—and established a three-man court to regulate labor-management relations in these categories. Workers were to receive "fair wages and moral working conditions," and the judges could establish rules and regulations concerning these situations. Strikes, boycotts, picketing, and intimidation were outlawed, but the right to quit a job was generously guaranteed. Employers could not discharge, discriminate against, or blacklist employees for utilizing the court. If the court determined that conclusive action was necessary, then the judges could ask a state court for permission to take over and operate an industry. The statute had the usual separability clause, that if any section or provision should be unconstitutional, this would not affect the validity of the other clauses.[10]

Allen toured the nation touting his plan as the correct solution to labor-management strife not only in America but everywhere. His message was well received in many quarters because the country had just witnessed a wave of strikes caused by wages failing to keep pace with the wartime inflation rate of 100 percent. Allen successfully debated AFL president Samuel Gompers on the issue. On the other side the well-known liberal Frank Walsh of Kansas City told listeners that the program would render collective bargaining a farce and could ultimately doom organized labor, calling it "state socialism in its worst form."[11]

Alex Howat was determined to oppose the law until courts declared it unconstitutional. Late in June 1920 his miners staged a "Saturday holiday." There was a continual, predictable shortage of railroad coal cars, and, as the miners operated only when they were available, several locals voted not to work on Saturday and take a two-day weekend to permit coal cars to accumulate. This decision conflicted with the coal contract, which called for a penalty of $1 for every day lost to illegal stoppages. Operators had not enforced this provision previously, but now they did. Howat considered this an outrage, and many miners struck in protest. The mine leader belligerently challenged state officials to compel the men to return to work.[12]

Concurrently, the Mishmash strike was developing. Mishmash was a boy employed in the mines, and when he turned nineteen he requested a man's pay, which his family of a mother and five siblings needed for survival. When the increased pay was not forthcoming after protests, Howat called a strike. The industrial court investigated and sustained Mishmash's demand, ordering the money to be paid through the clerk of the court and calling for an end to the strike. Howat countered that the money had to be paid at the company office, where all miners received their pay, and defiantly continued the walkout. Howat insisted on ignoring the legitimacy of the court or its orders, but, in the meantime, he and Dorchy had to begin serving their jail sentences for contempt of court arising out of issues in the strike of 1919.[13]

Miners then walked out in protest over Howat's imprisonment. With the sheriff's permission, Howat addressed the striking miners from the jail, directing some of his choicest epithets at the governor. Judges of the industrial court wanted to send in the militia and strikebreakers, but Allen wisely persuaded them that there was no current emergency in coal supplies and applauded when UMW president John L. Lewis suspended District 14 for court disobedience. Lewis and Howat were locked in combat over control of the UMW, a struggle that would finally end in 1930, when an Illinois federal district judge ruled that Lewis, not Howat, was the legal president of the UMW and his rebellious organization. Meanwhile, this incident gave Lewis his reason for suspending the president of District 14, and under the leadership of Van Bittner, Lewis supporters took over the district.[14]

In February 1921 a federal judge sentenced Howat and Dorchy to prison for contempt of court over the Mishmash strike, while the state brought similar charges against the two. The state supreme court rejected Howat's appeal, and he and Dorchy took their case to the US Supreme Court. This tribunal ruled that the industrial court did not have jurisdiction over the coal industry. In *Dorchy v. Kansas*, the justices decided that coal mining was not included as a "public interest" of Kansas. The state supreme court sustained Howat's conviction, based on the validity of the separability clause. At one point Howat and Dorchy were serving three concurrent sentences for contempt of court.[15]

The industrial court became a political issue in the election of 1922. Republicans named W. Y. Morgan, who supported Allen's labor concepts, for governor on a platform affirming the law. The Democrats named Jonathan Davis, who campaigned in opposition to the court. A powerful combination of aroused laborers and farmers, previously unknown, who were angry over agrarian conditions and approved Davis's promise of tax reduction gave the Democrat the victory. Davis, only the third Democratic governor in Kansas history, commuted Howat's sentence and reduced his fine to $1.[16]

The case of *Wolf Packing v. Court of Industrial Relations* had an interesting journey from Topeka to Washington and back to Topeka twice. In 1921 the state supreme court sustained the constitutionality of the law by asserting that the state could compel obedience on setting wages under the statute and the company could be forced to pay a "living" wage even though it might operate at a loss. The meat-packing company appealed the decision to the US Supreme Court the following year. Led by Chief Justice William Howard Taft, the court adopted a narrow interpretation of businesses affecting the public interest. Taft's opinion destroyed the industrial court by holding that there were only three types of business that fell into this category: public utilities; inns, grist mills, and cabs; and monopolies. The state merely asserting that a business was in the public interest, Taft insisted, did not make it so. Therefore it could not set wages in the meat-packing industry.

In a subsequent case, in 1923 the company took the issue again to the state supreme court where it denied the industrial court's order to allow one day off per week if an eight-hour day was established. The court heard the case a second time later that year. The industrial court, in controlling overtime, had set it at one-and-a-half pay if the men worked nine hours daily, but the men could not be worked such long hours more than twice weekly. If the company worked the men over forty-eight hours weekly, all the hours constituted overtime pay. The court sustained this clause, and it was not appealed again.

In a closely related issue the supreme court coupled an Industrial Welfare Commission law of 1915 with the industrial court statute. Using the welfare law, state factory inspector Linna Bresette proceeded to establish a shorter workday and a minimum regulation for female workers in Kansas. The law was challenged by the laundry industry, a notorious exploiter of women, and the justices split four to three, with the majority striking down the Bresette regulations based on the US Supreme Court's ruling in the *Wolff* case and in *Adkins v. Children's Hospital*, which held unconstitutional a minimum wage law for the District of Columbia. Justices Harvey, Johnston, and Hopkins dissented. As one authority noted, the court ultimately failed because "there seems little doubt that a fundamental purpose of the law was to reduce unions to a state of impotency" by depriving them of collective bargaining rights.[17]

This narrow interpretation was significant in the short term for Howat and labor because it vindicated his theory of unconstitutionality, but it was a victory for conservative judicial thought in the long run because it placed most businesses out of the reach of state regulation. Not until over a decade later did a revamped US Supreme Court begin to broaden interpretation of constitutional powers during the New Deal and permit wide-ranging regulation of economic issues.[18]

The automobile continued to revolutionize Kansas. It lessened the distinction between rural and urban life, required the building of service stations and highways, assisted school consolidations, and encouraged suburban developments, travel, vacations, and the construction of resort areas. Beginning in 1916 and continuing with the Federal Highways Act of 1921, the national government initiated an interstate highways program. The states built the roads, which meant they had to find new sources of revenue, and the government in Washington matched the costs dollar for dollar but insisted that the highways meet its construction standards and be connected with each other. With the stimulus provided by the Good Roads Association, Kansas became a leader in paved road mileage, a trend that continued into the depression years that followed. To assure the continued flow of federal dollars, the legislature initiated a gasoline tax. A turning point came in 1928 when the state approved a constitutional amendment establishing a state highway system and allowing the taxation and licensing of motor vehicles. A short time later a driver's license requirement was added.[19]

The Roaring Twenties witnessed the revival of the post–Civil War Ku Klux Klan. This new KKK was different. In addition to being anti-Negro, it was anti-Jewish, anti-Catholic, and anti–anything liberal, and it was opposed to the beliefs of approximately one-fourth of the Kansas population. It enjoyed a rather peculiar support from labor because workers disliked Allen, and the governor repudiated the Klan. It grew rapidly and reached a membership of as many as sixty thousand in the state. Its bigotry and racism enraged William Allen White, who labeled it "an organization of cowards" and "a self-constituted body of moral idiots." When the Klan began succeeding in Emporia elections, White became so disgruntled that he ran for governor in 1924 on a program of opposition to the robed and hooded riders because he believed the two major candidates would not stand up firmly enough to the KKK. Republican Ben Paulen won, and White came in a strong third with about 150,000 votes. In 1925 the state supreme court ruled that the Klan was a foreign corporation, chartered in Georgia, and had to have a charter to function in the state. When the secretary of state refused to issue one, this eliminated the Ku Klux Klan in Kansas.[20]

Silent movies were gaining rapidly in popularity, and by the end of the decade average weekly attendance at theaters reached 95 million out of a national population of 120 million. There was no censorship of the industry in its early years until Kansas became one of seven states to establish the State Board of Review of Motion Pictures in 1915. Two years later the law was revised and the name changed to Kansas Board of Review. The board's work was supported by a tax of $2 per reel, and it soon was collecting some $20,000 annually. Governor Arthur Capper and his highly influential *Topeka Daily Capital* supported the board's efforts. They sought to ban scenes of drinking, sex, nudity, women smoking, gambling, cruelty, and indecent language, leaving little of the original scenes in many movies.

The statute required the censorship fees to be paid to the superintendent of public instruction, until the state treasurer cast an envious eye on the revenues. By 1917 fees of $70,000 to $75,000 annually exceeded the board's costs of administration of $50,000 to $55,000, and movie producers joined the treasurer in questioning this money-making feature. The court agreed that the law was not intended to be a revenue measure, and the state won its case, with the excessive revenues going into the state treasury.[21]

The state continued its ban on the classic *Birth of a Nation* for over nine years. This struggle was supported by the National Association for the Advancement of Colored People (NAACP), which persuaded the state film censors to prohibit showing the movie because of its racial prejudices. The US Supreme Court ruled that it was an accurate portrayal of the Civil War and Reconstruction era, but the state censors continued to determine what films were acceptable for its citizens to see. The board's rejection of *The Easiest Way* was appealed to the supreme court, where Chief Justice Johnston, speaking for his brethren, decided that the court could not "substitute its judgment for that of the board." The board had not acted arbitrarily or capriciously in this instance, and it must be assumed to have acted in good faith. Mason, joined by Porter, concurred that the statute did not require the court to be the final arbiter on movies, but the legislature could have imposed this duty on the judges. The board also banned *The Marching Amazons of the Kansas Coal Fields* in 1922, an anticorporation and prounion propaganda film of women supporting their men during the great coal strike.[22]

The movie industry was revolutionized in 1927 with the production of *The Jazz Singer*, starring Al Jolson. The new "talkie" movies did not sweep the state immediately but had done so by the time of the Great Depression. Movies reflect their times and help mold the future, and during the Roaring Twenties they were deeply involved in promoting the new social revolution that saw increased emphasis on sex, drinking, and smoking. Talking movies again revolutionized the industry as it adjusted to the profound problems of sound, and this in turn created new challenges for the board of censors. In 1931 the legislature extended the censorship power to include all aspects of a film. At that time talking movies were on two disks, one for the visual and one for the sound. It was difficult for the board to extract the sound disk and then replace it in synchronization. In addition, board members had no script to guide them, so they had to listen for double entendres and other subtleties. In 1930 the film industry adopted the Production Code of the Motion Picture Producers and Distributors of America, and this greatly assisted Kansas censors if not moviegoers.[23]

The oil and gas industry continued to add substantially to the state's economy and the growing legal opinions on leases. Gas production in the Roaring Twenties reached five trillion cubic feet, much of which was piped to metropolises in the East. Petroleum output grew in the El Dorado area, but new fields were discovered in Marion and Greenwood Counties and also near Russell. In addition, refineries sprang up in those regions to process the oil that often accompanied natural gas. After Harry Truman gave up on oil exploration, or "chance," as he called it, and went to war, major oil companies moved in on his lapsed leases and discovered the great Teeter pool of oil where he had formerly leased.[24]

The judiciary committee of the state bar association continued its studies and recommendations for improvement of the legal system. At its 1926 annual meeting the bar association urged creation of the Judicial Council, which the legislature established the following year. This body served as a clearinghouse for suggestions from the bar and was composed of judges appointed by the chief justice plus chairs of the senate and house judiciary committees. Member J. C. Ruppenthal of Russell, who was instrumental in organizing the first annual conference of Kansas District Judges in 1908, was a key figure in this council. Among other topics, the council developed rules of procedure for district judges, including acceleration of preparing cases for trial and selection of juries and trial procedures. A committee composed of Ruppenthal, A. T. Ayers, and James McClure condensed the rules, and the state supreme court adopted their suggestions in 1929.[25]

The Judges

Several new justices were appointed or elected to the court during this conservative period. William West Harvey was born in Madison County, Kentucky, in 1869. His farm family moved to Shawnee County, where he alternated between teaching and attending the State Normal School in Emporia, finally graduating in 1896. He studied law and practiced it for twenty-five years, serving as a state representative for three sessions and rising to speaker, a promotion Governor Allen opposed but accepted upon assurances of cooperation, before being elected to the court in 1922. He was elected chief justice in 1945, and he served in this position until his retirement in 1956. During his thirty-four-year tenure he wrote 1,652 opinions. He chaired the Judicial Council from 1927 to 1941, and after his elevation to the position of chief justice, he regularly attended the Conference of Chief Justices.[26]

William Easton Hutchison was born at Oxford, Pennsylvania. A farm boy, he attended public schools and taught before practicing law and moving to Kansas in 1887. The Hutchisons had no children, and when his brother and wife were killed in an auto accident, the Hutchisons adopted their three children. He received a doctor of laws degree from the College of Emporia and practiced in Garden City. Governor Ben Paulen appointed him to replace Henry Mason. He was twice elected to the position and retired in 1940. His opinions were distinguished by long sentences, sometime two pages in length, but a colleague insisted that they were "clear and easily understood."[27]

William O. Joachims was born and raised in Topeka and attended Kansas State Normal in Emporia from 1903 to 1907. He received his bachelor of laws degree from the University of Kansas City Law School in 1910 before practicing in Wichita. In 1929 he was appointed to complete Richard Hopkins's term and served one year, declining to stand for election to the position.[28]

E. R. Sloan was born in 1883 in Seward, Nebraska. The family moved to Kansas in 1886. He attended Kansas State Agricultural College for one year and completed a law degree at Washburn Law School. He first practiced law in Hoxie, then moved to Horton in 1911. Sloan was appointed to fill John Marshall's term and served for twenty-one months. He then returned to law practice in Topeka.[29]

Richard Joseph Hopkins was born at Jefferson City, Missouri, in 1873. Six years later the family moved to Kansas, west of Garden City. He attended the University of Kansas from 1893 to 1896 and received a law degree from Northwestern University in 1901. Hopkins had an interesting political career, becoming a most controversial figure. He served as lieutenant governor in 1911 and as attorney general from 1919 to 1923 under Governor Allen. He was elected to the supreme court in 1923 and while on the bench wrote 468 opinions. As attorney general he enforced the industrial court decisions against coal miners with a relish. He was a strict enforcer of the law and was strongly opposed by both organized labor and Kansas corporations. As attorney general he implemented "ouster" suits against corporate officials, and they raised a hue and cry over President Hoover's consideration of him as district judge for the Sunflower State.

The opening came up in 1928, and the Kansas Bar Association pressed for the nomination of W. F. Lilleston, but his opposition to Prohibition led Senator Arthur Capper to persuade President Calvin Coolidge not to appoint him. The Anti-Saloon League then pressured Hoover, through Capper and the new senator Henry Allen, to name its favorite, Richard Hopkins. Despite pleadings from Kansas lawyers and laymen that Hopkins was unqualified as a lawyer, Hoover sent the appointment to the Senate. Members of the Kansas Supreme Court endorsed him, including Chief Justice Johnston, although one associate explained that the purpose of his recommendation was to rid the Kansas court of Hopkins's presence. The fight was not yet finished. Evidence was presented at the Senate confirmation hearings that Attorney General Hopkins did not keep accurate records of his fees. The Kansas State Federation of Labor submitted state and district court records of two counties where Hopkins reported state fees of $3,000 less than those collected from the two counties alone. The Senate Judiciary Committee recommended against his confirmation, but Capper pressured the full Senate to confirm him forty-nine to twenty-two.[30]

The Cases

The Great Crusade created litigation, as wars usually do, because of expansion of administrative powers. Some citizens of Germany and Austria-Hungary living in Topeka had declared their intention of becoming US citizens, and they sought to vote in an election. The state's constitutional requirements permitted "every [white] [male] person of twenty-one years" to vote if they lived in the state for six months and the township for thirty days. This included any US citizen or one who was of foreign birth but had declared his intention of becoming naturalized. The war was still in progress, so the court determined that "there are aliens and there are aliens." Alien friends can become citizens, but enemy aliens cannot, so the latter could not exercise the franchise. The court left unanswered the question of whether these enemy aliens could receive the franchise if they later became citizens.[31]

German citizen William Wolf took out his first citizenship papers in 1885, but they were destroyed in a fire, and he did not pursue the matter. He was employed by Cudahy Packing before the April 1917 declaration of war, and the federal authorities allowed him to continue to work there and to live in the packing-house district. An accident at work left him permanently injured. His employer argued that he was an enemy alien, and thus he was ineligible for workmen's compensation. The court determined that he did not fit this classification under the terms of the Alien Enemy Act of 6 October 1917, so he could recover damages.[32]

Victor Vietti was an eighteen-year-old who was mining coal to support his parents, who were Italian citizens. A rock fell from the roof of the mine and killed him. His parents sought workmen's compensation and received $4,435.12. His father had filed for first papers but did not pursue citizenship, although he signified his intent to remain in America. The company argued that under a law of 1917 aliens were limited to an award of $750. A treaty between the United States and Italy stipulated that their nationals should have the same rights as Americans "provided that they submit themselves to the conditions imposed on the latter." The court held that a treaty took precedent over any federal or state law, and the family was entitled to the larger award.[33]

Following the Armistice, many states decided to reward the sacrifices the veterans had made by voting them a cash bonus. Kansas voters approved such a measure in 1921, and two years later the legislature agreed by enacting a measure to raise $25 million in bonds for its soldier and sailor veterans of the Great War. The question taken to the supreme court involved the state defraying the "extraordinary expenses" those men incurred in leaving good-paying jobs to go to France to fight. The court concluded that they were "defending Kansas in France." The debt owed to veterans could not be computed in dollars, but they had defended Kansas as much as if "the armies had been facing each other in New York, or across the Mississippi or Missouri rivers, or on the prairies of our own state." The justices had been as vulnerable to the Creel Committee propaganda as anyone, and they entertained no doubt that the people and the state could constitutionally approve this bonus.[34]

The issue of illegal booze continued to rear its ugly head, and it would until repeal of Prohibition. J. H. Born violated the intoxicating liquor law and was sentenced to sixty days in jail and fined $100 and costs. He served his time but was unable to pay all of the fine, so the county commissioners assessed him twenty-one days at labor and credited him with $21, and he paid the remainder. He sought a writ of mandamus because the state constitution required all fines to be paid into the school fund, and it required equal rates on assessments and taxes. The law of 1917 on vagrancy permitted the county commissioners to compel work on streets, highways, and public works or at the poor farm. The court held the vagrancy law to be valid and denied mandamus.[35]

In 1919 the legislature provided that an automobile used in violating the prohibition laws would be declared a public nuisance and could be seized, forfeited, and sold by the state. Oscar Peterson and Fred Martin owned an automobile dealership and used one of their cars to run liquor from Brown to Nemeha Counties. The auto was seized and sold, but the Farmers Auto Company had a mortgage on it for $500. Most state laws allowed the mortgagors to receive their money, but Kansas law differed in allowing a claimant to show cause why the property should not be forfeited and sold. This was to help in determining ownership so that a later purchaser could receive clear title at a sheriff's sale. In this case, when the issue was taken to court, it was discovered that the bootleggers held the mortgage on their own car, so the lower court's decision was affirmed.[36]

A purchaser called at Reece Ford's house to buy whiskey. The following day Ford brought a jug in his car and sold it to him. He was convicted for illegal possession and also for illegal sale. He appealed on the grounds that this constituted double jeopardy. The court rejected his claim because he had to have possession in order to sell.[37]

Kansas City residents Mary and Steve Koska endured a chilling experience with bootlegging. Steve worked nights at the Frisco rail yards, and Mary's brother often spent the night with her and her children for moral support. The Kaska family lived next door and was well known in the area for selling liquor and offering gambling. One night four men came to see Kaska at the Koska house. The four children were sleeping on pallets on the floor. The men stepped in, walked on the children, ransacked the house looking for liquor, broke open a trunk, and stole valuables and money, with the brother watching helplessly. The Koskas sued the city on the grounds that they received no protection from this "mob." The majority of the justices decided that this was no "mob" in the sense of the state law requiring protection. The statute was not intended to create civil liabilities on cities, the majority stated, and this was not a "mob" in the sense of the law, so judgment against Kansas City was reversed. Justices Burch and Hopkins dissented on the basis that these men constituted a "mob" with their uncontrolled actions.[38]

Rolla Harvey was a thirty-nine-year-old employee of a bridge company who made a good salary and had a wife, Rebecca, and two children. He was not known as a violent man. One night at 11:30, Harvey and a friend left his house with the intent to acquire some more liquor. They were immediately accosted by City Marshal Easling, who demanded, "Ain't you out kind of late tonight?" "None of your damn business," responded Harvey. "I will make it some of my business," retorted the marshal. One of the men hit him, knocking him into the street. Easling responded by firing two shots, but he hit nothing, and Harvey returned to his home. As he stepped out of the house the next morning, a mob met him. One man fired and wounded Harvey. He responded by shooting one of them. Things quieted down, and Harvey left to find a doctor for his wound. He was unarmed but soon met the men, and one of them shot and killed him. Knowing Harvey fairly well, the sheriff had told Easling to go back and watch the house for the night until Harvey sobered up, then arrest him. Instead, the deputy raised a posse, and when Harvey left the house the next morning, Easling announced that Harvey was under arrest. The posse turned into a mob when Harvey shot one of them. Rebecca sued the city, and the jury agreed that the family had faced a mob. On appeal, four of the justices reversed the jury's opinion. The court was badly divided because three judges, Johnston, Marshall, and Dawson, dissented, believing that the episode constituted mob action.[39]

Determining what constitutes a mob is often difficult. F. F. Moore was "a law-abiding citizen" of Wichita. One night at 11:00 an off-duty policeman knocked on his door. Moore asked who it was, and the policeman responded that he wanted whiskey. Moore said that his house was not a joint, and when another man emerged from the weeds, Moore got his shotgun, and both men left. Four men then returned and broke down the back door of his house and rousted him, his wife, and his daughter out of bed. When they assaulted Moore, he told his daughter to call the police. The four men responded that they were the police. The wife had a nervous breakdown as a result, and their medical bills amounted to $250 plus damage to the house. Moore sued, and the jury determined that this was a mob and awarded $2,000. Five justices determined that "a man's home is his castle" but believed the award was too high. They gave Moore a choice of accepting $500 or enduring a new trial. He took the $500. Johnston dissented without opinion, and Marshall dissented from the majority, calling the policemen a "mob."[40]

Sam Hendren was "an admitted simpleton" with delusions of grandeur. One day he envisioned that Hollywood producers were seeking him for a movie but that other men were trying to kidnap him to prevent his golden opportunity. Thirty to thirty-five men and boys humored him by beating the bushes in the city park for "imaginary kidnappers." Good-natured ridicule soon turned ugly, and they began beating Hendren. The sheriff explained that this sort of ridicule had happened before, but when someone got a rope and pretended they were going to hang Hendren, things went too far. What began as razzing turned ugly, and he suffered two or three teeth knocked out and a disjointed arm with a piece of bone chipped from his radius. A jury awarded Hendren

$1,000, and the court affirmed the judgment. The city should have prevented this violence.[41]

Autos began as a rich man's sport, but as their number multiplied, they became a necessity that required extensive rules to promote full and indiscriminate safe use. Sixteen-year-old Dorothy Noble had her father's permission to drive his auto, and she used it to haul voters to polling places. She was accompanied by a friend when she struck and injured Minnie Stafford, and the jury awarded Minnie $2,500. The court decided that Dorothy was acting not as her father's agent but for the election committee, so he was not negligent. They agreed with the jury but believed the award was too much, and they lowered the amount to $1,800.[42]

Homer and Myron Christensen borrowed Quincy Blosser's car to drive to Manhattan to have the head of a cat that had bitten their father analyzed for hydrophobia. Charles Blosser, a minor who often drove his father's car, accompanied them and drove it home, although his father was unaware that he would do this. The auto had a noisy, bad muffler, which the Blossers knew about. They met Halvorson, with his wife and daughter, in a surrey. The horses were frightened by the noise and jumped. The surrey overturned, injuring the wife. Halvorson brought suit against Quincy Blosser and lost. The supreme court decided that owner Quincy Blosser had no connection with the injury, as his son had taken the initiative in accompanying the Christensens and thus was not the servant or agent for his father.[43]

A collision between cars driven by W. B. Fox and an employee of O. McCormick occurred at 10th and Morris in Topeka. A streetcar was in the middle of the street and came to the intersection at the same moment as did Fox in his Ford. When McCormick's employee swerved to pass the streetcar, he hit Fox's car. The city ordinance giving the right-of-way to the car on the right side superseded the old rule of right-of-way to the one who arrived first at the intersection. The court supported the ordinance as valid, and Fox could sue because of the driver's negligence.[44]

August Mader operated a taxi service in Topeka. The city ordinance forbade the solicitation of business on city streets without the consent of property owners. Mader parked and waited for customers at the train depot, but the Payne Taxicab Company was operating under an agreement with the Rock Island and Union Pacific Railroads to conduct this business. Mader was convicted of violating the ordinance. He appealed on the grounds that the ordinance was unconstitutional. The court denied his appeal, noting that no one had the right to set up such a stand anywhere without the permission of the city. Later cities would permit greater competition among taxis by denying this kind of monopoly.[45]

R. C. Jones farmed some twenty miles from Larned. He employed E. W. Naglo, a mechanic, to work on his tractor and drove him to the farm, agreeing to pay him $1 per hour and transportation both ways. Jones drove the car 35 mph on the way to his farm. The car skidded, and he righted it and continued. Then he reached 60 mph, skidded, and wrecked, injuring Naglo. The mechanic was an experienced driver, but he failed to warn Jones of his speed or reckless driving because he did not want to correct an older man. The court, however, ruled that the passenger must warn of reckless driving or speeding and, if necessary, ask to leave the car. Naglo could not collect damages because of his neglect.[46]

Two automobiles were carrying glycerin from a factory in Oklahoma to Kansas. One caught fire on a hill, and the driver, in his excitement, abandoned the car without securing it. The car rolled down the hill and exploded half an hour later. Mary Barnhardt was 1,100 feet away at the time, and the shock and poisonous gases affected her nervous system. The jury awarded her $1,500 in compensation. The driver argued that the fire was not his fault and that in his panic he forgot to secure the auto. The supreme court agreed with the driver and reversed the judgment.[47]

Martina Barzen and three other University of Kansas students were driving from Lawrence to Kansas City. After they passed Tonganoxie they overtook a caravan of trucks. The last one was hauling huge timbers, projecting eight feet in front and thirty feet in back. It was dark, and the truck had no red lights or warning of the timbers. Fred Ward was driving his father's car at a reasonable speed when he ran into the timbers, and Martina was injured. The supreme court could find no errors in the lower court's judgment for the girl, so the decision was affirmed. These dangers on a highway must be sufficiently marked with warnings to others.[48]

E. W. Hull operated a Standard Oil truck, delivering coal oil in the country. When he was ready to leave a farm, a six-year-old boy asked for a ride to the gate to open it. His mother said no, and the driver said no. As Hull was driving away, he noticed the boy on the running board and shouted at him to hang on. He hit a large bump and discovered that the boy was gone. The truck had run over his right leg, causing a "green stick fracture." Hull carried the boy home, and the mother sued. The award was appealed, and the court agreed that the boy was a trespasser. But the justices believed that the driver should have stopped when he first saw the boy on the running board. They reversed the lower court's judgment and held against Hull.[49]

O. C. Harlow purchased what he thought was a gallon of coal oil, which he alleged turned out to be gasoline. He poured some on cobs he was using for kindling, and a fire accidentally broke out, causing damage. The jury found dealer Propes guilty of negligence in not testing his product after others had made the same complaint. On the other hand, Harlow's negligence was the proximate cause of the accident because he did not test it before he poured it on his kindling. The court held that this was a case for the jury to decide, and Harlow subsequently lost.[50]

On a foggy morning a milk truck drawn by a team of mules was parked with the team untethered. Frank Phillips drove by in his car. The noise panicked the mules, and they ran into the automobile, injuring Frank. In defense, the truck driver said that Frank was drunk, there was sufficient light to see and avoid the driver's team, and Frank was driving on the wrong side of the road. The jury verdict awarded Frank $1,000. The justices agreed with the verdict, observing that the team should have been tethered.[51]

Ida Allen, a widow with three children, worked in a cement plant one mile from her home in Bonner Springs. She was walking home from work when a car driven by Taylor in which her relatives were riding drove by, and the driver signaled that he would pick her up and drive her home. Some witnesses testified that she looked at the car, and others said that she took a step toward it and came in line with traffic. Taylor's car tried to avoid a truck that had room to pass and that could have prevented the accident by not passing, but Taylor struck and killed Allen in an attempt to avoid hitting the truck. The jury awarded her estate $10,000. The supreme court affirmed the lower court's judgment, observing that Ida had as much right to travel the highway as did the truck driver.[52]

Building roadways was a necessary corollary to use of automobiles for transportation. A law in 1917, amended two years later, provided for building and improving country roads. Douglas County approved $472,970 to build a road from Topeka to Lawrence. This would be the county's match for federal aid of $147,150 for roads. Kansas law required the matching money to be apportioned 50 percent from the county, 25 percent from the township, and 25 percent from the district. The program was challenged, as the constitution forbade the state from building internal improvements. Opponents also questioned the statutes because the state set building standards and because townships did not have a voice in these decisions. The supreme court sustained this road construction because the state was not directly involved in the building. The state does have the power to control standards, but this was not a delegation of power to determine them. The county commissioners could issue bonds for this construction because it was a county project with assistance from other governmental units.[53]

On the other hand, the court was not always supportive. Rice County had $54,000 in reserve collected from the gasoline tax. It had no projects to spend the money on, as it could spend only 25 percent of the amount on a project with federal aid, and no such program was proposed. A friendly suit was initiated to determine if the county could transfer these funds to other purposes in the general road fund and the general bridge fund. The court responded negatively, because the county could not subvert the intention of the legislature in its road construction regulations.[54]

Saline County accumulated $210,000 and wanted to use the fund to assist the state highway commission to blacktop some roads in the county. The highway law of 1929 provided for this type of work but forbade borrowing to achieve it, and this project would require the state commission to match these funds. The high court held that this was unconstitutional because the county was using funds acquired through taxation for other purposes. Improving roads through use of money derived from taxes for other purposes was the same as borrowing, so this would be unconstitutional.[55]

Franklin County voters approved a petition for a road and created a district for financing it. By 1923 one and two-thirds miles had been completed when the county halted construction because of a recall petition. The county had received federal aid funds, so federal officials rerouted six miles at the southern end of the project, thus eliminating aid funds for the original road. Supporters of the road sued for a writ of mandamus to force county officials to complete the project. The supreme court approved the writ.[56]

The constitution forbade the state from "carrying on any work of internal improvement," but highways were becoming vital to the state and its people. The legislature created the State Highway Commission in March 1917 but found it necessary to remove the constitutional bar on internal improvements that had been put in place in the original constitution. On 6 November 1928 the voters approved a constitutional amendment by vote of 493,989 to 117,596, a significant majority, to add to Article 11, Section 9, the phrase that state power should extend to "maintenance of a state system of highways" but that no general property taxes nor general bonds could be used for this purpose. With this change Kansas proceeded to build a fine highway network, with the Highway Commission overseeing the work, using federal aid grants and county, district, and township funding for finances.[57]

Railroads continued to provide an endless source of litigation for the high court. A multipurpose toll bridge connecting Leavenworth to Drydal, Missouri, was used by railroads, vehicles, and pedestrians. John Cook and a friend purchased tickets to use it and were halfway across when a train approached. There was insufficient room at that spot between the train and the guard rail for safety, and as the train passed, the hot and burning steam "blinded, burned, and confused him." A bridge official testified that Cook was inebriated. The agent had warned the two men that a train was approaching, but they were not concerned because they had met trains on the bridge in previous trips and had no difficulty. Speaking through Justice Dawson, the court ruled that a public service corporation owed no higher duty to a drunk than to a sober person, unless he was so inebriated that he "cannot take care of himself." The agent should not have let them on the bridge when he knew the train was approaching, but he proved to the jury that he had warned them sufficiently so as not to be negligent in his duty.[58]

Fifty-year-old C. E. Akins was a railroad carpenter earning approximately $125 per month. He was working in the roundhouse in Parsons on an engine used in a run from Parsons to Kansas City, Missouri, so the engine was involved in interstate commerce. The hostler in charge recklessly ran an engine into the one Akins was repairing, and the accident took off a leg four inches below the knee. He could no longer work at his trade. The jury awarded him $18,000 for the loss but nothing for pain and suffering. Speaking for the court, Porter ruled that this was an excessive amount and ordered him to accept $12,000 or face another trial.[59]

Martin Wilbur Flanagan was a switching crew foreman who was killed while helping switch a defective car from a bad-order track to the repair track. The car needed repairing because it had no drawbar, and the crew had to use chains to pull it. Flanagan was killed while holding a lantern to help the brakeman attach the chains. His estate brought suit for compensation under the Federal Liability Act, raising the question that he was engaged in interstate commerce. The jury found no contributory negligence on his part, so the administrator of his estate had to choose between the Federal Liability Act and the state Safety Appliance Act. The court decided he was not in interstate commerce but could get redress under the Safety Appliance Act, and thus the case was remanded for a new trial.[60]

On 22 December 1918 two railcars in southwestern Kansas were reserved to haul cattle to market in St. Joseph, Missouri. After they were on their way, a blizzard struck, and the train crew left the cattle on a siding under the best shelter they could find by a large elevator. A passenger train was stuck in a snowdrift, and the heavier freight engine was uncoupled and used to pull it out of the drift, causing further delay. They finally got the cattle to the market in Kansas City, Kansas, and sold them on 30 December. Meanwhile the livestock suffered "great and unusual shrinkage." Was the railroad liable for the delays and loss of weight, or was this an "act of God"? The jury decided that this was not an unprecedented blizzard or "an irresistible superhuman case" that one could not anticipate, and the supreme court agreed that the railroad was not negligent in causing the delays.[61]

A significant question arose over the status of abandoned railroad land. Owners sought to sell a piece of land that included a land grant of 3.81 acres in 1887 for a railroad right-of-way. The court concluded that, once a railroad was abandoned, the grant of land reverts to the owners of land adjacent to the right-of-way.[62]

Richards worked in a strip mine as a shot-firer, or coal shooter. This job involved using a small amount of dynamite to create a cavity in the seam, then a shot of black powder to break the coal loose. The firing was done with a plunger and electricity from a battery located eight feet from the plunger for safety purposes. His battery was in need of repair, so Richards requested the kind of plunger batteries that he usually used but was told to use two dry-cell batteries. He then attached wires to the dry cell while he was carrying the dynamite, and the dry cell battery exploded. State regulations prohibited use of dynamite in deep shaft coal mining as well as other safety regulations for shaft mining. The union and operators tried to apply shaft-mining regulations to the new type of strip mining. Richards argued that the contract between the miners and the operators was not legal because it did not have the endorsement of the state mine inspector, who had approved the shaft-mining rules. In addition, Richards argued that he was employed in strip mining and thus was not really mining but using the explosives to assist in getting to the strip of coal. The supreme court held that the regulations on mining applied to both strip and shaft mining and rejected his appeal for compensation.[63]

Montee Everitt worked as a linotype operator for the Haldeman-Julius Publishing Company in Girard. He lost a part of a finger in his work. An arbitrator was appointed, and he recommended that Everitt should be compensated under the Workmen's Compensation Act. The jury awarded him $2,160. His employer offered him an operation to remove another portion of the finger to permit him to work again at his old job. He refused. The publisher also argued that the award should be $120 for the loss of his finger plus $6 per week for fifty weeks of lost work, or $420. Marshall, speaking for the supreme court, supported the jury decision.[64]

As with alcoholic beverages, Kansas was the nation's leader in curbing the use of cigarettes. In 1889 the legislature made it illegal for anyone to "sell, give or furnish any cigar, cigarette or tobacco of any form . . . to any minor under sixteen (16) years of age." In 1909 this was drastically broadened to include the sale or "giveaway" of cigarettes and cigarette papers. In 1917 reformers again changed the law to ban cigarette products completely, just in time to face the challenge of the military, which was insisting on promoting the use of tobacco products for servicemen in World War I. This, combined with the increased use of cigarettes by women during the Roaring Twenties, led to a repeal of the ban in 1927, with a continuation of the prohibition of sales to minors. The law, however, forbade the advertisement of cigarettes.[65]

The 1917 law was challenged when a jury found Earl Nossaman guilty on seven counts of violations. He argued that the law was an unconstitutional exercise of the state police power. The supreme court disagreed, noting that it was a proper use of the power.[66]

Attorney General William Smith brought a quo warranto suit for a declaratory judgment on the cigarette tax in the 1927 law. Also, he wanted an opinion on the ban on advertisement of tobacco products. The *Alma Enterprise* and the Kansas Press Association joined the suit on behalf of themselves, arguing that it infringed on the right of contract. The group also insisted that it violated the Fourteenth Amendment's equal protection clause. Cigarette products were imported from another state to Kansas, the supreme court insisted, so this was a matter of interstate commerce and beyond the reach of state power. This judgment included the ban on advertising cigarettes for the same reason.[67]

Shawnee County commissioners asked for and received a bond issue of $150,000 for the erection of the Public Welfare Institution, as provided by the legislature. It was intended for the homeless, the diseased, and especially tubercular victims. The law required it to be situated on an acreage "as near as practicable" to the county seat. The commissioners subsequently located it on ten acres of the county poor farm. A group of taxpayers sued to halt construction because of the location. The institution, of course, would require water and sewer lines, and this location was three miles outside the city limits of Topeka, which could provide these services within city limits. Justice Burch spoke for the court in assuring the board that it had exercised proper discretion in its activities but had misconstrued its powers in locating the institution on the wrong site. The new law was not intended to be a supplement to poor laws or the poor farm. Justices Marshall, Johnston, and West dissented without opinion.[68]

A law of 1907 concerned the support of "lunatics, idiots, imbeciles, distracted persons, feeble-minded persons, drug habitues, and habitual drunkards." John Bateman's son was committed to the state hospital for the insane in 1912. Two years later he celebrated his twenty-first birthday. When he died in 1918 the state sued his father to recover the costs of maintenance and care for him while he was in his majority years. The father argued that this violated the Fourteenth Amendment by taking his property without due process of law. The court held that the state should care for Bateman's son while he was a minor, but his father was responsible for his son's care after he reached twenty-one.[69]

Decreasing numbers of cases tested the homestead law in the twentieth century than earlier, but two arose during the Roaring Twenties that established new principles. A widower with four children signed an antenuptial agreement with a widow with seven children. If she survived him, she would receive one-fifth of his estate. She also agreed to care for his children as if they were her own. In addition, she would put her children to work as soon as possible as independents. These terms were included in their will. When he died, she sought an equitable division of his estate on the basis that she could not read, so this invalidated the agreement and the will. His estate was valued at $23,000, including $8,000 for the homestead farm in Jackson County. The court held that no fraud was practiced on her despite her illiteracy, and she had consented in writing to the agreement and will. These arrangements eliminated her from sharing the homestead farm.[70]

A couple on a Saline County farm separated in 1906, sold the farm, and made a financial settlement. Two years later they divorced. Their four children seldom visited their father thereafter. In 1914 he married widow Isabella Erickson with an antenuptial agreement that each would retain their own properties and leave them to their own children. They revoked this agreement before he died "suddenly" in 1922. The court held that Isabella's consent to execute a deed on their homestead was sufficient to make a contract with him to revoke their decision before marriage, and his children could not exclude her from claiming their homestead estate.[71]

Two important cases on rape came to the court during the 1920s. Myron Morrison was charged with three counts. He raped Loretta Morris in her home in Iola, he persuaded her to go to another part of the town for fornication, and he persuaded her to go to Kansas City, Missouri, for fornication. At his trial, Morrison argued that count one had nothing to do with counts two and three. Justice Hopkins wrote for the court that rape and fornication belong to the same family of crimes because illicit intercourse is the foundation for both. Letters were introduced to sustain the charges on counts two and three, providing good corroborating evidence, and the judgment of the lower court was affirmed.[72]

Lawyer H. N. Casement was convicted of statutory rape and was disbarred because of the felony. In arguing to be reinstated, he insisted that practicing law was a form of property, and the decision to disbar him deprived him of Fourteenth Amendment due process of law. Speaking for the court, Justice Dawson reminded him that it was a privilege, not a right, to practice law, and thus his disbarment was not a penal punishment. This was not a ministerial duty the court was performing in deciding the case, and his disbarment stood.[73]

The homeless IWWs and other radicals who caused problems for officials in prosecuting World War I led Governor Capper and others to promote the concept of enacting vagrancy laws. "Put them to work," Capper observed, "and they will avoid Kansas." The legislature enacted such a law in 1917. John Clancy was an IWW organizer in McPherson County in 1922 and showed no other visible means of support. A justice of the peace found him to be a vagrant and fined him $100 and thirty days in jail. He sought and received a writ of habeas corpus by posting a five-hundred-dollar bond to demonstrate he had means of support. The state again charged him, and in his trial he argued that he had been denied the right to counsel, had been denied the right to face his accuser, and could not be forced to be a witness against himself when he faced the justice of the peace. Upon appeal the court affirmed his sentence. The legislature had decided that the public peace and welfare demanded that this type of offense be tried quickly. He was also charged with being a loiterer as well as a vagrant (but he showed means of support), and he could have had a jury trial, but he did not request one.[74]

Sedgwick County commissioners announced an election for a bond issue of $120,000 to build a jail. The law required such elections be advertised for thirty days, and this one was held on the regular general Election Day, which constituted less time than required. The Eberhardt Construction Company sought a writ of mandamus to force the commissioners to proceed with the building. The court decided that failure to notify properly voided the special election. The law prohibited erecting the building without a legal vote of the people, so the contract with Eberhardt Construction was unenforceable.[75]

J. L. Beck leased his land near Augusta to an oil company. The contract stipulated that if the land was sold before drilling commenced, this would cancel the lease, and the lease money would be repaid. The drilling company entered the land, located a place to drill, and placed a boiler nearby to run the drilling operations. This appeared to be optimistic on the part of the driller, and Beck decided he could improve on the lease. He orally agreed to sell the land to Hennig for $8,000 and accepted a mortgage of $2,500 as part of the agreement. Beck argued that he had acted legally under the terms of the lease in making a bona fide sale, insisting that marking a spot and placing a boiler "does not constitute a commencement of operations" to drill. The oil company demanded its right to drill, but the court supported Beck.[76]

State law made it illegal to drill or operate a gas or oil well within one hundred feet of a railroad right-of-way. Winkler had a lease on a strip of land adjoining the Atchison, Topeka and Santa Fe. Another operator had a producing well eighty-three feet from the right-of-way on the other side. Plaintiff's lease was worthless if the state law was approved. Justice Burch said that this was a narrow question, but the state police power includes health, safety, and morals questions and covers "promotion of the common convenience, prosperity, and welfare." Oil and gas wells, he observed, can "become detrimental to a high degree." The law did not contravene the national or state constitutions.[77]

The art of embalming was many centuries old but of limited use until it became popular to embalm bodies before public display of them for funerals during the 1920s. Like all innovations, this one required controls. Kansas established the Board of Embalming to regulate this practice, including licensing and making rules. A major rule of the board required the embalming of a body before it could be moved from a city, and a mover had to receive a permit from the proper official and place a yellow tag on the body to announce this. A citizen of Geneseo died in Little River, about fifteen miles away, from no communicable disease. Relatives asked licensed practitioner Guy Miller to bring the body home and then embalm it. He complied, and the board removed his license because he failed to follow its rules, which were consistent with state law. Miller sued to regain his license. The court decided that in this type of case, these rules were unreasonable and constituted "undue interference with the rights of the relatives" of the deceased and the plaintiff.[78]

A state law of 1915 forbade discrimination in an "inn, hotel, or boarding house" where a city required a license for operation. Gerald Brown denied William Bradshaw, a Negro, lunch in his restaurant. The court held that a restaurant license did not fall under the category of one "required by any of the municipal authorities" of the state, so Brown's discrimination was a personal decision and not justiciable.[79]

Attorney General Hopkins seized documents of President Smithmeyer's Poehler company with a subpoena duces tecum to use in the prosecution of an antitrust suit. The supreme court held this to be an illegal search and seizure and ordered Hopkins to return them. He declined, and the following year the case reappeared in the supreme court. The company this time pleaded for a return of the letters, papers, books, telegrams, and records because it needed them to prepare for the antitrust charges against it "tomorrow" in Douglas County District Court. Hopkins insisted that some of these documents were instrumental in showing how the company's illegal trade was affected, and he could not relinquish them. The company asked for a continuance of the trial until it had the documents for the time necessary to prepare for trial. Citing the case the year previously, Justice Burch issued a writ of mandamus "without condition" to return the illegally seized papers.[80]

As a part of the Populist program that failed of enactment earlier, Congress passed the Smith-Lever Act in 1915 to establish an extension education program for farmers and extended this in 1919. In 1915 the state legislature approved this federal aid plan and provided for implementation, including the requirement that each unit have a minimum of 250 farmers and receive a minimum of $1,200 annually in aid from the county. Beginning in 1916, the Cloud County farm bureau received over $1,200 annually from the county commissioners to implement this education. When they made application in 1927 for the annual appropriation, the commissioners refused the money on the grounds that the program did not have the minimum of 250 bona fide farmers and also that they did not need the funds because they had some $800 in reserve from previous appropriations. In addition, the commissioners claimed that the program violated both the state and national constitutions. The bureau sought a writ of mandamus to force compliance with the law. The supreme court concluded that because it was constitutional to require counties to pay for a state road plan, counties should also support this education program. The mandamus was approved.[81]

Thomas Stone owned an eighty-acre farm in Cowley County, and in 1908 he signed an agreement with the Wichita Natural Gas Company. It could lay a gas line along the highway adjacent to his land and pay him 10 cents per rod, and he could purchase gas from the company at 27 cents net. Later the gas company signed this line over to the Empire Company, and it proceeded to charge Stone the full rate for natural gas. The justices ruled that the gas companies could use the highway right-of-way without fee, so they could charge full rate for their services. Stone could not receive a rate change from the new company without approval from the Public Service Commission.[82]

The court interpreted an old Sunday Blue Law in 1930. This Kansas statute forbade working on Sundays, but C. B. Kelly sold tickets and showed a movie, which he had advertised in the local newspaper. The justices affirmed his conviction, but Harvey, joined by Joachims, dissented. The dissenters believed this law was "an old one" designed to prevent slaves, apprentices, or family members from being compelled to work on the Sabbath. In addition, there was no evidence that the theater owner had done any physical work, which they thought the law intended.[83]

Henry Bertram owned two farms, one on each side of Joe Burton's farm. Henry and his hired man drove a 1,200-pound bull from one farm to the other. When they arrived at Joe's feedlot, where he was full-feeding some steers, the bull went up the driveway to the feedlot, where he smelled food and strangers. Joe's steers gathered around the strange bull, and it lunged at them, badly rupturing one of them. With the help of Joe's son, they got the bull out and on their way. The following morning the injured steer was found dead. In addition, the excitement threw the other steers "off their feed" for a few days. Joe sued for damages and won under the state herd law, which required farm animals to be contained. The court ruled that while the bull was not technically running loose, and he was not vicious at home, Henry should have known what happens when a bull meets up with strange animals, and he was negligent in controlling his huge animal. The judgment was reversed and the case remanded for new trial.[84]

During the 1929 harvest season, Taylor contracted with two farmers to harvest their wheat for 8 cents per bushel and windrow their barley for $2 per acre. He worked for twelve days before the sheriff appeared with a writ of attachment for the wheat harvest. Four days later Taylor filed a harvester's lien and began action against Sheriff White. In the meantime, White had employed E. E. Howlett to windrow the barley. Dawson, speaking for the court, reiterated the old principle that "first in time makes first in right" and supported Taylor's lien as first in time.[85]

Airplanes were becoming more common following the war, much like automobiles two decades previously. Stratford and Petticord entered into a contract that stated that Petticord would buy eighteen shares in Wichita Aeroplane Service company and agree to take out an insurance policy of $2,000 on one of the company's planes. One plane wrecked, and Petticord insisted that it was the one he insured. The problem lay in not specifying which plane he insured. The court held that he should have specified or else insured them all. The contract was so indefinite that he was incapable of recovery of damages.[86]

At the end of the decade, a crash took place on Wall Street that resulted in the worst depression in history descending on the nation. Many people were left destitute and faced the problem of depending on the assistance of others in order to survive. It was a desperate time for many until the arrival of World War II, which brought a return of prosperity with the production of war matériel.

6. The Devastating Depression

The Political Scene

The Great Depression created a new relationship between the state and its citizens in the form of direct government action, especially in the category of relief for families and businesses enduring economic hardship. Article VII of the Kansas Constitution requires that "the respective counties of the state shall provide as may be prescribed by law for those inhabitants who, by reason of age, infirmity, or other misfortune, may have claims upon the sympathy and aid of society." So reads the poor law clause in the constitution, a statement that was implemented and reinterpreted over the next eight decades of statehood as economic circumstances evolved.

In 1862 the legislature tried to fulfill this obligation by copying poor laws of other states that, in turn, had their roots in the English Poor Law, which was designed to meet the requirements of the seventeenth century. The legislature, fortunately, failed to make family members legally responsible for keeping relatives off the poor law program, but this implication was always present prior to the Great Depression and even later in the minds of some taxpayers. An agrarian state, Kansas made counties responsible for this obligation, and, in turn, this sometimes became a principal function of the commissioners. They early provided for apprenticing boys who had been raised in an orphanage or in a home with no father or breadwinner to be "bound out" until age twenty-one, at which time each would receive a new Bible, two suits of clothing, and $10 for their years of work and learning a trade. In addition, counties often provided for "poor farms," which were farmed out to the lowest bidder to care for the insane, the feeble-minded, and others in need.[1]

In 1872 the legislature authorized counties with more than thirty thousand population to appoint a commissioner of the poor for two-year terms. In 1891 the population minimum was raised to forty-five thousand, then lowered in 1901 to twenty-eight thousand and again in 1913 to twenty-two thousand, but the poor farm continued to be the most popular means of caring for indigents, especially in the eastern part of the state. This law was tested in the supreme court in 1875, with Justice Brewer writing for his brethren. The Osawkee Township voted $6,000 in funds for relief from a grasshopper plague. Two taxpayers brought suit to restrain the bond issue. Brewer noted that there were "poor" relative to "rich" and poor as in objects of charity. He pointed out that the statute made provisions for the destitute and grain for seed to farmers, not "food to the hungry, clothing to the naked or fuel for those suffering from the cold," so the law could not be sustained. Instead, the legislature thereafter followed a policy of grants to private charities to sustain the destitute.[2]

Following the stock market crash in 1929, an unprecedented harsh depression settled over America. At this time, three-fourths of all production of wealth in Kansas still came from agriculture. By 1932 the price of wheat had plummeted to 20 cents, cattle sold at 5 cents per pound, and hogs sold at $2 per hundredweight. Unemployment nationally skyrocketed to 25 percent or more of the eligible workforce. In April 1930 Kansas had 36,000 idle workers, and when Franklin D. Roosevelt was elected president in 1932, this had reached a staggering 235,000 out of a population of about 2 million, or over 10 percent. As agrarians lost their farms to drought and depression, the number of economically helpless grew, and Kansans discovered that farmers could starve the same as urban laborers. President Roosevelt established the President's Emergency Council on Employment (PECE), and Kansas Democratic governor Harry Woodring was forced to appoint the Kansas Employment Relief Committee (KERC) to gather economic information required for compliance in acquiring the state's share of borrowed federal funds for relief through the Reconstruction Finance Corporation (RFC).[3]

In 1931 the supreme court again had the opportunity to interpret the state's responsibility for support of the poor. A deserted wife and her five children in Stafford County moved to Barton County, where the family was supported for six months. Despite their protests, the justice of the peace removed the family back to Stafford County, where that county sued Barton County commissioners. The justices held that the family had become the legal responsibility of Barton County officials. Obviously, the legal costs of all this litigation would have furnished the family with ample means for quite some time.[4]

After Franklin D. Roosevelt's election as president in 1932, he immediately called Congress into special session to deal with the crisis. The Hundred Days session established the Civilian Conservation Corps (CCC) and the Federal Emergency Relief Act (FERA) to assist states in their relief efforts. Crawford and Cherokee Counties in the tristate mining region were particularly hard hit. KERC found that merchants there were forced to eliminate purchasing on credit, and some area families were living on bread and water. Children were not attending school because they had no shoes and insufficient clothing. One area welfare officer had to limit families on relief to $1.50 weekly. PECE representatives found children wearing newspapers for insulation and stealing food routinely, and some families were forced to bootleg alcohol to survive. They had survived two bitter winters, and another one was approaching.[5]

Kansans used their FERA funds to build roads through county sponsorship and Highway Commission supervision. In 1933 the legislature authorized the Highway Commission to provide contracts for work projects funded by FERA and county appropriations, with counties limited to one-fourth of 1 percent of assessed evaluation. They could issue bonds for the projects if the maximum levy was adequate. FERA required matching state funds of $3 for every $1 in its grants, or a 75–25 division. A major transition took place in April 1935 when Congress enacted the Emergency Relief Administration, and from this President Roosevelt created the Works Progress Administration (WPA, in 1939 changed to

Works Projects Administration). The WPA spent about 85 percent of its funds on labor, striving to give workers a "security wage of 30 cents or the prevailing local hourly rate, with a monthly schedule of 120 to 140 hours work." Eventually sixty thousand Kansans worked for the WPA.[6]

In 1934 Kansas received $21,652,249 in federal relief funding. This compares to $118,139,000 in state agricultural production that year. While state legislators complained bitterly over "being told what to do," they were forced to comply in order to receive this vital federal funding. But WPA created problems. Work relief had long been a county responsibility, and WPA was structured to operate through six divisions in the state. In addition, KERC had trained inexperienced workers for certain types of jobs and assigned the handicapped to lighter work so they could "avoid the stigma of unemployment." These practices conflicted with WPA definitions of "employable persons." These issues came to a head in 1936, when Roosevelt came up for reelection against Kansas governor Alf M. Landon. In July 1936 WPA announced it would employ twenty-five thousand needy farmers in Kansas on work relief in one day and fifty-five thousand in one week. But politics was increasingly influencing relief measures.[7]

After Kansas received its first FERA allotment, Governor Landon asked Harry Hopkins, Roosevelt's minister for relief, for additional funding above the legal limits. He called attention to his state being "largely agricultural," and not only did his farmers suffer from low crop prices like agrarians elsewhere, but drought hurt garden crops in three-fourths of his state during the current dust bowl. Drought in eighteen to twenty-nine counties ranged from "excessive damages" to "extreme drought." Landon informed Hopkins that his state constitution forbade the state from providing counties with relief assistance, and they had to rely on their own meager financial resources. The governor asked Hopkins for 40 percent of his relief needs rather than the three-to-one ratio, or 25 percent. Hopkins approved his request because he admired KERC secretary John Stutz of Kansas, and he penciled in a notation at the bottom of Landon's letter. "yes 40 percent ok Hopkins." This cozy feeling did not last.[8]

When the legislature approved the relief measures for highway construction, Attorney General Ronald Boynton declared this action to be unconstitutional. He insisted that Article VII, Section IV invested relief in county jurisdiction and forbade state assistance in this category. This explains why Landon asked for increased federal aid, because he believed the state could not help, and the burden was too great for counties to carry alone. When the highway bill passed, the governor asked Boynton to bring a quo warranto suit in the supreme court to get a declaratory judgment on the validity of its interpretation. The two officials, of course, were certain they knew the justices' forthcoming opinion.

Much to the officials' consternation, in 1934 in *Kansas v. State Highway Commission* the court ruled that "our constitution nowhere prohibits the state from making provision for the poor and needy." The case challenged a seventeen-million-dollar bond issue on the basis that Article II, Section VIII of the state constitution forbade the state from "carrying on any works of internal improvements." The court held that the amended constitution also provided for the state to build highways, and in this instance it was "assisting" the counties in constructing them. To the extent, therefore, that the bill in question "attempts to, or does furnish relief to the poor and needy, it violates no constitutional provision." The justices added that "there is necessarily vested in the legislature a discretion as to what may be prescribed by law." To continue his policy now, of course, Landon had to ignore this high court ruling and hope federal officials did not discover it. In fact, Landon returned to Hopkins at this time with outstretched hand, explaining that he needed more funding to assist his schools, which were underfunded because of reduced income from property taxes resulting from the terrible drought.[9]

Meanwhile, back in Washington, a department memorandum surfaced that pointed out that Kansas had "fared comparatively well" in not having to provide money for relief as had all other states. The Sunflower State had only to appropriate money for administrative purposes because of the "40–60 agreement," and Kansans had received millions in relief funds to which they were not entitled. At the same time, the director of the Social Science Research Council wrote Hopkins, alerting him to the Kansas Supreme Court decision in the *Boynton* case. Hopkins was enraged over the deception and the fact that Landon was asking for even more money for his schools. "Wish I had known it at the time," he muttered, referring to the court decision and his "40–60" note. The attitude of federal officials toward the Kansas relief program took an abrupt 180-degree turn.

A few days later a *Kansas City Star* reporter asked Hopkins about Landon's candidacy for the Republican presidential nomination, noting that it should help his chances greatly that he had balanced his state budget (Kansas law, in effect, required balanced budgets). Hopkins shot back that Kansas had "not put up a thin dime for unemployment relief." Another reporter then asked if the governor was not balancing his budget, and Hopkins responded, "Oh, yeah, and he is taking it out of the hides of the people." Being unaware of Landon's deception, reporters concluded that this was an unfair attack on Landon. A *New York Times* editorial, for instance, insisted that the New Dealer had his facts wrong and that he had made a partisan assault on the innocent Kansan. Columnist Arthur Krock noted that this attack "quickly became celebrated" because Hopkins had singled out Landon "unfairly."

Hopkins suffered a further loss of credibility when he reacted to a question about New Deal tax and spending policies. The Roosevelt administration believed in the Keynesian principle of spending to stimulate the ailing economy, which required high taxes and borrowing for financing. Hopkins predicted that in the upcoming election, people on relief would give victory to Roosevelt and the New Dealers. Political pundits revised these exchanges to assert that the WPA director believed in the success formula of "tax and tax, spend and spend, elect and elect." A writer for the Hearst chain of newspapers, which supported Landon, expressed the belief that Hopkins's attack on Landon clinched the Republican nomination for the Kansan.

Under Landon's prodding, the legislature enacted the cash basis law, which forced all state government units to limit their spending to the amount of funds available during the current fiscal year. Although Landon never emphasized budget balancing, the issue received widespread media coverage when he addressed the National Economic League in the summer of 1935. In this speech he credited the Kansas people with fiscal responsibility and warned that "we must so guard the use of public funds that government does not become such a burden as to destroy that which it is designed to protect." His fiscal philosophy received widespread news coverage and was especially popular with business interests that feared New Deal budget deficits.[10]

Landon continued the fiction of the constitutional ban on state aid for relief until the summer of 1936. After the wheat harvest was completed, as he explained it, he summoned a special session of the legislature to consider amendments to allow the state to enter this mythical "forbidden" territory. One change would add to the clause on county support for the poor the proviso that "the state may participate financially in such aid and supervise and control the administration thereof." A second would authorize the state to "provide by law for unemployment compensation and contributory old age benefits and may tax employers and employees therefore." The latter was to provide for state participation in the Social Security program enacted the previous summer by Congress. Social Security established federal programs for unemployment compensation, a compulsory savings program for retirees, and assistance to state old-age pensions.

The two houses quickly endorsed the leadership's contention that the situation constituted an emergency, so they could dispense with the normal legislative procedures. Democrats were outnumbered almost two to one and were unable to slow down the majority juggernaut. When a small group, led by Joseph MacDonald of Wyandotte County, tried to expose the farce that they were making unnecessary changes to the constitution, the majority ignored him. Democrats also sought, unsuccessfully, to debate other vital issues, but the majority was in control. At one point MacDonald was still talking when the Republican leadership temporarily adjourned the session. When he later attempted to insert the *Boynton* decision in the record, Republicans derided the chief justice's opinion as "mere dicta." Both houses approved the amendments, as did the voters in the election of 1936.

Alf Landon won the privilege of running against "The Champ" for the presidency in 1936. He received the Republican nomination because he was a westerner, he was popular with businessmen, some Republicans wanted to turn the party in a more liberal direction, and he was believed to be a "vote getter." He was the only Republican elected governor west of the Mississippi in 1932 and the only Republican governor reelected anywhere in 1934. Landon, in turn, campaigned fruitlessly against what he called the "slipshod" management of the New Deal policies and promised to balance the federal budget. Late in the campaign he struck a political nerve when he warned of the difficulty of keeping track of millions of accounts in the Social Security system. The Hearst chain of newspapers printed a picture of a bare-chested man with a chain around his neck labeled "YOU." Landon, however, never had a chance. Roosevelt asked voters, "Are you better off than you were four years ago?" The answer was a resounding yes, and he carried all but two states. Landon did not even win his home state, and the Democrats also swept the gubernatorial race.

To raise desperately needed revenue for the new Social Security programs, Democratic governor Walter Huxman promoted the allowance of 3.2 percent beer under the liquor laws in 1937. The legislature agreed after being persuaded that this type of beer and "near beer" were "nonintoxicating" and this became the first break with Prohibition since 1880. The succeeding governor, Republican Payne Ratner, also persuaded the legislature to create a pioneering body, the Legislative Coordinating Council. This was a modernization of Governor Landon's Legislative Council. The new board assisted the legislature through research, working out details of policy or principles, and streamlining proposals, immediately reducing the number of bills the legislature needed to consider by half.

The New Deal never completely resolved the great issues of depression and unemployment, although it made great headway until 1937, when Roosevelt cut relief in an attempt to balance the budget, and all the gains made since 1932 were erased. The coming of World War II settled the unemployment question, and soon there were widespread labor shortages. In Kansas, Governor Ratner took the economic order in a startling new direction by creating the Kansas Industrial Development Commission to promote industry. With its establishment, the state had an agency in place to attract lucrative war contracts. This gave the state's pioneering aviation industry a great boost, especially after federal officials took steps to encourage relocating the industry inland. Kansas also profited from the numerous army air bases the federal government constructed around the state. These bases became important training sites for corps personnel.[11]

The New Deal legislation created increased litigation because of the expanded role of government, both national and state, to battle the depression. This was accelerated by wartime regulations that began clogging federal courts. Guy Helvering, along with Harry Woodring, worked hard for Franklin Roosevelt's victory in 1932. Woodring was rewarded with the post of secretary of war until 1940, and Helvering became commissioner of the Internal Revenue Service for eleven years. Helvering was then appointed the first Democratic district judge in Kansas to succeed Richard Hopkins. He apparently worked himself to death in three years, trying to handle the heavy caseload. In 1945 Arthur Mellott was appointed to a second temporary judgeship, and his health, too, "eventually broke under the load." This temporary position became permanent with the appointment of Delmar Hill in 1949.[12]

Republican representatives in the US Congress, U. S. Guyer, W. P. Lambertson, and Ed Rees, testified before the House Judiciary Committee that this Democratic effort to obtain another judge for Kansas was "originated by the Doherty interests and members of the 'Pollock crowd' to discredit Judge Richard J. Hopkins." Henry Dougherty of Teapot Dome fame and president of Cities Service, which provided Kansans with natural gas, was feuding with then attorney general Hopkins over regulating rates and the latter prosecuting under the antitrust law. Democratic legislators such as John Houston, of course, supported adding the extra judge.[13]

Politics, as usual, played a role in judicial appointments, only this time, for a rare change, New Dealers dominated. Helvering was a Roo-

Fig. 6. Kansas Supreme Court Justices (undated): Harry K. Allen, Walter O. Thiele, Hugo Wedell, Homer Hoch, William West Harvey, John S. Dawson, William A. Smith. Image from the Kansas State Historical Society.

sevelt appointee, and Mellott benefited from being one of Harry Truman's instructors when he attended night school at the University of Kansas City Law School. Hill was chairman of the Kansas Democratic Party Committee and a supporter of Truman during the election of 1948. Walter Huxman was elected governor during the Roosevelt landslide in 1936. When he lost his reelection bid, the president appointed him to the Tenth Circuit Court. Mellott, Hill, and Huxman would play a role during the postwar period in the revolutionary transformation of civil rights.[14]

The Judges

William Amos Smith was a capable jurist who became one of the most controversial characters in the history of the bench because of his blatant involvement with Republican Party politics while serving as a justice. As Brian Moline observed, "Few persons sought office on the Republican state ticket without first consulting him and securing his support. Indeed, legend has it that Smith would persistently draft the Republican state ticket from his chambers in the Supreme Court."[15]

Always known as "Bill," Smith was born in poverty in Valley Falls on 3 December 1888, the younger brother of two sisters. He invariably wore a suit of clothes that his mother made from hand-me-downs until he was fifteen. Once he was forced to wear a pair of girls' pointed-toed shoes to school. He proved to be slow in school work, and some teachers spoke of his stupidity until the high school principal sensed his possibilities and encouraged him in debate. Smith discovered that he could think on his feet, and after graduation he went on to Washburn College and graduated from that college's School of Law in 1914.[16]

From then on, it was one political office after another, interrupted by military service in the Mexican Border War in 1916 and action in France, where he participated in the Argonne offensive and was promoted to captain. Returning from the war, Smith served on the Court of Industrial Relations as assistant attorney general and then as attorney general from 1926 to 1930. While in the latter office, he fought the Ku Klux Klan. More important to him, he opposed the political career of John R. Brinkley, the "Goat Gland" doctor from Milford.[17]

Doc Brinkley made a fortune operating on elderly men whose sex life had passed them by. He was a pioneer in the new medium of radio and advertised his questionable operation and his lucrative medical prescriptions over his radio station, KFKB, in Milford. He quickly became so popular and successful that the state medical organizations began investigating him. The state medical board removed his license to practice on the basis of fraudulence in his application for a license (he had misrepresented his medical education), and they persuaded the Federal Radio Commission to revoke his radio license on the basis that he was using it for personal gain, not the public welfare.[18]

Attorney General Smith detested Brinkley and saw his opportunity when the doctor decided to run for governor in 1930 in order to name a new medical board. Brinkley made his decision too late to get his name printed on the ballot and had to stage a write-in campaign. Running on that same ballot for a supreme court seat, the attorney general ruled that if the voters wrote "Mr. John Brinkley," "Mr. Brinkley," or "Dr. Brinkley" on the ballot and marked an X in the correct box, their votes would count. Anything else or any other mark would invalidate the ballot. Despite this handicap, Brinkley effectively used his radio station, as well as the relatively new airplane, for campaigning and almost won. Contemporary experts reported that the Republican Party and the Democrats illegally counted him out and gave the election to Democrat Harry Woodring.[19]

Alf Landon asked Smith not to run for the court position because he wanted him available to run for governor in 1932. Landon, of course, was rebuilding the weakened Republican Party after its disastrous split in 1930 and was successful enough in his efforts to capture the governor's seat for himself in 1932. Smith won the judicial seat of W. D. Jochims in 1930 and always referred to his fights with the KKK and Brinkley as the "proudest" events of his life.[20]

Smith served as a justice for twenty-six years and wrote 1,031 opinions. He supported the controversial right to work amendment and the workmen's compensation law, and he vigorously fought to keep supreme court justices on the partisan ballot. He actively supported Albert Cole against Tom Wilson for the First Congressional District seat, declaring that Wilson was on the payroll of Emperor Haile Selassie of Ethiopia. When Wes Roberts, National Republican Committee chairman, used his influence to help the Ancient Order of United Workmen sell a building to the state that it already owned for a commission of $11,000, Smith defended his old friend.[21]

This period enjoyed a succession of capable judges. Walter G. Thiele was born in 1885, son of the man who was the first white child born in Marshall County. He had four brothers and four sisters. He earned a law degree from the University of Kansas in 1910 and practiced in Lawrence. He was elected to the supreme court in 1932 and reelected three times. Thiele wrote six hundred opinions during his four terms on the bench. He was interested in the administration of justice and served as chairman of the Kansas Judicial Council from 1941 to 1954. A colleague described his "kindly, jovial, and happy disposition." Another noted that he consistently condemned arbitrary actions and recalled his "remarkable memory and quickness of perception."[22]

Harry Kyle Allen was born in Gallatin, Missouri, on 20 December 1872. He received a degree in law from Washington University in St. Louis and moved to Kansas City to join his brother in law practice. His specialty was land titles, and President Theodore Roosevelt appointed him to examine Indian land titles in Oklahoma. While in the Sooner State he assisted in writing Oklahoma's constitution and served as a state senator before moving back to Kansas City in 1913. Allen moved to Topeka in 1918 to teach at Washburn Law School, where he proved to be a good teacher, inspiring young lawyers. He was appointed dean in 1922. Elected to the supreme court as a Democrat in 1936, he returned to his law practice in the capital city when his term expired.[23]

Hugo Wedell was a native Kansan, born in Hillsboro on 3 January 1890. He attended Kansas State Normal and played on Emporia's championship basketball team in 1912. He became a professional baseball player for a while, and this made him ineligible for athletics at the University of Kansas. Wedell received a bachelor's degree from Kansas in 1915 and a law degree there in 1920 before practicing in Neosho County. Governor Landon appointed him to investigate the Finney Bond Scandal, and he was an unsuccessful candidate for the US Senate in 1930. Justice Wedell was appointed to Justice Johnston's seat when he retired in 1935. Wedell was elected to the position in 1936, 1942, and 1948, retiring at the end of that term.[24]

Jay S. Parker was born on 1 July 1895 in Morland and educated in the public schools in Hill City. Parker became interested in crippled children and was the main sponsor of the Kansas Crippled Children's Law. He graduated from Kansas Law School in 1918 and practiced in Hill City, serving several terms as county attorney. He was appointed assistant attorney general and then elected attorney general in 1938 and 1940. In 1942 he ran against incumbent Allen and won every county in the state. Parker was reelected in 1948, 1954, and 1960, becoming chief justice in 1957. Known as a hard-working justice, he proved most considerate of his fellow justices as their chief, retiring in 1966.

Allen B. Burch was born in Carthage, Missouri, on 18 June 1895. He received his law degree from the University of Kansas in 1917 and practiced in Wichita. He was elected to the supreme court in 1944 and wrote seventy-two opinions before he died unexpectedly in May 1948. He had "a keen and rare sense of humor," according to a colleague, and his opinions were marked by "clear statement and logical treatment."[25]

Homer Hoch was born in Marion on the Fourth of July in 1879. He graduated from Baker University in 1902 and worked with his father on the family newspaper. He ultimately received a law degree from Washburn University and then returned to Marion to practice and edit the *Marion Record*. He was secretary to his father, Governor E. H. Hoch, served in the lower house of the legislature from 1918 to 1933, served as state corporation commissioner until 1938, and possessed a good background in all three branches of government when he was elected to the supreme court in 1938. He was a good scholar and fluent speaker, writing 271 opinions before he died in 1949.[26]

The Cases

Motor vehicles continued to produce their share of litigation during the 1930s. Early in the decade the unique sales system of the Auburn-Kansas Distributor of Wichita came under scrutiny. The company required its salesmen to buy a car on condition for $886.20; the car would sell for $1,270.50. After the sale the agent would receive some of this difference as a commission. If the car had not sold within ninety days, the salesman would return the demonstrator, and it would be "reconditioned" for sale. Ross Conklin bought one of these models on conditional sale and executed a note for the $800 to the Finance Corporation of America for its advance of $796.67. These payments were cashed by the home office in Philadelphia. After ninety days Conklin returned the car to the dealer, who reconditioned and sold it but soon had to repossess it. The dealer finally sold it to Walpole in exchange for his Buick Brougham, worth $750, plus his note for $418. The distributor then went bankrupt. Justice Dawson, speaking for the court, held that when Conklin returned the car it was a repossession, and his conditional sales contract obligation was discharged.[27]

After Daniel Seigler bought an Essex it proved to be unsatisfactory, or what would be later described as a "lemon." He drove around town with a sign on the car reading "Buy an Essex and worry with me. I bought this Essex from Davidson Brothers, Kansas City, Kansas and I am sorry now." An employee stopped him on the street and told him to bring the car to the garage, and he would fix the problems. The mechanic was working on the vehicle when some employees began gathering around and removing the sign. When Seigler ordered them to leave his sign alone, a fight broke out, and the seven men "struck, kicked, and beat" him, injuring him severely. The jury awarded him $8,000. Justice Marshall agreed that this constituted mob action but decided the award was too high. Seigler could either accept $5,000 or face a new trial.[28]

Children, especially those who lived in rural areas, needed to learn to drive an automobile as early as possible. Ella Powers was a widow with six children. She drove two of them, ages thirteen and eleven, to Ellsworth in her Model T Ford. This model had the hand feed for gasoline on the steering column, the emergency brake on the left side of the driver, and three foot pedals to operate. After they left town on the way home, she decided to teach the eldest, Ethel, to drive. Ella sat in the middle of the front seat. As they approached a bridge, Ella cut the speed with the hand control. Midway across the bridge the left front fender or wheel caught a post. The car went through the railing and fell fifteen feet to the creek below. Mrs. Powers was killed, and Ethel suffered a broken arm and damage to her mouth. The justices reversed the trial court, saying that Ella contributed to the negligence that caused the wreck, and the township was not at fault for the condition of the bridge.[29]

Myrtle Cherry was a working woman who lived with her sister, Mrs. Gladys Gibson, in a Wichita apartment. The two women, along with Jack Hays, were drinking "spiked" beer and became "loud, boisterous, and vulgar." Gladys feared someone in the building would object, so she asked Hays to drive them for an "airing." He gave her his car keys, and the three drove to Newton, where they ate. Jack became more boisterous there and knocked dishes off the table. On the return to Wichita, a Ford on a side road failed to stop at the sign, and Jack grabbed the steering wheel. Gladys lost control, and they wrecked. Myrtle was seriously injured, and the jury awarded her $1,000. Jack was held negligent, but the jury disbelieved Myrtle's testimony, and the supreme court affirmed the lower court judgment.[30]

Seven-year-old Robert was visiting family friends in Lindsborg. On the spur of the moment the family decided to drive to the Black Hills without the knowledge or consent of his mother. His relative, P. A. Anderson, had hands and arms crippled to the extent that he could move the steering wheel only a short distance. On an "S" curve in Wyoming he could not maneuver the steering and wrecked and killed his two sisters. The boy was seriously and permanently injured. At his age, the court had to conclude that his mother had consulted with him about his visit in Wichita. The facts in the case showed that Robert was a "guest" in the car and was being transported without pay. Anderson, therefore, was not liable for his injuries.[31]

The state continued to build a superior highway system for these vehicles. A law in 1929 vested the powers of "construction, reconstruction, and maintenance" of the state highway system under the control of the State Highway Commission. The section of the constitution forbidding the state to build internal improvements was revised to permit the construction of highways, with the costs apportioned 60 percent to counties, 25 percent to townships, and 15 percent to the commission, with federal grants supplementing the costs of the units. The law limited the "high type" of highways the commission could build to one hundred miles annually. The Johnson County commissioners and voters had approved a highway to be paved with either brick or concrete and asked for state assistance. The commission responded that it had already committed its one-hundred-mile limitation that year. The question presented the court was, could the commission be forced to assist in the construction of a "benefit district highway"? Yes, the justices responded, because the Johnson County project was undertaken before the 1929 law was enacted, so it must be completed under the old road system. Johnson County voters had met all their requirements. Within fifteen days of the court issuing its writ, the commission must determine the type of material to be used and construction to continue.[32]

Likewise, on 1 April 1926 the Neosho County commissioners contracted for a hard-surface road to be constructed. It was completed in 1927, but full payment had not been completed when the 1929 law was passed that required the Highway Commission to assume liabilities for this type of construction. Speaking for the court, Justice Harvey decided that the commission had to assist in payment because the law required the state to assume liability for all such existing contracts for highway construction.[33]

Maintenance of the system was also litigated. A plaintiff was driving his car between Meade and Liberal on Highway 54 during a snowstorm. He came to a sign saying Road Closed and another reading Detour One Mile North to Liberal. When he followed these directions, he came to a temporary road barricaded with a stop sign. The barrier had been knocked down, and traces of car tracks indicated that previous drivers had ignored the warning, so he continued. He subsequently fell into a hole filled with snow, suffered injuries, and sued, charging the contractor with negligence. The jury decided in his favor. Upon appeal, the supreme court held that the law does not require a company to keep a guard on duty to protect warning signs, freeing the contractor from negligence in this instance.[34]

In 1934 the state sued the Highway Commission in a quo warranto proceeding. The commission was preparing to borrow $17,000 from the RFC, and the state wanted an interpretation of the county using these funds under Article VII, Section IV, enabling them to provide for the aged, infirm, and other unfortunates. The justices determined that the legislature had the power to enact this road legislation because the counties would perform the construction, and the governor or the commission had the power to carry out the will of the legislators. But did the use of taxes on vehicles and on motor fuel to build roads violate Article II, prohibiting the state from building public works? The court held the constitutional amendment of 1920 permitting the construction of highways by counties to be valid.[35]

The Arkansas River runs eastward through Hamilton and Kearney Counties. In 1857, before Kearney County existed, Hamilton County built a bridge over the river in Kendall township. Kearny County was organized in 1887 and included part of Kendall township. In 1895 Kendall township in Kearney County and Kendall township in Hamilton County raised $3,000 to build a bridge in Hamilton County half a mile upstream from the old bridge. In 1917 the legislature brought these bridges under the control of the county commissioners involved. By 1935 a new bridge was needed that would cost $27,448, and they could receive a federal grant of $12,000 in assistance. Kearney County commissioners declined to pay their part. In a writ of mandamus proceeding, the court held that this was part of a county line highway, and Kearney County had to support its share of it.[36]

Foes of prohibition continued to find different ways to test the law. George Vedder was charged with maintaining a nuisance and was fined $100 and thirty days in jail. He was issued a restraining order from maintaining the nuisance; in Kansas it was customary to use this term and "temporary injunction" interchangeably. During his trial it was disclosed that D. W. Hills was not the owner of the property used illegally as charged, so the assistant attorney general promised to file an amended petition. He never did file one, so Vedder never filed an answer and continued to operate his nuisance. In 1929 authorities filed a proceeding against Vedder again. Several terms of the court had lapsed since the first order, but the justices ruled that their order did not lose its force with the lapse of time, and he was convicted again.[37]

Mrs. M. F. Wheat owned a drugstore in Zenda in Kingman County. Her sixteen-year-old son, Donald, was a pharmacy student who helped her in the store, as did several temporary clerks during the Christmas season. They sold California Padres Wine Elixir, which contained 25 percent alcohol and was much in demand during the holiday season. Authorities discovered deliveries of three to four cases of the beverage to the drugstore "every few days" and many empty bottles scattered around the countryside. A "local toper" was using it to celebrate, and his daughter complained to authorities. Evidence also was presented that "toper" John Schulte was drunk at home from consuming "Medco," purchased at another location. The evidence was presented to the jury, including the empty bottles strewn around the small town and the deliveries to the drugstore. Apparently some members of the jury were quite aware of the evidence and disliked voting to convict their neighbors. After four days of discussion, the judge told the jurors to ignore the street talk they were hearing. Despite complaints of the foreman referring to the drink as "booze," the jury finally rendered a guilty verdict, which the court affirmed. Justice Joachims dissented on the grounds that he sympathized with the judge's concern over the length of deliberations, which he thought violated the speedy trial requirement.[38]

W. O. Blake was charged with three violations: driving a vehicle without a tag showing it was licensed, driving under the influence of alcohol, and driving at a speed higher than was "reasonable." The jurors quashed charge number 1 and failed to arrive at a verdict on number 2. On number 3 the jury accepted the evidence of Wade Gupton, who had turned on Highway 54 going east when Blake came from the east. Gupton had swerved to miss him, and Blake hit Gupton's right fender with his left fender. Blake sought to show the jury that Gupton instituted his prosecution because he declined to pay for the repair of Gupton's car. The jury found Blake guilty, and the court affirmed that while no evidence of speed was introduced, it was enough to say that Blake's speed was not "reasonable."[39]

Sarver and Beiber were driving from Osborne to Salina when they had an accident near Minneapolis. Officers saw one of them throw out a mostly empty alcohol bottle. They found that Sarver did not have control of his facial muscles, his eyes were blurry, and he had no control over his feet. When asked if he had been drinking, he replied, "I never dropped a drink in my life." Beiber staggered, had bloodshot eyes, and smelled of corn whiskey. Sarver said he thought he hit a bridge when the accident happened. The justices found guilty whoever was the driver, and the other was an accessory.[40]

The Hutchinson Country Club had a clubhouse, swimming pool, golf course, and tennis court, and it operated privately with membership fees. It was located near Highway 96, seven miles from Hutchinson and five miles from Nickerson, with most of its membership coming from Hutchinson. Management applied for a 3.2 beer license, and the county commissioners approved it. The operator needed the license to compete with surrounding sellers, and the Nickerson township objected to licensing. The court held that the liquor regulations derived from the state's police power, and the law authorizing townships to determine this question was not an unlawful delegation of legislative authority. The justices sustained the Hutchinson County commissioners.[41]

A man was arrested on liquor charges, and the car he was driving contained several pints of intoxicating beverages, so it was confiscated. R. G. Owens responded that the car belonged to him, and it had been used without his permission. The justices refused to confiscate it because the liquor laws were designed to prevent schemes or subterfuges in preventing confiscation of vehicles. This was a different case than normal, Justice Smith insisted. If this car could be confiscated, the automobile of any law-abiding citizen whose car was stolen could be confiscated if used illegally. Justice Harvey dissented on the basis that the law made no distinction between innocent and knowing owner or mortgagee. Its *use*, he maintained, had always been the test.[42]

The state workmen's compensation law was tested frequently during the depression, with the justices usually being generous toward the laborer. Henry Conner received a fractured rib that previously had been damaged, resulting in a "partial permanent injury." His compensation was based on 60 percent of the difference in his earning power before and after the accident, but not to exceed $18 weekly. The district court modified the trial decision and lowered the amount to $6 for 407 weeks. Conner appealed this decision, arguing that he should have total disability. His witness testified that he earned $5 to $6 weekly for the same work at the same mine. Hutchinson, speaking for the court, rejected his appeal, noting that the district judge was correct in assessing the lower amount because Conner did not have total disability.[43]

Linnie E. Knuth's husband, George, migrated from Germany in 1875 with his parents to Minnesota. He enlisted in the army in July 1898 and retired in 1930 with an honorable discharge. He married Linnie in 1905 and was stationed at Fort Leavenworth in 1909. The couple lived there with a son until George retired. Minnesota passed a compensation law in 1919, so he applied, giving his residence as Leavenworth, and received benefits. The Kansas compensation law went into effect in 1923, but officials denied him funding because he was a Minnesota resident. He died in September 1931, and widow Linnie appealed the denial of compensation. The justices decided that on 6 April 1917, when Congress declared war, there was no doubt that Knuth was a Kansas citizen living in Leavenworth, so their judgment was in favor of his widow.[44]

Oscar Miles was a caser for oil wells and worked only when a new well needed casing. He was killed one day while at this work, and his compensation was computed on the basis that he worked fifty-five days the previous year, earning $517.55. He also earned an additional $192.85 at odd jobs. Officials computed his compensation on the basis of working days, not days worked, because of the nature of his specialty. He left a widow and three children, so the commissioner calculated the family's loss at $4,000. The plaintiff argued that the commissioner should have computed on the days worked, and the sum should be $2,131. The supreme court sustained this award on the grounds that it was not Miles's fault that he lost working days when the company did not call him. It was the nature of his job, and he was killed working on the job. The statute called for $4,000, so his widow should receive it.[45]

Orville Stapleton was an employee of the State Highway Commission. He was in maintenance, but, specifically, he was an "oil section man," who patched breaks in the mat surface. This job had irregular hours and required he live near the work area because he was on call day and night. He suffered no deductions in pay while in transit. He was moving to Garden City, his new assignment, during a dust storm when he became unable to see the road, and his car overturned, killing him. Did his death arise from his employment? The justices held that he was killed while moving his household goods, and this was as "essential in the performance of his duties" as was moving his road machine.[46]

City lineman Rupp slipped on a wet floor, hit his back and hip on a car bumper, and injured his spine. In order to recover, his physician said he must stabilize his fifth lumbar vertebra. He was compensated $30 in

August, and the respondent paid his medical fees. He was then ordered to go to Kansas City, Missouri, for further examination, where he was told he had strained muscles. Work was the best therapy for this, so the city put him on a job with lighter duties, and he received his usual $22 weekly. The lower court held this to be wages, not compensation. The supreme court decided that the court was in error in determining this to be wages. The court's interpretation of the unemployment law meant that this was compensation because of the higher pay for lighter work.[47]

Catherine Piggue's husband worked for the Missouri Pacific Railroad and presented the justices with an opportunity to deliver a broad interpretation of the interstate commerce power. He worked in the switch yard of the line, moving a pile of cinders left by an engine, shoveling them into a wheelbarrow, when he suddenly slumped over and died within moments. This was a "receiving" track for engines from the Katy and Santa Fe Railroads, so the justices interpreted his work as coming under the interstate commerce category. Because of this he was covered by the Federal Unemployment Act, which had better benefits for his widow than the state compensation law.[48]

Following the declaration of war in 1917, the nation's railroads were in such chaotic confusion that goods were not moving as needed for the war effort. The national government took over the lines and operated them as one unit under the control of the Railroad Administration from 26 December 1917 to 1 March 1920, when the government returned them to the owners. Frank M. St. Clair was an employee on the Katy line in Parsons. During a collision of trains in the switchyard, he lost a leg. He employed plaintiffs as counsel to recover damages, and they notified the director-general of the lines that they were filing for $75,650 in damages. Meanwhile, St. Clair, arguing that he was mentally sick and physically weak when he signed this contract, employed a different counsel. Two weeks later the director-general, through his agents and attorneys, settled with this firm for $7,650. St. Clair insisted that he had sent the first law firm a telegram notifying them he was represented by new counsel, but they pursued their attorney's fee. The case went to trial in 1930. When control of the railroads were returned to original owners in 1922, plaintiffs were given two years to file claims. The original legal firm met this requirement, filing an attorney's lien against the director-general. The trial jury ruled that St. Clair was competent to sign a contract with them. The justices, on the appeal, decided the federal law did not bar attorney liens as provided by Kansas law, and the original contract must be fulfilled.[49]

W. P. Huston operated a playhouse and entered into a contract with a labor union covering the period 9 March 1939 through 31 August 1940. He agreed to pay a union operator $39.60 for a six-day week of six-hour days, plus overtime for additional hours. If he decided to close the playhouse, he would give two weeks' notice. Huston closed his operation on 20 December 1939 without notice, and Swart sued for wages from that time until 16 March 1940. The supreme court decided that the plaintiff could quit the job at any time, so the employer could fire him at any time, and Swart lost the wages he was demanding.[50]

Congress proposed a child labor amendment in 1924, and Kansas, among other states, voted not to ratify on 30 January 1925. Congress did not place the usual time limit on ratification, and thus the amendment is currently pending. During the Great Depression sweatshops and child labor again posed problems for the unemployed, and the amendment again appeared in the state legislature. This time it raised interesting legal questions. The house approved it by the necessary vote, but the senate tied, with twenty-two for and twenty-two against. Lt. Gov. W. M. Lindsay then cast the deciding favorable vote, and twenty-one senators and three representatives sought a mandamus to compel the secretary of state to erase endorsement of the amendment. They appealed this action for a supreme court interpretation of its legality. Two questions required interpretation. First, can a state reject an amendment and later reverse positions? Other states had rejected proposed amendments and then reversed and given approval, so this precedent applied in this case. Second, the lieutenant governor was not a senator and therefore could not vote on this issue. The justices held that ratifying an amendment to the US Constitution was a federal function and thus transcended any limits placed on the process by a state. The state constitution authorized the lieutenant governor's vote in case of a tie in the senate, his vote here was legal, and the writ of mandamus was denied. In 1938 the Fair Labor Standards Act prohibited child labor, and the Supreme Court approved the law in *U.S. v. Darby Lumber*, 312 U.S. 100 (1941), so the pending amendment is unnecessary.[51]

Five thousand banks failed during the first three years of the depression, and several cases arose out of this disaster. J. W. Miller and his relatives owned about 80 percent of the Midwest State Bank of Fort Scott, where he was a director and president. He was charged with twenty-five counts of "knowingly" and "unlawfully" receiving withdrawals and deposits when he knew his bank was insolvent because of bad loans. The bank was carrying as cash items his check for $6,200. The Farm and Home Savings and Loan Association had its offices in his bank building, and he allowed the company to issue checks for $18,661.61 for the purpose of "rescuing" its money from the bank before it collapsed. The court found no error in the trial court proceedings, noting that the legislature has authority to determine the organization and supervision of its chartered banks and rules for their solvency. The court approved the decision of his guilt according to law.[52]

The People's State Bank of Fort Scott was in receivership, and ten depositors brought suit to obtain preferred claims on funds of the insolvent bank. Hattie Cheyney deposited $5,000 in the bank at 6 percent for one year, but the bank never invested it for her and used the money instead to cover losses. Bank officials also sold $1,000 in Kansas City, Kansas, bonds to cover their deficits. The trial court awarded Hattie $6,000 for principal and interest. Hutchison, speaking for the court, found no error in the trial court proceedings and affirmed judgment against the bank.[53]

The Bank of Superior in Nebraska brought suit against a Kansas depositor. The president and cashier of the bank improperly placed $5,608.50 in his account, and he spent all but $101.42 before the bank failed. He insisted that the amount was a loan at 7 percent, he had repaid it, and the officials erred in placing the amount in the wrong account. The bank sought to recover the money and appealed to the supreme court. The justices found that a debit slip had been entered on the transaction, but there was no evidence to show that bank officials attempted to bring this to the attention of the defendant. The court affirmed judgment against the bank.[54]

Samuel Babcock made deposits on 15 June 1924, 9 February 1925, and 9 and 12 March 1925. The bank closed its doors two weeks after the last entry, and Sam brought suit to recover his money. He argued in the trial court that the bank officials should know about their financial condition, and they failed to comply with the information and suggestions the bank commission and examiners gave them about removing "bad" paper and "securing additional security on all loans." Upon appeal, the supreme court could find no errors in the record, so the jury verdict for depositor Babcock was affirmed.[55]

H. F. Dierking owned the Bank of Alta Vista until it closed its doors on 5 March 1932. He owed his son Arthur $3,168 on a loan and deeded him 109.5 acres of land to cover it. Arthur owed his son's wife $1,000, so he deeded her land for repayment. A. H. Radlef loaned the couple $1,200 on this land and secured it with a mortgage. Dierking also owed his daughter Bertha $1,317, so he deeded her 55 acres. He owned thirty-eight shares in the bank, and he and other directors knew about its financial problems. It declared bankruptcy, and the receiver sought to set aside the deeds of Arnold and Bertha because he believed, rightly so, that the deeds were given to set these lands beyond the reach of creditors. The supreme court decided that, regardless of their relationship, Dierking owed his children this money. The justices could find no evidence of fraud, deciding this was just a preference of the creditor for "certain debtors."[56]

President Franklin Roosevelt sought to inflate the economy by tinkering with the price of gold. The Gold Reserve Act of 1934 gave him further monetary controls by impounding bullion but allowed people to keep gold coins as collector's items or as keepsakes. Christopher Schmidt rented a safety-deposit box and placed in the box $2,000 in currency and $1,024 in gold coins, some of which belonged to a friend. On 28 September 1935 he opened his box, and when he did not return within a reasonable time, an employee found he had fainted and fallen on the floor. Several weeks later he returned with his attorney, and they found a package of nails in the box. An expert was summoned, and he found no evidence of forcible entry. A former employee, Yearbin, had been convicted of embezzlement, and discussions disclosed that he had handled the box for the plaintiff on several occasions. The plaintiff had two keys, and the bank had a master key. It also was discovered that the plaintiff had not reported the gold to federal officials, nor had he been given permission to keep the coins. Upon appeal the supreme court held that the bank should have taken "reasonable care and diligence" in preserving the contents of the box, but the renter could not make the bank a guarantor of the contents without giving officials exclusive control over access to the box.[57]

Foreclosures on land and homes proceeded apace with these desperate economic conditions, and many states and the national government enacted mortgage moratorium laws. Kansas enacted one in 1933. It authorized the governor, if he deemed it necessary and proper, to extend mortgage foreclosures for six months to allow the borrower time to repay. Velma Bolin signed a mortgage in 1925, and her application for an extension was denied. The trial court approved the denial, and the supreme court held that the extension powers granted to the governor were an unconstitutional delegation of legislative powers to the executive branch. This violated the concept of separation of powers, and the justices affirmed the lower court's decision.[58]

President Herbert Hoover's Reconstruction Finance Corporation authorized loans to states and their agencies for building infrastructure. The Kansas Forestry, Fish, and Game Commission took advantage of this program to borrow $200,000 to build necessary reservoirs, dams, and lakes and use fees collected from hunting, fishing, and trapping licenses to repay the loan. This action was challenged and taken to the supreme court, where the justices found several faults with the plan. First, it violated the constitutional ban on building internal improvements, as this action was limited to building roads and highways. It also conflicted with the constitutional limits on indebtedness at $1 million without the approval of the voters. Finally, the justices noted that there were too many variations in license fees to permit any certainty of paying off the debt from this source.[59]

Taxpayers had to trim their personal budgets and were concerned that a "spendthrift" legislature might violate the limit on state indebtedness, so Governor Alf Landon advocated a graduated income tax law based on the constitutional amendment the voters had approved in 1932 to raise increased revenues. This would operate in tandem with the "cash-basis" law of 1933 that required all governmental units to limit their spending to the anticipated revenues of each fiscal year. Administrators adhered to this guideline carefully, as they knew they could be removed from office for deviations.[60]

A company challenged the income tax on a technicality over deductions. A Delaware corporation transported natural gas from Kansas to Nebraska, Iowa, and Illinois. Company officials received a bill for an income tax that they did not file because they deducted the interest they paid to stockholders on a bonded debt held for capital expenditures necessary for conducting business. They appealed the tax bill, and the supreme court decided that the law provided for these expenditures to be deductible, but not on the interest on bonds held by stockholders. The legislature held plenary power to levy an income tax and to provide for deductions. The legislature can, and did, differentiate between stockholders and nonstockholders.[61]

Needless to say, the cash-basis law also met a challenge. The city of Valley Falls sued Jefferson County for $5,026.83 for maintaining city streets that served as connecting links to county highways. The county had never paid the city for this type of maintenance, but it became important to the city because of the new cash-basis law. The county separated its claim to begin with expenditure on those streets on 31 March 1933 but did not file the claim until October 1937. The court decided that the law barred claims prior to the time it went into effect, but the city claim was valid. The justices found no error in the trial court proceedings, and its decision was affirmed.[62]

Many companies added various ingredients to their products in order to make them look more attractive or try to increase their volume. The national government and thirty-one states passed laws to curtail this practice. In 1935 the Kansas legislature tried to help dairy farmers by enacting the filled milk law, based on the state's police power, which made it illegal to add any derivative to the dairy farmers' product other than a milk fat product. For some time a Michigan company was marketing Carolene and Melnut, a product to which the company added coconut oil to milk to make it more nutritious and healthful. Many retailers handled the product, and it was popular. The supreme court, however, decided that the Kansas law came under the prevention of fraud and deception with adulterated compounds and was constitutional and must be enforced.[63]

During the Hundred Days session Congress enacted the National Industrial Recovery Act, which contained two titles. The first established the National Recovery Administration to organize business and labor to defeat the depression. Title II created the Public Works Administration to build infrastructure and to encourage business in supplying the necessary materials. These programs in Kansas could be funded by federal grants or by city bonds under the terms of the basis of the cash-basis law. A special session of the legislature authorized cities to issue revenue bonds to pay the costs of the construction of utilities. The NRA program stated that if the president proclaimed the end of the emergency in two years, Title II would terminate. So the legislature, in creating the new type of bond, stipulated that if the NRA was terminated, the revenue bond authorization would end also, and this type of bond must be kept separate from the emergency type of bond. The city of Pittsburg sought a writ of mandamus to require the state auditor to register its revenue bonds. The supreme court decided that, because Title II was still operating in Kansas, registering these bonds did not violate state law. In addition, the justices said, this type of control over financial obligations did not constitute delegation of legislative powers.[64]

Like many counties suffering from the financial burdens of maintaining a program of welfare for the needy, Brown County was attempting to move Lucian Lange, his wife, and two children to the state of

Washington because the migrants were likely to become a public charge for the county. This action was based on the 1862 law making provision for those "likely to become a public charge" to be moved to the place where they "belong." The district court dismissed the action to quash the motion because the law of 1862 was "completely superceded by the Social Welfare Emergency Act" of 1937, which made provision for migrant welfare cases with funds from sales tax revenues. In awkward phraseology, the court held that the 1862 law "has thereby been impliedly repealed" by the depression act.[65]

The depressed economic conditions made pinball machines popular because they provided cheap entertainment with the five-cent cost to play them. Dale Waite was charged with operating a gambling house because his pinball machines gave free games for winning. The gambling law forbade machines or devices that provided for winning money or property. The court decided that this was a harmless prize of winning another "game" and was not "gambling."[66]

Movies also provided a depression form of escape with a relatively cheap ticket that took the viewer to faraway China or a dream world of Hollywood palaces where beautiful, rich people lived and played. During the 1930s a Colorado enterprise created Bank Nite to increase attendance. Customers over sixteen years of age could play by selecting a bank of their choice. Ticket purchasers would receive a number, and a drawing was held on Wednesday night for the weekly prize to be deposited in the winner's bank. If the owner of a winning number was not present, the amount would be added to the next week's drawing. The state brought a quo warranto suit, claiming this constituted a lottery. Justice Hutchison spoke for the court in citing *Davenport v. Ottawa* (54 Kan. 711), where the court defined the locked box with cash in the window of a business. Customers received a key, and the one with the correct key could open the box and take the money. The justices held this to be a lottery, and Bank Nite fell into the same category.[67]

Another world war brought new litigation. World War I had produced a 100 percent inflation rate, and Congress sought to control this problem in January 1942, days after the attack on Pearl Harbor, with the Emergency Price Control Act. The problem soon became acute with the great housing shortage of the war period. B. H. Johnson had several rentals in Salina, a defense-rental area with limited housing. As long as the renter paid his obligation, the law provided that he could remain in the housing without an increase in rent. If the owner wished to increase the rent, he had to appeal to the program administrator. Three cases came to the court at the same time. The US Supreme Court had upheld the constitutionality of the law, so the Kansas justices held the statute to be binding on the state.[68]

During this period of dedicated patriotism the Jehovah's Witnesses became highly unpopular because their teaching forbade worshiping any graven image, and they included saluting the American flag as a graven image. A state law of 1917 had provided for raising the flag and saluting it in public schools as part of opening ceremonies, a tradition that continued to the next war. In conformity with their teaching, the Smith children refused to participate in this exercise, so the Lawton school board ordered the teacher to expel any student who declined to salute. The teacher did not want to embarrass the children publicly, so she went to the parents and told them their children were expelled. The Smiths hired a competent teacher with a Missouri certificate to tutor the children. This did not satisfy the truant officer, who filed a complaint, and the parents were tried and convicted for their children's truancy. The state supreme court cited the US Supreme Court cases dealing with this issue that found the beliefs of the cult were not unreasonable, and the children could not be compelled to salute.[69]

The Jehovah's Witnesses were distributing their literature in Olathe and were arrested for loitering and for violating a city ordinance forbidding three or more people from assembling in public and annoying passers-by or in the use of sidewalks. They challenged their arrest, and the supreme court found no evidence of violating the ordinance. They could not be charged with loitering, because they were selling or giving away their literature, the *Watch Tower*, which was protected by freedom of the press in the First Amendment.[70]

Dr. John R. Brinkley sought to enjoin the state medical board from withdrawing his license to practice. State law established the board of seven physicians in good standing in the profession, appointed by the governor, to license doctors of various types. They must be of good moral character and produce proof of their legitimate medical studies. Applicants could be denied approval for committing felonies, gross immorality, or drug or liquor addictions. Brinkley asked the board for a hearing, and when board members came to his hospital in Milford, he demonstrated his operation to them. They remained adamant about retrieving his license, and he appealed to the supreme court to reverse their decision on the basis that this action of license removal took property, or his practice, without due process of law. Speaking for the justices, Burch fell into his occasional habit of using unprofessional language by noting that the doctor's famous operation provided that "dotards having desire without capability may cease to sorrow as do those without hope." The decision concluded that the board was a legitimate creation under the state police power, and the decision did not deprive property without due process of law.[71]

A Burns farmer went to Dr. Brown with spots on his scalp and face. Brown diagnosed his problem as syphilis and sent a blood sample to the El Dorado laboratory. The result came back negative, but Brown told the farmer it was positive, and his treatment would cost $150. The farmer asked Brown for a copy of the report and was informed that the lab did not keep records. When Brown was at the lab, he stole a form and filled it out to show that syphilis was the diagnosis. Still disbelieving, the plaintiff took his case to the state medical board, and the decision was that Brown's actions constituted a "gross immorality," and the board revoked his license. Brown appealed, and the supreme court sustained the board's ruling.[72]

It was well known that two farmers in the neighborhood possessed $24,000 in government bonds. Pyle committed murder while stealing these bonds in 1934. The state convicted him of murder in 1935 and sentenced him to life in Leavenworth. The state supreme court sustained his conviction in 1936, denying him a writ of habeas corpus. He studied criminal law while in prison, decided he had a good case for appeal, and prepared his own brief to present to the US Supreme Court. His brief showed that the state had used perjured witnesses to convict him and suppressed testimony favorable to him. The Supreme Court, speaking through Justice Murphy, reversed the Kansas decision and, through a writ of certiorari, ordered the Kansas Supreme Court to review its decision to deny him habeas corpus.[73]

The two major political parties cooperated in harassing minor parties and making it more difficult for them to participate in elections. The Union Party organized nationally on 28 June 1936 and held a convention in Topeka on 29 August to select a slate of presidential electors. The secretary of state refused to file the party's certificate of candidacy for the general election because it had missed the 20 June deadline for filing. The secretary notified party officials that they could get on the ticket for the general election only by paying a ten-dollar fee by 20 June 1936 and entering the state primary election. The party sued for a writ of mandamus, and the supreme court decided that the manner of selecting presidential electors was determined by each state. The Kansas legislature had established election laws for the direct primary and the general election for this procedure, and its actions were constitutional. The justices insisted that if the procedure was not followed, innumerable candidates would appear, and "enormous costs of printing and distributing ballots" would result. All of the justices, of course, were Republicans, except one Democrat. The identical question arose four years later when the Communist Party (CPUSA) attempted the same process and received the identical decision.[74]

The school board of Topeka contracted for buses to carry colored children to school from remote areas and to transport underprivileged ones to a special school set up for them. A disgruntled taxpayer challenged the arrangement. There were 6,428 whites and 947 coloreds in Topeka schools exclusive of junior high. They required nineteen grade schools for whites and four for coloreds, plus the special school for the underprivileged. Citizen Foster insisted that this arrangement for transportation was "an extraordinary function" that was beyond "the ends of legitimate education." Speaking for the court, however, Joachims denied the injunction because the school board had "implied power and authority" that legalized such an arrangement.[75]

Colorado sued Kansas over usage of Arkansas River water. In 1931 the legislature appropriated money for the attorney general's office, including funds to employ attorney C. S. Luper to defend Kansas claims. Governor Woodring signed the appropriation measure but objected to $5,000 for each of the years 1932 and 1933 for this litigation and $900 to the state architect to employ an engineer, yet he failed to explain his reasoning for this necessity. The state sued for a writ of mandamus to require the state auditor to audit the voucher for $5,000. The constitution requires the governor to stipulate his objections to items he dislikes in appropriation measures. He failed to do so, and the writ was approved.[76]

Maggie Atkinson was a forty-seven-year—old widow who rented a house in Wichita. Previous tenants and neighbors told the landlord they smelled leaking gas. He reported this to the gas company, and it promised to repair the problem. The leak continued, so he called again, and the company said the leak had been repaired. Repairmen had turned off the gas to work on the leak, and Maggie called to have the gas turned back on. The next day an explosion injured her by throwing her to the floor and causing "a nervous prostration." The jury awarded her $7,500. The defendant found a witness who testified that Maggie was going through "a natural stage of life" and that she had hallucinations. The court, however, found no errors in the trial and held the gas company liable.[77]

Janie Miller was married to Sam Moore, and he sued for a divorce in 1919, but the action was dismissed for want of prosecution. Assuming Sam had received the divorce, Janie openly and notoriously "took up" with George Miller as his common-law wife, and for eleven years "they shucked their shoes together," as Justice Burch expressed it so elegantly, from Ardmore, Oklahoma, to Butte, Montana. George was a truck driver and was killed in a collision. Janie became the administratrix of his estate. Sam also had a wandering eye without a yen for marriage, because before he was killed he met eighteen-year-old Helen in 1930, and they "commenced to common law together." In addition, other girls caught his eye, but he always returned to Janie, although less frequently and with shorter visits. Helen contested Janie's right to administrate, but she quieted her title and then sued for $10,000. The jury awarded her $3,000, and the supreme court affirmed this judgment. Burch observed, however, that "the social problem presented by the record must also remain unsolved."[78]

Defendant operated a cigar store and lunch counter in Wichita. A hallway in the building he rented led to a public toilet, a requirement for a restaurant. Across the hall was a shoe-shine spot that also had access to the toilet. The hall contained a trap door halfway from the diner to the toilet. The plaintiff, a regular customer who had used the facility for years, started for the toilet, fell into the open trap door, and broke an arm. That Sunday the trap door was left open for ventilation preparatory for work to reinforce the floor. The court held that this situation complied with the requirement for a public toilet. The landlord was not responsible for the tenant lifting the trap door.[79]

Mills operated a theater in Chanute and contracted to exhibit or show the movie *Devil Dancer* until he discovered that the censors had not approved it for Kansas viewing. United Artists contended that this censorship constituted a direct burden on interstate commerce. It also should be voided because it violated the prohibition against price fixing of the state antitrust law. The supreme court denied a rehearing because the state police power cannot "be emasculated by a private contract."[80]

Kenneth, a junior, and Eleanor, a sophomore, brother and sister, enrolled in Graham County High School. They attended during the first month, and on 20 September they "absented" themselves to attend a Friday football game. They returned to school on Monday, but principal M. H. Templeton refused them admittance, even using force to push them out of the building. Their father asked the school board several times to meet and resolve the issue, but he was refused. He applied for a writ of mandamus because the law limited suspension to sixty days, or this amounted to expulsion, and the plaintiff had no other remedy. In the litigation that followed, however, it was shown that the school board had relented and admitted them on 21 November, and the principal failed to inform them. By the time the case reached the supreme court, the question had become moot.[81]

The Finney Bond Scandal also reached the supreme court during the depression. Warren and Ronald Finney of Emporia, father and son, were successful financiers of the Fidelity State Savings Bank of that city who were charged with embezzlement of state bonds, and their Neosho Falls Bank closed as a result of the bad publicity. Every embezzler, Justice Smith observed, will insist that he meant to return the money, as the Finneys claimed. Smith could find no prejudice or misconduct or error in admissible evidence and affirmed the lower court's judgment.[82]

Following World War II, the state was challenged over its century-old law on school segregation, leading to the modern civil rights movement. Also a curious political episode demonstrated the questionable practice of justices continuing their political operations while on the bench, leading to the first significant change in their selection as justices since the constitution was written.

7. The Revised Selection System

The Political Scene

The landmark US Supreme Court decision of *Brown v. Topeka* in 1954 arose from the historic tradition of segregation of public schools in Kansas. With very few blacks in territorial Kansas, no provision was made for their education. Besides, most early settlers were interested in obtaining good land, not in promoting the rights of blacks. With statehood, local school districts determined their own policies. The state school laws were codified in 1876 without an express authorization for integrated schools, "creating the inference that the state permitted segregated schools."[1]

This situation changed significantly in 1878 and 1879, when the Exodusters arrived in the Sunflower State in great numbers. Fleeing the oppression of the Black Codes in the Reconstruction South, some thirty thousand penniless blacks appeared in the Kansas City area and were encouraged, often forced, to move on westward in search of communities that would allow them to settle. Many found a haven in "Tennessee Town" in North Topeka. In 1879 the legislature enacted a law permitting, but not requiring, first-class cities to segregate their elementary schools. The US Supreme Court gave legal sanction to this policy in *Plessy v. Ferguson* in 1896. While this was a transportation case, the principle of "separate but equal" was subsequently applied to all "Jim Crow" laws spreading across the nation as blacks continued to flee the "reconstructed" South. In Kansas the *Plessy* principle was challenged several times, but the state supreme court always ruled against those seeking integration of the public schools.[2]

Segregation began to face inexorable challenges nationally by the

1930s, first in higher education, where it was most vulnerable because it was a greater financial burden to the state than the public schools. It was becoming increasingly difficult to maintain "separate but equal" facilities in colleges, especially in professional and graduate education. In most instances, schools were separate, but the black ones were woefully unequal in quality; in many cases the cost of professional schools was so expensive that states paid out-of-state tuition to send their black students to a northern state for this level of education. This practice was challenged in *Missouri ex rel. Gaines v. Canada*, in which the court ordered the state to provide equality in its higher education if the state wanted to segregate it. Separate but equal meant exactly that. Oklahoma had established Langston University for its blacks, but Ada Sipuel defied this arrangement as being unequal and forced the state to admit her to the University of Oklahoma's School of Law. Finally, in *Sweatt v. Painter*, the law school for blacks in Texas was struck down on the basis that to separate facilities into two schools made the black one "inherently unequal." The stage was thus set to challenge the massive problem of segregated public schools across the nation.[3]

Topeka maintained Monroe, Washington, McKinley, and Buchanan schools for African American children for kindergarten through eighth grade. On 28 February 1951 the local chapter of the National Association for the Advancement of Colored People (NAACP) brought suit against the board of education in the name of Reverend Oliver Brown to enroll his daughter Linda in Spencer, a white school. The case went to the district court, headed by former governor Walter A. Huxman, who held a two-day hearing in Topeka in late June. Regardless of personal feelings, the district judges faced the fact that the US Supreme Court had repeatedly refused to overturn the *Plessy* opinion, and they believed they had to base their decision on that precedent. Their denial to Brown bypassed the circuit court of appeals and was appealed, of course, to the US Supreme Court, headed by President Dwight D. Eisenhower's nominee, Earl Warren. Curiously, in an identical case in South Carolina a few weeks earlier, Judge Waties Waring had daringly ruled for the plaintiff.[4]

NAACP counsel Thurgood Marshall included the *Brown* case with four others from the southern states of Virginia, South Carolina, and the border state of Delaware on the basis that segregated schools violated the equal protection clause of the Fourteenth Amendment. He included a fifth case from Washington, DC, based on the principle that segregating public schools in the city controlled by Congress contravened the Fifth Amendment. Marshall used the "Brandeis brief" approach, insisting that segregation not only violated the Constitution but also had adverse and lasting psychological effects on black children, who were thus consigned to an inferior position in life. The Kansas case, assigned first by random choice, was presented by Paul Wilson, whom Attorney General Harold Fatzer had delegated to write the brief. It was a fascinating charge for the future law professor who had no appellate experience.[5]

The Supreme Court heard the case in 1953 but was unable to reach an agreement, so it held a rehearing a month later. In May 1954 a unanimous court declared that separate schools for the races are "inherently unequal." Warren's famous footnote 11 extensively cited the sociological studies of Kenneth Clark to show the effects of segregation on little children. Knowing the enormity of implementing this opinion across the nation, the Warren Court requested the attorneys to reappear the following year with advice on remedies. It then handed down *Brown II*, which stated that American schools should be integrated with "all deliberate speed." Unfortunately, in the South the course pursued was very deliberate and completely lacking in speed. In Kansas the revolutionary decision was accepted, in no small part because Communist Russia was using segregation as an ideological weapon against America in the Cold War, and Kansans were staunch cold warriors.[6]

President Truman had integrated the armed forces by executive order in 1948, although it required the military necessity for troops of any color in Korea to end literally the segregated army. In 1947 his committee on civil rights issued a report, "To Secure These Rights," and efforts to fulfill this document propelled the civil rights movement for the next several decades. The *Brown* decision was a milestone in this campaign to live up to America's promise. As Kansas counsel Paul Wilson stressed, 1954 was "a time to lose." A unanimous Supreme Court committed the country to the proposition that rights of US citizens would be asserted against restraints of individual states to abridge the equal protection clause of the Fourteenth Amendment. This was another step in incorporating the Bill of Rights into that amendment. The following doctrine of interposition, whereby the individual state would inject its authority between its citizens and national authority, proved a failure in the twentieth century, as had secession a century before. In 1963 the Supreme Court concluded that the nation had experienced enough "deliberate speed" and ordered schools to integrate "at once."[7]

CORE and NAACP chapters had won few victories against segregation until July 1958, when students in Wichita, led by political scientist Ronald Walters, staged four weeks of sit-ins at a Rexall drugstore lunch counter. Walters and followers gathered in a church basement and practiced their routine, taking turns playing the white segregationists. This action opened up a few downtown restaurants and attracted national notice. It also drew the attention of a local motorcycle gang, which abused the protesters, and the police offered no protection to the "sitters." The crisis finally ended when carloads of people from the black community arrived to offer support.[8]

Kansas City activists achieved an antidiscrimination ordinance in 1960 but faced massive resistance from small businesses that challenged the ordinance in court. Opponents also succeeded in branding the activists as Communists and built a grassroots movement of resistance. The activists countercharged that these critics were in league with white southern racists, an accusation that hit home, as this period produced many televised images of the white supremacist violence against civil rights protesters during the Kennedy presidency. In a tense referendum battle with a high black voter turnout, voters upheld the ordinance by only 1,614 votes of 90,000 cast.[9]

Soon thereafter, the state supreme court and Kansans endured a traumatic experience that led to a new system for selecting future justices in what was termed the "triple switch" in Kansas politics. The story begins in late 1956, when Chief Justice Bill Smith became seriously ill in December and was hospitalized with a high fever and abdominal pain. Doctors diagnosed uremic poisoning caused by a kidney stone and operated immediately. On his hospital bed Smith made the decision to retire immediately, which signaled the resignations of two other officials. The timing was crucial, because if his surgery had been earlier, he might have recovered sufficiently by Christmas to decide to finish his term of two more years. Had his surgery been a week later there would have been insufficient time to plan the triple switch.[10]

Frederick Lee Hall, the second protagonist, had a tempestuous political career. Born in Dodge City in 1903, he was educated in the public schools, and his debating ability won him a scholarship to the University of Southern California, where he also took a law degree in 1941. He returned to practice in Dodge City, and, relatively unknown in Kansas politics, he ran for lieutenant governor in 1950 by campaigning as one of nine candidates. This split permitted Hall to win "west of 81" because he was strong in western Kansas. Edward Ferdinand Arn, his running mate, was a conservative who resigned as attorney general to accept a seat on the supreme court and then resigned from the court to run for governor. *Pageant* magazine described him as one of the five worst governors of his time.[11]

The more liberal young lawyer was completely incompatible with Arn, and the two squabbled continuously. Hall was unpopular with the conservative branch of the Republican Party because he had a "foreign" law degree (for some reason Michigan and Harvard Law Schools were acceptable in the Kansas pecking order), he had no military experience because of a minor physical problem, and many considered his personality to be disagreeable. In addition, Arn and his supporters thought Hall to be too pugnacious and aggressive, and they decided to run Arn's friend, Wayne Ryan, against him in 1952. Hall won reelection, though, campaigning as the victim of the "machine," an appeal to younger Republican voters. Because of Hall's complaints of "government by crony," Arn and his supporters determined to defeat Hall in the primary when he ran for governor in 1954. They supported George

Fig. 7. Fred L. Hall. Image from the Kansas State Historical Society.

Templar, who had to resign his position as US attorney to become a candidate. Hall narrowly won, though, with 52 percent of the vote on a platform of "Let's Clean Up Topeka as President Eisenhower Cleaned Up Washington" and went on to dispatch his Democratic opponent, George Docking of Lawrence, in the general election. Hall won with a large majority of forty thousand votes.

While governor, his program stressed items that the conservative faction opposed. When Hall called recalcitrant legislators "SOBs" to their faces, they formed the SOB Club, and as a result, Kansas "did a belly laugh and Hall was the victim." The Old Guard decided to run Warren Shaw, whom the governor had successfully opposed for election as house speaker two years earlier, against Hall in the 1956 primary, and Shaw won, only to be defeated in the general election by Democrat George Docking by over one hundred thousand votes. With the Republican Party badly divided, Docking would become the first Democratic governor in Kansas history to succeed himself.

Hall wrote the attorney general following the election that his opponents' charges had exposed him to "public hatred, ridicule and deprive[d] me of public confidence." He planned a governor's investigation of these activities, prompting speculation over his political future. He was searching for work when Smith was debating whether to resign. Docking's election confirmed the chief justice's inclination to heed his family's request to quit. Smith was certain the Democratic governor would replace him with A. Lewis Oswald, who ran against him for the supreme court seat in 1952. "You can rest assured I won't let George Docking name my successor," he proclaimed, and he began searching for an alternative. Hall suggested himself as the alternative, and as Smith's son was a member of Hall's law firm in Dodge City, he had no objection. This led the two to consult the third member of the triad, Lieutenant Governor John McCuish.

McCuish was an experienced politician who published a newspaper in Newton. As Republican county chairman, he had worked for the election of Governor Payne Ratner, and the governor appointed him to the newly established Department of Revenue and Taxation.

Chief Justice Smith helped the new chair "operate a smooth-running machine" for the governor by serving as his "brains." In late 1956 the lieutenant governor was also hospitalized for high blood pressure, but he consulted with his wife, and they agreed to participate in the plot. A highway patrol car took them to Topeka, where they joined Hall to visit Smith in Stormont-Vail Hospital. Hall announced Smith's resignation and then his own, and McCuish was sworn in as governor. His first official act was to name Hall as Smith's replacement on the high bench. All this took only minutes to transpire, and the new governor was recognized with a hastily assembled National Guard unit and the traditional twenty-one-gun salute.

While there was nothing illegal about this episode, and there were perhaps more sinister ones in supreme court history, Kansans were outraged over this "immoral" travesty. Many Republicans agreed with Democratic state chairman Frank Theis, who said he thought he was "a pretty good title attorney, but this is the greatest shift of titles I have ever seen in such a short time." Former governor Woodring had no comment, but Alf Landon was generous with Hall, believing he would "make a good justice," although he stated his opposition to using the supreme court "as a stepping stone for other political offices." The Salina newspaper described it as the "Topeka Taffy Pull" and predicted that Hall "is a bright enough lawyer to make a good justice if he wants to be. But this cozy little party confirms the suspicion that he is a bum politician." The *Kansas City Times* predicted that there would be two results from the switch: the senate would give "close scrutiny" to over fifty appointees Governor Hall had just sent it for confirmation, and there would be a renewed effort to enact a constitutional amendment to take the supreme court out of politics.

Alf Landon observed that, "by and large, over the years, the Kansas judiciary ranks with the best in the country." He correctly predicted that "when the governor picks our judges, it will put the Kansas judiciary more into politics instead of less." The current problem with the Kansas Supreme Court was not in the caliber or quality of its justices but with those justices being burdened with overwork. It was noted that the seven-member Kansas Supreme Court at that time was grinding out twice as many decisions annually as the nine-member US Supreme Court.[12]

Missouri pioneered the so-called merit plan in 1940 for selecting judges in a nonpartisan manner, but Kansas voters seemed reluctant to relinquish their control over the political process of choosing judges. The Kansas Bar Association (KBA) had been working on a plan similar to that of Missouri. This was killed by the house judiciary committee in 1953. Proposed again in 1955, it was defeated this time by the senate judiciary committee. The "triple switch" made this approach more acceptable, because this episode would never have happened under the commission system. A number of senators endorsed the KBA scheme, although two railed against the proposal on the floor for twenty-five minutes, with one insisting that this would remove the people's "God-given right to elect their own judges." He further warned that, under the Missouri plan, Boss Pendergast selected the judges for Kansas City. (Pendergast was the notorious political boss who ruled Kansas City for many years.) On 1 March 1957 the upper chamber voted thirty-three to four to support its concurrent resolution to present the voters with a referendum on the question. At the end of March the lower house endorsed it eighty-eight to thirty-four, barely the two-thirds necessary to propose a constitutional amendment. The voters rather narrowly approved the change in the next general election by a vote of 132,000 to 96,000.[13]

The plan called for a statewide supreme court nominating commission composed of members of the state bar from each of the four congressional districts as well as a nonlawyer member from each district. The lawyer members were to be selected by a vote of the members of the bar in each district, and the governor appointed the nonlawyer members. A statewide vote of all the bar members would select the chair for the commission. The commission would review all candidates for the state courts and nominate three to the governor. The governor would then select the new judge within sixty days. If he or she fails to make the selection within the time limit, the chief justice makes the choice. The judges then must stand for retention at the next general election and then stand for reelection every four years thereafter. This would allow the voters to become aware of a candidate's judicial record (assuming voters would take the time to do this). An examination of one of the plan's supporters revealed that under the current partisan system, about 70 percent of "Kansas judges today get their seat by appointment."[14]

Smith retired on his pension of $6,500. If he had remained on the bench another two years until mandatory retirement, the law would have awarded him $8,450, a sum he probably needed, as he was never a wealthy man. His decision to retire in 1956 was personally costly and also failed ultimately to prevent a Democrat from taking his seat on the supreme court.

The Judges

Governor Andrew Schoeppel appointed Austin Cowan in 1948 to complete Justice Burch's term. Cowan served on the court for one year. He was born in Valley Falls in 1885, and twelve years later the family moved to Parsons, where he attended public schools. He graduated from the University of Michigan Law School in 1911 and practiced in Wichita for thirty-seven years. After his year on the bench he returned to law practice. He and his wife died in an airplane crash in 1949 while performing a mission for a client.[15]

Edward Ferdinand Arn was born in Kansas City in 1906. He earned a law degree from the Kansas City School of Law in 1931 and served in the navy during World War II. He replaced Justice Hoch, who died in 1949, and resigned from the court a year later to run successfully for governor.[16]

Robert T. Price was born in Burlingame in 1903, attended the public schools there, and received a law degree from the University of Kansas in 1927. During his career he served as a juvenile court judge in Osage County and was elected district judge of Wabaunsee and Osage Counties from 1934 to 1940. He practiced law in Topeka with a stint in the navy in World War II and returned to his practice at the end of the war. Price served as a prosecuting attorney in the Japanese war crimes trials. Meanwhile he married Caroline, daughter of Frank Doster. In 1949 he took Burch's position on the supreme court and served as chief justice until he retired in 1971.[17]

William J. Wertz was born in Bedford, Pennsylvania, in 1896, and the family moved to Wichita in 1908. Wertz attended Ottawa University and served in the navy in World War I. He received a law degree from the University of Kansas in 1919 and moved to Wichita to set up a law practice. He served as Sedgwick County attorney and was elected to the state senate in 1940. He worked in the judge advocate general's office during World War II and was appointed to the supreme court to replace Ed Arn. Wertz was subsequently elected to the position in 1950, 1956, and 1962, retiring in 1965. During that period he wrote 471 opinions. A colleague noticed that Wertz caused excitement during oral arguments when he questioned counsel from the bench, or "perhaps challenged would be more correct."[18]

Lloyd M. Kagey was born in Beloit in 1902 and attended public schools there. He enrolled in the University of Kansas for three years and then received a law degree from Washburn in 1927. Kagey practiced law in Beloit and served as a district judge. He was stricken with polio in 1940, paralyzed from the waist down, but he continued to be active in his wheelchair. He served as assistant attorney general of Sedgwick County from 1941 to 1947. He was appointed to fill Justice Arn's position on the court, completing a five-week term, perhaps the shortest in court history.[19]

Claire E. Robb was born in Wichita in 1905. The family was poor, and he had to work as a newsboy, in a drugstore, and at other jobs to help support the family. He attended the local schools, living for a time with Justice Allen's family. He attended Washburn Law School, receiving a degree in 1933, and practiced in Wichita. He served as district judge in Sedgwick County, being reelected twice before being elected to the supreme court in 1955. He wore Justice Allen's robes during the swearing-in ceremony. Robb was known as a "fair and honest" justice and as a "Christian gentleman," high praise indeed![20]

Harold R. Fatzer was born in Edwards County in 1910. He and his twin brother, Hubert, attended Kansas State University, then received law degrees from Washburn Law School in 1933. They enjoyed playing the usual identical twins pranks on people. Harold served as county attorney and attorney general before Governor Hall appointed him to the supreme court in 1956 to replace Justice Harvey. He wrote 575 opinions during his tenure and 95 dissents. As was the custom of the court, he wrote his share of majority opinions, even when he dissented from the opinion. He became chief justice in 1971 and was active in the Judiciary Advisory Study Group, established in 1972.[21]

Alfred Schroeder was born on a farm near Newton. He attended Bethel College for two years, transferred to Kansas State, and was awarded a degree in agricultural economics. After receiving a law degree from Harvard in 1940, he enlisted in the army air corps during World War II. Schroeder served as judge in the juvenile, probate, and county courts of Sedgwick County before being elected to the supreme court in 1956, the last year of partisan elections. With Justice Fatzer's retirement, he became chief justice, retiring in 1987.[22]

Schuyler W. Jackson was born in Eudora in 1904. He grew up in a political family, with his father serving as attorney general for two terms and then being elected to Congress. Schuyler attended Topeka High and received a baccalaureate degree from Washburn. After earning his law degree from Harvard in 1930, he practiced law in Topeka from 1930 to 1939, lecturing part-time in Washburn Law School. Jackson served as supreme court reporter until being appointed dean of Washburn Law School in 1945. Governor George Docking appointed him to the supreme court during the triple switch episode in 1958, and he became the third Democrat to serve on the court.[23]

The Cases

African American students in Kansas were attempting to break down the color bar in public schools before the *Brown* decision. Several sought a writ of mandamus to attend white schools in Johnson County. When the question arose, the court appointed a commission to study the problem and make a report. The group found that "several years ago" the board of education had set up Walker school for black students because of pupil "congestion." Over the years the school had deteriorated and become outdated. Based on the study's recommendation, the board made plans to upgrade Walker to make it "equal" to South Park, the white school. This included remodeling or replacing the Walker building, with its outdoor toilets, and fireproofing it, providing the same programs for music, hot lunches, and other facilities so that by 1949 the two schools would be equal. This was in keeping with the half-century-old *Plessy* case, which required "separate but equal" facilities. Meanwhile, students of color could attend South Park until Walker was brought up to par with South Park.[24]

Following *Brown II*, several African American students sought a writ of mandamus to enroll in a white school in Bonner Springs. The state supreme court noted the recent rejection of "separate but equal" by the US Supreme Court and issued the writ, ordering the school district to "proceed with reasonable diligence" to integrate but to achieve this no later than the fall of 1958. Over the next several years Kansas schools rather rapidly integrated, ending almost a century of segregation in the Sunflower State.[25]

Massive population shifts during the 1930s and world war created great problems with student enrollments and state support of local education systems. Many farmers were forced to abandon their farms during the depression and seek a means of support for their families in California or other beckoning meccas. Thousands more sought employment in the new defense industries springing up in certain Kansas industrial centers during the Great War. These massive shifts in population left the resilient old red schoolhouse with enrollments of three or four or five students, a relic of the nostalgic past. The legislature was forced to recognize realities and to pass a school consolidation program in 1945, with amendments following two years later.

This law created a reorganization committee in each county to make recommendations for consolidations, with a state committee to supervise the plans. This was "unquestionably" an "agency" that the men who "molded the constitution" never contemplated, the high court noted when the law was challenged. The Kansas Constitution required "a uniform system of schools," the justices observed, and this area was not a subject of "local legislation." The justices found the law to be unconstitutional because it failed to establish a standard to guide the local committees. The court admitted that it was "cognizant of the complicated consequences" of its opinion, because probably there was "nothing more essential to the welfare of the state than the continued maintenance of adequate schools." The legislature was forced to enact amendments to meet the court's objections.[26]

Thinly populated Meade County reorganized its system by dissolving three schools and merging them into the Meade city system. The affected school boards sought to enjoin this action on the basis of the unconstitutionality of the law. In designing its amendments, the legislature had stipulated that plans made before February 1947 would be "operative and effective and validated," and the district court sustained the proposal on this basis. Upon appeal, the supreme court supported the district court decision.[27]

The county superintendents of Lyon and Coffey Counties planned to merge rural districts in both jurisdictions to create a joint rural high school district. State superintendent of schools Adel Throckmorton approved the merger, but the opposition sought to enjoin this action because the district would cross county lines. Speaking for the court, Justice Wertz noted that legislative intent called for separate methods for the formation of districts lying wholly in one county and another for joint districts lying in two or more jurisdictions. If there was a conflict between a statute dealing with a subject generally and one treating specifically with a phase of it, he noted, "the specific legislation controls." On this basis, the court sustained Throckmorton's proposal.[28]

The Lost Springs school district presented a different situation. This district lay in Marion County, two miles south of the Dickinson County line. Prior to 1951 twenty-eight of the Lost Springs sections of land were in Marion and seven were in Dickinson. Both Lost Springs and Herington had accredited high schools, but when voters in the seven sections decided to join the nearby Herington district, this left them with double taxation by the two counties. The court held it to be a legitimate decision to join Herington under the reorganization program, and Marion County could not tax them.[29]

Tenure for teachers, although unpopular with school patrons, was becoming a common demand, especially in districts where there was a strong concentration of members of the American Federation of Teachers (AFT) or Kansas Teachers Education Association (KTEA). The legislature recognized this movement and attempted to supervise it with the Tenure of Instructors Act of 1949. In April 1955 a tenured Wichita high school teacher was advised of her incompetency and neglect of duties, according to the guidelines of the Tenure Act. Following this warning, that August she received a contract with the automatic four-hundred-dollar raise provided by the salary schedule. In October the superintendent notified her of her termination for incompetency. Agreeably to the process, she was given a hearing, and she hired an attorney to represent her. This hearing in December resulted in her dismissal, and she was denied a rehearing. Precedents held that courts would not intervene in this process unless the school acted "arbitrarily, unlawfully, oppressively, or was guilty of bad faith or gross abuse of its discretion." Her only basis for appeal was the contention that the process of her dismissal denied her a thirty-day notice and an immediate hearing. The supreme court concluded that, "when construed as a whole," the board had acted "in substantial compliance" with the Tenure Act.[30]

The Daughters of the American Revolution (DAR) of Kansas established a trust fund of $1,250 for scholarships at Washburn College in memory of Victor Blakely, who died in World War I. A full tuition scholarship was given annually to a student until 1941, when the trust was transferred to the new Washburn Municipal University. The scholarship was continued but without the express consent of the DAR. The chapter brought suit for return of the $1,250 and interest earned on it since 1941, arguing that Washburn College had ceased to exist. Washburn University officials responded that the trust was a gift, they had invested the money wisely over the years, and no mention was made about revoking it. The court concluded that both Washburn and the DAR were incorporated institutions. If Washburn was exceeding its corporate powers, the state could raise this question, but not the DAR. It could revoke the gift only when the agreement included this proviso.[31]

The state regents of higher education issued self-liquidating bonds to build dormitories on the campus of Kansas State College of Agriculture and Applied Sciences. With this type of bond, the state did not incur indebtedness, and the bondholders had to rely on revenue from the dorms to pay the self-liquidating plan. When this program was challenged, the supreme court held that the state legislature had authority to determine if the dorms were necessary. These "nonprofit" dorms were "public buildings" and not internal improvements, which the state was prohibited by the constitution from building. Therefore, the 1947 law permitting construction of the dorms through this process was legal. This concept and ruling were of great value in assisting colleges in efforts to accommodate the post–World War II boom in student enrollments.[32]

Finally, the College of Agriculture was assisted by another ruling on its land grants. The act of 1862 authorized Congress to establish land-grant colleges through granting federal lands up to ninety thousand acres for each school. The law stipulated that the funds from the sale of these lands must "remain undiminished," and in Kansas the money had to be deposited in the College Permanent Fund to comply with this. Four thousand of these acres in Kansas lay in Morton County, not very valuable agrarian real estate, and they remained unsold. The picture changed during World War II when oil and gas deposits were discovered in southwestern Kansas. The state legislature in 1943 permitted the regents of higher education to lease oil and gas rights on these lands, by which they acquired $342,012.80 in lease rights. This sum did not include future royalties. The regents wanted to use these funds for building dormitories, and this policy came before the court because of the requirement to deposit any such funds in the College Permanent Fund. The justices ruled that the regents could use both the lease and royalty funds for dorms because the money was not from sale of the grant lands and thus did not come under the requirement of depositing the funds in the permanent fund.[33]

Racial discrimination helped promote the passage of the Taft-Hartley

Act in 1947. Railroad laborers were regulated and protected under separate legislation, the Railway Labor Act of 1934. Workers in the Santa Fe Railroad workshops in Argentine organized a union under the auspices of the Mediation Board provided by that act in November 1943, the Brotherhood of Railroad Carmen. This was to be the collective bargaining agent for blacks and whites. In January 1944 bargaining agent Mott L. Fox held a meeting to organize separate white and black unions, with the latter "under the jurisdiction and represented by" the former. Six blacks representing the one hundred African American workers there brought suit against this arrangement on the basis that they could not attend the white meetings or vote in them, and this discrimination was based on color, not ability. Justice Hoch wrote for the court, asserting that this was a denial of equal rights protected by the Fourteenth Amendment as well as the Kansas Constitution, which forbids exclusion on the basis of race or color. This practice, he asserted, "affects the economic welfare of all employees involved," and the discrimination was "arbitrary and unlawful."[34]

A. J. Porth had been a member of the Wichita Carpenters and Joiners Union since 1941. He was elected business agent and financial secretary in 1943 but was ousted from his membership in 1947 "unlawfully and maliciously," according to him. In 1946 he was a delegate to the AFL national convention, where he angered the national officers with reference to certain "controversial and offensive resolutions." National officials pressured his local to revoke his membership from the union as a punishment. Porth sued for $50,000 in punitive damages and $50,000 for actual damages. He agreed that he had failed to seek remedy for his grievance through the union appeals procedures but that he had written an appeal to the national office. The nation president "refused" it and sent notice that he must follow union rules and appeal through the established process. He decided this took too long and filed suit instead. The supreme court affirmed the lower court decision that he must first follow the union procedures, then resort to the civil courts for redress.[35]

During the 1950s a Senate investigating committee explored illegal activities of the Teamsters Union and its president, Jimmy Hoffa. When the Teamsters called a strike in Wichita, this brought union scrutiny close to home to Kansans. This fifty-day strike involved Rex Bullough, president of two taxi companies, who fought the Teamsters' recruiting activities on the grounds that his cabbies were independent drivers who declined to be organized. Fire and paint bombings of his taxis soon followed, and the use of stench bombs was particularly effective because they left a smell that patrons found obnoxious and, the company discovered, was especially difficult to remove. The violence was finally settled when a newly formed company union enlisted most of the independent cabbies and defeated the Teamsters. Meanwhile, with the help of the legal branch of Kansas government, an unusual investigation was undertaken.[36]

Paul Kitch was appointed special county attorney to head the investigation, aptly called an "inquisition," which was like a grand jury except that it was limited to the one issue of violence in the current strike and did not follow the usual procedural rules. Hearings were held before District Judge Howard C. Kline, who offered immunity to three of the Teamsters organizers for their testimony but denied them counsel, and they refused to testify. He sentenced two of them to one year in prison for contempt of court. Former governor Payne Ratner represented the men in their appeal to the supreme court.

Ratner agreed that while the "inquisition" might be legal because the legislature specifically authorized it, including the power of subpoena, the hearings were conducted in an illegal manner. They violated the Fifth Amendment protection of testifying against oneself and the Sixth Amendment of right to counsel, Ratner asserted, while the state denied this, as it was not a criminal proceeding, and those amendments would not apply. The supreme court agreed with the state's argument and denied the writ of habeas corpus because witnesses could be compelled to testify to the "inquisition."[37]

The Teamsters used a secondary boycott to force an asphalt paving company to agree to collective bargaining. The company had gross annual work worth $200,000, it did no work for the state or cities, and it bought all of its materials in Kansas. Secondary picketing was especially effective for the Teamsters because it put pressure on companies not involved in the dispute that were subcontractors. In addition, the Hoisting Engineers also picketed in sympathy for the strike. The paving company made no attempt to resolve the issue through Taft-Hartley procedures, yet the law prohibited secondary boycotts. The district judge issued an injunction, and the union appealed to the supreme court. The justices agreed that the secondary boycott was illegal, but this fell under the jurisdiction of Taft-Hartley, or the National Labor Relations Board (NLRB). The justices noted that even the plaintiff alleged that it was an unfair practice involving interstate commerce. This automatically made it the exclusive jurisdiction of the NLRB.[38]

In a similar case, the Amalgamated Meat Cutters filed suit in 1955 in Shawnee County against the Ohse Meat Company because it was trying to organize its workers, and the company refused to negotiate. The union stationed pickets at the rear of the business, so district Judge Beryl Johnson issued an injunction against this peaceful activity. The NLRB became involved and warned Ohse officials that a representation election could not be held before the injunction expired. The union argued that this quarrel came under NLRB jurisdiction, so the district court could not act, which the supreme court accepted. This subject, the justices agreed, "is very much alive." The district court had exceeded its jurisdiction, and the employer had no resort except to the NLRB.[39]

A case was brought to the supreme court in 1957 testing the Factory Act of 1949. W. W. Sutton had a sawmill in Pleasanton. Employee H. F. Bortzfield was operating an edger that lacked a belt-shifting device. He was removing a scrap of wood when his clothing was caught, and the saw injured him. The court sustained the lower court's decision that the company violated the Factory Act by failing to provide safeguards, Sutton was negligent, and the case was remanded accordingly.[40]

Several employees had reason to apply for workmen's compensation during this period. Employees at the Boeing assembly plant in Wichita, during lulls in their work, wagered on lifting "a large roll of wax paper" above their heads. Byron Neal, an "expediter" who kept production moving in his department, was doing this when the roll slipped and injured his neck. The assistant foreman for the area had warned the men to desist before someone got hurt. Writing for the court, Justice Hoch held that the unemployment compensation law covered only personal injuries "by accident arising out of and in the course of employment." Neal was not covered, because his injury arose out of "horseplay," and there was no negligence on the part of the employer.[41]

Mark McMillen was employed by the city of Salina in its water works division. He was not feeling well, and his doctor diagnosed a bad cold. While reading water meters, he slipped on mud and fell into a manhole. Even though McMillen was spitting blood, his doctor diagnosed his problem as a worsening cold. He died suddenly three weeks later. His death was caused by an aneurysm in his aorta when he fell. The supreme court sustained his widow's claim for compensation because his work accident aggravated an existing physical condition that led to his death.[42]

George Abbott, a minor, worked for a grain elevator during harvest season. His brother Lester was the manager, and George lived with him during the summer vacation. They quit work and went home to supper one evening. The weather looked threatening, and Lester told George to go back to the elevator and close two hatches in the roof of a storage bin. On his way across town, George talked a friend into giving him a ride. They hit an unlighted parked truck, and George lost partial use of his right arm. George never claimed employer negligence, but the court majority ruled that the compensation program did not include injuries sustained while he was on his way to his employment. Justices Parker, Harvey, and Smith dissented, because the law contemplated round-the-clock service in such cases, and he was on his way to work to carry out special orders of his boss when the injury occurred. To the dissenters, he should have compensation.[43]

Fifteen-year-old Robert worked for his parents delivering ice in the summer. Three days before he was to quit and return to school as a sophomore, he fell out of the truck when the seat moved under him, and a wheel ran over him. The parents had failed to get a work permit for him required by a 1935 law that applied to youngsters under age sixteen. Otherwise, they had treated Robert just as another employee, paying him a regular salary and withholding taxes. They paid his subsequent medical bills. When the issue came to the supreme court as a compensation case, the question was raised whether this type of work was "dangerous," as stipulated by the work permit law. The justices found no collusion between parents and child but said the parents were negligent in not obtaining a work permit anyway. This failure, however, did not relieve an employer or the insurance carrier of blame, so the insurer was liable.[44]

The state experimented with an approach different from that previously used in building highways following World War II. After studying the operation of the Pennsylvania turnpike, the legislature created the Kansas Turnpike Authority (KTA) in 1953. It authorized the KTA to issue revenue bonds, construct a turnpike charging tolls, and maintain the highway until the bonds were retired. If public funding was unavailable, the KTA could raise private funding for construction as long as the program was self-liquidating. The state instituted a quo warranto suit to prevent the KTA from initiating new roads. It was proposed that the KTA represented an unconstitutional delegation of legislative power, there was no standard for location of roads, the KTA had uncontrolled discretion as to employees, there was no limit on the revenue bonds, and the State Highway Commission was the agency authorized to make preliminary studies. The supreme court responded that the legislature did not have the technical expertise to decide and implement these necessary features, so it created the KTA to perform them. Questions also were raised as to creating a debt without a decision from the voters, which constituted a delegation of executive powers, appropriations would extend for periods longer than the constitutional restriction of two years, the bonds and the revenue the pike would produce were exempt from state taxation, and the law gave the KTA power to take property under eminent domain. The supreme court answered all these issues in favor of the KTA on the basis of the police power. Surveys were made and construction began to connect the large cities of Kansas City, Lawrence, Topeka, Emporia, and Wichita to the Oklahoma line. For some time the turnpike ended in an Oklahoma wheat field until the Sooner State built Interstate 35 to connect with the pike.[45]

During the construction process, surveyors entered the land of the Anderson Cattle Company and "annoyed and excited" 352 head of cattle that were being intensively fed a concentrated feed. When the company sued, the KTA argued that it was an agency of the state and possessed legal immunity. The court responded that it was not immune to this type of action. The 1953 law required compensation to be paid for all private property "damaged or destroyed." While the act was constitutional, it contained no waiver of immunity from tort liability.[46]

The "sport of kings" was replaced by dogs and automobiles in the Sunflower State in the twentieth century. Car racing, which appealed primarily to the male working class, can be a dangerous sport to spectators. An eighteen-year-old attended the races in Cejay Stadium in Sedgwick County. A car on a curve threw a piece of debris into the stands, and it injured his right eye. The mother sued for her son, but the justices could find no specific acts of the racing company that caused negligence, so the court rejected their suit.[47]

Clarence Cessna lived in a house on the fairgrounds, where he cared for the horses kept for racing on the nearby track. The same track also was used occasionally for car races, and a wheel came off during a race and struck the barn forcefully. Despite warnings, the racing company refused to provide banking on the track, which would ruin it for the horses, or provide a stout fence for protection. Soon a wheel again came flying off a car, struck Cessna 227 feet away, and broke his leg. He sued for $55,136.75. The racing association demurred but was overruled. Cessna argued that the cars should be inspected before races. The supreme court opinion observed that "sic utere tuo ut alienum non laedas" is one of the oldest legal maxims, and it had lost none of its potency "with the coming of new agencies of destruction and injury." Translated, the phrase means "you should use your property in a manner as to not damage that of another." The lower court's finding for Cessna was affirmed.[48]

An act of 1949 again outlawed lotteries but made an exception of pari-mutuel betting. Al Bissing owned land outside Wichita and conducted dog races as the Wichita Greyhound Club. Admission was 50 cents, and pari-mutuel betting was available. When challenged as a lottery, the club responded that this was not "chance." Bettors had to apply certain skills to pick the winner based on breeding, training, and handling of the dogs. Some states had this same system, while others banned all types of lotteries. The supreme court held that this system constituted a lottery and thus was illegal.[49]

Prohibition declined as a legal question after the legalization of malt beverages, but it still continued as an issue. The city of Newton seized Hannegan's auto because he violated a city ordinance in using it to transport illegal liquor. He then purchased the car at public auction for $1,600 and brought suit in district court to regain title to the car because the city had no authority to seize it, and he won his case. On appeal, Justice Wedell spoke for the court when he held that the state legislature "did not expressly confer power upon municipalities" to enact such ordinance. The law of 1919 on abatement, the court averred, "should be instituted and maintained by the state and not by a city" and then concluded that the auto was the property of the state because of its illegal use.[50]

The legislature changed the law on the sale of "nonintoxicating" beverages in 1949 by providing that those who held a license to sell cereal malt beverages could not possess over two quarts of alcoholic liquor in unstamped bottles. Eva's Tavern in Olathe at the junction of Highways 7 and 10 included a filling station, cabins, and a drink and dance hall. There was a kitchen in back and access to stairs leading to her sleeping quarters upstairs. Eva kept alcoholic beverages upstairs in her quarters and also in a closet under the steps. She was raided by officials with a search warrant, and they found two cases of whiskey and seven bottles of gin without Kansas tax stamps. The prosecution, however, had only a pint of whiskey and a bottle of gin (size unknown) that it offered as exhibits. The supreme court ruled that the other bottles in her possession might not have the proper stamps, but this could not be determined from the evidence. The possession of other liquor, however, violated the intent of the law to prohibit retailers of malt beverages from possessing intoxicating liquor anywhere on their public premises.[51]

Pete Larkin operated a beer tavern. When business declined he agreed to organize a club "for social and recreational benefit," known as the Merchants Club in Wyandotte County. He leased the first floor and basement of his building to the club, and he managed it for a weekly salary. He received articles of incorporation from the secretary of state in 1951. If members desired liquor, they purchased a coupon book. Larkin would buy and keep a supply of beer and liquor, and members could draw from this supply by coupons. The charter specified that "no liquor or beer shall be sold, bartered or given away at any time." The club was closed to the public, and entrance was gained by an electric door device that required a membership card to open. The Kansas Liquor Control Act of 1949 was designed to abolish the "open saloon" and prohibit illegal traffic in liquor. This idea of Larkin's was not new, as the supreme court had dealt with this concept as early as 1889. In this case, the supreme court said, the "membership club" was merely a "subterfuge" to evade the law.[52]

Adah Chambers, a Wichita licensee for retail sale of malt beverages, was ill and hospitalized from April until late July 1950. Adah gave her husband authority over her store, and as she continued on medication until September, he remained as the operator during this period. He entertained an out-of- town guest one day, an undercover agent testified, and fourteen cases of alcoholic liquor were loaded into an Oklahoma licensed automobile in his garage. The undercover agent of the Federal Alcohol Tax Unit testified that Barnett, an Oklahoma bootlegger, and Arthur Chambers drove into his double garage and transferred the liquor to Barnett's car. The agent stopped Barnett at Lincoln and Broadway and arrested him. Although the serial numbers on the cases were removed, the agent could identify the liquor by their brand names. This violated Kansas law, but there was no evidence that licensee Adah knew of the transaction. By the time the case reached the supreme court, the question had become moot, as her license had been revoked. The State Alcoholic Beverage Control Board of Review, by vote of two members with one absent, had decided to revoke. Justice Price, for the court, ruled that the licensee was responsible for what happened in her retail business, even though she was in the hospital or on medication. Otherwise, the whole system of enforcement would break down.[53]

Air travel was increasing in popularity for both passengers and pilots. Oscar Moritz operated the Moritz Flying Service and, among other students, taught veterans under the GI Bill of Rights of 1944. William L. Rivers, a licensed pilot, had an agreement with Moritz that they would use each other's planes when necessary. Rivers was flying below five hundred feet and, during an improper turn, collided with a Moritz student, Roland Scott, killing both men. Moritz sued the Rivers estate for the value of his airplane of $7,040. The Civil Aviation Board (CAB), a national agency, investigated and reported that Rivers was at fault. Moritz won in lower court based on this report. Upon appeal, the plaintiff argued that during the trial no evidence was entered "to the effect that this report was competent evidence," and the CAB investigation in this action was "hearsay and inadmissible." The supreme court, though, decided against the Rivers estate, as CAB was a responsible federal agency.[54]

William Boyle was a passenger in Franklin Hayden's airplane when he flew in a negligent manner in a low and dangerous altitude near Goodland, crashed, and killed the passengers. There were three men flying in the four-passenger Bellanca. The supreme court admitted that there were few precedents for handling this case, but the rules applying to passengers in automobiles were applicable to airplanes. An aircraft is different from a car, and, in this case, the plane had dual controls. According to the seating upon takeoff, Hayden was in control, and his negligence caused the crash. Widow Dorothy Boyle had standing to sue.[55]

The rate of divorce declined during the Great Depression because of legal costs but accelerated significantly during and after World War II. Much of this increase stemmed from war marriages, when the decision was often made on the spur of the moment to marry before the fellow left for war, and many made the marriage decision while serving overseas. Many war brides or their husbands later decided a mistake had been made during the glamour of serving in a foreign country or the glitz of marrying a foreigner. At war's end the divorce rate in America rose to an incredible rate of one in three and would climb to a fifty-fifty ratio at the end of the century. Legal reasons for divorce increased, and no-fault divorce arose in California in 1970 and spread rapidly across the nation. The by-product of divorce, child custody, also grew, with the tendency of awarding custody in the best interests of the child. Social Rehabilitation Services (SRS) and other agencies stood ready to intervene to help make decisions on custody cases.[56]

In 1918 Mary Watts willed part of her estate to Gardner Watts and part to be put in a trust for his son, Corwin. She was not directly related to Corwin but had raised him from infancy. Corwin married Nellie in 1924, and they had a daughter, Imogene, born in 1926. In 1931 a district court ordered the trustee to pay $50 monthly to Nellie to support her and her daughter and $50 monthly for Corwin. Nellie filed for divorce in 1944 on the grounds that she and Corwin had not lived together since 1932. She was given a lump-sum settlement of $6,500 from the trust, and Imogene received $50 monthly. Nellie asked the trustee to pay for the alimony and her attorney fees from the trust, and Corwin agreed. The trustee refused, however, because the fund was receiving $90.07 from oil royalties, and he believed it was irresponsible to assume that the royalty fees would continue at this rate. At the same time, Corwin asked for an increase to $100 monthly, and the trustee again declined because Corwin was "a spendthrift." The supreme court supported the trustee because the justices decided he had not abused "his discretion" in handling the trust for twenty-six years.[57]

Husband Brita divorced wife Christie in California in 1937. He received custody of the two children, ages four and two and a half, and Christie received visitation rights. Brita moved about in his work but remarried and again divorced. During this unhappy interim he left the children with Christie, who filed twice for modification of the divorce settlement and finally won custody because she could show she could give them a proper home and they would no longer be moved about. She lived with her parents in a six-room house, but she had leased another and was repairing it for their future home. In 1941 Brita moved to Wichita and brought the two girls with him without Christie's consent, and she filed a suit in Kansas to retrieve them. The judge asked the oldest girl where she wanted to live, and she responded in California and Kansas. The supreme court supported the judge's decision to award custody to Christie because the California court had done so, but the justices were distressed over the issue of "deep, human, personal values" involved in the case.[58]

Henry and Nannie Troemper were married in Kansas in 1910 and moved immediately to Nebraska. They had no children and made no adoptions. She filed for divorce in 1941, and in the settlement they agreed she would get fifty shares of stock in the Lancaster Company that they jointly owned and the household goods. He would pay $50 monthly for six months in alimony. Twenty-three days later he died intestate. In 1944 she filed suit as his heir for 240 acres of land in Wabaunsee County that was left in the estate because under Nebraska law the divorce was not finalized for six months, and she was legally his wife when he died. The supreme court decided that although Kansas law held divorces to be effective immediately, she was under the jurisdiction of Nebraska law, so she was legally his heir and entitled to the land in Kansas.[59]

Juanita and J. Blood Coates received a divorce in 1944. She was given custody of Jr. (twelve) and George (nine), and Blood received visitation rights and paid $80 monthly for child support. In 1945 she asked the court for permission to move to California and grant J. Blood a month each summer with the children. He asked for custody, and when she won, he appealed because she was moving the children out of state. Chief Justice Harvey and the court decided for Juanita and cited the precedents of Brewer's decision in *In re Buller* (28 Kan. 781) to move the children to England and *White v. White* (160 Kan. 32) to move the children to California to live.[60]

Pat and Ada McCarty married in 1937, and she filed for a divorce in 1941 on the grounds of extreme cruelty. He presented no defense, and she received custody of Sharon and $30 monthly for child support. Both remarried in 1942, and Ada and her husband, Bronte, were drowned in a capsized boat in Cody, Wyoming. Pat and his wife asserted that they were "fit and proper" persons and should get custody of Sharon. Ada's parents had kept the girl while Mr. and Mrs. Bronte vacationed in Cody. W. R. and Ada Urquhart of Ottawa sued for her custody. The court concluded that because Patrick had been divorced by two wives for "extreme cruelty" and W.R. was a Baptist minister, it would be best for Sharon to live with her grandparents.[61]

That same year the court had to make another hard decision on custody. Harold received a divorce from Anna May in 1945, and she received custody of the children, Dorothy and Kent. Anna died the next year, and Harold sued for custody. Following Anna's death, her sister Sylvia Tenpenny of Perry kept the children, and she also filed for custody. Both children wanted to remain in the Perry home. Dorothy was now seventeen and could do the housework for Sylvia. The court decided that Harold was a "fit" person and gave him custody of Kent, and he had to pay $30 monthly for Dorothy's support. With Justice Thiele speaking for the court, the justices concluded that it would be best for the children to remain together, so they gave Harold custody over Dorothy also.[62]

Charles and J. M. Marshall were married during World War II. She was an Australian citizen, they lived there for some time during the war, and Leon Charles was born there. After they moved to Kansas, Charles sued for divorce on the grounds that she committed adultery, frequented bars, and was periodically drunk. He claimed she was not a "fit" person for custody of Leon. She countersued for custody. The legislature knew the public loved lurid details of love affairs, so it enacted a law in 1935 that said that the charge of adultery was sufficient for divorce without details unless the defendant wanted them. The supreme court held for Charles, observing that the law was constitutional, and there was no need for eye witnesses on the adultery charge.[63]

In 1948 the Douglas County district court granted Mildred Ramey a divorce from Alvin on grounds of extreme cruelty and gave her custody of Charles (seven) and Carol (six). Seven months later she married "a colored man by the name of McCoy." The maternal grandparents, who also lived in Lawrence, instituted suit in juvenile court "within a few days" to receive custody of the children, who were "dependent and neglected." The following year the district court gave the father custody and permitted him to take them to his home in Portland, Oregon. Both the grandparents and the mother appealed this decision. It was established Kansas law that persons having an interest in custody cases could appear and present evidence. The supreme court, again in a difficult situation, failed to find either the father or the mother "unfit" persons and used the legal precedent that if a parent was able to care for the children, that parent should have them. The justices awarded custody to the father in Portland.[64]

Leon Jackson divorced Vena in 1955, and she received custody of Stephen (seven), James (five), and Dianne (three). Leon was given visitation custody for the months of June and July and was required to pay $50 monthly for each child's support. He paid her attorney fees of $300, and the court retained jurisdiction over the case. Leon became upset over Vena's raising the children in the Jehovah's Witnesses faith but in his quest to secure custody used the reasons that she was emotionally unstable and a poor housekeeper and cook and that she nagged the children. He charged also that this religion upset the children emotionally and would eventually make them unpatriotic citizens. His evidence was replete with Jehovah's Witnesses materials, and he won the judge's support. The lower court had abused judicial discretion in making the judgment for the father. This decision, the court noted, violated her rights in the First and Fourteenth Amendments and the Kansas Bill of Rights, Section VII, guaranteeing freedom of religion. The lower court judgment was set aside because the justices found too much evidence of religious pressure.[65]

David Whitcomb was nine and his brother Dennis was twelve. Both lived with the family in Wichita. Ira Huffington became interested in their mother, Barbara, knowing that she was a married woman. He embarked on a campaign "intentionally, maliciously, and systematically" to impose himself on her, with the result that she fell in love and divorced her husband, Norman. Consequently, David suffered "mental pain and emotional anguish" over his mother's actions and the loss of the protection of "a secure home." He sued for $25,000 actual and $10,000 punitive damages. The question of a minor child bringing such an action had never previously been before the supreme court. Justice Price delivered the opinion that family rights consist of those among themselves and those against the world. Common sense tells one that the boy did not bring this suit by himself, and if the court upheld this action, a one-year-old could do the same. If the court affirmed, then "we would be opening up a new field of litigation" between child and parent or grandparent, so David's suit was denied.[66]

Doctor of osteopathy V. A. Leopold performed acts of surgery and prescribed drugs for a fee, so the Finney County attorney brought action to enjoin him from practicing medicine. Leopold resisted this action on the grounds that the county attorney was not a party with an interest in the issue. He demurred, was overruled, and appealed. The State Board of Medical Examiners controlled the licensing of doctors. Leopold insisted before the supreme court that the action was brought not to protect the public health but "to protect the professional interests of the members of the medical profession." The justices disagreed with this, holding that the county attorney had the power and authority to bring this action in the name of the state. The law establishing the board was rooted in the police power, and county attorneys were agents of the state.[67]

The chiropractic unit of the State Board of Medical Examiners licensed Forest Leland as a chiropractor on 14 October 1950, and he established his practice in Protection, Comanche County. A year later he was accused of acts of moral turpitude. He denied the charges at his hearing, so an investigation was ordered. Leland received no notification of the new hearing, and no stenographic record was made of it. The board found him guilty and revoked his license. The justices decided that this was a decision involving a criminal act, and such a decision must be determined by a jury in a criminal action by the state. The board had exceeded its powers with this decision.[68]

Wichita city health officials held Pauline and Fern Welch on suspicion of having a venereal disease but actually charged them with vagrancy and drunkenness and jailed them without benefit of counsel, bail, or speedy trial. The health officer noted that they had been frequenting "places bearing a poor reputation." During the twenty-two days they were incarcerated without charges they refused to allow the county health officer to examine them. The supreme court decided that the health officer had the power to force the examination but had failed to do so, and the court thus ordered a writ of habeas corpus to free the pair.[69]

Goldie Harris sued dentist G. E. Exon for failure to use "proper care or skill" when removing a bridge from her lower left jaw. His saw slipped and cut nerves, tendons, and tissues in her lip. She had a licensed dentist in Wichita testify that Exon should have used a Liberty depressor to protect her lower lip during the procedure, although the "expert" allowed that there were several other methods, and each dentist "did his own thing." Speaking for the high court, Justice Thiele noted that a dentist is a dental surgeon, and the rules applying to surgeons apply to dentists. A dentist does not need to use "extraordinary skill and care" but the "ordinarily possessed and exercised." The trial court held for the defendant, and the supreme court could find no error in that litigation.[70]

Annis Brown, a quack, performed an abortion on Joy M. Joy. The procedure was not necessary to save her life, and it had not been prescribed by a medical doctor. It proved to be a careless operation that lacerated the placenta, and Joy died. The plaintiff sued for $5,000 and costs. Joy had consented to the procedure, so the defendant cited *Herman v. Julian* (117 Kan. 733) as the sole Kansas precedent that held no recovery if the woman consented. Kansas law required a first-degree manslaughter charge if it involved a willful killing of "any unborn quick child" and resulted in the death of the mother. The justices decided that "no person may lawfully and validly consent" to an act "to destroy human life." Joy's next of kin could "maintain an action for her wrongful death."[71]

Robert Ross and his wife were riding in their truck two miles north of Lawrence when they approached a railroad crossing with two tracks and stopped. Robert was driving on that misty, foggy evening, and he listened for a whistle. When he heard nothing he proceeded across, and a train struck his side of the truck, killing him. Wife Beulah brought suit, and the supreme court held that her action "could not be had" because of the doctrine of "last clear chance." This rule held that a person could avoid an accident by exercising "reasonable care in the final moments" before it happened. The engineer could assume that the truck would remain in place after it stopped. Trains have the right-of-way over road travelers, and there is a presumption that persons approaching a railroad track will use caution before crossing.[72]

The Kansas Corporation Commission (KCC) denied the Rock Island line permission to discontinue service of two passenger trains between Bellville and Goodland. This was the only available connection in this area to Colorado. In urging its discontinuance, the company included claims in 1953 of $50,000 as part of its operating costs and also the costs in "dieselizing" its motive power. Otherwise, the railroad was making money, and it appealed the decision to the supreme court. The justices responded that they did not try these cases but sat as an appellate court to decide on the judgment of the trial court. The justices added that the KCC decision did not deny the line property without due process of law.[73]

In 1928 the Ancient Order of United Workers (AOUW), an insurance company, asked and received permission to build a facility on the grounds of the state tuberculosis sanitarium near Norton. This would provide current medical facilities for the order's members who suffered from the terrible disease. The AOUW never paid taxes on the building because it was located on state land, but if it had, it would have contributed $100,000 by 1951. The state also paid for food, utilities, nursing, and medical costs for the patients on the basis that it would have incurred these costs if they were housed in the sanitarium. In 1951 the AOUW sought to sell the building to the state for $110,000, and the State Board of Administration agreed to the purchase. The issue became a political as well as a legal one because Republican National Committee chairman C. Wesley Roberts was to receive a commission of $11,000 for "facilitating" the sale. A legislative committee revealed the details of the story, and this incurred the wrath of President Dwight Eisenhower, who was trying to "clean up the mess in Washington" and did not appreciate this scandal in his party. Other party officials also objected.[74]

It also became a legal issue, as the state took the question to the court to decide the status of the building. The state argued that it owned the building because it stood on state land, and buildings belonged to the owner of the property on which they stand; therefore, the AOUW had nothing to sell. The issue came to the supreme court on the question of the authority of the State Board of Administration to permit the AOUW to build the structure because there was nothing in the agreement that the AOUW would hold title to it. In rather curious reasoning, the court held that the arrangement was constitutional until it was proven otherwise.[75]

A quo warranto proceeding challenging the Urban Renewal Act of 1956 came before the court that same year. The purpose of the law was to eliminate slums and blighted areas injurious to the health, safety, morals, and welfare in cities with populations over seventy-five thousand. Was it permissible for the legislature to enact a general law on this and delegate the specifics to be determined later? The court reported that it would not strike down a law unless it violated the constitution "beyond reasonable doubt." This law did not constitute an express infringement, and it was for a public use and purpose and therefore unconstitutional.[76]

The state brought action for a writ of mandamus to compel the secretary of state to publish a proposed amendment to the constitution. It provided that no person could be elected a county sheriff or treasurer for more than two consecutive terms. But the concurrent resolution providing for it was not published in the house journal. Both sides on the issue agreed that the resolution published in the statutes was not the one the legislature accepted because the printed resolution omitted the phrase "this resolution shall take effect and be in force from and after its publication in the statute books." The court denied the writ because neither the secretary of state nor the supreme court knew which proposal should be published. The secretary of state was correct in refusing to publish.[77]

In the August 1948 primary John Hardwick and Jim Kelly were the

Democratic nominees for office, and there was no Republican candidate. But the spot for the Republican on the ballot was blank with a square so that voters could write in a nominee and make a cross. Kelly won the Democratic vote, but enough Republicans wrote in Hardwick's name to give him the victory. The supreme court ruled that a person cannot be the nominee of more than one party, but this does not preclude his write-in votes. The county clerk had to print Hardwick's name on the ballot as a candidate in the general election.[78]

Jack Conrad was riding a horse east of Parsons on Highway 160 when Wayne Dillinger drove his truck into the horse and seriously injured the animal. It was a dark night, and the horse carried no light. The court ruled that the legislature defined "vehicle" so broadly as to include automobiles, animal-drawn vehicles, and every other device upon or by which people or property was transported. Therefore, the laws on traffic included ridden animals while "using highways for the purpose of travel," and Conrad was negligent in not having a lighted horse at night.[79]

A case came before the court in 1947 that presaged the *Miranda* decision of 1966. James Wiley, age seventeen, broke into and entered a grocery store in Pittsburg with another boy one night, and they stole $25.25 in goods. He was sentenced to the Kansas State Industrial Reformatory for a term not to exceed ten years. He sued for a writ of habeas corpus from Lansing prison on the grounds that he had been denied counsel and did not waive his right to one. In addition, he was held incommunicado from 2 through 7 November before sentencing. The Crawford County attorney denied his being abused or threatened in order to persuade him to plead guilty. He also was held in Lansing state prison instead of the reformatory. The reason for the latter complaint was that he was initially paroled in 1943, convicted of another burglary in Missouri, and sentenced to that state's penitentiary. He was then given conditional release and delivered to the Kansas prison. The Kansas warden insisted that the law required James specifically to request a lawyer. Justice Burch, speaking for the supreme court, observed that a sixteen-year-old boy "is not possessed of sufficient comprehension of his constitutional rights" in a felony case to waive them. The court was "cognizant of the great amount of juvenile delinquency which appears to be prevalent in the country at the present time." The boy could not have his complete freedom but must be returned to Crawford County for appropriate proceedings in a new trial. This was basically the ruling that the US Supreme Court would hand down two decades later.[80]

The cases the court heard during these Cold War years demonstrated that it was on the cutting edge of many of the legal issues of the period. The tenor of the justices' opinions give no indication that the change in selecting them for their positions had altered during this period. During the next decade and a half the justices would continue to decide questions based on new developments in state and national legal trends.

8. Modernizing the Law

The Political Scene

The US Supreme Court under Earl Warren seemed determined to reform America by itself, but when Warren Burger followed as chief justice of the United States, the Court retreated to its former conservative stance. The growth of the civil rights movement, the questions of obscenity, reapportionment, and criminal law made revolutionary changes in the legal system. Under the more temperate Burger regime, equal protection remained an important guideline, and the issue of sex and gender arose without prompting by the Supreme Court. The Kansas Supreme Court generally acquiesced in this national leadership, even though justices often found the guidance disagreeable. Racial issues, the rights of women and children, the rights of criminal defendants, and privacy readily come to mind.

The Kansas judiciary underwent a number of significant changes in the period following approval of the new system for selecting justices. Many voters were not pleased with the system of electing judges, and others were particularly upset over following this process for district judges. The electorate found it difficult "to make reasoned choices" without the assurances of party labels as a guide. As a result, the procedure was again changed in 1973 to allow districts that chose to do so to follow the old system of selecting partisan district judges. Those districts that elected to keep the commission could do so, and, as a result, seventeen judicial districts decided to retain the new process, and fourteen used the partisan election plan. The question of nominating judges would surface again in 2000, when the Kansas Justice Commission reopened the issue.[1]

The Kansas Bar Association (KBA) established a committee to investigate and to respond to a number of issues regarding public opinion. Following its recommendations, over the years justices began dressing more formally in robes. An improved retirement plan was put in place in 1953 for financial security for older judges. For administrative purposes this plan was merged in 1975 with the Kansas Public Employees Retirement System.[2]

There was a "dramatic increase" in district court cases, both civil and criminal, from 1950 to 1960. As a result, in 1959 the KBA endorsed a revision of the code of civil procedure and rules of evidence, which had scarcely been changed since the 1860s. In order to familiarize judges with the new procedures, Chief Justice Jay Parker called a conference at the University of Kansas in 1963. This successful meeting resulted in annual conferences summoned by later chief justices for the same purpose. The Judicial Department Reform Act was passed in 1965 to supervise district courts and to establish a judicial administrator for the lower courts.[3]

Following the adoption of a new Article III of the state constitution, the legislature implemented this amendment by abolishing the justice of the peace system, adopting a new procedure for municipal (police) courts, and authorizing the Judicial Study Advisory Committee to analyze the Kansas judicial system and make recommendations for improvement. From this advisory body came the creation of an intermediate court of appeals and the establishment of legislative guidelines for the nonpartisan selection of district judges. This change was followed two years later by the supreme court revising its rules governing appeals to it and to the newly created court of appeals.[4]

In 1965 publication began of *Pattern Instructions for Kansas*, which provided uniform procedures for criminal jury instructions in 1971 with additional supplements. Chief Justice Harold Fatzer established an advisory committee in 1973 to advise the state's bench and bar on "matters affecting the administration of justice, including the area of judicial discipline." The committee was composed of Judge Frederick Woleslagel, chairman, Justice John Fontron, state senator Harold Herd (later on the supreme court), and a number of district judges and attorneys. The commission made studies in the sensitive area of judicial conduct, particularly the new code adopted by the American Bar Association (ABA) in 1972. Out of this emerged the Kansas Commission on Judicial Qualifications and the seven canons of judicial conduct and discipline of the House of Delegates of the ABA. The commission was authorized to "admonish" judges in their conduct, but all other disciplinary action was reserved to the supreme court.[5]

The commission was authorized to investigate complaints concerning violations of the canons, make written reports, and recommend discipline to the supreme court. The canons it used were adopted by the House of Delegates of the American Bar Association and included disqualification where a judge might be unable to maintain impartiality, declining to use the judicial office to promote self-interest, refraining from extralegal activity that might question impartiality, and other mundane observations that meet commonsense requirements but that some judges might occasionally betray.[6]

A citizens' conference on Kansas courts was held 11–13 September 1974 in Manhattan, resulting in a committee of nonlawyers to lobby the legislature to implement judicial reform. The group also sought to inform the voting public on the system of nominating district judges. Two years later an office for a single court for appellate cases was created, effectively reducing appellate expenses and court delay.[7]

Future chief justice David Prager delivered a significant address to open this citizens' conference that detailed a number of problem areas in the judicial system. He noted that "justice, like religion and democracy, is not automatic." Reform, therefore, could not come only from lawyers and judges but requires the participation of concerned citizens.[8]

A decade earlier, he reminded his audience, the Joint Committee for the Effective Administration of Justice established a valuable credo. It included the points that effective justice must be fairly administrated without delay by competent judges, and it must operate within a modern judicial system and under "simple and efficient rules of procedure that facilitate the discovery of truth." In 1964 a similar citizens' conference recommended a unified court system that led to the rewriting of Article III of the state constitution. The question now to be addressed was how to effectuate truly a unified court system that had never materialized.[9]

Prager called attention to the fact that there were currently 105 probate courts, 105 juvenile courts, 93 county courts, 8 city courts, 5 magistrate courts, and 1 court of common pleas in addition to numerous municipal or police courts (no one knew how many because they did not file reports). In 1973 there were 37,000 cases in district courts, 190,000 cases in courts of countywide jurisdiction, and 200,000 cases in police courts, most of which involved traffic violations. Thus, the total number of cases meant that many Kansans had been involved in some sort of court proceeding. In addition, the cases affected profoundly "the offenders appearing before them from a crime prevention point of view."[10]

This litigious society, Justice Prager further observed, must provide every litigant with at least "one fair trial and one fair appeal." In Kansas there existed only one "true appellate court," the supreme court. During the previous year, this court with seven justices received 592 notices of appeal filed in the district courts. Prager lamented that in this situation "there is not sufficient judicial manpower" to handle this caseload. As a result, the average time from notice of appeal to decision in criminal cases was 19 months. The time lapse for civil cases was 15.9 months. A study of the current delays in litigation concluded that this was "probably excessive and unacceptable." The national advisory committee recommended that "a criminal case should be ready for initial action within 30 days after the imposition of sentence. Cases containing only insubstantial issues should be finally disposed of within 60 days after imposition of sentence. Cases presenting substantial issues should be finally disposed of within 90 days after imposition of sentence." The lapse in criminal appeals in Kansas does not contrast well with this national study.[11]

As a result of this backlog, the Judiciary Study Advisory Committee recommended the creation of a seven-man court of appeals. Panels of three of these judges could utilize district court facilities. This would mean that appeals could be handled within sixty to ninety days of filing. The committee recommended that these judges, and district judges, be selected by the governor from a list of two or three nominees developed by a commission of lawyers and nonlawyers. The judges would then run for election at the end of each four-year term on their record.[12]

Prager presented a chart showing that twenty-five district judges "now sitting," or 40 percent of the sixty-three, were appointed by the governor "with no confirmation of any kind by anyone." Eleven, or 17 percent, were selected in uncontested elections, so that a minority of the judges "were originally selected by choice of the people." The proposed change would alter this by making the district judges run on their record after an initial term of at least one year.[13]

Disparity of workloads contributed to the problem of backloads. In 1968 the legislature phased out five rural district courts and created five new urban ones. Less than a decade later the legislature unified all trial courts in a county into a single district court, except for municipal courts. All judges, except for the latter, became district court judges. State districts were then grouped into departments, with a supreme court justice assigned to oversee their work.[14]

There was an apparent lack of judges in the system to handle the appellate docket. This situation was relieved partially by the appointment of two commissioners to help write opinions and thus increase the supreme court's opinion-writing capacity by over 28 percent. Although these commissioners did not participate in the process of deciding cases, they carried the same burden of writing opinions as the justices. Beyond these cases, in 1973 this resulted in each justice writing 33.1 opinions annually. Each justice, of course, has responsibilities and commitments beyond this load, and it is inaccurate to state that each judge wrote one-seventh of the total opinions or that each wrote 33.1 percent of the annual caseload, but the Kansas justices carried 26 percent more cases than the national median.[15]

A computerized routine of logging the age and location of pending cases with rankings of fewest pending civil cases over two years old was established to address this problem of delay. The system is accompanied

Fig. 8. Kansas Supreme Court Justices (1978). Back row: Richard Winn Holmes, Kay McFarland, and Robert H. Miller. Front row: David Prager, Alex M. Fromme, Alfred G. Schroeder, and Perry L. Owsley. Image from the Kansas State Historical Society.

by a quarterly report labeled "the hit parade" that lists the twenty-five oldest cases pending in the state. This proved to be an effective prod, as judges, "like other people," want to be number one, and this stimulates them to keep their docket up-to-date. There remained, of course, inadequate compensation for Kansas judges. In recent years they have ranked in the fortieth range, resulting in making it more difficult to attract the more qualified candidates for judges. Kansas won a ten-thousand-dollar prize in 1987 from the National Foundation for Improvement of Justice for its delay reduction program.[16]

The legislature of 1976 provided, as one authority expressed it, "the most revolutionary change in the judicial system of Kansas in the history of the state." It reviewed the judicial configuration of district courts and recommended changes, especially in the northwestern and south-central areas of the state. By 1980 the number of districts had been reduced to twenty-nine, comprised of from one to seven counties each, with seventy judges. In addition, a second court of appeals was created in 1977. This court was authorized to sit en banc or in panels in various locations to give added impetus to expediting the appellate process.[17]

In planning for the future it was noted that Kansas, like other Great Plains states, should experience a steady increase in population. Expectations of continued growth in manufacturing should lessen the pattern of emigration from the state. The economy was stable, but the position of agriculture relative to manufacturing should witness the latter playing an ever increasing role. "Growth and change of this kind produces additional litigation," it was noted.[18]

The Judges

John F. Fontron was born on 2 December 1903 in McPherson. He attended the public schools there until 1915, when the family moved to Hutchinson, and he attended that high school. He enrolled in the University of Kansas in 1921 and in its law school, receiving a degree there in 1926. He practiced in Hutchinson, served in World War II, then returned to his practice. Fontron served as a county attorney and as district judge before Governor John Anderson appointed him to the supreme court in 1964. He worked on judicial rules and served on the Advisory Rules Committee of the Kansas Judicial Council. He had, according to one colleague, "a philosophy based on logic and equity and written in a style that is all his own and one that holds the reader's attention." The justice was well known for creating Fontronisms, such as "cancer of injustice" and "shoe of prejudice."[19]

Robert H. Kaul was born on a farm east of Holton on 28 August 1911 and graduated from the University of Kansas Law School. He practiced in Holton, then moved to Wamego, serving as county attorney of Pottawatomie County before joining the navy in World War II. After the war he was appointed as one of the youngest judges on the district court level. He was elected and reelected to the position from 1950 to 1964. He was appointed to the supreme court and served until he retired in 1977. While on the court he wrote 335 opinions.[20]

Earl E. O'Connor was born on a farm on 6 October 1922 near Paoli. He walked three-quarters of a mile daily to a one-room school for his elementary education. After he enrolled at the University of Kansas, his reserve unit was called up in World War II, and he did not complete his degree until 1947, earning his law degree there three years later. He practiced law in Johnson County and served as county attorney. Soon he was elected district judge, and he was believed to be the youngest to serve in that position. In 1965, when he was forty-two, Governor William Avery appointed him to the supreme court, the second such appointment under the new selection system. In 1971 he was sworn in as US district judge for Kansas. He was described as "stern, reserved, and strictly business" as a judge, but he was known for his humor and kindness when he took off his robe.[21]

Alex M. Fromme was born in Hoxie on 11 March 1915. He was educated in the public schools and enrolled in the six-year curriculum of undergraduate and law courses at Washburn College, graduating in 1939. While there he played on the Washburn football team. He returned to Hoxie to practice and served as county attorney. Governor Bill Avery appointed him to the supreme court in 1966. His opinions were "meticulously researched, well-organized, and obviously the result of vigorous penetrating thought." He taught legal ethics at Washburn and authored over 550 opinions while on the court.[22]

Perry L. Owsley was born in Pittsburg on 3 April 1915. He was educated in the public schools and attended Pittsburg State University, where he played basketball. After receiving his law degree from Washburn he practiced law in Pittsburg. He also served as city, county, and district judge and chaired the Kansas State Board of Tax Appeals. Governor Robert Docking appointed him to the supreme court in 1971. He was an experienced trial lawyer and while on the court demonstrated his wit, humor, and use of satire.[23]

David Prager was born on 30 October 1918 in Fort Scott. He was educated in the public schools and enrolled in Fort Scott Junior College. After attending the University of Kansas and being elected to Phi Beta Kappa, he enrolled in the law school there, being selected for the Order of the Coif, one of the school's highest honors. He was admitted to the bar in 1942, just in time to serve in the navy in the Pacific theater of World War II. He returned from the war to practice in Topeka. He served as district judge and lectured at Washburn Law School, teaching future justices McFarland, Lockett, and Allegrucci. Democratic governor Robert Docking appointed him to the supreme court in 1971. He was reelected to that position in 1974, 1980, and 1986. The following year he replaced Alfred Schroeder as chief justice and wrote a total of 637 opinions.[24]

The Cases

Tom Lee of Riley County was arrested in Manhattan on a driving while intoxicated (DWI) charge. He was requested to take a blood test but refused. His driver's license was suspended, and he appealed. The law of 1959 required submitting to a chemical test for breath, blood, urine, and saliva to check the level of alcohol content. If the driver was over the limit, his or her license would be suspended for no more than ninety days. The law stipulated that the test would be administered at the direction of the arresting officer because there were few other areas of the state with the necessary equipment to handle it. Lee argued that he was diabetic and should have had a choice over the blood test, contending that drawing blood is "brutal and offensive." His claim of diabetes was unsubstantiated, and the court refused to accept his claim. This test did not violate the Fifth Amendment on self-incrimination because it gave him a choice and a hearing. He did not retrieve his license for three months.[25]

The Private Club Act of 1965 divided drinking clubs into Class A, under which members did not buy drinks but their membership provided them from the fee without profit for the manager, and Class B, which provided that clubs could provide drinks to be "lawfully consumed." The Tri-State Hotel sought to enjoin enforcement of the law on the grounds that it violated Sections I and II of the state constitution and the Fourteenth Amendment, which provided equal protection for citizens. It was an unreasonable and arbitrary use of the state police power, the hotel insisted, it was "vague, uncertain, and ambiguous," and it penalized differently for acts by one class of citizens. The court cited precedents for upholding the Twenty-First Amendment, so the federal question was removed from this case. In addition, a club with a "liquor pool" is the same as the "open saloon" that Prohibition sought to destroy. The court cited *State v. Larkin*, which struck down the "Merchants Club." The legislature was trying to bring the "key" or "private" club under control by distinguishing between a public club that anyone could join by paying the membership fee and the private, or "key," club. The court held that the law had uniform operation throughout the state and was constitutional because the legislature was competent to determine the places where alcoholic beverages could be sold.[26]

The US Supreme Court, in *Miranda v. Arizona* (384 U.S. 436), ruled in 1966 that a person must be informed of his or her rights against self-incrimination in clear and unequivocal terms, that he or she could remain silent, and that he or she had the right to counsel at the time of arrest. Any coerced confession could not be used in court. This protection against self-incrimination dates back to English common law in the seventeenth century and became part of the Fifth Amendment in the Bill of Rights. After passage of the Fourteenth Amendment in 1868, the US Supreme Court began reviewing increasing numbers of criminal procedures cases. Then in 1897 the court decided *Braun v. United States* and held that any confession that was not voluntary was not admissible in court. A major change came during the Roaring Twenties, when the Court applied most of the Bill of Rights to the states through the Fourteenth Amendment's due process clause.

In the following decade the police methods of Nazi Germany repulsed the American people. They then began to learn that the police in many American cities were using similar tactics to extract confessions from their prisoners. After the passage of the *Miranda* ruling a hue and cry arose across the nation that the courts were coddling criminals and that Moscow was the instigator of the directive, but law officers soon discovered that they could extract confessions without using the "third degree," and the *Miranda* proceedings became an accepted part of police procedures.[27]

The Kansas court accepted this concept when Harold Faidley was convicted of DWI after Patrolman Lee Schuler stopped him on Highway 81 north of Wichita. Schuler saw Faidley's pickup weaving, and when Schuler stopped Faidley he could smell alcohol. Faidley showed Schuler his driver's license, then failed the heel-to-toe walking test. Schuler put him in the patrol car and read him his rights. Faidley argued that he had been denied his right against self-incrimination. The justices informed him that his rights were not violated because he was not forced to testify orally, just take the sobriety test. His right to counsel began in the police station, not out on the highway.[28]

The Taft-Hartley Act of 1947 listed unfair labor practices that unions could no longer pursue, such as requiring a company to conduct a closed shop, where workers had to belong to a union before they could get a job in their craft. Section 14b of the law permitted states to restrict their activities even further by banning compulsory union membership altogether. Nineteen agricultural states proceeded to take advantage of this by enacting so-called right-to-work laws, or what unions described as "right to wreck." In the election of 1958, Kansas voters approved an amendment to add this guarantee to the state constitution. The amendment was not a necessity but involved a campaign to take advantage of the great antiunion sentiment in the state for political purposes. Union security provisions "were already prohibited by statute unless a majority of the employees to be governed authorized it by secret ballot."[29]

Floyd Higgins soon brought suit to determine if this change extended to prohibiting the agency shop, a procedure that required workers to pay initiation and membership fees but not claim membership in the union, in other words, to carry their weight in the costs of achieving job benefits without actually becoming a union member. Kansans held two conflicting views on this: a worker should not have to belong to an union he or she does not support, but there should be no free "riders," or people who enjoy the fruits of organizing and would not support the union that fought and sacrificed to achieve these rights. The supreme court justices came down on the side of employers by sustaining the right-to-work forces, holding that the agency shop is a form of compulsion and thus illegal.[30]

In 1959 Harry Clark reached age sixty-five and retired from Skelly Oil Company. The company gave him a pension of $124.50 monthly, and he could draw retirement from OASI (Social Security) of $116 if he did not earn over $100 monthly. He applied for unemployment benefits but was rejected because he was unavailable for work and had not tried to find employment. The justices decided that he failed to comply with the requirements of unemployment compensation because he was on a pension, and the law was intended to protect people against "involuntary unemployment."[31]

Employees of the LMW Company, an iron and steel foundry, belonged to the United Steelworkers union. A strike was called, and pickets were placed. The company, determined to crush the union, demanded that workers sign an unconditional return to work agreement. Most of the strikers signed, but fourteen did not and sought unemployment benefits. The Employment Security Board denied their applications. The district court supported their claims, but the supreme court held that the lower court had erred. The justices rejected the strikers' claim because they had to demonstrate that their unemployment was not due to a strike but to "conditions beyond [their] control."[32]

Marian Seibert sought compensation for an unusual reason. Husband Donald worked in Topeka for Hoch Dairy, which delivered milk house to house daily. Donald was known as a "good worker" who supervised other employees. His wife was the bookkeeper, and she helped him after hours to load the trucks for his early-morning run. His employer visited the dairy weekly and called Donald to check on the business almost daily. Just before Donald's death, his wife left him. On the evening before his death, he had returned to work after dinner as usual to load trucks. The next morning he was discovered at work with a .22 caliber slug in his left temple. His younger brother, James, was in love with Donald's wife, but she did not return his affections. James knew Donald carried a .22 pistol in his glove compartment. James saw

Donald beat his wife just before she left him. He offered to drive her to Wisconsin, but she had to remain in Emporia, where he worked, until Saturday, when he could arrange the trip. The Topeka police never found the killer. His widow sought compensation. Workmen's compensation required that the death or injury must come "in the course of" or "arise out of" a worker's employment. She lost her appeal and took it to the supreme court. The justices agreed with the denial, noting that she failed to show that Donald's murder arose "in the course of" his employment.[33]

The Fair Labor Standards Act of 1938, commonly called the wages and hours law, was tested by school custodians, although the measure exempted state employees. The program was amended in 1961 to cover state workers and any who worked in any way that was affected by interstate commerce. The custodians worked in a school district located in Butler and Sedgwick Counties. They could work as many as sixty hours weekly, but they turned in their hours to the superintendent, who determined their overtime. The workers argued that many materials for their work, including what went into the construction of the buildings, involved them in interstate commerce. The trial court held against them, and the supreme court sustained that judgment because in any given week the employees were not producing goods involved in interstate commerce.[34]

Two hot mix asphalt plants in Kansas City, Kansas, were under union contract. Inland Industries was owned by the same person who owned Inland Hauling, which received 52 percent of its income by servicing the sister company. The Teamsters staged a secondary picket on Inland Industries to compel Inland Hauling to accept union organizing, and the trial court granted an injunction against this activity. The company appealed on the basis that Inland Hauling was a "neutral" company. The supreme court decided that placing these pickets was an "unfair labor practice," and this fell under the jurisdiction of the National Labor Relations Board. Kansas courts held no jurisdiction over this violation of federal law.[35]

An appellant filed for articles of incorporation as the Kansas Hometown Stamp Company to issue bonus stamps with purchases that were redeemable in cash or merchandise. The secretary of state refused the application because these stamps were made illegal under the act of 1958. The trial court cited *State v. Wilson* (101 Kan. 789), which held the issuance of these stamps to constitute criminal action. The old law of 1917 allowed merchants to redeem the stamps for cash or use in purchasing goods from them at market price. The supreme court decided that the law of 1958 was constitutional because the redemption in a merchant's goods was legal. The law would not allow the redemption in the merchandise of others because it would foster the belief that the stamps were free merely by patronizing the store that awarded them.[36]

A Michigan corporation that owned radio station KTSB in Topeka notified the attorney general of its intent to begin broadcasting a program called *Dialing for Dollars*. In this game the white pages of a telephone directory were cut into sections of twenty names. A slip would be drawn at random, and a person listed on that slip would be called. If the call was answered, the person had to respond with the code number, the word "up" or "down," the correct number from one to ten, and the amount of the jackpot. If the person had been listening, he or she would know these answers. If the person knew or guessed all the answers, he hit the jackpot; if incorrect, she received a consolation prize of $1. The plan, of course, was to increase the number of listeners. The attorney general responded that this was a lottery, but the trial court rejected this interpretation. The supreme court had previously held that a lottery must involve a consideration, a prize, and a chance, and it cited as a precedent the early "Bank Night," which attracted patrons to movies. The new criminal code of 1 July 1970 declared that radio and television programs requiring answering or calling in on the telephone would not fall within the category of a lottery, which was banned by the constitution. In the case of this show, no consideration was being paid, so it was not a lottery in the sense of the term at the time the constitution was adopted.[37]

Criminal charges were filed in Iola as a result of a gambling raid on the five slot machines of the local American Legion. This was a Class

A club that was exempt from federal income taxes, and the money the machines raised went to the club treasurer. In 1971 the legislature enacted the "bingo" exemption, which made "bingo and games of comparable characteristics" exemptions from gambling. In *State v. Myers* (152 Kan. 52) the supreme court decided that slot machines came under the category of gambling. Did the bingo exemption change this? The supreme court held the bingo law to be unconstitutional because the legislature sought to eliminate the "consideration" by saying that the restriction should not include money paid to play the game. This was gambling, and a tax-exempt organization was not immune. Justice Kaul concurred but insisted that the majority should not consider a constitutional question like this, because neither side in the litigation raised this issue. Constitutionality, he insisted, should not arise unless injected by one of the litigants.[38]

Jack Smith stole some valuable copper in Coffeyville and was convicted of two counts of larceny. He had two previous felony convictions, so he came under the habitual criminal act of 1949 and thus received twenty-five years on each count to run concurrently. He confessed to the crimes and was represented by competent counsel, but at his trial he showed that his brother, a junk dealer, gave him the copper. On appeal the supreme court decided that his rights were not "prejudicially affected" and affirmed his convictions.[39]

In November 1958 Lowell Andrews, a student at the University of Kansas, came home to Wyandotte County for the Thanksgiving break. He used his Ruger .22 and semiautomatic .22 rifle to shoot his father, mother, and sister in the living room. His wounded father tried to escape, and Andrews finished him off in the kitchen with his rifle. He dismantled the guns, returned to Lawrence, and threw them in the Kaw River. The police arrested him and advised him of his constitutional rights, and he made a statement, pleading insanity. A commission found him competent to stand trial, but Sir Joseph Satten of the Menninger Clinic found him insane in regard to ability to commit murder. His Baptist minister testified at his trial that he committed the murders in order to inherit the family estate. In instructing the jury, the judge told the jurors to keep in mind the question of his knowing right from wrong. Dr. Satten and Andrews's minister said he expressed no regrets over his actions. The supreme court decided that the trial court had applied the M'Naghten rule correctly when the jury concluded that Andrews understood that what he had done was wrong. Society must hold him responsible because he knew the actions were wrong when he committed them.[40]

On 15 November 1959 Herbert Clutter, his wife, Bonnie Mae, his sixteen-year-old daughter, Nancy Mae, and his son, Kenyon, were brutally murdered in the family farm home in western Kansas, near Holcomb. Two weeks later Richard Hickok and Perry Smith were arrested in Las Vegas, Nevada, for the murders. While Hickok was serving a sentence in the penitentiary, a fellow convict told him that Clutter was a wealthy farmer who kept his money at home in a safe. After his release from prison Hickok planned the crime with Smith, expecting to tie the family up, rob the safe, and leave no witnesses. They left Holcomb with nylon rope, adhesive tape, and rubber gloves. They committed the crime and fled to Mexico, where they sold Clutter's car. There was a tremendous amount of publicity about the crime, and they appealed their conviction because they could not receive a fair trial in Finney County. The justices, however, could find no errors in the trial court procedures and affirmed the judgment. Novelist Truman Capote immediately traveled to Holcomb, studied the evidence, did interviews, and wrote *In Cold Blood*, a pioneering work of the nonfiction novel genre.[41]

It fell to Justice Prager to write the opinion for the last case of hanging for murder in Kansas. James Latham and George York were arrested in Tooele County, Utah, and the Kansas Bureau of Investigation (KBI) returned the pair to Wallace County to stand trial for the murder of Otto Ziegler on 9 June 1961. Ziegler was a road master for the Union Pacific railroad and was found shot with four bullets, three of them in the head, and all fatal. Latham and York were held without bail, and the trial judge was careful in insisting on proper procedures. They received court-appointed counsel and a change of venue from Sharon Springs to Russell County, and the court examined 275 potential jurors, qualifying 60 of them. The jury found the two men guilty of deliberate and premeditated murder. The supreme court, Prager wrote, "is neither authorized nor does it have any disposition to debate the question of the wisdom of capital punishment." The criminal code empowers the jury to prescribe life imprisonment or death, depending on the circumstances of the crime, and this does not deny equal protection of the law. The justices also denied the refusal of the legislature to reapportion itself to have any bearing on the case.[42]

A grocery store in Lansing was burglarized of one hundred cartons of cigarettes. A witness testified that he saw the accused and two others in a car that evening parked in front of the store. The next morning a radio news bulletin described a 1950 blue-over-yellow Oldsmobile with "three colored occupants" who were wanted for questioning. The Kansas City police found the car with two men in it and the cigarettes in the back seat. When the owner returned, he and the two men gave conflicting stories about the cigarettes. The two men were taken to the police station, and three of the cartons were removed for evidence. There was no search warrant, but the court later upheld this action on the basis of "probable cause." When asked about his employment, the accused said he had worked for a service station for eight of the last ten years. The police had an FBI report of his being in prison from 1959 to 1961, so in an attempt to prove that he had committed a false statement about his employment, they asked him if he had ever been convicted of a felony. The defense objected and asked for a mistrial. The judge sustained the objection but denied a mistrial and told the jury to disregard that question. Upon appeal, the justices decided that the question was asked in good faith. They could discover no prejudice, and the judgment was affirmed.[43]

Lonnie Lee Jackson was charged with statutory rape of a nine-year-old, found guilty, and sentenced to prison for three to fifteen years. Ten years later he appealed his conviction in the district court of Wyandotte County. He learned just enough law in the prison library to write an appeal in pencil to vacate his sentence. Counsel was appointed for him, and he based his action on the fact that the court reporter died before he could transcribe the case, and no transcript was available. Jackson alleged in his appeal that errors *might* have occurred, such as the suppression of the testimony of Dr. A. P. Taliaferro of the Kansas City Police Department that no attempted rape had occurred. The supreme court ruled that Jackson failed to raise the double jeopardy issue "in a timely manner" and affirmed the lower court's decision.[44]

Kenneth Roth was convicted of robbery and murder in the first degree of a Yellow Cab driver in Topeka. He received ten to twenty years for robbery and life for murder, the terms to run concurrently. The jury that convicted him was drawn from the assessment roll of property owners, and ten prospective jurors were excluded because of their opposition to the death penalty. The principal witnesses against Roth were two codefendants, who testified that the three were together. Roth appealed because he was denied a representative and impartial jury. The supreme court held that the jury could not be challenged except on the grounds of serious misconduct or palpable disregard for the law. The exclusion of jurors opposed to capital punishment cannot be presumed to result in an unrepresentative jury. Also, Roth was not denied due process of law when the jury determined guilt and then passed on the sentence of death or life in prison. The jury must decide this on the basis of the creditability of witnesses. The justices found no errors in the trial court procedures, and the sentence was affirmed.[45]

Randall and Sharon Hill and murder victim Robert Koon, aka Bob Evans, arrived at the Red Slipper Club in Wichita one evening at the same time. An argument soon broke out over money to pay for drinks and over Hill's putative wife. Randall Hill pulled a gun on Evans, forced him into his car, and drove to the Hill residence. Hill then shot Evans because of his alleged relations with Sharon and buried his body under a stock tank on a farm. Hill was found guilty of robbery, kidnapping, and killing in the first degree, while Sharon pleaded the Fifth Amendment. Several witnesses were afraid to testify at the trial because of Hill's well-known temper, and they feared retaliation. The supreme court could find no errors in the trial court procedure and upheld Hill's conviction.[46]

James Sharp was charged in Sedgwick County with first-degree kidnapping and rape. Sharon Lucille Louthan, her husband, and their baby were driving one night when their car stalled. Sharp came by and took the husband to a friend's house for help. He returned, told Sharon the friend's car would not start, and offered take her to her husband and friend. Instead, he took her to a country road and raped her. She identified him in court as the perpetrator. Sharp pleaded guilty on the advice of appointed counsel. The Kansas kidnapping law required infliction of bodily harm. He claimed double jeopardy because he was accused of both kidnapping and rape. The supreme court held his plea to be voluntary. Justice Fontron dissented because the case should be remanded with instructions for an evidentiary hearing to see if Sharp's pleas of guilty and acceptance of sentence were coerced by his counsel.[47]

In 1958 James English was charged with the forcible rape of a Wichita housewife. He pleaded guilty and was sent to Larned State Hospital for observation and treatment. The superintendent was ordered to report to the court, and he said that English was competent to stand trial because he knew what he was doing. He had "a sociopathic personality disturbance," and there was no cure for this, only confinement. The court committed him to Larned. English dismissed his counsel, withdrew his guilty plea, and rejected the request of habeas corpus. Instead, he argued that the court had erred because he failed to receive equal protection and due process of law. The state responded that the action was a commitment to Larned, not a referral. The supreme court upheld the trial court, observing that English had received due process because the Kansas law on commitment for sex offenders was "humanitarian in purpose and a proper and valid exercise of the state's police power." This was not a cruel and unusual punishment, and the court confirmed his conviction.[48]

Albert DeLespine was convicted on two counts of molesting a child under fifteen years of age (the child was thirteen) under the Habitual Criminal Act and received fifteen years on each count to be served concurrently. The girl, her three girlfriends, and the school principal testified at the trial. The girl had gone to Albert's house because two of her friends told her that he always gave them money when they asked. When Albert started molesting her, the friends began kicking and pinching him, and he desisted. The next time she visited, he gave her $5 to go upstairs with him, and again he molested her. Albert testified at his trial that nothing happened. The supreme court ruled that when Albert testified, this permitted the state to cross-examine as to his previous convictions. In addition, it was permissible for a nine-year-old girl to testify after the court established her competency. Judgment was affirmed.[49]

Adelheed Jackson consulted a medical doctor, who told her that she was six to eight weeks pregnant but that there was no evidence that she needed an abortion. She persisted in wanting one, so a friend gave her the telephone number of what she thought was a medical doctor in Wichita, but Raymond Darling turned out to be a former licensed chiropractor. He said that an abortion would cost $400 and told her to take castor oil and pills ("mikren [Phonetically]," according to the case) to loosen the fetus. She also took aspirin and tranquilizers, overdosed, and aborted. This required a D & C (dilation and curettage of the interior of the uterus). Darling was charged with using a metal instrument and electric device to induce an abortion that was not necessary to save Jackson's life. An abortion was legal in Kansas only if it was performed to save the mother's life. An investigator for the State Medical Board testified that Darling was "the doer of the unlawful acts" that led to the board's decision to revoke his license for chiropractic because he also performed illegal abortions. The justices affirmed the lower court's judgment of conviction.[50]

The Garbers were of the Amish faith. LeRoy failed to send his fifteen-year-old girl to the public schools, arguing that this compulsory school attendance violated his religious freedom. Daughter Sharon completed the elementary school in Reno County and enrolled in a Chicago correspondence school. The compulsory school attendance law of 1965 covered children up to age sixteen. The Amish in Reno County had established Harmony School for their children who had completed the eighth grade but were under age sixteen. All classes were in English, except a German reading course. The Kansas law exempted only students with a physical or mental disability. The supreme court held that this act did not infringe on religious liberty, and home schooling did not satisfy the law. Parents' rights are subordinate to the state's police power. The constitutional right to religious freedom guarantees "the absolute right to believe" but "limits the right to act." Without the right to act, though, there is little else left in religious freedom.[51]

The attorney general charged that the Kansas City school board repeatedly violated the Kansas Act against Discrimination. It refused to hire qualified African American teachers for white children; it segregated black elementary supervisors from white ones with separate offices; it had blacks working in black schools and whites working in both black and white schools; it gave sanction to separate teachers' associations and made membership in them compulsory; over objections, it refused to transfer a teacher from one school to another for the sole purpose of integrating or mixing faculties. An antidiscrimination committee found against the school board. Under the wording of the present contracts, the board could assign teachers anywhere. The justices affirmed the lower court decision that the law was intended to bar discrimination, not to integrate the school systems.[52]

John Foote held a medical license in Kansas by virtue of a Pennsylvania endorsement, and he used this to apply for membership as a surgeon at Beloit Community Hospital. The local board refused to accept him, and he sought a writ of mandamus in Mitchell County. After he received it, the hospital board appealed. The lower court sustained the hospital, but the supreme court reversed in *Foote v. Community Hospital* (195 Kan. 385). From 1 October 1964 to 21 September 1965 Foote operated on patients. The hospital board continued to complain, and the state board of health investigated. They found Foote "extremely incompetent" and "guilty of unprofessional conduct." His procedures in eleven cases included the removal of a gall bladder in which he left the cystic duct open, it poured gall into the stomach, he never checked on it, and the patient died. In a case of tubal abortion, he removed the appendix, and a month later the woman was diagnosed with an incomplete abortion. The staff surgeons voted ten to one to remove him. His license was revoked, he appealed, and the supreme court this time decided the that Board of Healing Arts could revoke on the basis of "extreme incompetence."[53]

The defendant appealed a felony conviction of selling lysergic acid diethylamide, or LSD, the drug that Dr. Timothy Leary of Harvard made famous with his experiments in testing its effects personally. Haupt appealed on the grounds of entrapment. The narcotics agent of Sedgwick County and an informant drove to the Nomar Theater parking lot in Wichita. The lower court said the evidence showed that the defendant demonstrated "instant willingness and ability" to complete the sale "as soon as the opportunity to do so was afforded." The supreme court agreed that there was no entrapment involved. In fact, he requested the drug.[54]

The Wyandotte County sheriff had a warrant for the arrest of Carroll Crouch because the office believed he had obtained narcotics through forged prescriptions. Officers went to Lawrence with a search warrant and arrested him. They advised him that they would search the remainder of his apartment, he consented, and they found cannabis, or marijuana, in a closet. Previously, in *State v. Blood* (190 Kan. 812), the court upheld a search after arrest. Crouch argued that in his case the search was exploratory and thus unreasonable. The supreme court determined that the search was conducted for discovering prescription blanks or bottles of narcotics. The record showed no abuse of discretion, and the Fourth Amendment does not prohibit this type of exploratory search.[55]

The court revised the common-law doctrine on marriage and division of property in a divorce proceeding. Noema filed for a divorce in Sedgwick County. Later she and William Burnett were married in Miami, Oklahoma, and lived for a while in Wichita and on his father's farm in Kansas. It was unclear how much time they lived together, but neither contested the fact that they were together after the six-month waiting period. William's father died, and he inherited half of a three-thousand-acre farm. Noema filed for divorce on the grounds of extreme cruelty and gross neglect of duty. William responded that their marriage in Miami was invalid because her Kansas divorce was not yet final. The trial court ruled that the Oklahoma marriage should be annulled and the property should be divided because of their common-law marriage. He appealed, and the supreme court determined that the trial court could not annul the Miami marriage because in an annulment the woman loses all property rights. The lower court should proceed with the decision on divorce and alimony on the basis of a common-law marriage.[56]

The common law was further revised when Charles Jackson left nineteen hundred acres of land in Comanche County to his wife, Josephine. When she died the land was divided into eight hundred acres for their daughter, Beatrice, and the remainder to son Robert, a widower with five children, and then to his heirs. Robert later married Mildred, so when he died, his heirs were Mildred and his five children. In 1961 Mildred brought suit to receive half the farm and Robert's children the remaining half. The children responded that she should only get one-sixth, as she was not the heir of Charles, as was their father. Upon appeal to the supreme court, Justice Parker spoke for his colleagues. The common-law precedent was based on the rule that the spouse cannot inherit over the claims of the bloodline children. The court revised this by announcing that she could claim dower rights, and the lower court was correct in dividing the estate half and half.[57]

Another great change in the common law came with a new rule on adoption. Arthur Scott married Loretta Brinkhoff in Idalia, Colorado. He sailed to Japan to be a teacher, and she soon followed. Son Kenji was born in Japan in 1956. The couple divorced with the agreement that Arthur would pay child support and could visit Kenji. Loretta left Japan with Kenji for America. She married Alvin Zweygardt, and they lived in Kansas. Alvin soon became attached to Kenji and cared for him like a natural son. After they left Japan, Arthur never saw Kenji, although he continued to send cards and gifts to his son while he was teaching in New Jersey. When Alvin petitioned to adopt Kenji, and his mother agreed, Arthur contested it. During this period Arthur withheld his child support to enforce his visitation rights, but he failed to attempt to visit the boy. The case was appealed to the supreme court, and it made a great change in the common-law rights of a father. The justices held that the duty of a parent goes beyond mere child support and approved

Alvin's adoption because a father-son relationship had developed between him and Kenji.[58]

Milton Katz sued for divorce from Frances on the grounds that she was insane. She had been in various institutions over the previous five years and was currently in Osawatomie State Hospital. Kansas law permitted a divorce after five years if the patient was examined by three physicians appointed by the court and they decided the patient was incurable. The divorce was appealed to the supreme court, and the justices observed that "years ago the mentally ill were simply put under custodial care and kept there [but] psychiatry is more experimental these days." The court further noted that the divorce decree did not have to show continuance for five years in the same institution.[59]

Jane Finney filed for divorce from John, and their son Gary was born one day later. She left the boy in the care of her sister and her husband, the Irvings, in Augusta. He lived with them thereafter and he knew them as his parents. The divorce settlement gave the thirteen-year-old boy to his father, and Jane received custody of the other three children, with John paying child support. Each parent later remarried, and custody of son Dwight was given to John. Jane's sister and her husband filed to adopt Gary, and John responded with a motion for custody of his son. The supreme court decided that both parents were unfit for custody, with John having undergone shock treatments for mental illness, and Gary became upset by his father's visits. The justices decided that the Irvings' custody of Gary was in his best interest because his father was "a stranger to him."[60]

During twenty years of marriage, Hazel Sinclair became increasingly devoted to her religion of Jehovah's Witnesses. Robert finally sued for divorce on the grounds that she admitted that, agreeably to her religious beliefs, she would allow their two boys to die if necessary rather than allow them to receive a blood transfusion. She also taught them that the world would end in 1975 and similar Witnesses' doctrines. Robert insisted that she was so obsessed with her religion that she neglected her duties as a wife and mother. He received the divorce and custody of the boys, paying her an alimony of $3,000. She appealed, and the justices cited *Jackson v. Jackson* (181 Kan. 1), which held that religion was no grounds for awarding custody of children. In this case Hazel's beliefs and their results precipitated the divorce. The trial court was in the best position to decide on custody, so that decision was sustained.[61]

During the nineteenth and twentieth centuries with the Industrial Revolution and world wars there was a massive shift in population from rural to urban in Kansas and the nation. This resulted in agrarian states especially in an imbalance in state legislatures, with agrarian interests continuing to dominate. Politicians dislike reapportioning according to the census, as they want to continue to control with the "silent gerrymandering" of population shifts. Change had to come from above, with the US Supreme Court decreeing reapportionment. Many states redrew their district lines to assure some equity for voters, but during the 1950s twelve states had not redistricted in three decades. Reformers sought to bring change on the basis of Article IV of the Constitution, which guarantees a republican form of government.

The Supreme Court had avoided the issue by determining that it would not answer political questions, but in 1960 in *Baker v. Carr* (369 U.S. 186) the High Court held that this issue was justiciable. In June 1964 the justices decided in the case of *Reynolds v. Sims* (377 U.S. 533) that the Alabama system of using both a population and a "federal" plan for the state's two houses violated equal protection. The court rejected this "federal" concept and ordered reapportioning on the basis of "one man, one vote" as nearly as possible. Finally, in *Lucas v. Colorado Assembly* (377 U.S. 713) that same year the court rejected a plan that provided equality in the lower house but a slightly weighted one for agrarians in the upper house. The issue soon came to the Sunflower State.

The Kansas legislature reapportioned itself on the latest census figures of 1963. The lower house was continued at 125 seats divided one for each county and twenty apportioned according to population. The upper chamber would remain at forty seats based on the equal population of 54,125 each. The last reapportioning, which was in 1947, was slightly over the constitutional requirement of acting every five years. This effort was challenged because the legislature later found 8,800 people left out in Leawood, and the bill signed by the governor was not the correct version for reapportioning. The court held this illegal law to be unconstitutional because it violated equal protection. The justices expected the governor to call a special session of the legislature to correct this and recognized that exactness was impossible, but the new apportionment should approximate the "one man, one vote" rule as nearly as possible.[62]

The governor called a special session that apportioned the state into 125 districts with 97 new ones within 6 percent of the mean average. The remaining twenty-eight, except two, were within 9 percent, as close as possible to the requirement of the *Reynolds* decision. The supreme court decided that the legislature did not act capriciously nor arbitrarily but had made a diligent, earnest, and good-faith effort to comply with its previous order to reapportion.[63]

Carl Rupp rented a house with the water supplied by a well to a family. The house sewer ran close to the well, and nine-year-old Vicki fell ill from nephritis, or a harmful bacteria in her kidneys. She sued through her mother, and Rupp responded that adults should know about this danger, and thus the parents were negligent. Justice Jackson said that the defendant had confused the child with her parents. She could not know of the danger, and if she won the case, the money would belong to her, not her parents. He believed the parents' negligence did not relieve Rupp of his responsibilities.[64]

In 1960 voters approved the home rule amendment, and the following year the legislature provided for cities to issue revenue bonds for promoting economic growth through attracting industries for expanded employment. They could use the money to provide buildings, recreation, and manufacturing facilities and to enter into leases. Pittsburg issued bonds of $130,000 to lease a site and buildings for the Trialloy Company to produce textiles. A quo warranto action was brought, and the court held this to be a valid exercise of the legislature's power. Courts, the justices said, were concerned with the power to enact laws, not to judge their wisdom. The court cited cases as early as those assisting railroad construction in the territorial period. Several of the judges "entertain[ed] serious misgivings and doubts as to the wisdom and propriety" of such action, but the law did not violate any constitutional provision.[65]

Ronnie Hill was the assistant manager of Safeway in Emporia. The store sold merchandise on Sunday. This violated the Kansas Sunday closing law, in effect since 1855. The act had its origins in the common law, the supreme court noted, and the justices found it to be so vague that it violated Section x of the state constitution, which requires informing the accused of the cause and nature of the accusation. It also contravened the Fourteenth Amendment by taking property without due process of law. Age, the justices observed, does not validate a law nor rob it of its validity.[66]

The court continued to interpret and apply the homestead law. Harley and Barbara Parr declared bankruptcy in 1960 in Tonganoxie. An insurance company sought judgment on their property for $30,721.36 on the basis that the couple had waived their homestead exemption with the company. The supreme court said that the district court erred when it failed to allow this indemnity agreement. The waiver the couple signed was valid.[67]

The common law on obscenity reaches back to 1663, when Charles II brought suit against Sir Charles Sedley, who, in a drunken condition, exposed his naked body to the multitude (*The King v. Sir Charles Sedley*). Kansas has long attempted to regulate morals. It used its police power to limit access to books and movies and to use of contraceptive devices, with each coming under the close scrutiny of those wishing to protect First Amendment freedoms. Gradually, American legislatures enacted statutes to define this crime. In *Roth v. U.S.* in 1957, the Supreme Court limited the First Amendment to protect speech and writing that had "social significance." In a later movie case, Justice Potter Stewart allowed that he could not define obscenity, but he added his classic observation that "I know it when I see it."[68]

A Kansas law of 1961 attempted to define obscenity. The attorney general had the district judge of Geary County read seven books. He then issued a warrant, and officers seized books at the P-K News Service in Junction City. The law defined printed material as obscene if the "dominant theme" would "appeal" to the "prurient interest" of the average reader in employing "contemporary community standards." This terminology was patterned after the US Supreme Court's definition of obscenity in *Roth v. United States* (354 U.S. 476 [1957]). The state supreme court cited Irvin S. Cobb that "if the depth of the dirt exceeds the breadth of the wit," then the material was obscene; the court also cited the *Roth* case, which decided that "sex and obscenity are not synonymous." These books sold in Junction City were "hard core pornography," and the young soldiers from nearby Fort Riley would find them so. The books had no literary merit and were "trash." Obscenity was not protected by the First Amendment nor by Section XI of the Kansas Constitution. There was no trial by jury because this was a civil case. The problem with this standard, on both the state and national levels, is that "beauty is in the eyes of the beholder," and the justices would now have to do a lot of reading to determine their standards of pornography. *State v. Quantity of Books* was appealed to the US Supreme Court, and the nine justices there "apparently found values which our Kansas judges had overlooked."[69]

County zoning laws on cattle feedlots became an issue as the practice increased with the growth of commercial farming. In *Dell v. Excel Packing* a couple in 1958 chose to live in an area adjoining a feedlot. When they sued the cattle company, the justices "admonished plaintiffs for such a choice" of habitat and denied their suit. In a similar suit two years later in *Carp v. County Commissioners* the court held hog raising to be a part of animal husbandry that a Kansas statute prohibited zoning as a means of control. The legislature responded the following year with a statute that authorized zoning for control of agricultural pursuits in cities but left intact the prohibition of the controls in counties.[70]

The Fields purchased a home one-fourth mile west of Emporia in 1957. At that time a cattle company operated one-half mile north of them, and the Santa Fe had two cattle barns there. The Fields occasionally caught a whiff of polluted air, but it was not particularly obnoxious. Then in 1959 the Blue Stem Company bought forty acres adjacent to their home for expansion of its feedlot. This placed the Fields adjacent to the Santa Fe and Cattlemen's feedlot, resulting in as many as fifteen thousand cattle and twelve thousand sheep being fed in their vicinity. They brought suit, and a jury awarded them $4,500 in damages against Cattlemen's and $15,000 against Blue Stem. The Fields argued that the Lyon County zoning ordinance forbade these feedlots in residential districts, and the companies appealed. The question presented to the supreme court was to determine if these feedlots were industrial or agrarian in nature. The justices reversed the abatement order for the purpose of holding a hearing on this issue. If the feedlots were agricultural, then the county zoning laws would not be valid.[71]

A cattle company owned 359.16 acres south of Topeka on the west side of Highway 75. The Kansas Turnpike Authority needed some land there for the South Topeka Interchange. A court-appointed committee allowed $69,406.14 as a fair price. The company thought this was insufficient and appealed the amount. The district court jury allowed $60,848 and decided that this taking did not damage the remainder of the highway frontage. The company appealed to the supreme court because it was "paid a grossly inadequate compensation for its property taken and allowed nothing for severance damages." Both sides presented witnesses who were expert on land values. The justices found that "nothing approaching prejudicial error" had occurred at the jury trial and affirmed the judgment.[72]

Three Kansas highway patrolmen operated a speed trap on Highway 81 north of Wichita, with two of them in an airplane, from which they could check speeds and then radio to the third one on the ground, who made the arrests. The two in the plane kept Clarence Cook in sight until an arrest was made. They clocked Cook speeding, he was arrested, his motion to quash was accepted, and the state appealed. The justices admitted that this was an unusual circumstance, but the law "sees inevitability of change and seeks to adapt itself to new conditions." They determined that Cook was "arrested" when the third officer stopped him, and this required him to appear before a judge for a hearing. "The answer," the court noted, "must take into account modern conditions and especially, the mobile nature of our people," and it sustained the state action.[73]

The court continued to hold the homestead law in a special place. Bellport was awarded judgment against the Harders for $2,150.72 on their two promissory notes secured by a mortgage on their real estate. The trial court enjoined the sale of their homestead in LaCrosse, even though Mrs. Harder had left it to go to Colorado to seek employment. The Harders could rent the home while they were away, and the court upheld Mr. Harder later selling it to their daughter. The homestead, the court ruled, "is something toward which the eye of the creditor need never be turned," and the lender never had a lien on their home.[74]

The Turkey Creek water district in Marion and Dickinson Counties developed a control plan in May 1965. This action was under the authority of an act of the legislature that provided for these plans to "inure to the benefit of all the taxable, tangible property" in such districts. The plan would cost voters $97,900 over a ten-year period and would be repaid with a general tax levy covering the entire district. The plan was in accordance with a legislative amendment of 1961 to authorize the US secretary of agriculture to assist these plans financially, and the federal government would supplement the district's money with $1,454,100. The plaintiffs charged that this would violate the state's cash-basis law, and there must be a resolution putting the question to a general vote of the district. The trial court agreed, and the subsequent election approved the plan. The plaintiffs wanted reimbursement of $1,350 for attorney fees, and the trial court agreed. The supreme court ruled that the financing plan did not violate the cash-basis law and approved recovery of the attorney fees.[75]

Augusta suffered a flood on 5 June 1965. An oil company sued Mobil Oil because the company's refinery and storage tanks dumped substances on its property. The plaintiff claimed that when Mobil shut down its refinery, this released oil and acids into the floodwaters. The trial court ruled that this was an "act of God." Upon appeal the supreme court described an act of God as being "an intervening cause which was not foreseeable and the consequences of which could not be prevented." If Mobil released these substances, the floodwaters were not an intervening cause. The trial court had erroneously determined the question on the basis of affidavits of experts. The liability of something caused by nature cannot be placed upon the shoulders of the defendants, and the justices remanded the case for retrial on this basis.[76]

Agricultural surpluses in the 1950s created a financial crisis for American farmers. The Eisenhower administration responded with the Soil Bank plan in 1954, which provided payments to farmers for taking acreage out of production. A farm owner leased a quarter-section of land in Stafford County on a share basis of one-third and two-thirds. In 1960 the two placed the land in the Soil Bank program for ten years and agreed to share the $2,119 annually on an equal basis. When the owner died, her son inherited the land, and he sold it in 1966 to Elsie and W. H. Dudrey. Elburn Thomas, the original lease holder, claimed that the title was deliberately put in Elsie's name so that her husband could be the tenant operator and the payments would go to the couple, leaving Elburn out of the arrangement. The justices decided that this kind of scheme was "frowned on." The Soil Bank officials insisted that these contracts were continuations, and the court concluded that Elburn's rights were recognized when the Dudreys bought the land, so they "intentionally" violated his rights by excluding him from his share of the payment.[77]

In 1967 both the state and Wichita enacted a law requiring protective helmets or headgear for motorcyclists. Upon appeal, the supreme court sustained the requirements on the basis that the machines were comparatively light, and a rider needed to be in control of his or her machine every second. There was considerable difference between a smashed fender and an accident causing serious injury or death. The justices noted that forty-one states had such requirements, and most of their courts had upheld the laws. The issue was a balance between individual rights and benefits to the public welfare. There was no constitutional imbalance here, as the legislature determines what regulations are needed for the public safety. The law was reasonable, applied equally, and related to highway safety.[78]

The Haysville school district adopted a dress code in 1962 that prohibited "extreme hair styles." Controversy continued over the style boys used, so in 1971 a committee of five parents, three teachers, five students, three administrators, and one school board member drew up a new code that stated that student hair could not cover the eyes, and the length for boys could be no longer than the bottom of their dress-shirt collar. A boy challenged this on the basis that it violated his liberty, equal protection of the law, and his free speech because hairstyle is an individual expression. A majority of judges in the federal courts had continued to insist that they would not "enter this tangled thicket of federal constitutional law which has suddenly sprouted and grown." A majority of the Kansas judges bravely entered this "thicket" and noted that school boards govern local schools. This dress code was not unreasonable and violated no rights. Justice Prager dissented by quoting US Supreme Court justice William O. Douglas that a student should be permitted to wear his hair like Yul Brynner (movie actor) or Joe Namath (professional football player) and cited *Tinker v. Des Moines School District* (393 U.S. 405) in 1969 that the state operates school districts, but they should not become "enclaves of totalitarianism." Justice Schroeder agreed with this dissent.[79]

The court entertained a case in 1973 involving an issue that "in days of yore, seemingly did not disturb the good people of this state." The defendant was in the business of raising and fighting gamecocks in Johnson County. The attorney general obtained a declaratory judgment against this enterprise on the basis that it violated the cruelty to animals statute. The justices delved into a history of the activity from ancient times to that of Washington, Jefferson, and Hamilton being devotees of the "sport." Kansas law forbade cockfighting on Sundays, but in 1970 the legislature lifted the ban on Sunday cockfighting, card playing, and horse racing. The court noted that it "could assume that those three forms of entertainment now are lawful on any day of the week." Experts from Kansas State University and Oklahoma State University testified that chickens are birds, and so cockfighting involved no cruelty to animals. The justices added, however, that citizens still could not gamble on the outcome of fights.[80]

A case that tested the state's "no fault" insurance law resulted in altering the "traditional tort liability reparation." The statute required every motor vehicle owner to purchase liability insurance of not less than $15,000 bodily, not less than $30,000 for the death of two passengers each, and $5,000 for property damage. The trial court held the law to be unconstitutional, and the case was appealed. The supreme court decided that operating a vehicle was a privilege, not a right, and the requirement did not violate due process. It was enacted under the state police power, so no violation of equal protection was involved because it was not arbitrary or unreasonable. The constitutionality of a government action can be challenged only by a person directly affected by a statute. The district court erred in its judgment.[81]

A proposed constitutional amendment would allow the governor to reorganize the executive branch of government and send his proposed changes to the legislature for approval. It would also extend his and the lieutenant governor's terms to four years and limit the governor's tenure to two consecutive terms. The voters approved the reforms in the election of 1970, but the decision was challenged because it contained more than one change and it violated the Fourth Amendment of the US Constitution, which guarantees a republican form of government to the states. The district court decided that whole sections of the state constitution could be altered if the voters approved it. The supreme court held the question not to be a political one and thus justiciable. The separation of powers is an inherent concept of a republican form of government. The justices cited the Home Rule Act of 1961 as an example transmitting some power to municipalities and affirmed the lower court's judgment.[82]

Sixteen-year-old Terry was a guest in a car operated by Tom Bauder. There was a collision, and Terry suffered injuries. The Kansas guest law of 1931 denied nonpaying guests any remedy, even when the driver failed to exercise reasonable care. She appealed because the law denied her "remedy by due course of the law" of Section XVIII of the state bill of rights. It also violated equal protection of the Fourteenth Amendment. The justices held that this law had resulted in "a crazy-quilt pattern of application of the guest act which permits recovery in many factual situations and denies recovery in others." The Fourteenth Amendment does not preclude the state drawing distinctions between differing groups, but the Kansas classifications of gratuitous passengers and paying ones are "arbitrary and discriminatory and have no rational basis." Justices Kaul, Schroeder, and Fromme dissented because the majority here "judicially abolished the statute rather than waiting for the legislature to act."[83]

The court during this period handed down many decisions protecting the rights of individuals, and the emphasis was on individuals, not corporations. For example, the index on criminal cases rose from two pages (1962) to sixteen (1971). This trend would continue into the next period of supreme court history.

9. Retreat to Conservatism

The Political Scene

Beginning with the territorial period, the categories of marriage, divorce, child custody and support, adoption, and abortion were left to state control. In the latter decades of the twentieth century, while the Kansas Supreme Court continued to recognize actions of sister states on marriage and divorce, it began modifying common law on these topics and processing children in need of special services. The Court Appointed Special Advocate (CASA) program was instituted to meet the needs of the latter and proved to be a great success, although it was hampered primarily by an insufficient number of volunteers and funding to support them.

The CASA movement began in 1977, when David Soukup, a Seattle Superior Court judge, discovered the difficulty of making decisions with insufficient information on behalf of abused and neglected children. He surmised that community volunteers who could speak for children's best interests could provide a solution. Fifty citizens responded to his summons, and the CASA movement was born. The program succeeded beyond his wildest dreams, spreading rapidly, and three decades later almost sixty thousand volunteers were helping these children in about a thousand state and local offices, some known by names different from CASA. These volunteers have helped over two million children find safe and permanent homes.[1]

After extensive training, CASA volunteers are appointed by judges to be advocates of abused and neglected children and to make certain they are not lost in the overburdened legal and social systems or do not languish in an inappropriate group or foster home. A volunteer remains with his or her case until the child is placed in a safe, permanent home, and often that volunteer constitutes the one constant adult who really cares about that child. The volunteer serves as a fact-finder for the judge, speaks for the child in the courtroom to represent the child's best interests, and continues as a "watchdog" for the child during the duration of the case to bring it to a quick and appropriate conclusion.

To prepare for their representation, CASA volunteers interview the child, the parents, other family members, social workers, and medical authorities. Volunteers review all school and case-worker files, creating a comprehensive examination to present to the judge along with a recommendation that serves the child's best interests. The CASA worker does not provide legal representation in the courtroom but advises the judge on the child's best placement: with parents or guardians, in foster care, or freed for permanent adoption. This also, of course, assists the attorneys in presenting their cases. CASA workers do not advocate the child's wishes; instead, they present the child's best interests as they view the situation. They explain to the child what is happening and the roles the judge, the lawyers, and the social workers play in deciding the child's future, all the while remaining as an objective advocate.[2]

These volunteers were divided nationwide in the late twentieth century at 82 percent women and 18 percent men. About half are employed in part-time or full-time jobs, work fifteen to twenty hours monthly for the children, and come from all walks of life. The success of the program is demonstrated by the fact that children who have been assisted by CASA workers tend to spend less time in the foster care system, and they also have increased odds of finding permanent homes. Most CASA programs are nonprofit and are funded primarily by various service organizations. It is a priority program of the Department of Justice's Office of Juvenile Justice and Delinquency Prevention.[3]

Kansas law requires those in healing arts, optometrists, teachers, social workers, law enforcement officers, and other professionals to report cases of suspected child abuse or neglect to the Department of Social and Rehabilitation Services (SRS). In 1988, the year of CASA's origins in the Sunflower State, the SRS reported almost twenty-five thousand cases of abuse or neglect. Anyone can file a petition to have a court assume jurisdiction over a child. The CASA volunteer may be engaged in issues of custody, protective orders, supervision, or severance of parental rights, although all involved are dedicated to the attempt to preserve the family unit. CASA volunteers are immune from civil liability.[4]

The Kansas CASA program was similar to an early one in Sedgwick County called Roots and Wings and owes its origins to the efforts of Chief Justice Alfred M. Schroeder to establish a system similar to the one in Seattle. The Roots and Wings program in Wichita caught the attention of Probate, County, and Juvenile Judge Jerry Mershon of Riley County, who was a trustee of the National Council of the Juvenile and Family Court Judges. He received the Kansas invitation for the fifty states to send delegates to Washington for a conference and was charged with naming the remaining delegates, consisting of a charitable benefactor, a member of the house and of the senate of the state legislature, an activist in children's issues, and an appellate judge. Mershon asked the judicial administrator to accompany him in calling on Justice Schroeder to discuss selecting an appellate judge. To Judge Mershon's surprise and delight, the chief expressed an interest in attending the conference himself, and he became the only state chief justice to participate.[5]

Judge Schroeder told the Kansas delegation that he intended to use his influence to press for creation of a full-time coordinator for the state CASA program. He inserted this item in the judicial budget, and the legislature authorized the position in its next session. This "genuine interest and clout" coming from the top judge in the state, Mershon was convinced, "was the winning edge or catalyst" for a successful CASA in Kansas. CASA directors began meeting periodically in 1986, and directors for the association were established the following year. The organization was incorporated in 1991, and its name was changed to Kansas CASA. There are currently twenty-three such programs in the state, and they have made a huge difference in the lives of vulnerable children.[6]

The burning political issue of abortion came to the US Supreme Court in 1973, and the justices defined it legally in *Roe v. Wade*. The court insisted that personal anatomy was of fundamental interest to a woman, and, in the process, the court invalidated all state antiabortion statutes. Justice Harry Blackmun spoke for a seven-to-two court in identifying a new substantive due process right for a woman and her physician to decide whether or not to terminate her pregnancy. He used the trimester module of the nine-month gestation period as a guide. In the first trimester the woman had an absolute right to an abortion; in the second trimester the state could regulate the conditions for such an operation; in the final trimester the state's interest in the rights of the fetus took precedence over the woman's rights.[7]

Politicians cannot resist exploiting personal issues or concepts that voters can be aroused over, such as religious beliefs, sexual preference, and educational subjects, and manipulate them for their own purposes. The question of abortion, which should be left to the woman, her spouse, her physician, and her minister to decide, soon became a divisive political issue across the nation and in Kansas. Conservative pro-life citizens and those concerned with protection of private rights immediately staked out their positions on the question and for the next three decades gathered together on the anniversary of the *Roe* decision to declaim vociferously their views on this consuming question. Thenceforth potential candidates for public office had to pass a litmus test and announce their views on what point life begins and to state legal and medical positions on it, whether or not they possessed pertinent information. Pro-life forces sought constitutional amendments and federal and state laws to carry out their views. They bombed abortion clinics, harassed personnel who worked in them, physically intimidated women seeking abortions, and occasionally committed murder in the name of their cause. Pro-choice forces were also vociferous in insisting on the protection of personal rights. The Roman Catholic Church and other organizations opposed to birth control joined the melee and resisted making exceptions for conception by rape or incest. The American Civil Liberties Union (ACLU) supported the extension of women's rights. Few neutral citizens criticized the justices for overreaching and imposing a legal solution before allowing the states to develop their own criteria, as had always been the usual case in legal history. Proponents of legal activism applauded the court's action, while those who urged judicial restraint were appalled over *Roe*. Pro-choice advocates sought governmental assistance for family-planning clinics and medical costs for abortions for the poor, while pro-life supporters cut funding for these activities through Medicare, Medicaid, and Planned Parenthood.[8]

The abortion issue in Kansas predates Margaret Sanger, who coined the term "birth control" in 1914 and often spent time in jail for distributing diaphragms and spermicidal jellies from her clinic. The debate over contraceptives intensified when the IUD (intrauterine device) was developed, and when "the pill" was marketed in 1960, the family-planning debate intensified. During the 1960s feminists defined abortion as a woman's right and founded such groups as Zero Population Growth (1968). Congress began restricting Medicaid funds for abortion, and state legislatures placed restrictions on abortion procedures. Most antiabortion groups confined their activities to rallies and peaceful demonstrations, but those on the fringes bombed abortion clinics and murdered physicians who performed that service.

The election in 1980 of President Ronald Reagan, an open foe of abortion rights, led to a rash of state legislation on the subject. A shift away from this trend began in 1992 (beyond the scope of this study) during the Clinton years. The debate climaxed, but did not terminate, when Rachelle Shannon shot Dr. George Teller of Wichita in 1993 and Paul Tiller murdered John Britton and his bodyguard, James Barrett, and wounded June Barrett. Following the failure of passive opposition, pro-life advocates organized Operation Rescue to use lethal force in the struggle. The debate had now arrived at the type of Orwellian doublethink that had arisen out of the jungles of Vietnam a few years earlier: "We had to destroy the village to save it."[9]

The Kansas legislature enacted a tough abortion bill in 1986. Girls under eighteen would have to obtain parental consent to obtain an abortion unless it was necessary to save the girl's life. Although these girls were old enough for sexual activity, legislators explained, the law was necessary to protect them from their immaturity and "to foster the family structure and preserve it as a viable social unit." The alternative offered girls was to seek permission of the district court, "where they would have to explain why they refused to seek, or were unable to obtain, parental approval." The law carried a harsh penalty of fifteen years to life in prison for a violating physician.[10]

Both sides began girding for battle right after *Roe v. Wade.* A group of twenty-seven Protestant, Jewish, "and other religious groups" formed the Religious Coalition for Abortion Rights in Kansas (RCAR) to cooperate in safeguarding "the option of legal abortion." The organization claimed that this was a religious issue because of the metaphysical question, when does life begin? The pro-life forces insisted that this constituted a religious issue and pressed for legislation that would declare parenthood beginning at the moment of conception. Pro-choice people were also convinced that this was a religious issue and believed that such a law would violate the principle of separation of church and state implied in the First Amendment. RCAR, its pamphlet proclaimed, was pro-choice, not pro-abortion.[11]

Pro-choice forces coalesced around Dr. William Roy, who differentiated in a legal journal between the two kinds of abortion: the criminal type, which was illegal because it was unjustifiable, and the therapeutic type, which was necessary for the mother. In the last trimester, he asserted, all fetuses are viable, or capable of living outside the uterus. Roy reported that at that point thirty state legislatures were considering new abortion laws, and eleven had enacted such legislation. Despite the advances in contraception in recent years, he estimated that 220,000 unplanned pregnancies occurred annually in the country, and he believed that there were from 200,000 to 1 million criminal abortions performed every year. Often these women would "end up in a morgue or seriously ill." He pressed for legalized, controlled abortion.[12]

After Dr. Roy completed his law degree at Washburn Law School, he entered politics and was elected twice to the US Congress from the Second Congressional District. When Roy ran for the US Senate, Protestant minister Sterling Lacy rose in opposition. When Lacy read of Medicare spending millions of dollars annually to finance 220,000 abortions, he "went outside to see if the American flag was still flying." This "murder had to stop," he concluded, and he set out to denounce the doctor and the fact that Kansas witnessed 12,612 abortions yearly, or 57 percent above the national average, and was becoming "the abortion capital of all America."[13]

The raging battle soon centered on Wichita, home of Dr. George Tiller, who was becoming notorious nationally for his late-term abortions. Randall Terry and his Operation Rescue were successful in demonstrating in New Jersey, and his forces gathered in Wichita for a six-day rally to protest and picket three clinics that performed legal abortions. The pro-choice groups responded, and both sides were full of Christian zeal, with pro-lifers believing they were following in the footsteps of earlier protest movements, such as abolitionists, civil rights activists, and antiwar protesters. Pro-choice people were adamant that their opponents were "terrorists." Blockading a clinic, pro-lifers insisted, was not civil disobedience but "a biblical act of obedience." A sociologist studying the movement concluded that fundamentalists were becoming more activist because the Jimmy Carter administration "gave a sense of respectability to born-again Christians," the Republican Party was attempting to broaden its base, and these "Christians" found in the issue "a reason to speak out." Their opposition denounced these activities as "illegal," and Democrats rallied around this faction.[14]

Operation Rescue members picketed Tiller's home and church. A spokesperson defended their actions on the grounds that they were holding the physician "accountable for what he does." A spokesperson for Tiller responded that the protests were "despicable and deplorable." One supporter compared the situation to Auschwitz, while another suggested that the protesters use their "money and efforts" instead to help the pregnant women and thus lessen the need for abortions. About three thousand protesters rallied downtown for a meeting and a march to a city park for speeches. Both groups, about evenly divided in numbers, assured their listeners that they "represented a majority of Kansans," and so the debate raged without resolution because both were convinced that God was on their side, and they had received no sign to indicate otherwise.[15]

The Judges

Robert S. Miller was born on 3 March 1919 in Columbus, Ohio. He attended Ohio State University and received his law degree from the University of Kansas in 1943. He served in the army during World War II, then practiced law in Miami County after the war. He was elected district judge and reelected twice. Governor Robert Bennett appointed him to the supreme court in 1975. He wrote an opinion on the contract clause that the US Supreme Court sustained.[16]

In 1977 Kay McFarland became the first woman appointed to the court. She was born on 20 July 1935 in Coffeyville. The family moved to Topeka, and she attended public schools there. She enrolled in Washburn University and received her degree in 1957. After receiving her law degree from Washburn Law School, she practiced in Topeka until her election as Shawnee County district judge in 1971. She rose to chief justice in 1995 and retired from the court in 2009 after twenty-three years of service.[17]

Governor Bennett also appointed Justice Richard W. Holmes in 1977. Holmes was born in Wichita on 23 February 1923. He was educated in the public schools and served in the navy during World War II. Graduating from Kansas State University summa cum laude with a business degree in 1950, he received a law degree from Washburn in 1953. He practiced law in Wichita with his father, specializing in probate and corporation law. Holmes was a founder of the North American Judges Association in 1959, chairman of the Kansas Judicial Council for two years, and a member of the Conference of Chief Justices until he retired and McFarland replaced him.[18]

Harold Shields Herd was born in rural Comanche County on 3 June 1918. He graduated from Protection High School and attended Southwestern College, lettering in football, track, and debate. He graduated from Washburn University in 1940, receiving his law degree there in 1942. Herd served in the navy during World War II and began practicing law in Coldwater after hostilities. He was elected to the state senate in 1964 and served as minority leader from 1968 to 1972. Governor John Carlin appointed him to replace Justice Owsley in 1979. After retiring, Herd taught constitutional history at Washburn.[19]

Tyler C. Lockett was born in Hutto, Texas, on 7 December 1932. He was educated in the public schools and graduated from Texas A&M. He moved to Wichita to operate a clothing store similar to the one his father had in Texas. After serving in the navy in World War II, he returned to Wichita to open a sporting goods store. He served for a while as sheriff and was an effective crime fighter. He received his law degree from Washburn in 1962 and served as district court judge. Governor Carlin appointed him to replace Justice Fromme in 1983.[20]

Donald L. Allegrucci was born in Pittsburg on 19 September 1936. He graduated from Pittsburg State University in 1959 and received a law degree from Washburn in 1963. He practiced law and served as district judge and on two special Kansas Court of Appeals panels. He served a term in the state senate when Carlin was speaker of the house. Governor Carlin appointed him to the supreme court in 1986, and, with Justices Prager, Herd, and Lockett, they constituted a Democratic majority on the court for the first time in its history.[21]

Fred Newton Six was born on 20 April 1929 in Independence, Missouri. He graduated from the University of Kansas in 1951 and received his law degree there in 1956. During the Korean War he was an intelligence officer on an aircraft carrier in the China Sea. He edited the KU law review and was awarded the Order of the Coif. He worked for a law firm in New York City for a year before returning to Topeka to practice law. He served as assistant attorney general and on the court of appeals and became the first appeals judge to be appointed to the supreme court. Governor Mike Hayden appointed him to replace Justice Prager, making the balance on the court again three Democrats and four Republicans. He was once described as an "independent thinker with a firm grasp of legal principles."[22]

The index for *Kansas Reports* for this period (1975–89) does not list a case on abortion, but the following year a case arose that allowed the justices to sidestep the question of when life begins. A couple brought suit against their doctor and the ALZA Corporation for the wrongful death of an embryo through the use of the company's IUD. At that time the Food and Drug Administration had approved the use of this device for a twelve-month period. Dr. Clinton failed to inform Brenda that she should replace her IUD within a year. Brenda became pregnant and suffered pain and bleeding during her pregnancy. He recommended terminating the pregnancy when the fetus was sixteen and a half weeks old. Following the abortion, Brenda suffered physical and psychological distress. Was this young, nonviable fetus a "person"? Herd spoke for the court in determining that the ALZA's warning for physicians was sufficient. Clinton just failed in his duty to warn Brenda. This fetus was not a person within the meaning of the wrongful death act of Kansas.[23]

William and Annetta were married in 1968, and Tracy was born in 1970 in Kansas City, Missouri. After delivery Annetta began working as a bartender in the Chatterbox Club. William worked for the Rock Island line. They eventually separated, and she left the baby with a sitter while she was at work. One day she told William that there was no sitter available, and she would have to take the baby to work with her. He objected and later took the child, and she was cared for by her paternal grandmother and still later by his new wife. In 1971 William divorced Annetta, who was summoned to the proceedings, but she failed to appear, and William received custody. Annetta learned of the divorce and married Michael Compton. In 1972 William married Deborah Ann, who petitioned to adopt Tracy. Annetta asked for visitation rights. The court held that Annetta had failed to assume parental duties for two years, and good policy demanded that, with adoption, "a complete break be made with old ties." The court denied Annetta's request.[24]

A couple divorced in 1970, and, during this process, the question arose of custody of their child. After evaluation, the State Welfare Department determined that it was in the best interests of the child to give custody to Leo, not Tammy, the mother. Leo was a rancher in Kansas and left the child with a couple named Kitchens. Leo and Tammy both remarried, and Tammy moved to California. She married a welder who had a good income, and they had one child before she had to have surgery, which left her unable to bear any children. Tammy decided she wanted her first child back, as did Leo and his wife. When asked why they did not try to take the child from the Kitchens, Leo and his spouse said that they did not want to "uproot" her from her happy home with the Kitchens. The supreme court decided that the child had a happy situation, and the trial court had made a good decision to leave her with the Kitchens, who wanted her.[25]

Irene was granted a divorce, with Frank paying her $150 per month for a year and then $30 monthly thereafter, contingent on her death or remarriage. Frank soon filed to terminate the alimony because Irene had entered into a common-law arrangement with Elmer Schlarnon. Frank was denied, reapplied, and was again denied. Speaking for the court, Justice Fatzer noted that there were three elements necessary for a common-law marriage. These included the capacity to marry, a marriage agreement, and, through circumstantial evidence, a demonstration to the public that a couple is husband and wife. Fatzer decided that there was no evidence that the couple had an agreement that they would marry. Justices Schroeder and Fromme dissented because the couple met all the requirements except that there was no marriage agreement. Frank lost and had to continue his alimony payments.[26]

Kenneth and Emily were married in 1969 and had two children. They moved to Topeka, where another child was born. Their marriage became increasingly strained, so they decided to move back to Tennessee, buy a new house, and begin married life anew. Emily moved the children to Tennessee. Kenneth signed a contract to buy a house there, then changed his mind, and filed for a divorce in Shawnee County. The children were in Tennessee, and the court there gave Emily custody. The supreme court used the "long arm of the law" concept to decide that Emily lived in Tennessee, Kenneth lived in Kansas, but the family had lived together in Kansas for some time, so this gave Kansas courts jurisdiction. The supreme court had long held that all issues in a dissolution of marriage should be determined at the same time, so it used the "long arm" concept to agree on custody for Emily. It served no worthwhile purpose, the justices noted, for two persons disenchanted with their marriage to dissolve their bonds in one state and fight for custody in another one. The trial court had denied jurisdiction, so the court reversed and remanded.[27]

Another custody case arose after a divorce. Catherine gave birth to Patrick in 1970. She married Stephen in 1974, and he adopted Patrick. Three years later they divorced, and she received custody. She moved to Wichita, and Patrick lived with her parents so that he could continue in the Haysville schools. In 1980 her parents sued for custody of Patrick and won because they had developed a parental relationship with him over the years. Catherine appealed this decision, and during the hearing she was found "fit" to be a mother. A law of 1980 permitted courts to award custody of minors to third parties even if mothers were fit. The supreme court found this law to be unconstitutional because it destroyed the fundamental right of due process to deprive the mother of her child as long as she was capable of being a good parent.[28]

In 1978 Congress enacted the Indian Child Welfare Act, which sought to protect the Indian family by placing these children in a foster or adoptive home that reflected Indian values and culture. A baby who was the illegitimate son of an Indian father and a white mother was adopted by the father's parents after the mother gave her consent. The grandparents received temporary custody. The father, Carmon Perciado, decided he wanted custody of the boy. Carmon was five-eighths Kiowa, but he was an inmate of the Kansas State Industrial Reform School at the time, so SRS recommended against this request. The supreme court sustained the decision to give custody to Carmon's parents because this ruling did not need the consent of the illegitimate parent.[29]

In a most unusual decision in 1980, the supreme court allowed a child to sue her mother. A three-year-old "unemancipated minor" was injured in an auto accident when her mother, who was driving, through negligence, collided with another car in Jackson County. Rosanna's grandfather pursued the case for her. The mother's response claimed parental immunity from an unemancipated minor. The supreme court listed nineteen states that had abolished the concept of parental immunity but announced that the old doctrine, which was considered necessary for "the tranquility and harmony of domestic life[,] misconceives the facts of domestic life." The primary disruption of family life by the suit, the new theory held, is not the lawsuit but the injury itself resulting from "the misconduct of a parent." The case was remanded for determination of the issues. Justices McFarland and Schroeder dissented.[30]

William G. Barclay was an ordained Baptist minister who refused to officiate at his chapel for a marriage between a black and a white because it violated his religious beliefs. He was charged with denying the couple their civil rights. The court held that if the civil rights act was intended to include an ordained minister refusing to perform his "personal or professional services" because of his religious beliefs, then the statute was unconstitutional. The justices concluded that the legislature did not intend to apply the act in this type of situation, and the charges were dismissed.[31]

Owen from Kansas and Peggy from Oklahoma were first cousins who were married in Colorado. Kansas law forbade first cousins from marrying, but they lived in Parsons, and the courts accepted acts of "sister" states. Owen and Peggy considered divorce, so they separated and made a property settlement. When Owen executed his will, he did not mention Peggy. He filed for divorce and died soon after. She filed for one-half of his estate. Their marriage, illegal in Kansas, was legal in Colorado, and he had filed for a divorce that was not yet completed, so the supreme court upheld her claim. Justice Herd, speaking for the court, sustained their legal marriage but noted that their separation agreement was "fairly, knowingly, and willfully made" where she retained all her property and Owen kept his, but the divorce was not finalized.[32]

Kevin McCune attended a party and left at midnight with a friend. He decided that the friend was too drunk to drive, so he got out and walked for about a mile. Four persons, two men and two women, picked him up in a car. Driver Thompson drove one of the girls home and then stopped on a dirt road. He pulled a gun and took McCune's wallet, jewelry, and suede coat. He then forced McCune to have oral sex with the three of them. When a police car stopped, McCune was clad only in a knit shirt. McCune claimed that they used force, and they responded that the action was consensual. The jury found Thompson and Pennington guilty of aggravated robbery and sodomy. Kansas law defined sodomy as "oral or anal copulation between persons not husband and wife or consenting adult members of the opposite sex, or between a person and an animal or coitus with an animal." The defendant argued that this law discriminated against consenting homosexuals and thus was an unconstitutional violation of the Fourteenth Amendment. The court denied his appeal.[33]

Jim was charged with attempted rape and aggravated battery. He admitted that he had consumed a lot of alcohol that night, but he was unable to remember anything after a certain point in time. At the trial his attorney insisted that his alcohol level was so high that it made him incapable of rape. The court ordered a mistrial because the defense failed to file notice of insanity. He was again charged, and at the retrial he claimed double jeopardy. Insanity and voluntary intoxication are two different defenses, and he never claimed intoxication to the point of insanity. The court held that in the mistrial after the jury was sworn, a retrial was constitutionally permissible "only where the trial court, in the exercise of its sound judgment, determine[d] the ends of justice require a mistrial." Jim was discharged.[34]

Scott was extradited from California and convicted of aggravated incest with his eight-year-old stepdaughter. Scott and his wife had separated, and the mother had returned to Kansas. Her daughter told a friend about the assault and was told she should tell her mother. The girl was afraid of Scott, and SRS agreed she should not face him in a trial. The police and SRS videotaped her testimony while she demonstrated with a doll what happened. Scott argued that this violated his Sixth Amendment right to confront his accuser. The prosecution then decided on using closed-circuit television with Scott behind a screen so that his presence could not intimidate the girl. The supreme court rejected Scott's contention that this denied him access to counsel. The justices agreed that it was true that during that period he was hidden, but "it was in Chisholm's best interest that he not confer with his attorney at that point" because he could only write a note or whisper in his lawyer's ear during the testimony.[35]

Floyd Carmichael told S.C., age fifteen, that he had been arguing with her mother and to come upstairs and talk to him about it. Once in the bedroom he told the girl that he had killed her mother, and then he raped S.C. twice. When the mother came home no one was there, so she drove to a coffee shop where she thought she might find her daughter and picked her up. When charged, Carmichael said that S.C. ran away from home, and he left work to find her. He was convicted of two counts of rape and one of kidnapping. While he was in jail he was told that S.C. had gonorrhea. The defense counsel requested the jail to take a culture for gonorrhea but was refused because the rape shield law was designed to restrict or prohibit evidence regarding the girl's chastity. Carmichael claimed that this test would prove that he never had intercourse with the girl. The supreme court decided that, while this evidence may have been helpful, there was no evidence to support his claim "beyond a reasonable doubt." A physician examined her and found cuts and bruises and seminal fluid in the pelvic area. Officials had also found handcuffs, a sleeping bag, rope, and tape in the trunk of his car, as she had testified. Her blood type samples supported her story, and his conviction was affirmed.[36]

Jimmie Collier entered into a contract to build an asphalt parking lot for Owens-Corning Fiberglass Corporation. A union representative asked if he was a union contractor. He responded no, and the union threatened to put a "banner," or picket, on him. Collier reminded the union that Kansas had passed a right-to-work law. The union picketed, and Owens-Corning informed Collier that if the pickets continued, its employees would honor it, and the company would have to shut down the plant. The Taft-Hartley Act specifically exempts the exclusiveness of the NLRB with regard to controlling right-to-work, and the supreme court held this to be an illegal secondary boycott.[37]

The Kansas Department of Transportation (KDOT) adopted the Davis-Bacon Wage Scale, which was enacted to put a floor under wages. This involved computing the current rate of per diem wages to prevent an employer from gaining an advantage on contracts by underpaying his employees. Under this provision, Kansas was divided into five areas or wage zones. A paving company argued that a carpenter is a carpenter no matter where the wage zone is; thus, the wages of all carpenters in the area should be considered. On appeal, the supreme court decided that KDOT had the authority to include Davis-Bacon in its specifications. This was not a delegation of authority to the Department of Labor because it was a decision of KDOT, not the secretary of labor.[38]

The Board of Public Utilities (BPU) of Kansas City managed the municipally owned water and electric utilities. The board voluntarily met and conferred with the carpenters, machinists, electricians, painters, and aerospace workers on hours and wages. The board then agreed to have maintenance on their turbines performed by Creole Products Services, and the board would utilize nonunion labor. An informational picket line was immediately established at the employees' entrance to the plant. Officials asked them to move to the contractors' gate, and they refused. When the machinists and electrical workers declined to come to work, this was enjoined, and they moved from the employees' gate to that of the employers. Union rules with the BPU prohibited strikes because they were municipally owned utilities. The state Employees Act restored the injunctive process to those who came under the entire act. BPU met and conferred with unions and refused to come under the entire act. The supreme court held that BPU thus denied itself injunctive proceedings and could not halt this picketing.[39]

During negotiations in Crawford County in 1978, the school board advised the teachers' association that nineteen of its proposals were "nonnegotiable." The association brought action to force the school board to negotiate the issues in good faith. After the trial court held a hearing, it ordered an injunction against the school board. In 1977 the legislature enacted "impasse" legislation that "some teachers, professional employees associations, and school boards" interpreted as beginning "a new ball game." This initiated numerous litigations, and Crawford County became involved in one of them. The supreme court affirmed the trial court's judgment in part and reversed it in part. The justices believed that this new situation of impasse created "a bewildering array" of choices and issues. Thereafter, the justices instructed, both sides should agree on whether all issues are negotiable, or they should mutually agree that they will negotiate. All judicial districts have more than one school district, so the same judge could reach different conclusions on identical proposals within a close proximity of time for different unified school districts. Thus the scope of negotiations would require "judicial determination each year on which school district rules would apply" and "there would be no judicial rules on which the parties could rely."[40]

A dispute arose from the professional negotiations in the Topeka school district for the 1978–79 year. The Collective Negotiating Law of 1970 required bargaining in good faith from both sides. The Kansas National Education Association (KNEA) asked for impasse because the school board was not negotiating in good faith. The board rejected the charge. Van Zandt, the executive director of KNEA, brought to court the correspondence, manuals, and other materials that were designed to help negotiating teams in order to show that the school board was forcing the association to impasse as part of its strategy, as these materials would demonstrate. The board argued that these were "sensitive" materials in the category of trade secrets and could not be used. The trial court agreed. Without these materials the supreme court could not determine if the court erred, but it did conclude that the school board did not refuse to bargain in good faith.[41]

Anna and Matthew Sawyer, ages eight and eleven, attended public schools in 1981–82. The parents were dissatisfied with the progress of Matthew, so they decided to homeschool the two the next year. Matthew had attended second grade in Tennessee, but the school refused to promote him. This homeschool situation was unaccredited, and there was no schedule for classroom activities. There were two more children, ages four and twenty-two months, at home. Mrs. Sawyer was the sole provider of child care, and she was acting as a teacher with no teaching experience and only one and a half years of college education. Between 1979 and 1982 Matthew's standardized learning achievement scores dropped from the 45th percentile to the 16th. The trial court held them to be "children in need of care." The justices determined that the only goal of the homeschool was to extricate Matthew from his failure in public schools. This arrangement violated the public school attendance law, and the Sawyer case had no merit.[42]

Parents of a handicapped student insisted that the school continue to mainstream his education in the public schools, but the administration insisted that he should be in the Kansas State School for the Visually Handicapped. The school district had worked with Kurt and his family for ten years, and it had provided him and his family with counseling services and with counseling from the Menninger Foundation. It cost the district $187,000 annually for his education. Testing showed that he had a normal intellect, and the district had consulted with the School for the Visually Handicapped. The district's efforts to help the boy were described as "herculean." Upon appeal, the justices upheld the school board's decision.[43]

Robert Achiya was employed as a full-time teacher and also as an assistant football and basketball coach. He was assigned six classes and one planning period daily. The second year of his employment he also was assigned the duties of head football coach and senior high girls' basketball coaching. But instead of teaching American history, he was assigned to seventh- and eighth-grade assistant physical education. In the third year he signed his contract and reserved the right to refrain from all athletic teaching. When the board reduced his primary contract, he sued. The justices decided that he was a tenured teacher, and the board had violated due process of law in his contract. It had to reinstate him with back pay.[44]

Jim Bauer taught shop for seven years but also was certified to teach the social sciences. The board had to institute a reduction in force, so it terminated him and hired a social sciences teacher. He protested that he was certified for that job, but the board responded that this was not the same as "qualified" and sustained his being terminated. The board never discussed this issue or anything about his contract with Bauer. The supreme court held that the board could terminate him only with good cause and ordered him reinstated.[45]

The state enjoined the showing of a film for being obscene and cited *Miller v. California* (413 U.S. 15), which updated the *Roth* rule in determining obscenity. If it incited the prurient interest of an average person, if it was patently sexually offensive, or if it lacked as a whole any literary, artistic, political, or scientific value, it was obscene. The new rule eliminated the phrase "utterly without redeeming social value." Also, one should apply local standards, not national ones. The supreme court ordered the film destroyed. The justices erred here in ordering its destruction because this would have the effect of prior restraint. Prager correctly dissented on the basis that the destruction was unwarranted and what happened to the film elsewhere "is of no concern to us."[46]

Randy Hughes was charged with selling obscene devices in his adult bookstore in Wichita. These devices included the SexPlorer Pleasure system, a vibrator with dildo (penis-shaped) attachment, and "Miss World, an inflatable doll with artificial vagina." Did these objects meet the definition of obscenity? The justices decided that the obscenity law was "unconstitutionally overbroad" because it subjected licensed physicians, psychologists, and sex therapists to possible criminal sanctions for performing their function. These devices provided legitimate therapy, and the law invaded the right to privacy in using them. Using these contrivances, the justices insisted, is "a constitutionally protected activity." Any interpretation of the obscenity law was too broad when it restricted their use.[47]

The plaintiff was driving her car along the turnpike west of Cassoday with her husband and three children. The car left the road and struck a guardrail, and the husband and three children were killed. She sued, alleging defects in the roadway and also that the "interstate" road markers constituted an expressway guarantee that the road conformed to standards of a federal interstate highway. The court ruled that the Kansas Turnpike Authority (KTA) is an arm or agency of the state, and thus constitutionality is assumed unless proven otherwise. The interstate sign is not an express warranty. There were no specific procedures for filing claims against the KTA, so she had to proceed as in any other civil action. The KTA had no immunity, as the legislature had intended for motorists to have recourse to action. McFarland, Schroeder, and Fromme dissented.[48]

The KTA bonds of $160 million issued in 1954 were to mature in 1994. In the 1984 refinancing, the earlier bonds were properly defeased, with the $36.6 million still outstanding. In 1984 the KTA issued $134.7 million in new special obligation bonds. Enough bonds were placed in escrow to cover this principal left over plus interest. The defendant argued that the 1984 defeasance violated the terms of the 1954 bond issue. The justices ordered otherwise.[49]

A bill passed the legislature just before it adjourned and was sent to Governor Robert Bennett. The secretary of state refused to publish it and was issued a writ of mandamus. In 1974 the people revised the constitution to extend the governor's time to veto from three days to ten. The supreme court did not want to limit legislative action in the absence of an express constitutional prohibition, so the ten-day limit was constitutional even though the legislature had adjourned.[50]

A quo warranto proceeding was brought to determine the governor's line item veto power, which the legislature gave him in 1974. The attorney general claimed that the governor's veto of sections of the Revenue Act of 1981 had exceeded his powers. He responded that his veto involved items that were general and had nothing to do with appropriations. The legislature had included an amendment to the School Equalization Act in the appropriations bill. The line item veto power thus negated the prohibition of more than one subject change in a proposal. The court held that this new power did not authorize including measures in a bill wholly unrelated. In this case the legislature was trying to control school budgets and spending, this was unconstitutional, and the governor's action was sustained.[51]

The Haven police chief issued a complaint against Donald Gregg for selling alcohol without possessing a license. He challenged his conviction because a majority of the city council had not voted for the ordinance as required. The evening of the vote, the mayor and one council member were absent. Two of the three members present voted yes, one abstained, and the mayor's substitute also abstained, leaving only two of the five voting affirmatively. The common law held that abstention is an affirmative vote, but Kansas law modified common law on this, so the ordinance never received a majority vote.[52]

As part of its attempt to protect consumers, the New Deal enacted the National Gas Act of 1938. The policy of Ronald Reagan four decades later was to deregulate by abolishing or modifying these New Deal laws, a program that often had disastrous results. It also forced states to reexamine their regulatory policies and modify them according to new federal laws. The effort of Kansas to regulate the production and price of natural gas led to a case being appealed to the US Supreme Court, where the law was sustained.

Under old Kansas regulations, the price of natural gas would be determined by seller and buyer in a predetermined contract in writing every two years, 120 days before the beginning of the contract year. On 19 November 1978 the state legislature passed the Kansas Natural Gas Price Protection Act to control prices in this hazardous industry and to promote an increase in the production of natural gas with "a drastically different approach." At this point the price of gas varied from 90 cents per MCF to $1.90, and experts anticipated "a sudden escalation of interstate gas prices" under deregulation, forcing the state to act. The new Kansas regulations, the state insisted, had "an important public purpose" that was "reasonable and appropriate" under the state's police powers. The Energy Reserves Group (ERG), a producer of gas, argued that this constituted "an impairment of contract" prohibited by the US Constitution, and it sought to break its contract with Kansas Power & Light. It appealed the state law setting new guidelines.

Speaking for the court, Justice Miller held that although the old law set the price based on predetermination, the state was forced to make "an appropriate exercise of its police power" in changing the regulations. The Kansas law was "justified" under the circumstances and was not unconstitutional, as claimed by the ERG, because of "retroactivity." The ERG appealed this opinion to the US Supreme Court, where the *Miller* decision was sustained. Speaking for the court, Justice Blackmun observed that the "regulation of energy production and use is of national concern." In deregulating the industry, Congress expected states to regulate intrastate markets in accordance with national policy. The Kansas law was "one State's attempt to balance the need to provide incentives for the production of gas against the need to protect consumers from hardships brought on by deregulation." Blackmun and the court saw "no constitutional or statutory infringement" in the statute.[53]

Van Turner pleaded guilty to welfare fraud, but he insisted that during his trial he had no counsel to represent him. He was sentenced and placed on probation, and when this was revoked he began serving time in the Kansas State Penitentiary. While in prison, he withdrew his guilty plea and insisted that he had not "knowingly and intelligently" waived his right to counsel. Later documents were introduced that showed that the judge had informed him of his right to counsel, and he had appeared with counsel sometime during his trial. The supreme court declared that, whether charged with a misdemeanor or a felony, the accused had received his *Miranda* rights. Where there was a question of waiver in a criminal case, some evidence was needed that he had had his rights read to him. The trial record showed in writing that he knew his rights.[54]

Two Salina policemen saw a vehicle pull into a parking lot. The passenger got out and went into the adjacent restaurant. The officers asked the driver for his driver's license and, while waiting for him to produce it, noted a hypodermic needle and a plastic bag of pills on the floor of the passenger's side. The pills were amobarbital. The passenger, Faulkner, was already in the restaurant. Faulkner, with prior convictions, was subsequently convicted of intent to sell 667 tablets of amobarbital and 616 other tablets. They were packaged in lots of one hundred with notations of strength on the package. Pharmacists do not distribute these pills on packages of over twenty-five. Therefore, the judges found an obvious intent to sell.[55]

When two officers searched Ricky Jaques's apartment they discovered heroin and found it necessary to use force when he put small bags of heroin in his mouth and refused to spit them out. One officer held him immobile while the other put his hand around Jaques's throat to prevent him from swallowing the bags. The officers were able to retrieve the bags for evidence. There was no indication of injuries of consequence, and, while mace was present, there was no proof of its use, as the accused claimed. The justices reminded in their opinion that if the arresting officer has probable cause, then "he has the right and duty to take reasonable measures to ensure the incriminating evidence is not destroyed." The officers remained within the rules in obtaining their evidence.[56]

Vernon Revis was charged with DWI (driving while intoxicated). The law referred to "certain alcohol and drug related traffic offences," and he argued that the act was unconstitutional because it contained more than one subject. The justices ruled that where the subject of the legislation is germane to other provisions, the act is not objectionable in regard to containing two or more subjects.[57]

Robert was convicted of aggravated robbery and illegal possession of a firearm in his robbery of two Quick Trips in Salina. He was sentenced to fifteen years for the robbery and one to ten years for the firearm, to be served concurrently. The Quick Trip manager had called the police immediately, and an alarm had been radioed out. A state highway trooper stopped Robert on suspicion and found a .22 caliber revolver under his car seat and a sack of coins in the car. The officer read him his rights and arrested him. Robert's defense was that the officer had no search warrant and no probable cause. Thus the gun and coins were "fruit of the poison tree" (the legal doctrine that barred evidence seized illegally because of a tip from an independent source) and inadmissible for evidence. The supreme court determined that the officer had "probable cause" from listening to the radio bulletin about the robbers. The modern development of automobiles and airplanes made mandatory the change in the rules of police procedure because of the quick escape factor.[58]

Another robbery led to a decision for a different kind of procedure. Robbers struck the Fourth National Bank in Wichita, tying up the employees with wire and covering their heads during the process of collecting cash. After the robbers left the bank, the employees freed themselves and called the police. Even with their heads covered, sometimes haphazardly, the employees could give a partial description of the robbers' clothing. A highway patrolman was helping two African Americans change a flat tire on the turnpike. After reviewing the events, he concluded that they acted suspiciously, and he radioed to the Oklahoma highway patrol to look for them. Oklahoma authorities captured them, and they were convicted of aggravated robbery and kidnapping the bank employees. The justices concluded that the employees could identify the men sufficiently so that their testimony was not circumstantial evidence. The Oklahoma officers had probable cause for seizure because they had a description of the car, its license plate number, and a summary of the clothing the men were wearing to justify their arrest. The robbers had committed kidnapping by forcing the employees into the basement of the bank, and they also were under a federal indictment for robbing a national bank, but this did not constitute double jeopardy. The supreme court affirmed the verdict of guilty brought in by the trial court.[59]

A quo warranto proceeding was brought to test the authority of the Alcoholic Beverage Control Board to issue a license to a Class B club where alcohol is served with food or a restaurant that has a license to sell alcoholic drinks by the glass. The justices described the long history of prohibition in Kansas and attempts at its enforcement, trying to determine what constituted the "open saloon" that the state was trying to prohibit. The justices concluded that restaurants authorized to sell liquor by the drink were "in no sense of the word 'saloons.'" This is permissible if the restaurant derives no less than 50 percent of its gross receipts from the sale of food.[60]

A truck driver was caught speeding on the turnpike and was stopped. He refused to accept this quietly, and a scuffle ensued. The patrolman called in a deputy sheriff for assistance, and, in addition to speeding and refusing to show his daily log book, the driver was charged with disorderly conduct, resisting an officer, and obstructing the legal process. In addition, the county attorney charged him with the above because the deputy sheriff was involved in the fray. The driver pleaded guilty to speeding and nolo contendere (no contest) to the log book charge, but he insisted that the remaining county charges constituted double jeopardy. The justices noted that he waived the right on double jeopardy when he failed to make this motion to dismiss these county charges within twenty days of his arraignment. The trial court had erred in dismissing these complaints because of this, and its decision was reversed.[61]

In June 1985 Brenda filed suit to divorce Eddie Adams. He moved to Kansas City, Missouri, and she began "seeing" the appellant. Both of them worked at the Western Missouri Mental Health Center. One day Frederick came home and caught Brenda and Eddie in bed together. He hit Brenda several times, left, and returned with his friend Monk and a gun. He kicked in the door and then tied up Eddie, leaving Brenda certain he would kill the two of them. Frederick and Monk left with Eddie, and the latter was never seen again. Frederick returned and took Brenda to the hospital to have her beating wounds checked. Based on her testimony, Frederick and Monk were tried, and Monk was acquitted. Frederick was convicted and received three life terms for kidnapping, murder, and possession of a weapon. Frederick tried to defend himself after he became disgusted with his attorney's conduct of Frederick's defense. The supreme court held that once the accused accepted counsel, he could not defend himself. His subsequent conviction of murder and the other felony counts did not constitute double jeopardy.[62]

Kansas law prohibited imprisonment for debt except "in case of fraud." Robert Jones was the owner and operator of Johnson County Motors, which handled Yamaha motorcycles. The Yamaha company in Japan retained title to the cycles until they were sold, and then the Johnson company paid for them. It was a nice arrangement for Jones, as he did not have to tie up funds in inventory. The state filed suit against JoCo because Jones owed the parent company $250,000 for bikes sold and money not remitted. Jones was liable because he intended to defraud, so this was not imprisonment for debt.[63]

William Minner filed a complaint with the state Civil Rights Commission against Sears for refusing him credit because he was black. The commission secured a subpoena duces tecum (or subpoena for production of evidence) on Lloyd Reynolds, Sears credit manager, ordering him to produce company documents on company policy, practices, and so on or be in contempt of court. Sears moved to quash the subpoena. The antidiscrimination law of 1953 was enacted with the object of preventing discrimination on the basis of race, creed, color, sex, physical handicap, or ancestry in public accommodations or places of business. On appeal the supreme court decided that intrusion of constitutional rights must be reasonable, and a subpoena for the company credit records constituted no violation of privacy. Sears argued that if it complied with the subpoena, doing so would subject the company to a damage suit. The justices responded that this would not occur if the information in the records did not violate constitutional rights.[64]

A question arose over whether a private club, Class A, with a federal income tax exemption, could receive a license to conduct bingo games. The revised law of 1974 permitted bingo for nonprofit charitable organizations such as religious, fraternal, educational, and veterans' groups. With the approval of the attorney general, the secretary for revenue began the process of issuing licenses to three clubs that he interpreted as being fraternal in nature. The supreme court overruled this decision because evidence showed that the clubs were "social clubs not qualifying as fraternal organizations." It came down to the question of interpreting the nature of these clubs.[65]

Raymond Hruska was convicted of theft of telecommunications services in Saline County. Southwestern Bell provided information to convict him by wiretapping his telephone to prove that he was using a "blue box" to avoid paying for long-distance telephone calls. On this basis the police obtained a search warrant. The supreme court decided that the law permitted Bell Telephone to tap for this type of information. The district court did not err in overruling the defendant's motion to suppress the evidence or in failing to give a requested instruction on attempted theft of these services. Judgment against Hruska was affirmed.[66]

The Federal Power Commission approved certain natural gas price rates, so the Phillips Petroleum Company paid suspense royalties but no interest for a nine-year period. A class action suit was begun seeking to recover interest on these suspense royalties. The trial court determined that members could bring a class action suit because they had not waived their claims, and on the theory of unjust enrichment, the court made an award of 6 percent compound interest. Phillips responded that members could not bring a class action suit because some of them did not live in Kansas or own land in the state. On appeal the supreme court decided that the class action suit was "a recognized exception for suits of a representative character." The company must pay the interest, but members of the suit could opt out, so the case was remanded for proceeding consistent with the foregoing conclusions.[67]

David Lines was appointed building inspector for Topeka in 1968. A city ordinance required management-level employees to live in the city. David married and moved into his wife's house in Perry, but he maintained his apartment in Topeka. The mayor recommended that Lines be terminated for poor job performance. The commissioners refused to accept this decision, so the mayor proposed firing him for failing to live in the city. Three of the commissioners, or a majority, agreed, so he was terminated. David brought suit to be reinstated with back pay. The district court held the city ordinance to be unconstitutional because of "vagueness and uncertainty," following the concept that the court should uphold rather than defeat the law if possible. The supreme court agreed that the ordinance was so vague as to deny due process of law. The city could require residence, and this did not violate the right to travel, as David claimed, and Topeka did not violate equal protection of the law. So the trial court was sustained in some parts and reversed in others.[68]

Virgil Fakes was injured when he was helping De Von Patterson move heavy well-pumping equipment. They were using Fakes's winch truck, which Alliance Mutual insured under a general liability contract. Alliance refused to protect Patterson, so Maryland Mutual ultimately paid the $20,981.10 and sued Alliance for the award. The trial court decided that Patterson was not covered within the meaning of insurance and held for Alliance. The supreme court determined that Fakes was asked by the foreman of Sunray DX to bring his winch truck, and DX would pay for its use, so the lessee or borrower was DX. The policy on the truck extended liability coverage to Fakes or anyone operating it with his permission. Patterson thus was not the borrower of the truck nor the employee of Fakes, and the justices approved judgment for Patterson's award.[69]

Lawyer J. R. Russell ran for a position on the Public Utilities Board in 1979. He placed an ad in a newspaper attacking Paul Haas, Public Utilities Commission member and Russell's opponent, claiming that Haas's statements were "false, deceptive, and misleading." Section 11 of the state bill of rights guarantees that people may speak or write freely, "being responsible for the abuse of such rights." In other words, people were protected in freedom of speech, but there were certain limits. A lawyer can speak out without losing his license, but his First Amendment rights are not "absolute." Russell paid for a three-column, full-page advertisement accusing Haas of signing an illegal contract for the Public Utilities Commission and "someone" of embezzling. The Kansas Bureau of Investigation had explored these charges and found no evidence to support them. As a result, the justices supported the action that Russell was being publicly censured for his dirty politics.[70]

Junction City had an ordinance prohibiting the possession of guns except on the owner's land or business. Another ordinance provided for the purchase of guns, which the first ordinance prohibited carrying. How could one purchase or carry a weapon to a gunsmith under this prohibition? The justices said that the carrying ordinance was "constitutionally overbroad" because the owner could not carry a weapon legally from the purchaser or the repairman.[71]

In 1974 the state legislature authorized the Board of Healing Arts to study the ancient Chinese practice of acupuncture. The board endorsed an experimental program to practice the art and exempted practitioners from criminal or civil prosecution. The plaintiffs were licensed chiropractors, and when the experiment ended in 1975, they agreed to wait on further rules from the legislature in 1976. When the legislature failed to act promptly, plaintiffs asked for a declaratory judgment that no special license was needed, as the procedure did not include surgery. The procedure did include the insertion of a nonhollow wire in the skin, and some argued that this was surgery because infection or injury sometimes occurred. Why and how the practice works were never explained to the scientific community, so there was much skepticism about the practice. The justices decided that because of the experimental program, the legislature was aware of acupuncture's value as an anesthesia and other achievements, and some chiropractors had adopted the procedure. The legislature knew of this and did not prohibit it in the 1976 law, so it was legally acceptable.[72]

The Douglas County sheriff was investigating a murder when a bulletin arrived of a stolen car with two occupants. Warrants were issued for their arrest on suspicion of murder. Sherry Pegg, a reporter for the *Topeka Daily Capital*, interviewed the county attorney, who refused to name suspects. She responded that she already knew them, so he advised her of the criminal statute prohibiting publicity until after warrants were executed and returned. In this case such revelation might alert the two, and they could escape. Pegg telephoned state editor Sands, who told her to go to the office of the district court and get the correct names, although the *Capital* already had them from monitoring the police radio. The newspaper subsequently published two articles on the episode. One suspect escaped, and the other was captured sometime later in another state. The supreme court held that criminal sanctions could not be imposed for publishing "truthful information properly obtained from public records."[73]

Stricklow and his wife were directors for Meadow Fresh Farms, which distributed Imitation Low Fat Dry Milk. This product contained partially hydrogenated coconut oil and therefore was a filled milk, which Kansas law prohibited. The national law against filled milk came in 1923 because it was believed that the butterfat portion of milk was the only source of vitamins contained in milk. Kansas passed a similar law the same year. The justices cited *Caroline Products v. Mohler* of 1940 (152 Kan. 2), which held the law to be constitutional. "Many courts in recent years," the justices noted, "have altered their positions due to changed conditions in the food industry." They sustained the lower court's decision in favor of Meadow Fresh Farms.[74]

In 1985 Billy Lee Thompson was charged with telephone harassment under the criminal code of 1969. The justices held that the state has a legitimate, justifiable interest in prohibiting intrusion by telephone by one who intends to harass the listener with comments, suggestions, or proposals that are obscene, lewd, lascivious, filthy, or indecent. Thompson's intent to harass was an element of the crime of harassment by telephone.[75]

The Heritage Baptist Temple operated a day-care center in Dodge City without a license from 1974 to 1979. The temple had been licensed, but the new minister did not renew it because, he argued, this function was part of the church's ministry. Claiming a genuine religious liberty, he objected to state licensing because the state prohibited corporal punishment. The justices held that day care is not a religious activity, and the temple's religious activities were not disturbed by licensing. Temple members cannot be exempt from the law in practicing their religion. The justices used the examples of polygamy, the use of poisonous snakes, and other dangerous religious practices and observed that mere licensing did not prevent members of the temple from following their religious beliefs.[76]

Plaintiff agreed to purchase Russell Kare Center and lease with option to buy Alfern Nursing Home, two adult care centers in Russell. Both had provider agreements, were required to participate in Medicare, and were licensed by the Kansas Department of Health and Environment. Following the purchases, new licenses were obtained. The SRS refused to reimburse for the period from the day of purchase to the date of issuing the licenses based on the experience that some centers never renewed their licenses after purchase. The district court reversed the SRS decision, and the supreme court sustained the lower court. Federal rules are controlling here, and once the state participates, it must comply with federal standards. Under federal rules there was an automatic transfer of regulations. The SRS must repay.[77]

A suit was brought to recover damages as the result of an incomplete transfer involving the sale of milo to purchasers in South Korea. After a group of Koreans toured Kansas milling operations and were convinced milo would be a cheap substitute for corn, Reginald Hurd telephoned the plaintiff's manager, William Warders, about purchasing some of the grain. Warders then purchased vast amounts of milo for $5 per bushel, above the market price $3.65, for what he considered to be a legitimate deal. Warders was given the plaintiff's name by the chairman of the Grain Sorghum Commission, whose function was to facilitate the sale of Kansas grain, and was led to believe that Hurd worked for the commission. Warders lost a good deal of money in the transaction, but the justices found that no legal breach of duty was owed him. This was the chance he took in speculating in hopes of profiting from the situation.[78]

Darryl Kulwin was a traveling salesman with a bag of jewelry for sale. He and Panoria Rustin rented rooms at the Red Roof Inn in Overland Park. They agreed to meet for dinner and discuss possible purchases. Kulwin left the bag of samples in the inn's office, telling the clerk it was valuable but not what it actually contained. An "unidentified person" stole the bag. Kansas law provided that inns were not responsible for losses unless the guest gave the clerk an itemized list of the valuables, and the inn could not be compelled to accept guests with valuables for sale. The law was designed to alleviate common-law liability, with a distinction made between valuables and valuables held for sale. The inn was responsible for the loss.[79]

Memorial Hospital filed suit to discover if it was subject to the Kansas Open Meeting Act (KOMA). It operated a nonprofit hospital owned by Riley County. The old board held open meetings, but in 1984 the board was restructured. It possessed no taxing power or eminent domain, and trustees decided how the funds were to be spent. The district court held that KOMA did not apply to this situation, and the attorney general appealed the decision. The supreme court determined that the legislature's intention was to apply KOMA where the county commissioners were the host. If the county leases the hospital to another, then KOMA does not apply if (1) there is no government decision making involved or (2) it is an independent entity, providing it serves under the lease of a hospital property from a board of trustee. The trustees are subject to KOMA, not the board of directors.[80]

The court during this era continued the process of modernizing the law. The justices updated the common law where needed and adapted new technology and processes to old procedures, but retreated to a basic conservative interpretation of the laws as delivered in the 1950s and 1960s.

Conclusion

The Wyandotte Constitution, with Article III establishing the judicial branch of government and the supreme court, was typical of its time and place in borrowing heavily from earlier state constitutions, especially that of Ohio, where many of the framers originated. These people wrought well, and little of their work needed change over the next dozen decades. Although the early justices had little formal legal training, this, too, was typical of the era. Luckily, most were self-trained in the fundamentals and were dedicated to the law as a profession and to applying it to Kansas circumstances. In the early decades the justices dealt with issues typical of an emerging frontier state that was flooded with litigation over removal of Indian tribes and quieting their land "titles," dealing with white land titles, settling county seat wars, and building railroads. The early court followed the national pattern of reliance on common law, the jury system, stare decisis, or precedents until new societal differences arose. The court significantly modified tort defenses to allow plaintiffs more leeway to collect damages in the post–Civil War era.

The emerging Industrial Revolution before, during, and after the Civil War produced sea changes in Kansas society. It reinvigorated and revolutionized the capitalist system and took it in new directions, produced the "labor problem," and exploited the laboring classes, both agrarian and industrial. Both groups rose in protest over their reduced status in society, laborers by organizing unions and farmers by attempting to improve their lot in life through political action. Either group, if politically cohesive, could control the state's political life, but certainly if they united, they could subdue the economic royalists and demand their rightful heritage of a part of the American Dream. Alas, they continued to reject cooperation and, through division, were defeated.

The farm organization and Populist Party came close to achieving power but, in the end, also succumbed to the "divide and conquer" approach. The capitalists continued to succeed in convincing agrarians that laborers were the enemy. Those in power cannot abide challenges to their authority or the inevitability of their achievements. The Populists disputed this but lost without other support groups.

In the long term, however, the Populists succeeded when the Progressives accepted their program and carried it out until World War I interrupted their success. War was followed by reaction, which was supplanted by the world's worst depression and even more devastating World War II, all in two decades. The Great Depression caused liberals to revive the reform movement with a new relationship between government and individuals and carry to fruition the earlier Populist and Progressive reforms. In recent history the emphasis has been more on personal rights of women, children, and minorities in contrast to the previous emphasis on property rights. During these epochs, the law metamorphosed in tandem with the alterations in society. Law in Kansas formed its society, and Kansas society, in turn, molded the law. When the Populists dominated the supreme court, the ruling class anticipated dire consequences to its world. But lawyers are universally conservative politically and are especially dedicated to precedent. This becomes even more pervasive when they become judges, as they are governed by the constraints of law. The Populist majority on the court disappointed their supporters and shocked their opponents by handing down decisions similar in effect to those of Democrats or Republicans. Politics seemed to play no dominating role in interpreting and applying the law.[1]

In its early history the justices began modifying the common law to give greater protection to women. This was later extended to protecting children in custody and in legal adoption. The issue of prohibition plagued law enforcement officials and courts until this sumptuary legislation was abandoned in 1948, when "the bootleggers and the prohibitionists" ceased marching to the polls together. During prohibition's nine-decade history the working man was convinced he had a God-given right to his liquor after a hard day's work, and clever suppliers experimented with a host of legalities to test the law, the enforcement officers, and the judges and to evade the ban. Most important in the long run, the experiment resulted in abolishing the terrible nineteenth-century open saloon.

The federal courts follow a firm rule against hearing "friendly" cases. Litigants must have "standing" to bring their case; in other words, one side or the other must have been "hurt" and need legal redress. The Kansas system includes provision whereby a state official may bring a quo warranto case to seek an interpretation of a legal or constitutional question. The governor or attorney general, for instance, might want to know the constitutionality of a recently enacted statute and bring quo warranto proceeding to receive an answer without testing it by litigants who have standing in regard to the law.

From its beginnings in 1882 the Kansas Bar Association (KBA) has played a major role in helping the judicial system remain modern and effective. In 1887 its judiciary committee established a clearinghouse to evaluate ideas for improving the judiciary. In 1899 the association recommended reorganizing the supreme court and increasing the number of justices to the current seven. In the 1950s the KBA developed the current process for selecting justices for the high court. Not least, in 1959 it endorsed a revision of the code of civil procedure and rules of evidence and made substantial recommendations in reducing delays in the state system of justice.

George Washington, the first president, made a major contribution with the precedents he established for executive action. Kansas was fortunate to have Samuel Kingman as one of its first chief justices. Kingman, likewise, set the tone and approach for Sunflower justice as he served with both kindness and astute judgment to chart the early court on a proper course.

Justice David Brewer also ranks among the great Kansas jurists. He usually sought to promote judicial self-restraint on the bench. After

Brewer's elevation to a federal court, President Benjamin Harrison promoted him to the US Supreme Court, the first Kansan to be so honored, where he served with distinction for twenty years.

Chief Justice Frank Doster was decades ahead of his time with his support of women's suffrage and his philosophy of "the rights of the user prevail over the rights of the owner." Much to the surprise of most leaders of the two major political parties, Populist justices Doster and Stephen Allen failed to display any radical philosophy while on the Kansas bench, leaving the casual observer to conclude that jurists are basically conservative in their judicial decisions, regardless of their political persuasion. Doster, like Brewer, urged judicial restraint yet observed in one of his opinions that "a state possesses all power not expressly withheld." He also expanded the "attractive nuisance" common-law concept to protect the dangerous behavior of boyhood play.

Chief Justice William A. Johnston was another great jurist. He supported the medical concepts of Dr. Samuel Crumbine, who led Kansans to the cutting edge of public health reform worldwide, and he promoted changes in the judicial system to bring Kansas into the twentieth century of judicial performance. This included expanding the number of high court members to handle the increasing workload, to promote the member with the greatest seniority to the position of chief justice, and to modernize the procedures establishing a system of rotating visitation of justices writing opinions to eliminating errors and misunderstandings in the court's decisions. Under his tenure, the state also experimented with the novel concept of combining judicial and administrative authority in the Court of Visitation and the Industrial Court of Kansas, both of which proved to be dismal failures.

Finally, David Praeger was an outstanding chief justice, especially in his efforts to modernize outdated court procedures. He promoted citizens' conferences to analyze workloads and have public support for legislation to improve the system of justice. During his tenure the court instituted a program of logging cases for age and pending location, which led justices to curb their delays in hearing cases. As a result, in 1987 the National Foundation for Improvement of Justice awarded

Kansas a ten-thousand-dollar prize for its delay reduction program. In addition, the legislature was persuaded to revise the state court system to accommodate shifts in population patterns to achieve a more equitable system of justice.

In the mid-twentieth century, Kansas modified its process of selecting justices by adopting the Missouri Plan, a nonpartisan committee to name choices for appointment by the governor, followed by retention elections. This issue resurfaced at the millennium with the Kansas Justice Initiative and a thorough debate over the merits of the Missouri Plan. Many voters resented their loss of control over justices, and judges and lawyers strongly supported the gubernatorial selection over competitive selection. The result was deadlock and inaction because of the attempt to reduce the complex process into simple choices.[2]

The Kansas court was able to adapt to new developments such as the telephone, the automobile, and the airplane that made law enforcement more difficult. At the same time, the justices were forced to adjust to new social mores that sought to increase privacy to the individual, more rights over control of their bodies for women, and increased protection against discrimination over that burning issue of race, which continues to haunt American society. The stars have yet to reveal a method for Kansans to discuss this crisis, let alone resolve it. In a less consuming realm, farmers and wage-earners have yet to reconcile their crucial differences.

Throughout Kansas history Republicans have dominated the supreme court, except for those rare instances when Democrats captured the gubernatorial chair. This has made no difference in rendering nonpartisan decisions. On the other hand, Kansas justices failed to follow the national pattern after the vain attempt to impeach and convict US Supreme Court Justice Samuel Chase in 1803, and this had an effect on national judges, who refrained from partisan activities thereafter. Some Kansas justices, on the other hand, were quite partisan until the 1950s, when the practice was carried too far, resulting in a change in the selection process.

Preparation in the law has tended to follow national trends from "reading" law, to professional training, to specialization. Few of the early justices attended law school but instead "read" law in a lawyer's office to prepare for the bar exam. The original court was composed of three justices, with one specifically elected as chief justice, elected for six-year terms. A constitutional amendment in 1900 expanded the number to seven, and the one with the greatest tenure was automatically elevated to chief justice. This number allowed the justices to sit separately in divisions of three each, with the entire bench hearing only those cases deemed vital for review by all. The path to these seats came through gubernatorial nomination or selection by the electorate. Thus, Republicans enjoyed 88.4 percent of the positions to the end of 1975.

Paternal occupation of these judges is difficult to obtain, and 67.2 percent must be listed as "unknown." From 1861 to 1900 most were in the professional category, while from 1900 to 1957 21.6 percent were farmers. The recent period revealed so little information that "no summary can be given." Most of the justices during the first period were native-born, and in all periods, a small-town community dominated their origins. Fifty-four percent attended a college or university, 3.3 percent went to an academy, and 18 percent enjoyed a public school education. Only the University of Kansas, Kansas State Normal, College of Emporia, Washburn University, and the University of Wisconsin had more than one graduate. Fifty-five and seven-tenths attended a law school. The University of Kansas and Washburn University law schools provided 43.5 percent of the justices.[3]

To receive election or appointment, the person must be well known across the state, and thus over 50 percent of the nominees held state government positions. The judiciary provided fifteen members, the executive branch nine, and four came from the legislature. A few served as county attorneys before elevation to the supreme court. Almost one-fourth had the experience of being a judge, over 26 percent were general practitioners of the law, 18 percent served as government attorneys, and 16.3 percent were primarily politicians before going to the high bench. In all this, the Kansas court appears to have followed the pattern established in other state judiciary systems.[4]

A number of Kansas cases were appealed to the US Supreme Court, where they created significant precedents in national law. *The Kansas Indians* set a precedent for law dealing with tribes, and *Ashbell v. Kansas* helped establish uniformity in criminal court procedure. *Brown v. Topeka* touched off a major social revolution in the United States, and *Energy Reserves Group v. Kansas Power & Light* helped clarify the contract clause in the US Constitution. Ironically, the largely agricultural Sunflower State provided several cases to clarify national labor law. These included allowing states or their agencies to establish work rules in their projects, sustaining the disallowance of the yellow dog contract, and protecting the rights of an IWW organizer. Finally, and not least, the high court clarified states acting in their own "public interest" in two other cases.

Appendix: Kansas Supreme Court Justices

Ewing, Thomas 1861–62
Kingman, Samuel Austin 1861–64, 1866–76
Bailey, Lawrence D. 1861–69
Safford, Jacob 1865–71
Valentine, Daniel Mulford 1869–93
Cobb, Nelson 1862–63
Crozier, Robert 1864–67
Brewer, David 1871–84
Horton, Albert H. 1876–95
Hurd, Theodore 1884
Johnston, William Agnew 1884–1935
Allen, Stephen Haley 1893–99
Doster, Frank 1897–1903
Martin, David 1895–1902
Burch, Rousseau Angelus 1902–37
Smith, William Redwood 1899–1905
Pollock, John C. 1901–3
Ellis, Abraham Halstead 1901–2
Cunningham, Edwin W. 1901–5
Graves, Charles Burleagh 1905–11
Greene, Adrian C. 1901–7
Benson, Alfred Washburn 1907–15
Mason, Henry Freeman 1903–27
Atkinson, William D. 1904
Smith, Clark Allen 1905–15
Porter, Silas Wright 1905–23
West, Judson S. 1910–22
Dawson, John Shaw 1915–45

Marshall, John 1914–31
Harvey, William West 1923–56
Hutchinson, William Easton 1927–39
Joachims, William O. 1929–30
Sloan, Edward Ray 1931–33
Hopkins, Richard Joseph 1923–29
Smith, William Amos 1930–56
Thiele, Walter G. 1930–56
Allen, Harry Kyle 1936–42
Wedell, Hugo 1935–55
Parker, Jay S. 1942–66
Burch, Allen B. 1945–48
Hoch, Homer 1939–49
Cowan, Austin 1948–49
Arn, Edward Ferdinand 1949–50
Price, Robert T. 1949–71
Wertz, William J. 1950–65
Hagey, Lloyd M. 1950
Robb, Clair E. 1955–65
Fatzer, Harold R. 1956–77
Schroeder, Alfred 1956–87
Hall, Fred L. 1956–58
Jackson, Schuyler 1958–64
Fontron, John F. 1964–75
Kaul, Robert H. 1965–77
Fromme, Alex M. 1966–82
O'Connor, Earl E. 1965–71
Owsley, Perry E. 1971–78
Prager, David 1971–92
Miller, Robert S. 1975–90
McFarland, Kay 1977–2009
Holmes, Richard W. 1977–95
Herd, Harold Shields 1979–93
Lockett, Tyler C. 1983–2002
Allegrucci, Donald C. 1987–2007
Six, Fred Newton 1988–2002

Notes

Preface

1. Francis H. Heller, "Lawyers and Judges in Early Kansas: A Prospect for Research," *University of Kansas Law Review* 22 (Winter 1974): 217–18. The point that the state courts affect our everyday lives comes from James W. Hewitt, *Slipping Backward: A History of the Nebraska Supreme Court* (Lincoln: University of Nebraska Press, 2007), 1.

2. Heller, "Lawyers and Judges," 217–18.

3. Michael H. Hoeflich, "Why the History of Kansas Law Has Not Been Written," *Kansas History* 26 (Winter 2003–4): 264–71.

4. James Willard Hurst, "Old and New Dimensions of Research in United States Legal History," *American Journal of Legal History* 23 (January 1979): 20; Morton J. Horowitz, "The Conservative Tradition in the Writing of American Legal History," *American Journal of Legal History* 17 (July 1973): 281.

5. Daniel R. Ernst, "Law and American Political Development, 1877–1938," *Reviews in American History* 26 (March 1998): 208.

6. Lord Bryce quoted in Ernst, "Law and American Political Development," 212.

Introduction

1. See Nicole Etcheson, *Bleeding Kansas* (Lawrence: University Press of Kansas, 2004), 12, for a description of this sectional balance.

2. Etcheson, *Bleeding Kansas*, 100–102, 122.

3. Howard v. Kansas City Railroad, 41 Kan. 402 (1889), 19 How. 393.

4. Kenneth M. Stampp, *America in 1857* (Oxford: Oxford University Press, 1990), 328–29. For the vote on the Lecompton Constitution, see G. Raymond Gaddert, *The Birth of Kansas* (Lawrence: University of Kansas Publications, 1940), 77.

5. Ernst, "Law and American Political Development," 223–24.

6. The president subsequently acquired this appointive power, and, as Peter S. Onuf notes, the president "through his appointive governor controlled territorial development" (*Statehood and Union* [Bloomington: Indiana University Press, 1987], 78). For the secession crisis and last-minute attempts to resolve it, see R. Alton Lee, "The

Corwin Amendment in the Secession Crisis," *Ohio Historical Quarterly* 70 (January 1961). For the six governors, see Arthur J. Stanley, Jr., "Lawyers in Politics," in *Requisite Learning and Good Moral Character: A History of the Kansas Bench and Bar*, ed. Robert W. Richmond (Topeka: Kansas Bar Association, 1982), 76–77.

7. "Executive Minutes of Governor John W. Geary," in *Kansas Historical Collections* (Topeka: Kansas State Historical Society, 1886–88), 4:602–3.

8. T. M. Lillard, "Beginnings of the Kansas Judiciary," *Kansas Historical Quarterly* 10 (February 1941): 96–97. For "agent nor attorney," see James Durham, "U.S. v. Lewis L. Weld: Judiciary Creativity or Judicial Subversion," *Journal of the Kansas Bar Association* 56 (1986): 8–11, an interesting account of this case.

9. James K. Logan, "The Federal Courts and Their Judges—the Impact on History," in *The Law and Lawyers in Kansas: A Collection of Papers Presented at the 116th Annual Meeting of the Kansas State Historical Society, October 4 & 5, 1991*, ed. Virgil W. Dean (Topeka: Kansas State Historical Society, 1991), 59–60.

10. Logan, "The Federal Courts," 61–62.

11. Paul E. Wilson, "The Early Years: The Bench and Bar before 1882," in Richmond, *Requisite Learning*, 32–35.

12. Ernst, "Law and American Political Development," 137; "last straw" quote from Stampp, *America in 1857*, 155.

13. Stampp, *America in 1857*, 154, 188.

14. Martha B. Caldwell, "When Horace Greeley Visited Kansas in 1859," *Kansas Historical Quarterly* 9 (May 1940): 115–27; see Stampp, *America in 1859*, 23, for "famine horse."

15. John A. Martin, "The Wyandotte Constitutional Convention," *Kansas Magazine* 5 (1911): 23–25.

16. Matthew H. Raney, "The Early Political and Military Career of Governor John Alexander Martin" (M.A. thesis, Kansas State University, 1991). Peter Cozzens, *This Terrible Sound* (Urbana: University of Illinois Press, 1992), is excellent on these battles and Martin's role in them.

17. Stampp, *America in 1859*, 29.

18. Article III, Kansas Constitution.

19. *Freedom's Champion*, 24 September 1859.

20. Stampp, *America in 1859*, 27–29.

1. The Kingman Court

1. Etcheson, *Bleeding Kansas*, 240–42.

2. Lillard, "Beginnings," 98; Gaddert, *The Birth of Kansas*, 125.

3. Edwin A. Austin, "The Supreme Court of the State of Kansas," *Kansas State Historical Society Proceedings* 13 (1913): 95.

4. Mary Scott Rowland, "Thomas Ewing: The Reluctant Chief Justice," *Journal of the Kansas Bar Association* 57 (February 1988): 31–32.

5. Wilson, "The Early Years," 38; Etcheson, *Bleeding Kansas,* 240–41; David McCullough, *Truman* (New York: Simon & Schuster, 1992), 32.

6. Joseph G. Waters, "Samuel A. Kingman," *Kansas State Historical Society Proceedings*, 9 (1904): 46–47.

7. "All men" quote from John Martin, "The Wyandotte Constitution," in the *Champion*, July 30, 1882; "a home is a home" from Howell Jones, "Judge Samuel Kingman," *Kansas State Historical Society Proceedings* 10 (1910): 57.

8. Roger L. Theis and Karl R. Swartz, "Kansas Homestead Law," *Journal of the Kansas Bar Association* 65 (April 1996): 20–27.

9. William E. Treadway, "The Gilded Age in Kansas," *Kansas Historical Quarterly* 40 (Spring 1974): 29.

10. Joseph G. Waters, "Samuel A. Kingman," *Kansas State Historical Society Proceedings* 9 (1904): 53.

11. Waters, "Samuel A. Kingman," 64–65.

12. Waters, "Samuel A. Kingman," 61.

13. Waters, "Samuel A. Kingman," 47, 62.

14. "In Memoriam," *Kansas Reports*, vol. 47 (1891); *Lawrence Daily Journal*, 16 October 1891.

15. "In Memoriam," *Kansas Reports*, vol. 56 (1895).

16. "In Memoriam," *Kansas Reports*, vol. 55 (1895).

17. Waters, "Samuel A. Kingman," 117–18; Wiley v. Keokuk, 6 Kan. 111.

18. 33 Kan. xi (1885).

19. Waters, "Samuel A. Kingman," 118–19; Brian J. Moline, "David Joseph Brewer, Kansas Jurist," *Journal of the Kansas Bar Association* 35 (January–February 1986): 7.

20. Waters, "Samuel A. Kingman," 99.

21. Waters, "Samuel A. Kingman," 96–97. The House also impeached State Auditor George S. Hillyer at the same time as the governor. The Senate convicted Hillyer, and he appealed to the supreme court in a quo warranto procedure in which Kingman wrote the opinion that detailed how the impeachment and conviction/acquittal process should operate constitutionally. See Kansas ex rel. Adams v. Hillyer, 2 Kan. 17 (1863).

22. Waters, "Samuel A. Kingman," 98.

23. Waters, "Samuel A. Kingman"; Kansas ex rel. Watson v. Cobb, 1 Kan. 32 (1863).

24. Judd v. Driver, 2 Kan. 455 (1864).

25. Legal Tender Cases, 123 Wall. 457 (1871) sustained the legality of this money, and Veazey Bank v. Fenno, 8 Wall. 533 (1869) upheld the tax on state bank notes.

26. Gordon Morris Bakken, "Law and Legal Tender in California and the West," *Southern California Quarterly* 62 (Fall 1980), is excellent on this topic.

27. Jones v. State, 1 Kan. 273 (1863).

28. Robert W. Richmond, *Kansas* (Wheeling IL: Forum Press, 1989), 151–52; see Henry F. Mason, "County Seat Controversies in Southwest Kansas," *Kansas Historical Quarterly* 2 (February 1933), for other county wars.

29. Kansas ex rel. Wells v. Commissioners of Neosho County, 6 Kan. 524 (1870); Brewer quote from Gossard v. Vaught, 10 Kan. 162 (1872).

30. 3 Kan. 123 (1865); Bronson v. Kingle, 1 How. 311.

31. Ward v. Ward, 5 Kan. 239 (1869).

32. Helm v. Helm, 11 Kan. 19 (1873).

33. McCracken v. Todd, 1 Kan. 148 (1862).

34. Summers v. Spybuck, 1 Kan. 313 (1863).

35. Irwin v. Paulette, 1 Kan. 394 (1863).

36. Lounsberry v. Rakestraw, 14 Kan. 151 (1875).

37. Blue Jacket v. Johnson County, 3 Kan. 299 (1865).

38. Hunt v. State, 4 Kan. 60 (1866). See Deborah A. Rosen, *American Indians and State Law: Sovereignty, Race, and Citizenship* (Lincoln: University of Nebraska Press, 2007), for an analysis of this confusing issue.

39. Johnson County v. Craft, 6 Kan. 94 (1870).

40. Hunt v. Kansas & Missouri Bridge, 11 Kan. 323 (1873).

41. Ephraim v. Garlick, 10 Kan. 280 (1872).

42. 13 Kan. 302 (1874); The Kansas Indians, 5 Wall. 761.

43. Craig Miner, *Kansas* (Lawrence: University Press of Kansas, 2002), 103.

44. Kansas Pacific v. Missouri, Kansas and Texas Railway, 15 Kan. 15 (1875).

45. Parker v. Winsor, 5 Kan. 362, 367–68.

46. Union Pacific v. Rollins, 5 Kan. 167 (1869). James W. Ely, Jr., *Railroads and American Law* (Lawrence: University Press of Kansas, 2001), 117–20, discusses the fence law issue.

47. Gordon M. Bakken, "The Development of the Law of Tort in Frontier California," *Southern California Quarterly* 60 (Winter 1978).

48. Union Pacific v. Davis County, 6 Kan. 256 (1870).

49. Leavenworth County v. Miller, 7 Kan. 479 (1871).

50. State v. Santa Fe, 6 Kan. 500 (1870).

51. Pacific Railway v. Nash, 7 Kan. 280 (1871).

52. Kansas Pacific v. McCoy, 8 Kan. 538 (1871).

53. Darling v. Rogers, 7 Kan. 364 (1871).

54. Michael J. Brodhead, *David J. Brewer: The Life of a Supreme Court Justice, 1837–1910* (Carbondale: Southern Illinois University Press, 1994), 24; R. Alton Lee, "The Populist Dream of a 'Wrong Way Transcontinental,'" *Kansas History: Journal of the Central Plains* 35 (Summer 2012).

55. State v. Stringfellow, 2 Kan. 263 (1864).

56. Wheatley v. Terry, 6 Kan. 427 (1870).

57. Commissioners of Leavenworth v. Lang, 8 Kan. 284 (1871).

58. Vail, Trustee v. Beach, Treasurer, 10 Kan. 214 (1872); Washburn College v. Shawnee County, 8 Kan. 344.

59. Kermit L. Hall, *The Magic Mirror* (Oxford: Oxford University Press, 1989), 165–66.

60. Harris v. Harris, 5 Kan. 46; last quote from Hall, *The Magic Mirror*, 20.

61. Anderson v. Anderson, 9 Kan. 112 (1873).

62. Brandon v. Brandon, 15 Kan. 342 (1875).

63. Anthony v. Haldeman, 7 Kan. 50 (1871).

64. Missouri Railroad v. Morris, 7 Kan. 143 (1871).

65. State v. McCord, 8 Kan. 232 (1871).

66. Lewis v. State, 5 Kan. 296 (1867).

67. Madden v. State, 11 Kan. 340 (1863).

68. Jones v. State, 17 Kan. 608 (1876).

69. Luke v. Johnnycake, 9 Kan. 350 (1872); *Atchison Daily Champion*, 5 January 1870.

70. State v. Millar, 2 Kan. 174 (1863).

71. State v. Smith, 3 Kan. 274 (1874).

72. State v. White, 15 Kan. 538 (1875).

73. Sawyer v. Sauer, 10 Kan. 466 (1872).

74. Clay v. State, 4 Kan. 49 (1866).

75. Robert Bader Smith, *Prohibition in Kansas* (Lawrence: University Press of Kansas, 1986), 20.

76. State v. Thompson, 2 Kan. 438 (1864).

77. Hagan v. State, 3 Kan. 89 (1866).

78. State ex rel. Price v. Sec. of State Laurence, 3 Kan. 88 (1864).

79. Nichols v. Weaver, 7 Kan. 373 (1871).

80. Lewis v. Bourbon County, 12 Kan. 186 (1871).

2. The Chief Justice as Politician

1. Quoted in R. Alton Lee, *T-town on the Plains* (Manhattan KS: Sunflower University Press, 1999), 14.

2. Lee, *T-town*, 14–15.

3. Cortez A. M. Ewing, "Notes on Two Kansas Impeachments," *Kansas Historical Quarterly* 23 (Autumn 1957): 281–85.

4. R. Alton Lee, *Farmers vs. Wage Earners* (Lincoln: University of Nebraska Press, 2005), chap. 1.

5. Bader, *Prohibition in Kansas*, 44–45.

6. Brian J. Moline, "Prohibition and the Attorney General, 1880–1900," in Dean, *The Law and Lawyers*, 39.

7. George Templar, "The Federal Judiciary in Kansas," in Richmond, *Requisite Learning*, 64.

8. Lee, *Farmers vs. Wage Earners*, 6–8.

9. Lee, *Farmers vs. Wage Earners*, chap. 2, "an uncommon governor."

10. Austin, "The Supreme Court," 116; *Atchison Daily Globe*, 16 July 1894. The LLD was an advanced law degree.

11. 65 Kan. ix.

12. 65 Kan. x.

13. Box 1, folder 2, Albert H. Horton Papers, Kansas State Historical Society, Topeka.

14. Box 1, folder 1, Horton Papers.

15. *Atchison Daily Champion*, 12 March 1879.

16. Burton J. Williams, *Senator John James Ingalls* (Lawrence: University Press of Kansas, 1972), 81–83.

17. Williams, *Senator John James Ingalls*, 94–95.

18. *Atchison Daily Champion*, 3–4 March 1880; box 1, folder 2, Horton Papers. The *Topeka Daily Capital*, 4 May 1880, also reprinted Ingalls's speech.

19. Box 1, folder 2, Horton Papers; Williams, *Senator John James Ingalls*, 111.

20. B. P. Waggener to Albert Horton, 23 January 1895, box 2, folder 2, Horton Papers.

21. Frank Hagerman to Thayer, 4 February 1895; Horton to Hagerman, 15 February 1895; Brewer to Horton, 7 February 1895, all in box 2, folder 3, Horton Papers.

22. B. P. Waggener to Albert H. Horton, 6 February 1895, and Walter Sanborn to David Brewer, 11 February 1895, box 2, folder 3, Horton Papers.

23. Austin, "The Supreme Court," 121.

24. Brian Moline, "Justice William A. Johnston, 'The Grand Old Man of Kansas,'" *Journal of the Kansas Bar Association* 56 (April 1987): 19–20.

25. First National Bank of Manhattan v. Warner, 22 Kan. 375.

26. Hixon v. George, 18 Kan. 25 (1877).

27. Blankenship v. Nancy, 19 Kan. 159 (1877).

28. Garnett Bank v. Bowen, 25 Kan. 82 (1881).

29. Atchison Savings v. Wheeler, 20 Kan. 625 (1878).

30. Grinter v. Kansas Pacific, 23 Kan. 455 (1880).

31. Brown v. Boston Steel, 23 Kan. 473 (1880).

32. Franklin County Commissioners v. Sarah Pennock, 18 Kan. 579 (1877).

33. Peter Karsten, *Heart versus Head: Judge-Made Law in Nineteenth-Century America* (Chapel Hill: University of North Carolina Press, 1997), 211.

34. Kansas Central v. Fitzsimmons, 18 Kan. 34 (1877).

35. Union Pacific v. Dunden, 37 Kan. 1 (1887).

36. Biggs v. Consolidated Barbed Wire, 60 Kan. 217 (1899).

37. Brown v. Santa Fe, 31 Kan. 1 (1883). See Ely, *Railroads and American Law*, chap. 5, for a good account of the development of railroad law. See Karsten, *Heart versus Head*, 201–33, for the development of the "attractive nuisance" rule (quote at 211).

38. Santa Fe v. Koehler, 37 Kan. 463 (1882).

39. Kansas Pacific Railway v. Joseph Peavey, 29 Kan. 122 (1882).

40. Atchison and Northern v. Flinn, 24 Kan. 447 (1880).

41. Union Pacific v. Henigh, 23 Kan. 244 (1880).

42. Mason v. Missouri Pacific, 27 Kan. 83 (1877).

43. Hopkins v. Pacific Railway, 18 Kan. 462.

44. Santa Fe v. State, 22 Kan. 17 (1879).

45. Prohibition Cases, 24 Kan. 499, 503 (1881).

46. Kansas v. Stormont, 24 Kan. 499 (1881).

47. Bader, *Prohibition in Kansas*, 65.

48. Ames v. Brudden Brupsden, 25 Kan. 524 (1881). Brodhead, *David J. Brewer*, 37–38, seems to confuse the Prohibition Cases with the Intoxicating Liquor Cases.

49. Kansas v. Schweiter, 27 Kan. 499 (1882).

50. Kansas v. Mugler, 28 Kan. 181 (1882).

51. Kansas v. Nickerson, 30 Kan. 545 (1883).

52. Kansas v. Topeka, 30 Kan. 653 (1883).

53. Kansas v. Topeka, 32 Kan. 452 (1883).

54. Crawford v. State, 28 Kan. 518 (1882).

55. Tuloss v. Sedan, 31 Kan. 165 (1883).

56. Kansas v. Brown, 38 Kan. 390 (1882).

57. Brodhead, *David J. Brewer*, 39–40; 20 Kan. 650.

58. Larson v. Berquist, 34 Kan. 334 (1885).

59. Powell v. Powell, 18 Kan. 371 (1877).

60. Townsend v. Nutt, 19 Kan. 282 (1877).

61. Spurgeon v. Spurgeon, 32 Kan. 171 (1884).

62. City of Council Grove, 20 Kan. 619 (1878).

63. Gilmore v. Hentig, 33 Kan. 156 (1882).

64. In re Dressler, 35 Kan. 678 (1886).

65. Fretwell v. Troy, 18 Kan. 271 (1877).

66. Winfield v. Winfield Gas, 37 Kan. 24 (1887).

67. State v. Baldwin, 36 Kan. 1 (1886).

68. State v. Jansen, 22 Kan. 349 (1879).

69. State v. Adams, 20 Kan. 311 (1878).

70. In re Payson, 23 Kan. 534 (1880).

71. New York Life v. Gowan, 18 Kan. 300 (1877).

72. Gross v. Bogard, 18 Kan. 288 (1877).

73. State v. Ruth, 21 Kan. 583 (1879).

74. State v. Mulkins, 18 Kan. 16 (1877).

75. Sewell v. Caruthers, 26 Kan. 724 (1882).

76. State v. Gilmore, 20 Kan. 551 (1878).

77. State v. Saunders, 19 Kan. 127 (1877).

78. Potawatomie v. Morrall, 19 Kan. 141 (1877).

79. Mayberry v. Sivey, 18 Kan. 291 (1880).

80. Kansas v. D. W. Stormont, 24 Kan. 483 (1881).

81. Board of Ed. v. Tinnon, 26 Kan. 2 (1881); Brodhead, *David J. Brewer*, 43–44; Knox v. Independence, 45 Kan. 152 (1891).

82. Privett v. Stevens, 25 Kan. 192 (1881).

83. Pruett v. Beckford, 26 Kan. 52 (1881).

84. Smith v. Martin, 20 Kan. 572 (1878).

85. Lee, *Farmers vs. Wage Earners*, 64.

3. The Populist Interlude

1. Elizabeth Sanders, *Roots of Reform* (Chicago: University of Chicago Press, 1999), 410.

2. Robert C. McMath, *American Populism: A Social History* (New York: Hill and Wang, 1993), 51–52.

3. See R. Alton Lee, *A History of Regulatory Taxation* (Lexington: University Press of Kentucky, 1973), for coverage of this unique use of the taxing power.

4. See R. Alton Lee, *Principle over Party: The Farmers Alliance and Populism in South Dakota, 1880–1900* (Pierre: South Dakota State Historical Society, 2011), chap. 1, for these agrarian problems that were similar throughout the Great Plains.

5. O. Gene Clanton, *A Common Humanity* (Manhattan KS: Sunflower University Press, 2004), 44.

6. Solon J. Buck, *The Agrarian Crusade* (New Haven CT: Yale University Press, 1920) is the standard account of the Grangers. Munn v. Illinois, 94 U.S. 113 (1877) sustained the so-called Granger laws.

7. Laurence Goodwyn, *Democracy's Promise* (Oxford: Oxford University Press, 1976) stresses the importance of the Alliance movement to the later Populist political activities. Clanton, *Common Humanity*, does not emphasize their importance in Kansas as I do their significance in South Dakota. See Lee, *Principle over Party*, chaps. 2 and 3.

8. John D. Hicks, *The Populist Revolt* (Minneapolis: University of Minnesota Press, 1959), 194–97.

9. Peter H. Argersinger, "Pentecostal Politics in Kansas: Religion, the Farmers' Alliance, and the Gospel of Populism," *Kansas Quarterly*, Fall 1969, 31.

10. Gene Clanton, *Populism: The Humane Preference in America* (New York: Twayne, 1991), 36.

11. Burton J. Williams, "The Kansas Alliance versus 'Mr. Republican,'" *Kansas Quarterly* 1 (Fall 1969).

12. Michael J. Brodhead, "Populism and the Law: Some Notes on Stephen J. Allen," *Kansas Quarterly* 1 (Fall 1969): 76–78. William Johnston noted that although this was a period of "turmoil and strife," he could find "no trace of the agitation . . . in their opinions and judgments" (box 3, William Johnston Papers, Kansas State Historical Society, Topeka).

13. Clanton, *Populism*, 107–8.

14. Clanton, *Populism*, 107–11, for coverage of this "war."

15. In re Gunn, 50 Kan. 155. William M. Wiecek, *The Guarantee Clause of the U.S. Constitution* (Ithaca NY: Cornell University Press, 1972) is the best source on the Dorr rebellion.

16. D. Brewer to Horton, 26 March 1893; B. P. Waggener to Judge Albert H. Horton, 1 March 1893, box 2, folder 4, Horton Papers.

17. Clanton, *Populism*, 223.

18. Clanton, *Populism*, chap. 13.

19. Michael Brodhead, "Visions of a Better World: Comparisons of Jurists David Brewer and Frank Doster," *Kansas History: A Journal of the Great Plains* 16 (Spring 1993): 44–46.

20. Brodhead, "Visions," 48–49.

21. Bar Association of Kansas, *Minutes*, 1907, 27.

22. Austin, "The Supreme Court," 117. The author wrote biographies of all the justices for the period before the Populists and of those added after the turn of the century when the court membership was expanded. For some unexplained reason he could not find it possible to write anything about Allen or Doster, and they were simply ignored, as if they never served on the court.

23. Michael J. Brodhead, *Persevering Populist: The Life of Frank Doster* (Reno: University of Nevada Press, 1969), 134. This is an excellent biography in which the author does justice to a complex figure.

24. Brodhead, *Persevering Populist*, 144–45.

25. *Kansas City Bar Bulletin*, March 1925.

26. Secretary of State, "Biennial Report," 1899; Biographical Sketches, Kansas State Historical Society, Topeka.

27. Supreme Court, Proceedings, 1945.

28. Thomas Amory Lee, "Judge John C. Pollock," *Journal of the Kansas Bar Association* 9 (February 1954): 219–25.

29. Virginia Noah Gibson, "The Effect of the Populist Movement on Kansas State

Agricultural College" (M.S. thesis, Kansas College of Agriculture and Applied Sciences, 1932), 20–37.

30. Gibson, "The Effect," 38–85.

31. R. Douglas Hurt, "The Populist Judiciary: Election Reform and Contested Offices," *Kansas History: A Journal of the Great Plains* 4 (Summer 1981): 138; 61 Kan. 265 (1899); Yoe v. Hoffman, 61 Kan. 265 (1899).

32. Taylor v. Bleakly, 55 Kan. 1 (1895).

33. Simpson v. Osborn, 52 Kan. 328 (1893).

34. Sims v. Daniels, 57 Kan. 556 (1896).

35. Railroad Commission v. Snyder, 53 Kan. 470 (1893).

36. 53 Kan. 207.

37. State v. Johnson, 61 Kan. 803; R. Douglas Hurt, "Populists on the Kansas Supreme Court," *Midwest Review* 4 (Spring 1982): 19.

38. State v. Briedenthal, 55 Kan. 308 (1895).

39. Householder v. Morrill, 55 Kan. 317 (1895).

40. Rogers v. Morrell, 55 Kan. 737 (1895).

41. Lease v. Clark, 55 Kan. 621 (1895); Brodhead, "Populism and the Law," 78, notes that, other than these decisions on Populists holding office, there was virtual unanimity on the court with Allen's appointment.

42. Briedenthal v. Edward, 57 Kan. 335 (1896).

43. In re Thomas Davis, 58 Kan. 368 (1897).

44. Kansas v. University of Kansas, 55 Kan. 389 (1895); Kansas v. Topeka, 59 Kan. 501 (1898).

45. State v. Johnson, 61 Kan. 803 (1900).

46. 65 Kan. 240; Smiley v. Kansas, 196 U.S. 447 (1905).

47. Cherokee Coal v. Wilson, 47 Kan. 460 (1891). These Populist prolabor laws are detailed in Lee, *Farmers vs. Wage Earners*, chap. 3.

48. Morback v. Home Mining, 53 Kan. 731 (1894).

49. R. Douglas Hurt, "Populist-Endorsed Judges and the Protection of Western Labor," *Journal of the West* 17 (January 1978): 19–20.

50. In re Dalton, 61 Kan. 257 (1899).

51. State v. Wilson, 61 Kan. 32 (1899).

52. 61 Kan. 146. See also Hurt, "Populist-Endorsed Judges," 24.

53. Bowen v. Phillips, 41 Kan. 364 (1889).

54. Moline, "Prohibition," 43.

55. State v. Fulker, 43 Kan. 237 (1890).

56. State v. Smith, 51 Kan. 120 (1893).

57. In re Sims, 54 Kan. 1 (1894).

58. State v. Yates, 52 Kan. 566 (1894).

59. State v. Stark, 63 Kan. 529 (1901).

60. Emporia v. Smith, 42 Kan. 433 (1889).

61. Smalley v. Hiawatha, 41 Kan. 550 (1889).

62. Hurla v. Kansas City, 46 Kan. 738 (1891).

63. Davenport v. Ottawa, 54 Kan. 711 (1895).

64. Long v. Emporia, 59 Kan. 46 (1898).

65. Consolidated Electric Light and Power v. Healy, 65 Kan. 798 (1902).

66. Price v. Atchison Water Company, 58 Kan. 551 (1897).

67. Roman v. Leavenworth, 90 Kan. 379 (1913).

68. Zagar v. Union Pacific, 113 Kan. 241 (1923).

69. Santa Fe v. English, 38 Kan. 110 (1887).

70. Santa Fe v. Randall, 40 Kan. 421 (1898).

71. 46 Kan. 415 (1891).

72. Chicago Railroad v. Ozark Township, 41 Kan. 403.

73. MKT v. Cook, 47 Kan. 216 (1891).

74. Long v. Chicago Railroad, 48 Kan. 28 (1892).

75. Missouri Pacific v. Finley, 38 Kan. 550 (1888).

76. MKT v. Haber, 56 Kan. 694 (1896).

77. Kinchlow v. Elevator Company, 57 Kan. 374 (1896).

78. Santa Fe v. Wiley, 57 Kan. 764 (1897).

79. State v. Lewin, 53 Kan. 679 (1894).

80. State v. Ashbell, 55 Kan. 398; text quotes from the *Topeka Daily Capital*, 8 November 1896.

81. 60 Kan. 51. In Ashbell v. Kansas, 209 U.S. 251 (1907), the US Supreme Court affirmed the Kansas decision.

82. Harrison v. Brophy, 51 Kan. 1 (1898); Hurt, "Populist Judiciary," 133–34.

83. Cattle Company v. Kline, 51 Kan. 23 (1893).

84. Acker v. Kimmie, 37 Kan. 276 (1887).

85. Harrison v. Brophy, 51 Kan. 1 (1898).

86. Kansas City v. McDonald, 60 Kan. 481 (1899).

87. Kansas v. Will Sholl, 58 Kan. 507 (1897).

88. State v. Pratt County, 42 Kan. 641 (1889).

89. Hornaday v. State, 62 Kan. 822 (1900).

90. Badger Lumber v. Marion Water, 48 Kan. 182 (1892).

4. The Grand Old Man's Court

1. Hall, *The Magic Mirror*, 232.

2. Peter Irons, *A People's History of the Supreme Court* (New York: Viking, 1999), 236–37.

3. Melvyn I. Urofsky, "State Courts and Progressive Legislation during the Progressive Era," *Journal of American History* 72 (June 1985): 65–66.

4. Urofsky, "State Courts," 66–67.

5. Urofsky, "State Courts," 84.

6. Robert Sherman LaForte, *Leaders of Reform* (Lawrence: University Press of Kansas, 1974), 2–3.

7. LaForte, *Leaders of Reform*, 4–6.

8. LaForte, *Leaders of Reform*, 7–12.

9. LaForte, *Leaders of Reform*, 4.

10. Richmond, *Kansas*, 207–9.

11. Lee, *Farmers vs. Wage Earners*, 91–104.

12. R. Alton Lee, *From Snake Oil to Medicine* (Westport CT: Praeger, 2007).

13. Miner, *Kansas*, 222, notes the number of female officeholders and lawyers.

14. Robert H. Kaul, "The Kansas Judicial System," in Richmond, *Requisite Learning*, 43–45.

15. Austin, "The Supreme Court," 101.

16. Austin, "The Supreme Court," 46n299; "The Supreme Court," box 4, Johnston Papers. The neighbor to the north, Nebraska, was also undergoing changes in its courts and personnel at this time. See James W. Hewitt, *Slipping Backward* (Lincoln: University of Nebraska Press, 2007), 8–9.

17. Austin, "The Supreme Court," 110–11.

18. Austin, "The Supreme Court."

19. Austin, "The Supreme Court," 95.

20. Austin, "The Supreme Court," 122.

21. Austin, "The Supreme Court," 124.

22. Austin, "The Supreme Court," 123–24.

23. *Kansas City Journal*, 14 June 1908; Kansas Judicial Clippings, vol. 1, pp. 88–91, Kansas State Historical Society, Topeka. For the J. R. Burton episode in Kansas History, see R. Alton Lee, "Joseph Ralph Burton and the 'Ill-Fated' Senate Seat of Kansas," *Kansas History: A Journal of the Central Plains* 32 (Winter 2009–10).

24. Kansas Judicial clippings, vol. 1, 1889.

25. Supreme Court, Proceedings, 1946; 91 Kan. iii–viii.

26. Supreme Court, Memorial Proceedings, 1946.

27. 147 Kan. iii. A doctor of laws degrees at that time was a graduate degree and not the same as a modern doctor of law or doctor of juridical science degree.

28. 144 Kan. iii.

29. Kansas Supreme Court, Proceedings, 1945.

30. 133 Kan. iii.

31. Moline, "Justice William A. Johnston," 19.

32. Moline, "Justice William A. Johnston," 20–21.

33. Johnston memorial, box 3, Johnston Papers.

34. Moline, "Justice William A. Johnston," 23.

35. Moline, "Prohibition," 55–56.

36. State v. Hickox, 64 Kan. 650 (1902).

37. State v. Peak, 66 Kan. 701 (1903).

38. State v. Durein, 70 Kan. 1 (1904).

39. Ziebold v. Renier, 73 Kan. 312 (1906).

40. State v. Pittsburg, 80 Kan. 710 (1909).

41. State v. Miller, 92 Kan. 994 (1914).

42. State v. Missouri Pacific, 96 Kan. 609, 612 (1915).

43. James A. Marone, *Hellfire Nation* (New Haven CT: Yale University Press, 2003), 311; 242 U.S. 211; 104 Kan. 742.

44. Santa Fe v. Concord, 66 Kan. 81 (1903).

45. Santa Fe v. Bancord, 67 Kan. 569 (1903).

46. St. Louis and San Francisco v. League, 71 Kan. 79 (1905).

47. 75 Kan. 56.

48. Santa Fe v. Coliati, 99 Kan. 544 (1907).

49. State v. Missouri Pacific, 76 Kan. 467 (1907).

50. Patterson v. Missouri Pacific, 77 Kan. 236 (1908).

51. Larabee Flour v. Missouri Pacific, 85 Kan. 214 (1911).

52. Vosburg v. Railway Company, 89 Kan. 114 (1913); Santa Fe v. Vosburg, 238 U.S. 56.

53. St. Louis Railroad v. Gorman, 79 Kan. 643 (1909).

54. Burke v. Santa Fe, 83 Kan. 144 (1910).

55. State v. Wilson, 65 Kan. 237 (1902).

56. State v. Atkin, 64 Kan. 174 (1902).

57. Atkin v. Kansas, 191 U.S. 207 (1903).

58. State v. Ottawa, 84 Kan. 107 (1911).

59. In re Williams, 79 Kan. 212 (1908).

60. Caspar v. Lewin, 82 Kan. 604 (1910).

61. Laffery v. Gypsum Company, 83 Kan. 349 (1911).

62. Henderson v. U.S. Gypsum, 84 Kan. 336 (1911).

63. Casteel v. Pittsburg Vitrified, 83 Kan. 533 (1910).

64. Sibley v. Kansas City Cotton Mills, 85 Kan. 256 (1911).

65. Roberts v. St. Marys, 86 Kan. 403 (1912).

66. Lupier v. Santa Fe, 86 Kan. 712 (1912).

67. State v. Coppage, 87 Kan. 752 (1912).

68. Coppage v. Kansas, 236 U.S. 1 (1915); Lochner v. New York, 198 U.S. 45 (1905); Adair v. United States, 208 U.S. 161 (1908).

69. 92 Kan. 146.

70. Francis v. Brock, 80 Kan. 100 (1909).

71. Williams v. Benson, 87 Kan. 421 (1912).

72. Corley v. Santa Fe, 90 Kan. 70 (1913).

73. Ellsworth v. Jarvis, 92 Kan. 895 (1914).

74. Fisher v. O'Brien, 99 Kan. 621 (1917).

75. Jacobs v. Santa Fe, 97 Kan. 247 (1916).

76. State v. Sherow, 87 Kan. 235 (1912).

77. Burlingame v. Thompson, 74 Kan. 393 (1906).

78. Topeka v. Crawford, 78 Kan. 583 (1908).

79. Kansas City v. Gilbert, 65 Kan. 469 (1902).

80. Kansas City v. Overton, 68 Kan. 560 (1904).

81. Billiard v. Topeka, 69 Kan. 53 (1904).

82. Reynolds v. Topeka, 66 Kan. 672 (1903).

83. Thomas J. Sugrue, *Sweet Land of Liberty* (New York: Random House, 2008), 173.

84. Williams v. Parsons, 79 Kan. 202 (1908).

85. Williams v. Parsons, 81 Kan. 593 (1910).

86. Rawles v. Wichita, 76 Kan. 361 (1907).

87. Cherryvale v. Harmon, 80 Kan. 170 (1909).

88. Cooper v. Goodland, 80 Kan. 121 (1909).

89. Chapple v. Kansas Vitrified Brick, 70 Kan. 723 (1905).

90. Natural Gas v. Neosho County, 75 Kan. 335 (1907).

91. State v. Ise, 91 Kan. 416 (1914).

92. In re Burns, 87 Kan. 19 (1912).

93. State v. Johnson, 84 Kan. 411 (1911).

94. Osborn v. Russell, 64 Kan. 507 (1902).

95. Miely v. Metzger, 97 Kan. 804 (1916).

96. State v. McCullough, 96 Kan. 786 (1915); 252 U.S. 516.

97. Moore v. Nah-can-be, 72 Kan. 169 (1905).

98. State v. Baker, 65 Kan. 117 (1902).

99. State v. Jehlik, 66 Kan. 301 (1903).

5. Reaction in the Roaring Twenties

1. David M. Kennedy, *Over Here* (New York: Oxford University Press, 1980), chap. 1, "The War for the American Mind," is a good introduction. See also Horace C. Peterson and Gilbert C. Fite, *Opponents of War* (Seattle: University of Washington Press, 1968).

2. Clayton Koppes, "The Industrial Workers of the World and County Jail Reform in Kansas, 1915–1920," *Kansas Historical Quarterly* 41 (Spring 1975), is an excellent account of these jail conditions.

3. 117 Kan. 69 (1907); 274 U.S. 562.

4. Lee, *From Snake Oil*, 245–51.

5. In re George Buckner, 105 Kan. 574 (1919).

6. *Topeka State Journal*, 3 April 1918.

7. Kansas State Federation of Labor, Proceedings, 1919, address by John P. Frey.

8. Lee, *Farmers vs. Wage Earners*, 139–42.

9. Lee, *Farmers vs. Wage Earners*, 143–50.

10. Lee, *Farmers vs. Wage Earners*, 151–54.

11. Lee, *Farmers vs. Wage Earners*, 152–53.

12. Lee, *Farmers vs. Wage Earners*, 159.

13. Lee, *Farmers vs. Wage Earners*, 159–60.

14. Lee, *Farmers vs. Wage Earners*, 160–61.

15. Dorchy v. Kansas, 264 U.S. 286 (1924).

16. Lee, *Farmers vs. Wage Earners*, 171.

17. Brian J. Moline, "Judicial Regulating in Kansas: The Rise and Fall of the Court of Visitation and the Industrial Court," *Journal of the Kansas Bar Association* 63 (December 1994): 35.

18. Wolf Packing Co. v. Court of Industrial Relations, 262 U.S. 522 (1923); 109 Kan. 629; 111 Kan. 501; 114 Kan. 304, 487.

19. Geoffrey Perrett, *America in the Twenties* (New York: Simon & Schuster, 1982), 122, 252.

20. William Allen White, *Autobiography* (Lawrence: University Press of Kansas, 1990), 330. The case was State v. Ku Klux Klan, 117 Kan. 564 (1925).

21. State v. W. D. Ross, 101 Kan. 357 (1917).

22. Gerald R. Butters, *Banned in Kansas* (Columbia: University of Missouri Press, 2007), chap. 4. The appeal to the court is at 102 Kan. 356 (1917). *The Easiest Way* decision is Midwest Photo Corp. v. Kansas Board of Review, 102 Kan. 356 (1918).

23. Butters, *Banned in Kansas*, 148–49, 176–82, 186–88.

24. Craig Miner, *Discovery* (Kansas Independent Oil and Gas Association, 1987), 149–86.

25. Kaul, "The Kansas Judicial System," 48–51.

26. Kansas Judicial Clippings, vol. 2, 157; Supreme Court, Proceedings, 1957, 187 Kan. vii–xiv.

27. Kansas Judiciary clippings, vol. 2.

28. 187 Kan. xxvi–xxix.

29. 197 Kan. iii.

30. *Journal of the Kansas Bar Association* 13 (August 1944): 28–31; W. G. Clugston, *Rascals in Democracy* (New York: Richard D. Smith, 1941), 211–20.

31. State v. City Clerk of Topeka, 103 Kan. 754 (1918).

32. Wolf v. Cudahy Packing, 105 Kan. 317 (1920).

33. Vietti v. Mackie Fuel, 109 Kan. 179 (1924).

34. State v. Jonathan Davis, 113 Kan. 4 (1923).

35. State v. Brewster, 101 Kan. 564 (1917).

36. State v. Peterson and Martin, 107 Kan. 641 (1930).

37. State v. Ford, 117 Kan. 735 (1925).

38. Koska v. Kansas City, 123 Kan. 362 (1927).

39. Harvey v. Bonner Springs, 102 Kan. 9 (1917).

40. Moore v. Wichita, 106 Kan. 636 (1920).

41. Hendren v. Arkansas City, 122 Kan. 361 (1927).

42. Stafford v. Noble, 105 Kan. 219 (1919).

43. Halvorson v. Blosser and Blosser, 101 Kan. 683 (1917).

44. Fox v. McCormick, 110 Kan. 91 (1921).

45. August M. Mader v. Topeka, 106 Kan. 867.

46. Naglo v. Jones, 115 Kan. 140.

47. Barnhardt v. American Glycerin Co., 113 Kan. 136 (1923).

48. Barzen v. Kepler, 125 Kan. 648 (1928).

49. Richard Foster Newlin (minor) v. Standard Oil, 122 Kan. 86 (1926).

50. Harlow v. Propes, 101 Kan. 424 (1917).

51. Phillips v. Meyer Milk, 129 Kan. 45 (1929).

52. Stotts v. Taylor, 130 Kan. 158 (1930).

53. State v. Shawnee County, 106 Kan. 196 (1920).

54. State v. Rice County, 117 Kan. 348 (1924).

55. State v. Saline County, 128 Kan. 427.

56. State v. Franklin County, 124 Kan. 141 (1927).

57. *Kansas Statutes Annotated*, 1988 ed.

58. Cook v. Leavenworth Terminal Railway, 101 Kan. 103 (1917).

59. Akins v. Federal Administrator of Railroads, 109 Kan. 474 (1921).

60. Flanagan v. Katy Railroad, 108 Kan. 133 (1920).

61. McKinley v. Hines, 113 Kan. 550 (1923).

62. Barker v. Lashbrook, 128 Kan. 595 (1920).

63. Richards v. Coal Co., 104 Kan. 330 (1918).

64. Everitt v. Haldeman-Julius Publishing, 124 Kan. 115 (1927).

65. R. Alton Lee, "The 'Little White Slaver' in Kansas: A Century Long Struggle against Cigarettes," *Kansas History* 22 (Winter 1999–2000): 258–67.

66. Kansas v. Nossaman, 107 Kan. 715 (1920).

67. Little v. Smith, 124 Kan. 237 (1927).

68. Beck v. Shawnee County, 105 Kan. 325 (1919).

69. State v. Bateman, 110 Kan. 546 (1922).

70. Burns v. Spiker, 109 Kan. 22 (1921).

71. Hoard v. Jones, 119 Kan. 138 (1925).

72. State v. Morrison, 121 Kan. 844 (1926).

73. In re Casement 129 Kan. 853 (1930).

74. In re Clancy, 212 Kan. 247 (1922).

75. Eberhardt Construction v. Sedgwick County, 100 Kan. 394 (1917).

76. Hennig v. Wichita Gas, 100 Kan. 255 (1917).

77. Winkler v. Anderson 104 Kan. 1 (1919).

78. Miller v. Board of Embalming, 110 Kan. 135 (1921).

79. State v. Brown, 112 Kan. 814 (1923).

80. State v. Smithmeyer, 110 Kan. 172 (1921); Poehler v. Hopkins, 111 Kan. 329 (1922).

81. County Farm Bureau v. Cloud County, 126 Kan. 322 (1928).

82. Empire Gas v. Stone, 121 Kan. 119 (1926).

83. State v. Kelly, 129 Kan. 849 (1930).

84. Bertram v. Burton, 129 Kan. 31 (1929).

85. Taylor v. White, 131 Kan. 791 (1930).

86. Stratford v. Petticord, 108 Kan. 775 (1921).

6. The Devastating Depression

1. Grace A. Browning, *The Development of Poor Relief Legislation in Kansas* (Chicago: University of Chicago Press, 1935), vii, ix.

2. State v. Township of Osawkee, 14 Kan. 322 (1875).

3. Lee, *Farmers vs. Wage Earners*, 176–79. Between 1 October 1932 and January 1933 Kansas borrowed $1,145,000 for relief, assuming for the first time a responsibility for the unemployed.

4. 133 Kan. 494 (1931).

5. Lee, *Farmers vs. Wage Earners*, 178–79.

6. R. Alton Lee, "Drought and Depression on the Great Plains: The Kansas Transition from New Deal Work Relief to Old Age Pensions," *Heritage of the Great Plains* 34 (Spring/Summer 2006): 8–10.

7. Lee, "Drought and Depression," 10–11.

8. Much of this relief material was published in R. Alton Lee, "[Not] a Thin Dime: Kansas Relief Politics in the Campaign of 1936," *Historian* 67 (Fall 2005). The author is grateful for permission to use this. When the FERA field representative recommended that Hopkins approve the 60–40 agreement, he noted that "we now have in Kansas one of the best State Relief Administration set-ups."

9. Kansas v. State Highway Commission, 138 Kan. 913, 914 (1934).

10. Peter Fearon, *Kansas in the Great Depression* (Columbia: University of Missouri Press, 2007), 53.

11. See Lee, *Farmers vs. Wage Earners*, chap. 7 for the impact of the war.

12. Logan, "The Federal Courts," 67.

13. *Kansas City Star*, 10 February 1938.

14. Logan, "The Federal Courts," 68.

15. Brian J. Moline, "Bill Smith the Jurist as Politician," *Journal of the Kansas Bar Association*, November 1988, 31.

16. Moline, "Bill Smith."

17. Moline, "Bill Smith," 31–32.

18. R. Alton Lee, *The Bizarre Careers of John R. Brinkley* (Lexington: University of Kentucky Press, 2002), chap. 4.

19. Lee, *The Bizarre Careers*, chap. 5.

20. 202 Kan. vii.

21. Moline, "Bill Smith," 33–34.

22. 202 Kan. ix.

23. 187 Kan. xxiii.

24. *Journal of the Kansas Bar Association* 23 (February 1955).

25. 165 Kan. vi; Kansas Judicial Council, Proceedings, October 1948, 39–40.

26. 168 Kan. v–ix.

27. Finance Corp. of America v. Walpole, 132 Kan. 250 (1931).

28. Seigler v. Kansas City, 131 Kan. 504 (1930).

29. Borman v. State Highway Comm., 139 Kan. 540 (1934).

30. Cherry v. Hays, 141 Kan. 346 (1935).

31. Morgan v. Anderson, 149 Kan. 814 (1936).

32. State v. Johnson County, 131 Kan. 403 (1930).

33. McCandles Construction v. Neosho County, 132 Kan. 651 (1931).

34. Cole v. Cook, 137 Kan. 250 (1933).

35. State v. Highway Commission, 138 Kan. 913 (1934).

36. State v. Kearney County, 146 Kan. 461 (1937).

37. State v. Vedder, 130 Kan. 472 (1930).

38. State v. Wheat, 131 Kan. 564 (1930).

39. State v. Blake, 133 Kan. 152 (1931).

40. State v. Sarver and Beiber, 134 Kan. 98 (1931).

41. Johnson v. Reno County, 147 Kan. 211 (1938).

42. State v. Goytle and Owens, 140 Kan. 732 (1934).

43. Conner v. Base Line Coal, 130 Kan. 534 (1930).

44. Knuth v. Kansas Compensation Board, 137 Kan. 392 (1933).

45. Miles v. Employers Liability Corp., 138 Kan. 863 (1934).

46. Stapleton v. State Highway Commission, 147 Kan. 419 (1938).

47. Rupp v. Jacobs, 149 Kan. 712 (1939).

48. Piggue v. Baldwin, 154 Kan. 708 (1942).

49. Stephens and MacCaskill v. Davis, 140 Kan. 221 (1934).

50. Swart v. Huston, 154 Kan. 182 (1941).

51. Coleman v. Miller, 146 Kan. 390 (1937).

52. State v. Miller, 131 Kan. 36 (1930).

53. Cheyney v. People's State Bank, 135 Kan. 521 (1932).

54. Dempster v. Douthit, 130 Kan. 349 (1930).

55. Babcock v. Newby, 133 Kan. 48 (1931).

56. Bank of Alta Vista v. Dierking, 143 Kan. 617 (1936).

57. Schmidt v. Twin City Bank, 151 Kan. 667 (1940).

58. Oakland State Bank v. Bolin, 141 Kan. 126 (1935).

59. State v. Forestry, Fish, and Game Commission, 139 Kan. 197 (1934).

60. Fearon, *Kansas in the Great Depression*, 51–53.

61. Natural Gas Pipeline v. Commissioner of Revenue and Taxation, 155 Kan. 416 (1942).

62. Valley Falls v. Jefferson County, 148 Kan. 429 (1938).

63. Carolene Products v. Mohler, 152 Kan. 2 (1940).

64. Pittsburg v. Auditor George Robb, 143 Kan. 1 (1936).

65. State v. Lange, 148 Kan. 614 (1938).

66. State v. Waite, 156 Kan. 143 (1942).

67. State v. Fox Kansas Theater, 144 Kan. 687 (1936).

68. Ritchie v. Johnson, 158 Kan. 103 (1944). The other cases are at 35 and 122.

69. State v. Smith, 155 Kan. 588 (1942). The national cases are Minersville School District v. Gobitus, 310 U.S. 586 (1940), and Jones v. Opelika, 316 U.S. 584 (1942).

70. Olathe v. Lauck, 156 Kan. 637 (1943).

71. Brinkley v. Haussig, 130 Kan. 874 (1930).

72. Brown v. Haussig, 136 Kan. 384.

73. State v. Pyle, 143 Kan. 772 (1936); Pyle v. Kansas, 317 U.S. 213 (1942).

74. Parsons v. Secretary of State, 144 Kan. 370 (1936). The CPUSA case is Wiggins v. Secretary of State, 152 Kan. 629 (1940).

75. Foster v. Topeka Board, 131 Kan. 160 (1930).

76. State v. Auditor French, 133 Kan. 579 (1931). The federal case was Colorado v. Kansas, 278 U.S. 574.

77. Atkinson v. Wichita Gas, 136 Kan. 854 (1933).

78. Hagaman v. Manley, 141 Kan. 647, 648 (1935).

79. Campbell v. Weathers, 153 Kan. 316 (1941).

80. United Artists v. Mills, 136 Kan. 33 (1932).

81. Jacobs v. Graham County High, 130 Kan. 248 (1930).

82. State v. Finney, 141 Kan. 12 (1935).

7. The Revised Selection System

1. Paul Wilson, "Brown v. Board of Education of Topeka: A Personal Perspective," in *Kansas Revisited*, ed. Paul K. Steuwe (Lawrence: University Press of Kansas, 1996), 280.

2. Plessy v. Ferguson, 163 U.S. 537. Interestingly, Fred G. Addis, "A Historical Study of Kansas Supreme Court Decisions for 1861–1957 with Respect to Public School Administration" (Ed.D. diss., University of Colorado, 1960), is narrowly limited to that topic and does not deal with public school segregation.

3. Missouri ex rel. Gaines v. Canada, 305 U.S. 339 (1938); Sipuel v. Board of Regents, 332 U.S. 631 (1948); Sweatt v. Painter, 339 U.S. 626 (1950).

4. Virgil W. Dean, "Walter A. Huxman: Leading by Example," in *John Brown to Bob Dole*, ed. Virgil W. Dean (Lawrence: University Press of Kansas, 2006), 224–25. See also Miner, *Kansas*, 344–47.

5. Paul E. Wilson, *Musings of a Smiling Bull: Selected Essays, Articles and Speeches* (Lawrence: University of Kansas School of Law, 2000), "A Time to Lose."

6. Bob Beatty and Mark A. Peterson, "Covert Discrimination: Topeka—before and after Brown," *Kansas History: A Journal of the Central Plains* 27 (Autumn 2004), presents a good coverage of the issue in the capital city.

7. Watson v. Memphis, 373 U.S. 526.

8. Sugrue, *Sweet Land*, 152–53.

9. Sugrue, *Sweet Land*, 153.

10. This material appeared in slightly different form in R. Alton Lee, "The Triple Switch: How the Missouri Plan Came to Kansas," *Journal of the Kansas Bar Association* 73 (January 2004). The author appreciates permission to reprint this.

11. "Sketches of Governors," *Topeka Daily Capita*l, 26 February 1976. "West of 81" refers to the highway that runs north and south through the state, dividing two-thirds of the state from the more populous eastern part.

12. *Topeka State Journal*, 15 February 1957.

13. Jeffrey D. Jackson, "The Selection of Judges in Kansas: A Comparison of Systems," *Journal of the Kansas Bar Association* 69 (January 2000): 34.

14. *Topeka Daily Capital*, 1 March 1957.

15. 168 Kan. ix–xi; Supreme Court Clippings, vol. 1, 15.

16. *Topeka State Journal,* 8 February 1949.

17. Supreme Court Clippings, vol. 2, 121.

18. 197 Kan. xxix–xxxv.

19. *Illustriana Kansas* (Hebron: Illustriana, Inc., 1933), 612; *Topeka Daily Capital*, 19 November 1950.

20. 197 Kan. xxiii.

21. 246 Kan. viii–xiii.

22. Supreme Court clippings, vol. 3, 77; 240 Kan. xviii.

23. Supreme Court clippings, vol. 1, 77.

24. Webb v. School Board, 167 Kan. 395 (1949).

25. Cameron v. Board of Education, 182 Kan. 39 (1957).

26. State v. Ethel Hines, 163 Kan. 300 (1947). Addis never pursued this question beyond 1948.

27. Remple v. Kobs, 166 Kan. 38 (1948).

28. State v. Throckmorton, 169 Kan. 481 (1950).

29. State v. Lost Springs High, 176 Kan. 378 (1954).

30. Mallion v. Wichita School Board, 181 Kan. 230 (1957).

31. DAR v. Washburn University, 160 Kan. 583 (1945).

32. State v. Board of Regents, 167 Kan. 587 (1949).

33. State v. Board of Regents, 176 Kan. 179 (1954).

34. Betts v. Easley, 161 Kan. 459 (1946).

35. Porth v. Carpenters and Joiners, 171 Kan. 177 (1951).

36. Lee, *Farmers vs. Wage Earners*, 256–58.

37. In re Ferris, 175 Kan. 704 (1954).

38. Asphalt Paving v. Teamsters, 181 Kan. 775 (1957).

39. Amalgamated Meat Cutters v. Judge Johnson, 178 Kan. 405, 414 (1955).

40. Bortzfield v. Sutton, 180 Kan. 46 (1957).

41. Neal v. Boeing, 161 Kan. 322 (1946).

42. McMillen v. Salina, 163 Kan. 575 (1947).

43. Abbott v. Southwest Grain Co., 162 Kan. 315 (1947).

44. Dressler v. Dressler, 167 Kan. 749 (1949).

45. 176 Kan. 683 (1954).

46. Anderson Cattle v. Kansas Turnpike Authority, 180 Kan. 749 (1957).

47. Cole v. Johnson, 177 Kan. 576 (1955).

48. Cessna v. Coffeyville Racing, 179 Kan. 766 (1956).

49. State v. Bissing, 178 Kan. 111 (1955).

50. State v. Hannegan, 161 Kan. 492 (1946).

51. State v. Wilson, 169 Kan. 659 (1950).

52. State v. Larkin, 173 Kan. 112 (1952).

53. Chambers v. Herrick, 172 Kan. 510 (1952).

54. In re Estate of Rivers, 175 Kan. 809 (1954).

55. Estate of Franklin Hayden v. Boyle, 174 Kan. 140 (1953).

56. Hall, *The Magic Mirror*, 299–300. See Glenda Riley, *Divorce: An American Tradition* (New York: Oxford University Press, 1991), chap. 7, for divorce in the post–World War II period.

57. Watts v. McKay, 160 Kan. 377 (1945).

58. White v. White, 160 Kan. 32 (1945).

59. Estate of Henry Troemper v. Nannie Troemper, 160 Kan. 464 (1945).

60. Coates v. Coates, 161 Kan. 307 (1946).

61. McCarty v. McCarty, 163 Kan. 427 (1947).

62. May v. May, 162 Kan. 425 (1947).

63. Marshall v. Marshall, 168 Kan. 169 (1949).

64. Ramey v. Ramey, 170 Kan. 1 (1950).

65. Jackson v. Jackson, 181 Kan. 1 (1957).

66. Whitcomb v. Huffington, 180 Kan. 340 (1957).

67. State v. Leopold, 170 Kan. 613, 616 (1951).

68. Leland v. Board, 176 Kan. 334 (1954).

69. Welch v. Shepherd, 165 Kan. 394 (1948).

70. Harris v. Exon, 161 Kan. 582 (1946).

71. Joy v. Brown, 173 Kan. 833, 840, 841 (1953).

72. Ross v. Rock Island, 165 Kan. 279 (1948).

73. Rock Island v. Kansas Corporation Commission, 177 Kan. 697 (1955).

74. Lee, "Triple Switch," 29.

75. State v. AOUW of Kansas, 178 Kan. 69 (1955).

76. State v. Urban Renewal, 179 Kan. 435 (1956).

77. State v. Shanahan, 173 Kan. 403 (1952).

78. State v. Tipton, 166 Kan. 145 (1948).

79. Conrad v. Dillinger, 176 Kan. 296 (1954).

80. Wiley v. Hudspeth, 162 Kan. 516 (1947).

8. Modernizing the Law

1. Jackson, "The Selection of Judges," 35.

2. Kaul, "The Kansas Judicial System," 52–53.

3. Kaul, "The Kansas Judicial System," 53–54.

4. David Prager, "The Road to a More Effective Judicial System," in Dean, *The Law and Lawyers*, 87–88.

5. Prager, "The Road," 54–56.

6. Prager, "The Road," 56.

7. Prager, "The Road," 86–87.

8. American Judicature Society, Citizens' Conference, copy in Kansas State Historical Society, Topeka.

9. American Judicature Society, Citizens' Conference.

10. American Judicature Society, Citizens' Conference.

11. *Washburn Law Journal* 13 (Spring 1974): 334–35.

12. *Washburn Law Journal* 13.

13. *Washburn Law Journal* 13.

14. *Washburn Law Journal* 13.

15. *Washburn Law Journal* 13:325–26.

16. *Washburn Law Journal* 13:96–98; 246 Kan. viii–xiii.

17. Prager, "The Road," 57–58.

18. *Washburn Law Journal* 13:330.

19. Supreme Court Clippings, vol. 3, 138; 232 Kan. liv–lviii.

20. Supreme Court, Proceedings, 16 October 1978; Supreme Court clippings, vol. 6, 178.

21. http:/www.10thcircuithistory.org, O'Connor biography.

22. 232 Kan. lxiv–lxxii.

23. 226 Kan. xli–xlvii.

24. 243 Kan. xiii–xxviii.

25. Lee v. State, 187 Kan. 566 (1961).

26. Tri-State Hotel v. State, 195 Kan. 748 (1965).

27. Lonnie Wilson, "Miranda v. Arizona," in *Law in the Western United States*, ed. Gordon Morris Bakken (Norman: University of Oklahoma Press, 2000), 118–25.

28. State v. Faidley, 202 Kan. 517 (1969).

29. Fred A. Beatty, "The Agency Shop Agreement and the Kansas Right to Work Law," *Journal of the Kansas Bar Association* 27 (May 1959): 349. See R. Alton Lee, *Truman and Taft-Hartley* (Lexington: University Press of Kentucky, 1966), for a political history of this labor law.

30. Higgins v. Cardinal Mfg., 188 Kan. 11 (1961). For a background of the issues, see R. Alton Lee, *Eisenhower and Landrum-Griffin* (Lexington: University of Kentucky Press, 1990).

31. Clark v. Employment Security, 187 Kan. 695 (1961).

32. Rickman v. LMW Mfg., 191 Kan. 543 (1963).

33. Seibert v. Hoch, 199 Kan. 299 (1967).

34. Razey v. Unified School District, 205 Kan. 551 (1970).

35. Inland Industries v. Teamsters, 209 Kan. 349 (1972).

36. Cushenberry v. Shanahan, 190 Kan. 720 (1963).

37. State v. Highwood Services, 205 Kan. 821 (1970).

38. State v. Nelson, 210 Kan. 439 (1972).

39. State v. Smith, 193 Kan. 299 (1964).

40. State v. Andrews, 187 Kan. 473 (1960).

41. State v. Hickok and Smith, 188 Kan. 473 (1961).

42. State v. Latham and York, 190 Kan. 222, 423 (1962).

43. State v. Hunt, 198 Kan. 222 (1967).

44. Jackson v. State, 204 Kan. 823, 829 (1970).

45. State v. Roth, 207 Kan. 691 (1971).

46. State v. Hill, 211 Kan. 287 (1973).

47. Sharp v. State, 203 Kan. 937 (1969).

48. State v. English, 198 Kan. 196, 209 (1967).

49. State v. DeLespine, 210 Kan. 348 (1968).

50. State v. Darling, 208 Kan. 469 (1972).

51. State v. Garber, 197 Kan. 567 (1966).

52. State v. Kansas City School Board, 199 Kan. 312 (1967).

53. Board of Healing Arts v. Foote, 200 Kan. 447 (1968).

54. State v. Haupt, 210 Kan. 778 (1972).

55. State v. Crouch, 192 Kan. 602 (1964).

56. Burnett v. Burnett, 192 Kan. 247 (1963).

57. Jackson v. Lee, 193 Kan. 40 (1964).

58. Waters v. Zweygardt, 195 Kan. 614 (1965).

59. Katz v. Katz, 191 Kan. 500 (1963).

60. Finney v. Finney, 201 Kan. 263 (1968).

61. Sinclair v. Sinclair, 204 Kan. 240 (1969).

62. Harris v. Shanahan, 192 Kan. 185 (1963).

63. Harris v. Anderson, 196 Kan. 450 (1966).

64. Becker v. Rupp, 187 Kan. 104 (1960).

65. State v. Pittsburg, 188 Kan. 612, 623 (1961).

66. State v. Hill, 189 Kan. 403 (1962).

67. Iowa Mutual Insurance v. Parr, 189 Kan. 475 (1962).

68. Honorable J. Richard Foth, "Judges Read Dirty Books," *Journal of the Kansas Bar Association* 47 (Fall 1978): 191–99. See also Hall, *The Magic Mirror*, 317–18, for a brief survey.

69. State v. Quantity of Books, 191 Kan. 13 (1966); Foth, "Judges Read Dirty Books," 197–98.

70. Dell v. Excel Packing, 183 Kan. 331; Carp v. County Commissioners, 193 Kan. 177.

71. Fields v. Anderson Cattle, 193 Kan. 558 (1964).

72. Cutting-Greenlease v. KTA, 185 Kan. 599, 600–601 (1959).

73. State v. Cook, 194 Kan. 495, 499 (1965).

74. Bellport v. Harder, 196 Kan. 294 (1966).

75. Barten v. Turkey Creek Watershed, 200 Kan. 489 (1968).

76. Smitherman Oil v. Mobil Oil, 203 Kan. 72 (1969).

77. Thomas v. Dudrey, 208 Kan. 684, 689 (1972).

78. Wichita v. White, 205 Kan. 408 (1970).

79. Blaine v. Haysville School Board, 210 Kan. 560 (1972).

80. State v. Claiborne, 211 Kan. 265, 264, 266 (1973).

81. Manzanares v. Bell, 214 Kan. 589 (1974).

82. Van Sickle v. Shanahan, 212 Kan. 426 (1973).

83. Henry v. Bauder, 213 Kan. 751 (1974), "crazy-quilt" quote at 756.

9. Retreat to Conservatism

1. http://www.nationalcasa.org/about us/history.htmc.

2. http://www.kansascasa.homestead.com/information-ns4.html.

3. Kansascasa.

4. Derenda Mitchell, "CASA: A Voice for Children," *Journal of the Kansas Bar Association* 58 (May 1989): 28–29.

5. Judge Jerry Mershon, address to the Riley County CASA anniversary dinner, December 1988.

6. Mershon, address, http://www.kansascasa.homestead.com/information—ns4.html.

7. Roe v. Wade, 410 U.S. 113.

8. Ted G. Jelen, ed., *Perspective on the Politics of Abortion* (New York: Praeger, 1995), is a good collection of essays on the subject.

9. Jelen, *Perspective*, 10–11.

10. *Topeka Daily Capital*, 8 February 1986.

11. Pamphlet, *Religious Coalition for Abortion Rights in Kansas*, Kansas State Historical Society, Topeka.

12. William R. Roy, "Abortion: A Physician's View," *Washburn Law Review* 9 (1969–70).

13. Pamphlet, *An Open Letter on Abortion*, Kansas State Historical Society, Topeka.

14. *Wichita Eagle*, 14 July 1991.

15. *Wichita Eagle*, 19, 22 July 1991. In 2010 an opponent murdered Dr. Tiller in his church as he served as an usher.

16. *Directory of State Officers*, 1982, 3; Berenece Wallace, "History of Paola, Kansas, 1855 to 1955," Kansas State Historical Society; KU Laws, fall 1988, 4.

17. *Directory of State Officers*, 1982, 25.

18. *Directory of State Officers*, 1982, 24; *Topeka Capital Journal*, 7 September 1999.

19. http://www.rootsweb.ancestry.com/-kscomanc_hs.html.

20. John D. Bright, ed., *Kansas: The First Century*, 4 vols. (New York: Lewis Historical Publishing Company, 1956), 407–08; *Topeka Daily Capital*, 4 February 1983.

21. *Topeka Capital Journal*, 25 December 1986.

22. Supreme Court clippings, vol. 3, 134–35; 243 Kan. v–x.

23. Humes v. Clinton, 246 Kan. 590 (1990).

24. Herbst v. Compton, 217 Kan. 164 (1975).

25. Trompeter v. Trompeter, 218 Kan. 535 (1976).

26. Fleming v. Fleming, 221 Kan. 291 (1977).

27. Varney v. Varney, 222 Kan. 700 (1977).

28. Aslin v. Seamon, 225 Kan. 77 (1978).

29. In re Baby Boy, 231 Kan. 199 (1982).

30. Nocktonick v. Nocktonick, 227 Kan. 758, 768 (1980).

31. State v. Barclay, 238 Kan. 148 (1985).

32. In re Loughmiller, 229 Kan. 584 (1981).

33. State v. Thompson and Pennington, 221 Kan. 165 (1976).

34. In re Mason, 245 Kan. 111 (1989).

35. State v. Chisholm, 243 Kan. 270 (1988).

36. State v. Carmichael, 240 Kan. 149 (1986).

37. Collier v. Operating Engineers, 228 Kan. 52 (1980).

38. Ritchie Paving v. KDOT, 232 Kan. 346 (1982).

39. Kansas City v. Carpenters, 237 Kan. 295 (1985).

40. Chee-Craw Teachers v. Crawford County, 225 Kan. 561 (1979).

41. NEA v. Topeka Board, 225 Kan. 445 (1979).

42. In re Sawyer, 234 Kan. 436 (1983).

43. Bailey v. Unified School District, 233 Kan. 714 (1983).

44. Achiya v. Unified District, 242 Kan. 572 (1988).

45. Bauer v. School Board, 244 Kan. 6 (1988).

46. State v. "The Bet," 219 Kan. 641 (1976).

47. State v. Hughes, 246 Kan. 607 (1990).

48. Flax v. TPA, 226 Kan. 1 (1979).

49. KTA v. Wheeler, 243 Kan. 602 (1988).

50. State v. Shanahan, 220 Kan. 589 (1976).

51. State v. Carlin, 229 Kan. 665 (1981).

52. Haven v. Gregg, 244 Kan. 117 (1988).

53. Energy Reserves Group v. Kansas Power & Light, 230 Kan. 176 (1981); Energy Reserves Group v. Kansas Power & Light, 459 U.S. 400 (1982).

54. State v. Turner, 239 Kan. 360 (1986).

55. State v. Faulkner, 220 Kan. 153 (1976).

56. State v. Jaques, 225 Kan. 39, 41 (1978).

57. State v. Revis, 233 Kan. 972 (1983).

58. State v. Mall, 216 Kan. 287 (1975).

59. State v. Smith and Miller, 224 Kan. 662 (1978).

60. State v. Kennedy, 225 Kan. 13 (1978).

61. State v. Fisher, 233 Kan. 29 (1983).

62. State v. Martin, 241 Kan. 732 (1987).

63. State v. Jones, 242 Kan. 385 (1988).

64. Civil Rights Commission v. Sears, 216 Kan. 396 (1975).
65. State v. Kalb, 218 Kan. 459 (1975).
66. State v. Hruska, 219 Kan. 233 (1976).
67. Shutts v. Phillips Petroleum, 222 Kan. 527 (1977).
68. Lines v. Topeka, 223 Kan. 772 (1978).
69. Maryland Mutual v. Alliance Mutual, 223 Kan. 674 (1978).
70. State v. Russell, 227 Kan. 897 (1979).
71. Junction City v. Mevis, 226 Kan. 526 (1979).
72. Acupuncture Society v. Board of Healing Arts, 226 Kan. 639 (1979).
73. State v. Stauffer Communications, 225 Kan. 540, 548 (1979).
74. Stricklow v. State Board of Agriculture, 232 Kan. 589 (1983).
75. State v. Thompson, 237 Kan. 562 (1985).
76. State v. Pringle, 236 Kan. 544 (1985).
77. Americare Properties v. SRS, 241 Kan. 607 (1987).
78. Farmer Co-op v. Department of Agriculture, 240 Kan. 355 (1986).
79. Nova Stylings v. Red Roof Inn, 242 Kan. 318 (1987).
80. Memorial Hospital v. Knutson, 239 Kan. 663 (1986).

Conclusion

1. Brian J. Moline, "The Populist Court," *Journal of the Kansas Bar Association* 58 (October 1989), especially makes this point about Frank Doster and Stephen Allen, the Populist majority at the turn of the twentieth century.

2. See Jeffrey D. Jackson, "The Selection of Judges in Kansas: A Comparison of Systems," *Journal of the Kansas Bar Association* 69 (January 2000).

3. Francis H. Heller, "The Justices of the Kansas Supreme Court 1861–1975: A Collective Portrait," *Kansas Law Review* 24 (1976).

4. Heller, "The Justices."

Glossary

abatement	reduction, as in a tax
amercement	inflicting a penalty at the court's discretion
amicus curiae	literally, "friend of the court"
caveat emptor	literally, "let the buyer beware"
common law	law developed by judges based on precedent
de facto	"in fact," referring to a situation that exists
defeasance	defeating the force or operation of some other deed or will
de jure	"in law," meaning consistent in law
demurer	a party's allegation may be true, but it lacks consequences
docket	list of cases for trial
en banc	the entire court
equity	a process to remedy a defect in common law
ex post facto	"after the fact," or making an act a crime after it has taken place
grand jury	called especially to investigate and charge
habeas corpus	literally, "you should have the body"; is there evidence to charge a person with a crime?
hotchpot	the combination of properties in an estate; the properties are then divided equally among the heirs
intestate	dying without a will
larceny	stealing
mechanic's lien	a worker's claim for labor, and he is paid for that labor
obiter dictum	literally, "beyond the saying" (the core decision); an opinion expressed by a judge that is not binding
per curiam	the unsigned opinion of the entire court
petit jury	an ordinary trial jury
prima facie	literally, "on the face of it"; presumably

pro forma	literally, "for form"
quash	to void or annul
quo warranto	literally, "by what warrant"; in search of information
replevin	an action by which an owner recovers goods
riparian	the right of owner to water under his land
seriatim	literally, "in a series"; in order
situs	the location of property or of an event
status quo ante	literally, "state in which previously"; the preexisting state of things
sui juris	literally, "of one's own right"; having complete legal rights
tort	a private civil wrong or injury
writ	a court order
writ of certiorari	to certify the records
writ of error	to appeal because of possible error
writ of mandamus	to order a public official to do public duty
writ of replevin	an action to recover property from someone who wrongfully possesses it

Index to Federal Cases Cited

Index to State Cases Cited

Index

In the Law in the American West series:

Federal Justice in California: The Court of Ogden Hoffman, 1851–1891
Christian G. Fritz

Practicing Law in Frontier California
Gordon Morris Bakken

A Germ of Goodness: The California State Prison System, 1851–1944
Shelley Bookspan

Flooding the Courtrooms: Law and Water in the Far West
M. Catherine Miller

Lone Wolf v. Hitchcock: Treaty Rights and Indian Law at the End of the Nineteenth Century
Blue Clark

Imperfect Victories: The Legal Tenacity of the Omaha Tribe, 1945–1995
Mark R. Scherer

The Trial of "Indian Joe": Race and Justice in the Nineteenth-Century West
Clare V. McKanna Jr.

Slipping Backward: A History of the Nebraska Supreme Court
James W. Hewitt

Law and Order in Buffalo Bill's Country: Legal Culture and Community on the Great Plains, 1867–1910
Mark R. Ellis

The Nebraska-Kansas Act of 1854
John R. Wunder and Joann M. Ross

Women Who Kill Men: California Courts, Gender, and the Press
Gordon Morris Bakken and Brenda Farrington

Called to Justice: The Life of a Federal Trial Judge
Warren K. Urbom

Sunflower Justice: A New History of the Kansas Supreme Court
R. Alton Lee